HARRY, TOM, AND FATHER RICE

HARRY, TOM, and FATHER RICE

ACCUSATION AND BETRAYAL IN AMERICA'S COLD WAR

JOHN HOERR

University of Pittsburgh Press

Published by the University of Pittsburgh Press,
Pittsburgh, PA 15260
Copyright © 2005, John Hoerr
All rights reserved
Manufactured in the United States of America
Printed on acid-free paper
10 9 8 7 6 5 4 3 2 1

Library of Congress Cataloging-in-Publication Data

Hoerr, John P., 1930-
    Harry, Tom, and Father Rice : accusation and betrayal in America's Cold War /
John Hoerr.
        p. cm.
    Includes bibliographical references (p.   ) and index.
    ISBN 0-8229-4265-8 (hardcover : alk. paper)
1. Anti-communist movements—Pennsylvania—Pittsburgh—History—20th century. 2.
Pittsburgh (Pa.)—Politics and government—20th century. 3. Cold War—Social
aspects—Pennsylvania—Pittsburgh. 4. Davenport, Harry James, 1902–1977. 5.
Legislators—Pennsylvania—Pittsburgh—Biography. 6. Quinn, Tom. 7. Labor
unions—Pennsylvania—Pittsburgh—Biography. 8. Rice, Charles Owen, 1908–9.
Priests—Pennsylvania—Pittsburgh—Biography. 10. Pittsburgh (Pa.)—Biography. I.
Title.

    F159.P657H64 2005
    974.8'86043'0922—dc22

                                            2005001793

For Mother

Also in memory of
Thomas J. Quinn
August 10, 1917–February 11, 2005

CONTENTS

Illustrations follow page 210

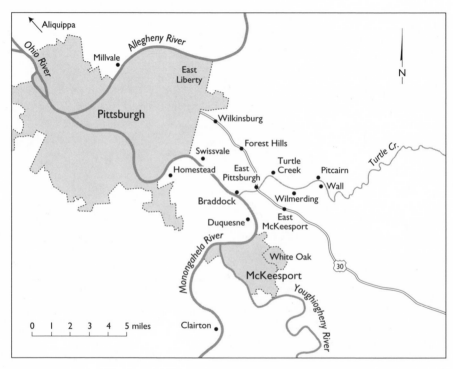

Pittsburgh and the Turtle Creek Valley

PREFACE

THE history of the McCarthy era, extending roughly from 1947 to 1957 and coinciding with the early years of the Cold War, has been told many times over in books, movies, documentaries, and scholarly articles. I wouldn't presume to change the contours of that history or offer a new interpretation of the period. Within that known history, however, are countless unknown tales of people swept up in the rush to expose and prosecute all who were associated with the Communist Party or its members and organizations. In this book, I tell one of those previously untold stories, involving a politician, a local union leader, and a priest.

The politician was my uncle, Harry Davenport, a one-term congressman who represented a Pittsburgh district in 1949–1950. His friendship with the union man, Thomas Quinn of the United Electrical Workers (UE), was put to the test when the UE came under attack by Congress and anti-Communist labor leaders. Events in that struggle linked Davenport and Quinn with the priest, Monsignor Charles Owen Rice, who worked indefatigably for years to root out Communists and their close allies in the labor movement—only to repudiate his own overzealousness in later years. Their intertwined story may fill one of the many voids that still exist in our understanding of the era when people informed on one another and the labor movement split asunder.

Parts of my story, especially those involving Monsignor Rice and to a lesser degree Tom Quinn, are known to labor historians. Harry Davenport, however, has been lost to history. I did not set out to place my uncle in any particular niche, merely to find out what happened to him. In the process, I came across his personal relationship with Quinn and their relationship with Rice. For historical background, my story relies on two excellent works on unions and labor relations in the electrical industry. They are *The Electrical Workers: A History of Labor at General Electric and West-*

inghouse, 1923–1960 by Ronald W. Schatz and *Cold War in the Working Class: The Rise and Decline of the United Electrical Workers* by Ronald L. Filippelli and Mark D. McColloch. For a history of the CIO (Congress of Industrial Organizations), I turn often to Charles H. Zieger's *The CIO, 1935–1955*. A biography of Father Rice, *Rev. Charles Owen Rice: Apostle of Contradiction* by Patrick J. McGeever, is useful for a chronology of Rice's life. But I do not rely on this author's judgments about Rice's conduct. *Fighter with a Heart: Writings of Charles Owen Rice*, edited by Charles McCollester, with its striking photographs, was a helpful guide to Rice's career and writings.

Harry Davenport and his sisters and brother were dead by the time I began writing, but I have many memories of stories told by my mother, Alyce Hoerr Clark, and her sisters, Annamae Osterman Krider and Sister Catherine Davenport. My sister Lynn and her husband Ronald McKay read portions of the manuscript and helped me align my memory with events in the life of the Davenport family; my sister disagrees with some of my interpretations. My Davenport cousins, Jake and Harry Osterman and Mary Kate (Bast) Gillespie, also refreshed my knowledge of certain events. Comments attributed to Harry Davenport come from my own memory, entries in my journal, speeches recorded in the *Congressional Record*, stories related by John Connelly and Tom Quinn, and newspaper accounts.

With only a few exceptions, noted individually in the endnotes, all comments attributed to Tom Quinn come from the more than two dozen interviews that I conducted over a period of four years. I tape-recorded lengthy talks on April 20, June 8 and 9, and December 5, 2000, and April 29 and October 15, 2002. Because we were separated by distance, other interviews took place by telephone, during which I transcribed his words almost exactly on a computer as we talked. Quinn's health declined in 2003 and 2004. I posed a final question in a phone call in December 2004, asking if he could recall the first name of a man he had known fleetingly in 1949. His memory still sharp, Quinn answered without hesitation. Two months later, he suffered a major stroke and died in a Pittsburgh hospital, attended by his family, at the age of 87.

Quinn's three sons, Charles, Ronald, and Stephen, furnished crucial and insightful details about Quinn family life. All four Quinns read the manuscript and corrected factual mistakes about their family but did not ask me to modify the way in which I positioned Quinn in the political context.

I owe a considerable debt to the professional staffs of various archives and libraries. I am especially grateful to staff members of the Archives Service Center, University of Pittsburgh, and particularly to David Rosenberg, curator and archivist of the UE Archives and Labor Collections. He guided me through archival labyrinths and read and commented critically on portions of the manuscript. Marilyn Cocchiola Holt, head of the Pennsylvania Department at Carnegie Library of Pittsburgh, helped me resolve a number of research quandaries. I also received assistance from Tim Corliss of the Special Collections and University Archives, Rutgers University Libraries, which holds the IUE Archives; Martha L. Berg of the Rodef Shalom Congregation Archives, Pittsburgh; the staffs of New York University's Tamiment Library and Newark, New Jersey, Public Library; Matthew Wasniewski in the Office of History and Preservation, U.S. House of Representatives; the staff of Congressman Steven R. Rothman; and archivists at the National Archives in Washington, DC. Gerard L. Boscia, a freelance historical researcher, provided invaluable help by finding and copying microfilm files of old newspaper articles and offering general guidance to research facilities in the Pittsburgh area. Ed Reis of the George Westinghouse Historical Museum in Wilmerding, Pennsylvania, located information about George Westinghouse and Wilmerding.

Several people read and commented on portions of the manuscript. My son Peter served as first reader, criticizing early drafts and helping me frame my story. My wife, Joanne, performed copyediting duties, over and over, on many versions of each chapter. I benefited especially from the pointed criticisms of historians who know the subject, Ronald Schatz and Charles McCollester. David Montgomery, who read most of the manuscript, called attention to gaps in my narrative and suggested a number of avenues for further research. A former UE member himself, Montgomery contributed some of his own experiences. Sam Lemon, a personal friend since college days and former labor negotiator for Westinghouse Electric Corporation, furnished observations and anecdotes for my profile of the UE leader James Matles. Lemon also commented critically on parts of the manuscript. He and I continue to disagree in a friendly way about aspects of the McCarthy era.

I am grateful for research suggestions provided by Ellen Schrecker, John Earl Haynes, Steve Rosswurm, and James Weber. John E. Connelly gave freely of his time in interviews that provided crucial information about Harry Davenport. The late James W. Knox, who also knew my uncle, gave me photographs and background information about the Democratic Party of Allegheny County and former Pittsburgh mayor David L. Lawrence. James Dodero helped me establish contact with Connelly and Knox. I received other research help from Thomas Duzak, Mike Locker, Cary Burnell, Ed Ayoub, Russell Gibbons, David Demarest, Tom Foley, Rev. Thomas J. Donaghy, Jim McKay, Laurence Lillig, Gerrie Mulooly, Father Gabriel of St. Nicholas Croatian Church in Millvale, and the McKeesport Heritage Center. My old friends Ruth Ann and Bill Molloy provided suggestions, companionship, and occasional lodging during my trips to Pittsburgh.

I want to give special thanks to Annabelle and Alex Staber, who shared with me several hours of reminiscences about their tribulations during the McCarthy era. A former UE member who was fired by General Electric, Alex was a target of congressional investigators through the 1950s. He died as I was writing this book, as did my cousin and friend, Jake Osterman.

HARRY, TOM, AND FATHER RICE

PROLOGUE

A DEATH IN MILLVALE

ULRICH'S Hotel in Millvale, Pennsylvania, is a place where solitary old men, living on a Social Security pittance, go to die. On a cold morning in December 1977, a long-term boarder named Bill Sitzman decided to turn up the heat in room 7. Bending over to adjust a heat-flow register on the wall near the floor, he happened to glance through the register into an adjoining room. He saw two inert bare feet, lying toes up on the floor of room 6. Knowing that his neighbor was in his seventies and was ill and drank too much, Sitzman notified the hotel manager, who unlocked the door to room 6 and found the man dead. His name was Harry J. Davenport, once a congressman of unusual promise, who had lost everything—career, family, and something of his manhood—during one disastrous term in Washington. His sudden downfall after an excellent start had never been explained, not by him or by the press or by anyone that I knew. He was my uncle.

In June 2000, I visited Millvale for the first time to see where my Uncle Harry had died. The town sits on the west bank of the Allegheny River across from Pittsburgh. Frame houses crawl up the hill from a tiny business district that is no more than a blur for motorists speeding up and down the valley on Route 28 along the river. The iron mill for which Millvale was named ceased operations more than a century ago, and most other industry trickled away, leaving Millvale a poor little place with four thousand mostly elderly residents and a healthy mortuary trade. Walking through the anemic business district, I came upon at least three funeral homes, including one located in a storefront with a sign offering "grief resources."

About a quarter of the way up the slope, on Howard Street, stood Ulrich's Hotel, a triangular, three-story brick building with a bar and small restaurant on the ground floor and thirteen guest rooms in two upper stories. Rooms were cheap and safe, protected by a steel door at the bottom of a staircase on the street level. The tenants were mostly elderly men, along with a few younger fellows who lived there on disability pensions while recuperating from injuries, or who had merely dropped out of the rat race for a time. Life was not demanding at Ulrich's. At eleven o'clock on the morning I visited, eight men were sitting at the bar, chatting and watching a game show on television. None had known my uncle. One helpful man took me upstairs to the room of the oldest boarder. When he opened his door, an overpowering stench of sweat puffed out of the small, cluttered room. A fetid shroud of melancholy fell over me. In a room such as this, perhaps this very room, my uncle had spent his last lonely years. This boarder, however, had arrived at Ulrich's after Davenport died. "I've known six or seven guys who died here but not him," he said, and closed the door.

At the time of his death, Uncle Harry had been on a downhill slide for a very long time—twenty-seven years, to be precise—since he lost his seat in Congress. He had lived most of that time in Pittsburgh, and I was still curious about his last years in Millvale. Informed that a former Ulrich's boarder named Bill Sitzman might remember Harry, I visited him at an assisted-living home in Millvale. Sitzman, eighty-three, a retired machinist and World War II veteran, sat with me on a bench in the vestibule. He was lean and grizzled and wore suspenders over a white T-shirt. Before answering questions, he insisted on telling me that he was merely a boarder at this home and needed no assistance from anybody.

He had lived next door to Davenport for at least two years at the hotel, Sitzman said. "We weren't too friendly, though. Harry *drank,* you know," he said, pouring a lot of alcohol into "drank." He told me of the morning he saw Harry's bare feet through the register and thought he might have passed out from drinking. "Harry wasn't friendly with many people," Sitzman continued. "He was sort of odd. You'd see him walking on the street reading a book. He must've been a good writer. I heard he wrote political speeches." What speeches? Sitzman shrugged and stood up. By his standards he had talked enough.

According to a death certificate that I received several weeks later, my uncle had had a bleeding ulcer and died of a gastrointestinal hemorrhage at the age of seventy-five.

Lonely deaths seem more poignant when they occur at the end of a long and wasted life. But learning more about Uncle Harry's death did not solve the central mystery of his life. Why, after a meteoric political rise as a liberal Democrat in the 1940s, and a ten-thousand-vote victory over the incumbent in a Republican district of Pittsburgh in 1948, did my uncle lose his bid for a second term in the House of Representatives, seldom work at a paying job over the next three decades, and sink to near homelessness? He lost a wife and young daughter through divorce and alienated family members who helped him. He lived in miserable lodgings, cadged money and drinks, and died on the floor of a pensioners' boarding house in the shell of an industrial town.

The question had nagged me for years. Harry Davenport was the younger of my mother's two older brothers. He had a successful early career as an advertising executive at department stores and Hearst newspapers in various cities. During this time he primed himself for a political career. He read voraciously; studied history and policy issues; learned how to write pithy, eye-catching prose; and taught himself public speaking. Harry Davenport the politician emerged as a self-educated intellectual skilled in the arts of self-display, a New Deal Democrat who planted his flag of social justice well beyond political lines earlier drawn by Franklin D. Roosevelt and Harry Truman.

I occasionally saw Harry when I was growing up in the 1940s in McKeesport, a steel town on the Monongahela River southeast of Pittsburgh. I recall when he was elected to Congress in Pittsburgh's old Twenty-ninth Congressional District. He defeated a prominent member of the House Un-American Activities Committee (HUAC), which was notorious for ruining more lives through guilt by association than the number of Communist spies it actually identified. Even the *New York Times* considered Harry's victory significant enough for separate notice in the paper's national election coverage on November 3, 1948. But something went terribly wrong in Washington during Harry's first term, and he returned to McKeesport a defeated man in 1950. There were rumors in the family of drinking and philandering, but no one could give a definitive answer to what had happened because Harry would not talk about it. He told me that he was writing a book to be titled "Death of a Congressman," hinting that it would be an indictment of people who caused his downfall. Nothing came of this.

I did not see my uncle for several years while I served in the army and later moved around the country as a wire-service and newspaper reporter. In the midsixties, a new reporting job took me to Pittsburgh, where Uncle Harry then lived in a bathhouse on Forbes Avenue (before such places became notorious as sex dens). We talked every few months over drinks in the evening or at holiday dinners at my home. Harry was in his early sixties and had not had a job, aside from occasional stints as a publicist for other politicians (who invariably lost their elections), since he left Congress. When he drank too much, he could be mean and vitriolic. Most of the time, though, I liked my uncle, even if I could not understand why he lived as he did. He was a witty, urbane man, and we talked about books and politics. He always wore a suit and tie, which he somehow managed to keep clean and pressed no matter where he lived, and he still looked and acted the high-flying politician, lording it over bartenders and waiters. Most played along with him, addressing him, tongue-in-cheek, as "Senator" or "Congressman." He was a secretive man and rarely volunteered anything about his life. I was reluctant to ask him about his years in Congress. How do you ask a man, what caused you to fall apart? Once or twice he spoke of those years. He was especially proud of having introduced the first resolution to abolish HUAC. Years later I found corroboration for this claim in the *Congressional Record.* About what caused his defeat in 1950, Uncle Harry spoke to me only once, and on this occasion he contended that he had fallen victim to the political hysteria arising out of the fear of widespread Communist subversion.

I last saw Harry in early 1975, just before I left Pittsburgh to work in New York. Two years later, my mother informed me in a phone call that Harry had died. By then he was living in Millvale, but she had no idea how he had gotten there.

My interest in Harry was revived in 1999 and 2000 by a curious succession of small discoveries that gradually opened a door on the past. My uncle, I found, had indeed been caught in a political squeeze between rival union groups of anti-Communists and Communists. He could not hold up under enormous pressures and may have betrayed a friendship.

The account of his rise and fall, which I present in this book, is only one of many untold stories of personal tragedy resulting from the anti-Communist hysteria of the McCarthy period. But my inquiry also uncovered a complex web of relationships and acts that tell much about the America of that era. I went searching for a story about my uncle and found a much broader one with several remarkable characters.

One was Thomas Quinn, a Pittsburgh union leader and friend of Harry's, who helped my uncle win election to Congress. But Quinn found himself bereft of friends when Red hunters accused him of being a Communist. Called to testify three times before congressional committees, Quinn defied his questioners on each occasion. After his first appearance in 1949, he was convicted of contempt of Congress. The U.S. Supreme Court overturned his conviction in the 1955 landmark case that bears his name, *Quinn v. United States.* Although Quinn worked closely with Communists in his union, investigators never presented indisputable evidence that he himself belonged to the Communist Party and no evidence of any kind that he engaged in subversive activities. Yet he was fired from his job and remained under FBI surveillance for twenty years. Quinn persevered without compromise. He became a labor mediator and went on to become director of the Pennsylvania Bureau of Mediation. As a reporter in the 1960s, I interviewed Quinn on several occasions and renewed my acquaintance with him while hunting for my uncle's past.

The protagonist's role in the story I tell in this book is shared by the two leading characters, Harry Davenport and Tom Quinn, whose lives intertwined at a crucial point. A more limited, supporting role is played by another man whom I became reacquainted with during my search. He is Monsignor Charles Owen Rice, probably the best known of a small cadre of prounion Roman Catholic priests who, in the 1940s, attacked Communist influence in American unions. Known as Pittsburgh's labor priest, Rice helped bring about a catastrophic split in the labor movement over the Red issue in 1949. In the same year, he influenced HUAC to summon Quinn and fellow workers to appear at hearings on trumped-up accusations. These hearings, among the most despicable in HUAC's long tenure, helped propel Harry Davenport down the road to political ruin and blackened Tom Quinn's name for more than ten years. Yet Rice was by no means a villain. His attacks on Communist-led unions were welcomed by many workers, who wanted to rid themselves of leaders seemingly in thrall to the Soviet Union. He later repudiated some of his more "overzealous" actions during that period. In the 1960s, he brought passion and conviction to the struggles against racial discrimination and the Vietnam War.

My story illuminates a dark corner of the Communist witch hunts of the 1940s and 1950s. Much has been written about the unraveling of Soviet spy rings in the United States in the 1940s, of Julius and Ethel Rosenberg, of Alger Hiss and Whittaker Chambers, of Senator Joseph McCarthy and McCarthyism, and of famous cultural figures such as the Hollywood Ten, Arthur Miller, and Lillian Hellman. Little attention has been paid to the thousands of ordinary Americans, working in all kinds of jobs, who suffered for no good reason in the effort to root out Communism. It was no crime to be a member of the Communist Party, although some lawmakers tried hard to criminalize political associations and to restrict free speech. Many workers in the Pittsburgh area lost their jobs because they were accused of belonging to the Communist Party or Communist-front organizations, or because they invoked the constitutional right against self-incrimination before congressional committees, or merely because they were subpoenaed to appear at a hearing. Their families were shunned, their children tormented; many of the accused never again held a good job.

The main events of this story occurred in Pittsburgh and outlying mill and factory towns during a twenty-year period extending from the middle of the 1930s to the 1950s. This may seem long ago and far away to many, but not to me. I grew up in one of those mill towns and have the look of that place and time burned into memory. Like most of my neighbors, however, I did not realize what was happening to those people—a relative few, but still far too many in a country where freedom of expression was a founding principle—who were swept up in the purges of the McCarthy years, from the late forties to the late fifties. While searching for my uncle's story, I also unearthed some of their stories.[1]

1

A TALE OF TWO HARRYS

THERE were not one but two Harry Davenport mysteries in the extended Davenport family. Congressman Harry J. Davenport, my uncle, was at the center of a political and psychological mystery, and his uncle, Harry F. Davenport, was the victim of an unsolved murder decades ago. I had not thought about either Harry for many years when, in the spring of 1999, I visited McKeesport to mourn the death of an aunt in the Davenport family. A conversation with my cousins one evening goaded me into an impulsive—and probably futile, I told myself—search for information about the older Harry, the murder victim. Next morning, with extraordinary good luck, I found a crucial account of that murder and also stumbled on a lead that put me on the trail of the younger Harry.

Harry the former congressman had one older brother and four younger sisters, including my mother, Alyce, who died in 1991. Her sister Annamae, the last survivor of this generation of Davenports, died in April 1999 at the age of ninety-four. Two days before the funeral, Annamae's sons, Harry and Jake Osterman, and others of us in the next generation, gathered at Jake's home in White Oak, outside McKeesport, to reminisce about Annamae and her brothers and sisters.

The Davenports were a colorful gang. Edward, the oldest, went into politics in Los Angeles after an advertising career and was serving his second term on the Los Angeles City Council when he died in 1953. The two oldest girls, Kate and Julia, were twins. Kate, a hospital nurse with a wry wit, died in 1965. Julia became a Roman Catholic nun, Sister Catherine, who spent six years in China as a missionary in the 1930s and was evacuated only a step ahead of Japanese invaders in December 1941. She died in 1997, insisting to the last that she was a year younger than her twin. Annamae, brassy and bossy, had worked for many years as an office manager for various employers, including her brother Harry in the early 1940s. She knew she had only a few days to live when my sister visited her at a nursing home. "Hiya, Lynn," Annamae said. "I'm on my way out." The youngest Davenport, my mother, Alyce, had a bubbling comic sense like her sisters, but unlike them she had no desire to work outside the home and claimed to know nothing about business. She learned quickly enough when my father died suddenly, leaving her with two children and a hotel deeply in debt.

And there was poor Uncle Harry, who had died alone in a place where none of us had ever been. As always, various theories about his decline were offered. He drank too much, or he ran afoul of David Lawrence, former mayor of Pittsburgh and Democratic Party boss in western Pennsylvania. As always we came to no conclusion. Harry was a mystery and would remain so, it seemed.

One of my cousins mentioned the other Harry Davenport, a ghost from decades ago. We had heard stories that he was a policeman in the nearby town of Wilmerding and that he had been murdered by a gang of bootleggers, probably in the 1920s. Was this merely a legend, or was it historical truth? We didn't know. Our family had not kept newspaper clippings and had lost touch with the older Harry's immediate family. We knew only that this Harry was the brother of our grandfather, John W. Davenport. It seemed absurd that we knew so little about our great-uncle who had come to such a mysterious death.

Next day, with a cold wintry rain beating down on my car, I drove to Wilmerding. Although it is located only a few miles from White Oak, getting there, as with so many small towns in the hills of western Pennsylvania, poses a challenge to outsiders. I had not visited Wilmerding in some years, and I had to feel my way, negotiating a series of hills, edging ever closer, until finally I happened onto a vaguely familiar back road that plunged down the north side of a ridge, landing me at the bottom in placid little Wilmerding. Surrounded by hills and bluffs rising to three or four hundred feet above the valley floor, the town straddles Turtle Creek. A shallow, muddy stream contained by concrete flood walls, Turtle Creek curls down the valley and empties into the Monongahela River at Braddock. Wilmerding was one of scores of small industrial towns that sprang up in the late nineteenth century either on the banks of Pittsburgh's rivers—the Monongahela, Allegheny, and Ohio—or in the hollows and valleys formed by their tributaries. Together, these towns and their factories formed a vast, interlocking system of mining and manufacture of steel and metal products that boosted America into the second phase of its industrial revolution. By 1999, industry had abandoned most of the towns, leaving only hulking structural remains, pensioners who once worked the factories and mills, and growing welfare loads.

I was fascinated anew by this remote valley, so far removed in space and time from the new, Internet-driven economy. I had the fanciful notion that if there existed parallel valleys roughly on the order of parallel universes, the Turtle Creek Valley would be such a place, eternally invisible to people in the widely known Monongahela Valley, whose banks were crowded, mile upon mile, with steel mills and furnaces constituting at one time the world's greatest concentration of heavy industry. While the Monongahela Valley received all the acclaim of industrial enthusiasts (and the contempt of Rust Belt haters), on the other side of the first ridge to the north, the Turtle Creek Valley remained hidden amidst towering hills, largely unknown and certainly unvisited by all except its residents. Yet a remarkable industrial system developed along this small stream, a system that was to electrical equipment and railroad braking systems as the Monongahela was to raw steel. In a sense the Turtle Creek Valley was the Silicon Valley of its time.

One man was responsible for this development: George Westinghouse, the prolific inventor and industrialist. In 1887, this valley was a long narrow strip of marshy, partly farmed land with tracks of the Pennsylvania Railroad running up the middle. That year, Westinghouse bought five hundred acres along Turtle Creek, reaching from the present site of Wilmerding to East Pittsburgh, a few miles downstream. In 1889–1890, he raised a factory to produce his patented railroad air brakes and built the town of Wilmerding for the employees of Westinghouse Air Brake Company (WABCO). A few years later, Westinghouse built a plant in East Pittsburgh to manufacture electrical equipment for another of his many firms, Westinghouse Electric Company. By the turn of the century, this hidden valley had become a great manufacturing center with a population of many thousands in a half-dozen towns lining the creek. Radical politics would find fertile breeding ground here in factories, union halls, and ethnic fraternal lodges.[1]

In April 1999, the air-brake plant consisted of several old factory buildings on the south side of the creek. WABCO had vanished in the economic maelstrom that felled many old-line industrial companies in the Pittsburgh area in the 1980s. A new company now operated the plant with a workforce of about two hundred, compared with seven thousand during WABCO's best years. Wilmerding had lost half its population, shrinking to about twenty-two hundred residents. But it was exceptionally clean and neat, displaying none of the rot and abandonment that marked the deindustrialization of so many other mill towns in the nearby river valleys.

I hoped to find information about the Davenport murder at the George Westinghouse Museum, located in the company's former headquarters building. This is a striking old brick-and-stone structure that sits at the top of a sloping, parklike greensward in the middle of town. Built as a community center, reflecting George Westinghouse's visionary, if paternalistic, social philosophy, the four-story building originally contained a library, restaurant, swimming pool, bowling alley, and meeting rooms. After much of the building was destroyed by fire, Westinghouse converted it into WABCO's general offices. Townspeople have always called it the Castle because of its imposing facade, including gabled roofs and a five-story corner tower with synchronized clocks facing in four directions.

The Castle was a marvelous artifact of turn-of-the-century industrial America. Visitors could wander through wide corridors and gaze into spacious offices still furnished with rolltop desks from early in the century. The museum, I found, was devoted primarily to Westinghouse himself, displaying examples of his inventive genius. All worthy exhibits for a museum goer, but of no help to me in my quest for news of a murder. Disappointed, I started to walk out the door. At the last moment, I caught sight of a framed newspaper article hanging on a wall behind a life-size manikin of a woman in an 1890s ball gown. I squeezed behind the manikin and began reading an article headlined "In Memoriam."

It was a clipping from the *WABCO News*, a company newspaper, mourning the loss of the company's chief watchman—and his name leaped out at me—Harry F. Davenport. He was murdered by unknown assailants on the night of December 12, 1926. By a stroke of luck, I had found my man. (The *WABCO News* piece is not dated by year, but it contains clues that later enabled me to find newspaper stories with additional details, confirming the year as 1926.) According to the company paper, Davenport settled in Wilmerding in 1892, became a policeman, and rose to chief of police. In 1914, WABCO hired him as chief watchman, but he continued to serve as a borough constable. It was in this capacity, the piece says, that he "had incurred the enmity and ill will of a gang of boot-leggers on account of his activity in enforcing the Prohibition law." On the night of his death, he was ambushed on a dark street while walking home from the plant. Witnesses said a car pulled alongside Davenport, and a shotgun blast knocked him down. Two men jumped out of the car, struggled briefly with the wounded man, then shot him in the chest. The car raced away before anybody could identify it or the men. Davenport's wife Katherine testified before a coroner's hearing that she heard shots, ran to the door and "saw the slayers speed away." Her husband was fifty-eight. A gang of racketeers headed by the Volpe family of Wilmerding, well known in western Pennsylvania, was widely suspected to be behind the murder. Despite a countywide investigation, no indictments were ever brought.[2]

After making arrangements to obtain a copy of the article, I strolled along a first-floor corridor and came to an office door with the words UE Local 610 painted on the window. I felt another breeze from the past. Once upon a time UE was one of the best-known acronyms in industrial America, standing for United Electrical, Radio and Machine Shop Workers of America. (The union's official name was rarely used, or even known to the members, and the union was universally known as the UE.) In the late 1940s, the union represented more than four hundred thousand workers at General Electric (GE), Westinghouse Electric, Sylvania, and many other corporations. WABCO workers belonged to UE Local 610, and the business agent of the local in the 1960s, I recalled, was a man named Tom Quinn. With quickening excitement, I also recalled that Quinn had known my Uncle Harry and once gave me a provocative lead about his political fate that I never pursued. With Davenports much on my mind, I felt an urgent need to locate Quinn—if he was still alive—and follow up on that conversation.[3]

A woman in the Local 610 office tried to be helpful, but of course she did not know Quinn, who had left the union nearly thirty years before. I began to think my luck had run out. She offered to call the UE national office in Pittsburgh, and rather quickly came up with an address and phone number. Quinn had retired and moved to Pompano Beach, Florida.

Diverted by other projects, I finally wrote to Quinn in December 1999, reminding him who I was and asking if he would repeat in more detail what he had told me about Uncle Harry in the sixties. Within days I received his reply, a six-page, hand-printed letter on tablet paper. Its short, pithy sentences mirrored the directness of Quinn's answers and— I would soon see—of Quinn himself. It was true, he wrote, that Harry was, in a sense, caught in the middle of a battle between the UE and its anti-Communist foes. But there was much more to the story, including a confrontation between Quinn and Harry, related in such understated terms that I could barely restrain my desire to know more.

I would need to interview Quinn at length. But his wife, Irene, was very ill. We finally arranged a meeting in April 2000 at the home of Quinn's son Ronald in the Pittsburgh suburb of Forest Hills.

To motorists passing through, Forest Hills appears to exist only as a pathway to other places. It has no mills or smokestacks, and its dominant physical feature is a divided, four-lane highway that splits the town in half. This is U.S. Route 30, the old transcontinental Lincoln Highway, known locally as Ardmore Boulevard. Lying just east of Pittsburgh, Forest Hills has indeed been a place passed through for more than two hundred years, first by an English army during the French and Indian War on a road hacked through the wilderness and much later by great armies of workers riding streetcars on Ardmore Boulevard to and from factories in the Turtle Creek Valley. At the east end of Forest Hills, one trolley line dipped down a steep incline to drop off workers at the Westinghouse Electric plant in East Pittsburgh, where Tom Quinn emerged as a union leader in the 1940s. Large numbers of Westinghouse employees, including many white-collar office workers and foremen, once lived in comfortable brick homes hidden in wooded ravines and hills on both sides of Ardmore Boulevard. The borough also lay at the geographical center of Harry Davenport's congressional district in 1948–1950.

I made my way from noisy Route 30 to Ron Quinn's home in a quiet, leafy neighborhood. Tom Quinn was standing on the front porch as I drove up. I had last seen him fifteen years earlier at a labor-history conference. He was now eighty-three years old, still slim as I remembered him, but with shoulders slightly bent. As a younger man he had stood about five-eight, not large by any measure. But he had had a wiry, agile, ready-for-anything look. A tilt to his body gave the impression of independence, of a cocky loner, sure of himself, an orphan boy who shouldered his way into a world often closed to orphans and made his own place in it. He had what I thought of as a quintessential Irish face, with pointed nose and protuberant cheekbones.

Tom had had a rough time in recent months. Irene, his wife of more than sixty years, contracted cancer while they were living in Florida. The Quinns' three sons, all Pittsburgh-area residents, brought their parents back to Pittsburgh and placed Irene in a nursing home. Quinn suffered a nervous breakdown and was hospitalized for a month. Strong-minded and resilient, Tom recovered sufficiently to leave the hospital and move in with Ron.

Knowing that I wanted to talk to his father, Ron had invited me to dinner. Another of Quinn's sons, Stephen, also was present. The Quinn brothers, I came to understand, had grown up in a close-knit family and were intent on protecting their father from any harm. Ron, fifty-eight, headed the Bureau of Employment and Training of Allegheny County. He also was a professionally trained bassoonist who played frequently with small orchestras. His living room bookcases were stuffed with books on art and art history. Steve, fifty-four, was a history professor at a local college. The oldest brother, Charles ("Chuck"), was principal of education at a state prison in western Pennsylvania.

We talked for two hours over dinner and dessert. When I switched on a tape recorder, Quinn responded to questions directly and simply, without exaggeration or rhetoric. The illness had left him feeling weak, but his extraordinary memory enabled him to recall events of fifty to sixty years ago in considerable detail. During one of my interviews with him in the 1960s, Quinn had told me that the UE helped elect Harry Davenport to Congress in 1948 and turned against him in 1950. I assumed this was merely a case of a union punishing a politician for casting a few wrong votes. I was wrong about that. I was also wrong in assuming that Quinn knew Harry only as a political acquaintance. I changed my mind when Quinn asked a question that startled me. Talking about Harry's congressional campaign in 1948, Quinn said, "He was very progressive, and we had high hopes for him . . ." He paused and asked, "Did he have a sister who was a nun?" Yes, I said, mentioning her name, Sister Catherine. Quinn nodded. "I thought I recalled that. Harry and I, you know, we became pretty good friends. We'd go out night after night around the clubs and bars to campaign. You'd go into the bar and buy everybody a drink, set them up. Harry did more than buy one. He had a few himself. Some nights I had to push him up the stairs to get him to his apartment. But I liked him. We had a real opportunity to have a damned good congressman from the Twenty-ninth District."

If Tom had retained the memory of Harry's sister for more than a half century, I thought, the two men must have been more than political allies who shook hands once or twice. They appeared to have been friends, and my uncle might have betrayed that friendship for political reasons. It was not nice to contemplate, but I pressed on.

Quinn had many other memories about the persecution of Communists and non-Communists alike in the 1940s and early 1950s. He told of friends who spiraled down hill after losing their jobs; informers who were acclaimed as heroes for accusing people, only to be discredited later as liars; FBI agents monitoring his (Quinn's) activities year after year; Father Rice and his machinations; newspaper sensationalism; and the steadfastness of his wife and sons, who put up with threats and harassing phone calls without complaint.

By the time I left Ron Quinn's home, I had decided to continue my search for the elusive Harry Davenport. Tom Quinn had provided pieces of evidence that needed to be verified and augmented by other details about the man and his times. Over the next few years I interviewed Quinn many times. Most other participants in those events had long since died, but I talked to a few who remained, including Monsignor Rice. I also read oral histories and old newspaper accounts and found much useful material in the UE Archives at the University of Pittsburgh's Archives Service Center. The National Archives in Washington provided access to HUAC records.

As the fruits of this research began to accumulate, I decided to construct a story. The very act of writing a story, I thought, would put the material in perspective and yield insights that otherwise would remain buried under the surface of events. I wanted to know what Uncle Harry did and why he did it. Quinn had told me that he first met my uncle in the spring or summer of 1948 during Harry's campaign for Congress. Since that year also happened to be an important one in my own life, it provided an excellent borehole to the past.

McKeesport in the summer of 1948: sultry heat, the hollow clang of pipe banging against pipe at the National Tube Works, men streaming to and from the mill gates three times a day, soot raining down, sidewalks often blanketed with glittering specks of graphite deposited during a volcanic "slip" in a blast furnace. It was a busy time. A series of industrial strikes had disrupted life in the Monongahela and Turtle Creek valleys for two years after World War II. But with labor peace more or less restored, the factory towns had settled into a plodding routine of producing more and more steel and electrical equipment for the surging postwar economy. Nationally, Harry S. Truman was running for reelection, and in Pittsburgh, a dozen miles downriver from McKeesport, Harry Davenport was making his second bid for a seat in Congress.

I did not see much of my uncle that summer because of family circumstances. I had finished high school in the spring and would go away to college in the fall. I was excited but apprehensive about a future bristling with menace. With World War II only three years past, the United States and its allies were siding against the Soviet Union in a new conflict called the Cold War. Great armies were massed and poised to strike from either side of an artificial line dividing Western and Eastern Europe. Meanwhile, America, England, and France were airlifting food, fuel, and medical supplies into West Berlin, which stood isolated behind a Soviet blockade. On any given day, war seemed imminent. In the United States, HUAC was accusing Alger Hiss, a former state department official, of spying for the Soviets. It was said that Russia soon would produce its first atomic bomb, with bomb-making secrets provided by agents in the United States. In retrospect, this political environment seems mild in comparison with the threats posed today by nuclear and biological terrorism, the AIDS epidemic, global warming, and human reproductive cloning. But it was all we had at the time, and it seemed darkly ominous to a seventeen-year-old boy.

On the other hand, the future for me and our family seemed promising. My father was entering a new line of business. His beer distributorship, buoyed by wartime wages, had done very well, but Dad craved the challenge of planning and building something new. In 1948 he bought the old Clinton Hotel, a six-story building on Fifth Avenue in the middle of the business district and two blocks from the Tube Works. McKeesport was booming in those early postwar days, when American steel had few competitors around the world. With construction crews and businesspeople crowding into town, Dad foresaw the need for more hotel space. That summer I pitched in as a carpenter's helper and painter's apprentice as Dad renovated the old Clinton from top to bottom and renamed it the McKeesporter Hotel.

The McKeesporter would become a haven for Uncle Harry at a difficult time, and I would come to know him better then. But in 1948 I perceived him only as a remote figure moving on the periphery of my immediate family. I had no informed opinion on his congressional campaign or his politics, though of course I knew he would be good for the country because he was my mother's brother. But I did not make personal plans based on Uncle Harry's election—aside, that is, from thinking vaguely about securing an appointment to Annapolis. Never mind that I was not a football star and that I lacked a quarter of an inch in height to qualify for education as a future Admiral Farragut. Congressman Davenport's influence, I may have thought, would somehow boost me over that shortfall.

I had been aware of Uncle Harry from the time that I was about nine or ten, when he would show up at Davenport family reunions, blowing in from some distant place, usually alone. He was not married then and shared an apartment in Pittsburgh with his mother, my grandmother, a widow for many years. In the early forties, Harry served as executive secretary of a chamber of commerce in the East Liberty section of Pittsburgh and also published a weekly shopper's guide called the *East Liberty Shopping News*. Before that he had worked in several cities as a retail advertising man and along the way had picked up a broad knowledge of politics, culture, and business as well as a large store of anecdotes from which he drew in relating explosively funny stories. When he felt like being charming, wit and humor seemed to burst from every pore. But just as often he radiated a moody darkness that concealed inner churnings of unknown magnitude. In his late thirties, Harry stood about five feet nine or ten inches and had thinning black hair and a thick chest. He looked impressive in a double-breasted business suit and walked about— glided, really—with all the dignity, grace, and certainty (already) of a powerful politician, as if he were chairman of a Senate committee.

My mother, father, sister, and I visited Harry and Grandmother every now and then on Marchand Street in Shadyside, right around the corner from Sacred Heart Church and adjacent to East Liberty. They had a capacious second-floor apartment with a large dining room and living room and a front sunroom with three windows set side by side. I would stand at the windows, gazing down on a vacant street. I remember those visits with some particularity because time seemed to stand still in that neighborhood of large homes and apartment houses and few children. When I went outside, there was nothing to do except kick the curb and stare back up at the windows in the sunroom. When Uncle Harry was home, he would bustle about in a starched white shirt and tie, talking on the phone or working at a desk in the corner of the dining room. His shopping-news layouts would be spread over the dining room table, and he would occasionally pause at the table and with quick, sure hands shift a few mocked-up ads from one place to another. He gave the impression of being much in demand and always on the move. When Mother and Grandmother took us on a tour of stores in East Liberty's prosperous shopping district, Uncle Harry's handiwork, the *Shopping News*, would be everywhere—in shoppers' hands, at street-corner kiosks, lying discarded on the sidewalk.

When Harry ran for Congress on the Democratic ticket in 1948, some of the Davenport in-laws were not happy with his liberal political views. My parents contributed to his campaign, though more out of familial ties than political passion. Mother was apolitical most of her life, except in 1952 when she voted for Eisenhower, believing that he would keep me out of combat in Korea. Dad and his father both had been Democrats at least since the early 1920s, in part because the Democratic Party supported repeal of Prohibition, an action devoutly desired by Granddad, who had made a good living in the wholesale beer and liquor business. They also gravitated naturally toward the party that espoused the cause of the common man, even though it did more espousing than accomplishing. Dad rarely talked about politics, but he had enthusiastically supported Franklin D. Roosevelt, probably because FDR, like Dad, did not sit around waiting for supply and demand to come back into balance when business slumped. Uncle Harry's liberal convictions comported with Dad's belief that every man (if not yet every woman) deserved an equal chance.

We were too busy at the hotel that summer to become involved in Uncle Harry's campaign. But one evening my dad took us to a Davenport for Congress rally at a meeting hall somewhere in Pittsburgh. Several dozen people were milling around. The men drank beer from a half barrel contributed by my father. We sat on wooden folding chairs and listened to the speeches. I remember that my uncle salted his speech with an Irish accent for the benefit of the Irish Americans in the audience. I thought he laid it on a bit thick. But then he was a politician. For years after that, politics to me meant laying on the brogue. I have no recollection of what issues Harry talked about, what promises he might have made or equivocated on. Politics held no interest for me at that age. Too young to vote, I was absorbed in heroic thoughts of sports and romantic notions about girls. That year's presidential campaign also confused me. President Truman was running against Republican Thomas E. Dewey and a third-party candidate, Henry Wallace. There was much muddled talk, as far as I was concerned, about the Cold War, Communist spies, the atomic bomb, and labor unions.

Tom Quinn was probably at this meeting, and very likely my gaze lit on him, then quickly passed on, as it wandered over the hall in search of girls. After renewing our acquaintance in 2000, I mentioned this meeting a couple of times. Based on the scanty evidence I offered, Quinn could not recall the specific event but said he attended most of Harry's rallies in 1948. As legislative chairman of the UE local at Westinghouse's East Pittsburgh plant, he organized voter support for UE-backed candidates. The union was pushing Davenport in particular because his victory in a Republican district would help swing control of the House of Representatives back to the Democrats after major losses in 1946.

In a sense, then, I was present at or near the beginning of Harry and Tom's political relationship and personal friendship, which, as it turned out, would be one of the few keys that might unlock the secret of Harry Davenport. Fifty years later, when Quinn told me his story, a remarkable one in its own right, I came closer to understanding how he and Uncle Harry became friends and how their friendship fell victim to a crisis in both of their lives.

Tom Quinn was born on August 10, 1917, in Pittsburgh. Within a year his mother, Lillian, and probably his father were swept away in the great flu epidemic of 1918. Tom never knew his father's name and, years later, failed to find a trace of him in the chaos of the birth and death records for 1918. As a young boy, Tom knew only that he had no father and that the woman he knew as his mother, a widow named Adelia, was a tall, robust, hard-working woman who had immigrated from Ireland. After her husband died, she operated boardinghouses of the kind that were common in working-class neighborhoods, offering tiny rooms or dormitory beds to single men who worked in factories or on construction jobs. Tom remembered in particular a big frame house on Wylie Avenue in the lower part of Pittsburgh's Hill District, a large immigrant neighborhood that sprawled across a hill just behind the city's business district.

The seven or eight boarders who lived in Adelia's house were mostly migrant construction men lured to Pittsburgh by work on new skyscraper headquarters buildings for major corporations. Young Tom performed many chores, such as shopping for vegetables and fetching chewing tobacco and White Mule moonshine from Adelia's larder when the boarders requested either. They were tough, weather-beaten men who wore soft caps and overalls with shoulder straps and carried their own tools. Tom liked to listen to them talk about their work. They seemed giantlike and heroic, and they treated him protectively. It was not the same as having a father. There was no towering father figure in his young life. But Adelia gave him love and made sure he received a good education, enrolling him in a Catholic grade school. In the 1920s, parochial schools generally were superior to public schools, and Tom's report cards usually had solid columns of A's.

This life came to a sudden end in early 1929. Adelia suffered a severe heart attack one night and died before morning. She had not yet turned fifty, and Tom was only eleven. Adelia had had the foresight to name her physician as Tom's guardian. He sent Tom to live with one of Adelia's sisters, Mary Layton, in Youngstown, Ohio, some sixty miles northwest of Pittsburgh. Mary, probably already in her sixties, also was a widow. She had six daughters, five already grown and married, and one son, and she worked nights as a cleaning woman in the offices of a utility. Mary had not had an easy life, but she was willing to give Tom a home. The sale of Adelia's boarding house had brought in a little money, which helped Mary care for Tom.

Sometime after he arrived in Youngstown, Tom learned a startling truth about his "mother," Adelia. She was really his grandmother, who had taken him in after his real mother died, Mary told him. Mary did not make this disclosure out of malice; she thought the boy was old enough to know the truth. Tom remembered being shocked, but the revelation did not change his feelings for Adelia. He still thought of her as Mother, who had done her best for him.

When Quinn told me this story in the summer of 2000, in one of my extensive interviews with him, seventy years had passed since his boyhood. He had had an eventful, sometimes stormy, life starting at a very early age. Yet he dredged up memories of tough times with equanimity rather than bitterness. Gazing levelly at me as we sat on the front porch of his son's home in Forest Hills, Quinn described each experience in simple, understated terms. When I suggested that he might have had an extraordinary amount of bad luck early in life, he shrugged. In this shrug I saw that he had long since crossed that hurdle and had no need to jump more. Later, when I read his words as I transcribed them from my tape recorder, it occurred to me that Quinn learned at a very young age to take a skeptical view of life as it presented itself to him. Very little was as it seemed, and one must question conventional beliefs about religion, politics, or anything else.

In Youngstown, Tom finished sixth grade at a Catholic school, served as an altar boy, and sang in a church choir. Impressed with his abilities, the nuns skipped him over seventh grade. After Tom completed eighth grade, Mary dipped into Adelia's small inheritance to pay tuition at Ursuline Academy, where he finished two years of high school. In the Layton home, he formed a close friendship with Mary's son, Charles, who, though only in his twenties, had already seen much of the United States. He had hopped freights and traveled to California, where he worked as a fruit picker. Tiring of this, he rode the rails back to Youngstown and found a job in a steel mill. Shortly after Tom arrived, Charles was laid off at the mill and came home to live with his mother. In the early 1930s, times were getting hard. Charles could not find steady work and began selling appliances door to door. With time to spare, he took an interest in Tom, talking to him, taking him to the library, encouraging him to read. Charles himself had developed a love of literature, especially works that illuminated the social condition. He introduced Tom to the novels of H. G. Wells and John Galsworthy and to the plays of George Bernard Shaw and Eugene O'Neill. Charles professed to be a Socialist and said the country had to find a new way; capitalism was not working.

"He [Charles] had quite a bit of influence on my life, even though I only lived with him for a short amount of time," Quinn would say of Charles many years later in an interview with historian Ronald Schatz. "I don't know that he was a union activist, but he was kind of a free spirit. He had a pretty good idea of what kind of society we live in. He talked about the lousy conditions in the mills, and he said we have to do something about these conditions. But everybody was talking about that at that point. The jobs just disappeared. Guys were out there scrounging around. I remember, about every three months he [Charles] was selling something different, vacuum sweepers, telephones, selling stuff."[4]

Under Charles's influence, Tom was drawn to books, especially social-protest literature. Dissatisfied with the reading assigned in school, he would play hooky some mornings and go to the public library to read more of Shaw. But this life was nearing an end. With family income dwindling and Tom's small inheritance exhausted, Mary Layton could no longer provide a home for him. She reluctantly appealed to Tom's guardian, and it was decided to transfer him to a Catholic orphanage in Pittsburgh, St. Joseph's Protectory. Charles argued against the move, and Mary cried and wrung her hands. Tom did not want to go to an orphanage, but he understood why it had to be so. Nonetheless, it was the third major separation of his young life. It could have embittered him or made him feel unloved, but he did not remember it that way. "Looking back, I'd say I was pretty fortunate," he told me in 2000. "There were always people there to help me. I was never hungry. I dressed well . . . got a good education." His great-aunt, he felt, had been more than kind to give him a home in the first place.

After moving to Pittsburgh, he heard occasionally from the Laytons in Youngstown. But Tom never saw Charles again—until his funeral. This occurred in 1933 or 1934. Charles committed suicide. "He never got a real job again," Quinn recalled. "His situation became intolerable, and he started drinking. He drank some terrible poison that ate him up inside. I went there for the funeral. It sure was heartbreaking."

St. Joseph's Protectory, located in Pittsburgh's Hill District not far from Adelia's boardinghouse on Wylie Avenue, was home to sixty-five or seventy boys, mostly orphans, ranging in age from about seven to twenty. The priests who ran the home were not Dickensian ogres who mistreated their innocent charges. The boys were not put to hard labor or abused in any way. There was, however, a price to pay for being an orphan, an intellectual price. Tom enjoyed learning and wanted to finish high school. But St. Joseph's could afford to pay tuition for only one or two boys each year at Pittsburgh's Central Catholic High School. Tom was not one of those chosen; he was enrolled instead in a welding course at the Connelley Trade School in the Hill District. His academic education came to an abrupt halt.

Even as he told me this story seventy years later, I could sense how deeply the loss had affected him. To be cut off from books and book learning went beyond the normal punishment that indifferent society metes out to orphans. Rationally, Quinn knew that no one intended harm in denying him an academic education; emotionally, he never forgot it.

At St. Joseph's, Tom and several other older boys were housed in a separate building where they supervised themselves. They prepared meals and ate together and formed baseball and basketball teams. Quinn became a leader on both teams, even arranging game schedules and buying equipment. Then and later in life, when something needed doing, Quinn would step in and do it.

When I first visited the Hill District a few years before the urban riots of 1968, it had become almost entirely a black community, seething with anger—justifiably, I thought, even as I nervously threaded my way through groups of sullen men on street corners. Tom Quinn spent most of his early years in the Hill during the 1920s and 1930s, when it was the most colorful, exciting neighborhood in Pittsburgh. Since early in the century the Hill had attracted the poorest of newcomers from many ethnic groups, including the Irish, Jews, Italians, Germans, Syrians, and especially African Americans. Cheap tenement housing and warrens of hovels and tiny homes proliferated on the hillside overlooking Pittsburgh's Point, where the Monongahela and Allegheny rivers join to form the Ohio. By the 1920s, a growing black population dominated the Hill's culture and politics. To the degree that a black middle class and black institutions existed in Pittsburgh, they were centered in the Hill District, Homewood, and a few smaller neighborhoods. The Hill was a paradoxical community where people depended on their churches and religious networks for moral and spiritual guidance and at the same time supported a widespread numbers racket led by chiefs who, at least in legend, were Robin Hood–like characters. Jazz music blared from speakeasies and notable nightspots such as the Crawford Grill, and musicians such as Duke Ellington often performed in Hill establishments. Baseball enthusiasts crowded into the home fields of the Homestead Grays and Pittsburgh Crawfords, great Negro League baseball teams. Whites and blacks lived in peace in the Hill during those years, partly because most were poor and were recent immigrants from Europe and migrants from the American South.[5]

Quinn enjoyed this diversity as he grew to manhood, and he learned much about the bleakness forced on many people by poverty and discrimination and about the fortitude needed to surmount these circumstances. He also developed a strong sense of self. Growing up without a father and mother making decisions, leading him along one path or another, Tom began to think for himself. However well he was treated by relatives and others who cared for him, he essentially was alone in life. He had to be responsible for himself.

Tom's grandmother had brought him up as a Catholic, and he had attended Catholic church with his relatives in Youngstown. At the same time his cousin Charles, who had quit the Church as a young man, was introducing Tom to literature and to rudimentary socialist concepts that scoffed at both capitalism and religion. By the time he arrived at St. Joseph's, Tom had decided that religion had not helped him much in the past and would not in the future. At the age of fifteen or sixteen he began skipping Sunday Mass at the Protectory. One Sunday a priest found him holed up with a book in the boiler room during Mass. The priest lectured him and told him to go to the chapel and pray to his mother. "I went to the chapel," Quinn said in 2000, "but I didn't have any feeling about the efficacy of prayer. Part of it was my cousin's influence. I didn't see the value of going to church. It may be that I saw all this misery [during the Depression] and wondered, what value is religion. I don't know. I just came to this conclusion." He became an atheist.

Turning eighteen in 1935, Quinn was placed in a work-school cooperative program, alternating two weeks of work with two weeks of schooling, at a small factory in the Pittsburgh suburb of Sharpsburg. In theory, a co-op program enabled a student to earn money while learning on the job, and the employer gained a low-wage apprentice who might become a valuable skilled worker. In practice, employers tended to exploit student-workers, demanding the equivalent of a full day's work for a half day's wage. With the streets full of unemployed men and boys, many employers felt entitled by the law of supply and demand to operate with cheap labor. But Quinn refused to be exploited. Thus came his first run-in with management.

He had been hired by the Sharpsburg firm as a welder at twenty-five cents an hour. When he demonstrated his proficiency, the company gave him a ten-cent raise and assigned him to a full-time work schedule.

Quinn said he would gladly work forty hours a week if management would pay him the regular welder's rate of eighty-five cents an hour. His boss did not like this attitude. There were plenty of other Connelley boys willing to take Tom's place. Quinn refused to back down because "what they were trying to do wasn't right." The situation reinforced Quinn's growing awareness that he was on his own. He still lived at the Protectory, but the priests were busy with younger boys. Connelley School administrators said they were powerless; Tom would have to abide by the employer's policy. He still refused. He was fired.

He was not alone. Everywhere he went around Pittsburgh he saw out-of-work men and boys, some standing in long lines to apply for a job, some wandering the streets in ragged clothing. When he got together with other young men, they usually talked about who was hiring and what they paid and what the conditions were like—not that you could change conditions. Finally, Tom heard that Jones and Laughlin Steel Corporation (J&L) was hiring at its huge plant in Aliquippa, some fifteen miles down the Ohio River from Pittsburgh. In January 1937, Tom and a friend from the Protectory moved a few belongings into a cheap room at an Aliquippa boardinghouse and went to work in the steel mill. Not for the last time, Quinn would be caught up in a historic event.

2

LABOR TURMOIL, 1937

A S 1937 recedes in time, its historical importance swells in my imagination. More than sixty years later, I still remember my parents lamenting about friends who were living hand to mouth in that seventh year of the Great Depression. Everybody, it seemed, was pursuing scarce jobs, and the New Deal acronyms WPA and CCC rolled familiarly off the adults' tongues as they talked of the out-of-work cousin who finally got a job sweeping streets in a WPA (Works Progress Administration) program, or the young man in the next block who went out West to chop down trees at a CCC (Civilian Conservation Corps) camp. People were driving Pierce-Arrows, old Model-T's, and roadsters with open rumble seats; riding streetcars everywhere in the Pittsburgh area; trying to make a comeback from disastrous reversals; listening to jazz and the new swing music; dancing the jitterbug to songs like "Chattanooga Choo Choo"; and joining unions in massive numbers. This last phenomenon, one of the great social movements in American history, swept up millions of people and eventually deposited Harry, Tom, and Father Rice at the same historical juncture.

My earliest memory of an outside world intruding on my boy's awareness is from 1937. I was six years old and a first-grader at George Washington School on Sumac Street in McKeesport. One Saturday morning, as I strolled past the school looking for playmates, I spotted two men on the sidewalk across the street, walking rapidly in my direction. Each had what appeared to be a sign hanging from his neck with large black words that said something like "Go, CIO." I stopped and gaped. Having read the adventures of Dick and Jane, I knew what go meant, but CIO stumped me. I had absorbed enough of American culture by this time to understand that the men were advertising something. To whom? I saw no one else on either sidewalk in that long block of Sumac; no adults, no other children. When they passed by, I saw that the signs on their chests had doubles that hung down their backs, with the same words. Unable to make heads or tails of this business, I went on my way.

Later that day, I probably asked my father and mother about CIO, and they probably gave a vague explanation, mentioning "the mill" and "the union." Dad rarely talked about unions and never about anything as hypothetical as the class struggle or as abstract as capitalism. I never heard him disparage organized labor or "mill men." A few years later, when he opened his beer distributorship, I am certain he would have been offended if his drivers and helpers attempted to form a union. He thought he treated them pretty well.

Eventually I came to understand that CIO stood for a union organization known as the Committee for Industrial Organization (changed in 1938 to Congress of Industrial Organizations). The story of its founding in the mid-1930s has been told often. Workers in mass-production industries were clamoring to be organized, but the American Federation of Labor (AFL) responded lethargically to this demand. In 1935, eight unions affiliated with the AFL formed a committee to initiate new organizing campaigns and a year later converted the CIO into a federation rivaling the AFL. Despite early difficulties, the CIO would grow to 4 million members by the late 1940s while establishing new unions in industries such as steel, autos, electrical equipment, rubber products, and others.

The men who marched down Sumac Street with the CIO signs were my introduction to the labor movement, a subject that would occupy me during most of my working life as a reporter. By 1937, the CIO was throwing large amounts of money and manpower into organizing the steel industry, and McKeesport steel mills and foundries were a major target. The National Tube Company, a U.S. Steel subsidiary, employed thousands of men in a large conglomeration of furnaces and mills strung along the banks of the Monongahela River. Smaller mills and factories scattered around the city employed hundreds more. At every mill and foundry gate, CIO organizers would collar workers at shift change, asking them to sign a pledge card and contribute fifty cents or a dollar. Occasionally men would parade around with picket signs. But this activity always occurred downtown in the vicinity of the mills, not in residential neighborhoods, where I spotted my first CIO men. Their appearance on quiet Sumac Street was so at odds with what I knew about the world at the age of six that I never forgot them.

Like those out-of-place men, the CIO itself was a once-in-a-lifetime occurrence. It took root in unlikely capitalist soil, sprouted, and produced a brilliant, if short-lived, flower that touched the lives of millions of families across the United States. The CIO today is all but forgotten. But in the first ten years of its existence, it was a ubiquitous presence in industrial towns such as McKeesport. By the time I was nine or ten years old, every school kid knew that the CIO was a mighty union organization of some kind. The CIO founded the United Steelworkers of America and remained a sort of domineering older brother to the fledgling steel union for several years. When the union struck the mills in the 1940s, people talked of the CIO being on strike, not the Steelworkers.

A mention of CIO conjured a very tangible sense of power, always countervailing power. Wherever you had a steel corporation or an automobile or coal-mining company, you also had the CIO—and its larger-than-life president, John L. Lewis. He was an imposing hulk of a man who scowled out from under thick black eyebrows, spoke in a sonorous voice, and threw down oratorical lightning bolts crackling with bits of Old Testament pronouncements borrowed from God. Just to speak the name John L. Lewis was to invoke, on the side of labor, a Herculean hero, and in the minds of the capitalist class, a ruthless ogre. As president of the United Mine Workers of America, he had been the prime mover in creating the CIO. He, more than all other union leaders in the thirties, knew that a great historical opportunity had arrived, and he had seized it.

I had no reason to venerate Lewis or the CIO, as did families whose livelihood depended on the ability of CIO unions to wrest wages and benefits from corporations. But I know now, if I did not in the 1940s, that my father's retail businesses benefited greatly from rising steel wages. The CIO represented more than economic power; its influence pervaded many aspects of life in a mill town. Men wore CIO caps and played on softball teams in a CIO league. Tube City Brewing Company, which had made the popular Tube City beer in McKeesport since the 1890s, introduced a CIO Pilsener in 1936 or 1937. But the brewery offered a choice to beer drinkers who hated unions—and there were plenty of these in McKeesport. The label on pilsener bottles suggested that CIO could be interpreted as meaning Choice Ingredients Only.[1]

The CIO's economic impact spread far beyond the mill towns. The Steelworkers, United Auto Workers (UAW), and other CIO affiliates conducted long, contentious strikes to establish concepts such as company-funded pension and health insurance plans, cost-of-living raises, multiweek vacations, and strong grievance procedures that protected workers from being fired without cause. In the years following World War II, these concepts and policies formed the bedrock of the employment contract for most large corporations, union or nonunion. In the Monongahela Valley, the CIO and the Steelworkers also brought political democracy to mill towns that had been under one-party Republican rule for three decades.

Despite these successes, the CIO did not endure as an independent federation. It merged with the larger AFL in 1955 after internal divisions had shrunk the CIO's ranks. As the 1940s drew to a close, the organization had burst into a self-devouring political firestorm. Metaphorically, it might be said that Father Rice helped ignite the fire, which seared many loyal members such as Tom Quinn—and consumed friendly outsiders who ventured too close, including my uncle, Harry Davenport.

Back in the 1930s, though, the rise of the CIO fired Uncle Harry's simmering passion for political reform. Working as an ad writer and salesman at a Detroit department store, he saw the misery caused by auto-industry shutdowns and layoffs in the Depression. Thousands of jobless workers wandered the streets looking for work and handouts. In 1933, about 13 million people, 25 percent of the national workforce, were unemployed. Harry read about general strikes that immobilized San Francisco and Minneapolis in 1934, and worker unrest and anger about corporate employment policies was spreading. Management could cut wages without notice, fire or lay off people for any reason (or no reason), and arbitrarily promote and demote workers; foremen could punish workers they disliked and reward toadies. Ordinary workers did not have medical benefits or health insurance, and pension plans existed only for managers or well-paid employees who could contribute a portion of their salaries to a pension fund. Unionization posed little threat because employers would fire union activists, and local police would run organizers out of town. Many factory towns abolished the right to assemble peacefully and speak freely in support of unions.

The federal government finally took action in 1935, when a Democratic Congress passed and President Roosevelt signed into law the National Labor Relations Act. The Wagner Act, as it was known, made union activity a right protected by federal law. It encouraged workers to join unions and raise their standard of living through collective bargaining. More than anything else, the new law gave workers hope—hope that by banding together they could bring about change. The CIO set out to convert this restless militancy into organized power. With five hundred thousand dollars of seed money from the Mine Workers' treasury, John L. Lewis hired hundreds of organizers and sent them to industrial towns throughout the East and Midwest to begin recruiting new members on a massive scale.

In early 1937, sit-down strikes waged by auto workers in Detroit and Flint, Michigan, pushed giant General Motors to recognize and bargain with the CIO's UAW. In Detroit, Harry Davenport cheered on the sit-down strikers, visualizing a new labor movement spearheaded by the CIO as an instrument for generating social and political reform.

Two months later, U.S. Steel surprised everyone by negotiating a first contract with the CIO's incipient steel union, the Steel Workers' Organizing Committee. In Pittsburgh, the recently ordained Father Charles Owen Rice, eager to demonstrate the centrality of the Catholic Church in the lives of working people, walked on picket lines and urged workers to join unions. Tom Quinn was even more directly affected when CIO organizers arrived at the Jones and Laughlin Aliquippa Works.[2]

In January 1937, the Aliquippa Works stretched two miles along the Ohio River and employed, at full strength, more than ten thousand workers. J&L had built the plant in the early 1900s, and the town of Aliquippa along with it. The company dominated the political life of the town with the same authoritarian zeal that it ran the mill. Local politicians owed their offices to J&L's endorsement. Police officers ran a campaign of terror against union activists at the company's behest. Although U.S. Steel had accepted unionization, J&L and other major steel producers, collectively known as Little Steel, refused to line up behind the industry leader. Contending that the Wagner Act was unconstitutional, these firms set up machine guns at the plant gates to keep picketing strikers at bay.

When the newly formed National Labor Relations Board (NLRB) found J&L guilty of illegally discharging ten employees, the company appealed the decision. The case eventually reached the U.S. Supreme Court, where *NLRB v. Jones and Laughlin Steel Corp.* became the crucial test case of the Wagner Act's constitutionality.[3]

Quinn was vaguely aware of this case, then pending before the Supreme Court, when he started as a maintenance welder in Aliquippa's tin mill. He received eighty cents an hour, a fair enough wage, he thought. But he did not like the bosses' arbitrary use of power. Men could be ordered to change shifts with little notice or assigned hard or menial tasks as punishment. Foremen often promoted friends or relatives, disregarding qualifications or seniority. Quinn saw that there was plenty of unrest in the mill, but at the age of nineteen he was happy merely to have his first well-paying job. He knew almost nothing about the union.

Leaving work one night, Quinn was stopped on the street by a man who whispered, "Hey, kid, want to sign a union card?" Quinn recalled, "We went into an alleyway, and he pulled out a card, and I signed it. I said, 'Sure I'll join the union, what the hell.' I didn't have any idea . . . what it was all about, or even what a union would do for us. Except that we had to do something, because of all the shit we were getting."

On April 12, 1937, the Supreme Court upheld the NLRB's decision and order against J&L. The Court declared that the federal government had the power to regulate labor relations in the private sector. While the employer has the right to hire and fire, the Court said, it "may not, under cover of that right, intimidate or coerce its employees." Despite the decision, J&L refused to recognize the union. Quinn remembered attending a union meeting one night at an ethnic hall. A union official told the men they would have to strike to force the company to obey the law.

The strike started at 11 p.m. on May 12. To enter the plant at the main gate, workers had to pass through a tunnel under a set of railroad tracks. The company commandeered a bus from the local bus line, which J&L owned, filled it with strikebreakers, and headed for the tunnel. It drew up at the tunnel mouth, where a huge throng of workers, Quinn among them, choked the passageway. A bloody confrontation might have ensued, Quinn recalled, had it not been for one person. "A little old lady with a black umbrella stood in front of the bus with umbrella pointed at it like a sword. They backed off the bus. She became well known, that little old lady in black. Later in the day, she tried to stop scabs from going onto an overpass that went into the plant. Some got through, but not many."

The mass picketing continued for a day and a half, and the situation remained tense until Pennsylvania governor George Earle entered the plant and talked with J&L managers. With federal law and the U.S. Supreme Court involved, management finally concluded that they could no longer run the town as a private fiefdom. They agreed to abide by the results of a representation election conducted by the NLRB. Six days later, workers at all J&L plants voted for the union, about seventeen thousand votes to seven thousand against the union. The company then signed its first union agreement, raising pay across the board by ten cents an hour and reducing the standard work week from forty-eight to forty hours. Despite J&L's capitulation, several other Little Steel companies lured strikers back to work and continued to operate nonunion until 1940–1941. But after the Supreme Court decision against J&L, no American corporation ever mounted a serious challenge to the Wagner Act on constitutional grounds. Eventually, though, company executives found weaknesses in the law that enabled them to resist unionization attempts.[4]

For Quinn, it was exhilarating to be part of such a victory. But he did not last long enough at Aliquippa to judge whether the new union would make a significant change in the lives of workers. Laid off in September because of a slumping economy, he moved back to Pittsburgh and took a short-lived job at Westinghouse Electric in East Pittsburgh. Laid off again in December 1937, Quinn would be out of work for several months as the Little Depression of 1937–1938 exacted a toll on Pittsburgh's manufacturing industries.

Although the CIO would experience many failures over the next few years, by 1937 it had arrived on the national scene with explosive power. That year turned out to be significant also in the lives of both Uncle Harry and Father Rice.

In 1937 Uncle Harry threw aside all political inhibitions and joined the Communist Party USA (CPUSA) in Detroit. He was by no means alone. Thousands of other Americans, convinced that capitalism had wrecked the country, turned to radical politics in the hope of finding a way out of the Depression. People yearned to take part in a political movement that would address unemployment, poverty, racism, and economic inequality. The CPUSA had abandoned a narrow sectarian approach and now was working to build a broad coalition with unions, New Deal Democrats, and other groups on the left. This Popular Front, as it came to be called, would attack America's economic and social ills and join a worldwide struggle, with the Soviet Union, against the rise of fascism in Germany, Italy, and elsewhere. Historians still disagree about whether the Popular Front was a response to American circumstances or an organizational shell that concealed the party's subservience to the Moscow-based Comintern, which coordinated the worldwide Communist movement. But in 1937–1938, the CPUSA and the Popular Front appealed strongly to some idealistic Americans, particularly in industrial cities like Detroit, who were relatively unaware of the murderous nature of Stalin's dictatorship and wanted to enlist in a fight to reform society.

Disillusionment would set in, especially after Stalin in 1939 signed a nonaggression pact with Germany, giving Hitler free rein to invade Poland. Many people dropped out of the CPUSA and continued to conceal their Communist ties. Exposure as a Communist or former Communist or merely a Communist sympathizer usually cost people their jobs, often destroyed careers, and frequently caused families to break up.

Harry disclosed his party association to me in the 1960s. By then, the hazards of being named as a former Communist were fading. A new kind of radicalism on the left—the student revolutionaries, Students for a Democratic Society, Maoism, and so forth—was making the old Communists seem a tame bunch. By this time Harry no longer had a career or a job or much of a future to protect. He voiced leftist-radical opinions on many subjects and did not care who heard him. The more shocked the reception, the better. He liked to drink at workingmen's bars, where he would burst into loud invective against President Lyndon Johnson and his conduct of the Vietnam War. Other men at the bar would throw belligerent stares our way, but Harry's age probably saved him—and me.

Uncle Harry then lived in a bathhouse on Forbes Avenue near downtown Pittsburgh, a situation that appalled my mother and her sisters. Short of a flophouse hotel, the bathhouse probably was the cheapest lodging available, and Harry particularly enjoyed the steam room. He made a little money as a book salesman and political publicist. Every two or three months I would invite him to lunch or dinner. I enjoyed talking with him about politics and books. I should say rather that he talked and I listened. I saw him as a tragic figure, a flawed man who had been overwhelmed by forces beyond his control. I had a vague hope of perhaps encouraging him to pick up the pieces of his life and—well, I am not sure what I expected him to do. I was not foolish enough to urge him, a man in his early sixties who had not had steady work in fifteen years, to find a job or to invite him to move in with me and my family. I just had a vague hope that something would happen for him. Most of all, I wanted to get at the heart of the mystery surrounding him and his truncated political career. But he was a secretive man who rarely volunteered anything about his earlier life, and I was reluctant to probe for details.

Harry portrayed himself in those years as scornful of American institutions and far to the left of all political parties, including the Communist Party and most radical splinter groups. He claimed to admire Communist China, singling it out particularly for having eradicated prostitution—in a country with 300 million men. I recall laughing aloud at what I considered an absurdity. He grinned but defended his position by quoting an obscure book on contemporary China. (I was surprised to learn much later that Chinese Communists apparently did make some headway against prostitution, although "eradicate" undoubtedly exaggerated what was accomplished.) Most of Harry's political declarations in that period were calculated to make himself appear the most radical of radicals.[5]

One day I asked a put-up or shut-up kind of question: had he belonged to the Communist Party in the 1930s? We were having lunch at the Venice Café on Fifth Avenue near the Allegheny County Courthouse. The date was June 29, 1967; at home that evening I wrote an account of our lunch in my journal. In those years, Harry spent much of each day strolling and sitting in bars in the courthouse area, where many people recognized and spoke to him as if he were still a big shot. Harry liked this. He also liked, as I did, the informal atmosphere of the Venice and its diverse lunch crowd, which included lawyers, midlevel county bureaucrats, black activists employed in Lyndon Johnson's War on Poverty, and construction workers. I noted that Harry was wearing a dark blue suit with a spotted tie and that he was in good humor. He started the conversation, as usual, by recommending a number of books. In this case, *On the Art of Writing* by Arthur Quiller-Couch, *Watch Your Language*, by

Theodore Bernstein, and "Strunk's little grammar." I dutifully jotted down all three titles, though I already had read E. L. Strunk's *The Elements of Style.*

We chatted a bit about politics. Then, emboldened by his relative openness and good mood, I asked, "Did you ever belong to the party?" I probably left out Communist to indicate my knowingness. He gave me a sly smile, as if to say, "You impudent brat!" but the answer came quickly. Yes, he had joined the Communist Party in 1937 in Detroit and resigned from it—ended his "formal association with," is the way he put it—in 1939. "In those days, in Detroit," he said, "that was where the action was. It was a romantic period of my life." Light blue eyes sparkled, mouth twitched in a wry smile, a very Irish wry smile. "During the Depression, when men slept under bridges and stood in bread lines, it was much easier to get into something like that. If you had any heart at all, that's what you did. But I was different from the rest. I was always neatly dressed and clean. I had a job in business. Most of them thought of me as a bourgeois outsider."

I did not press for details, such as his role in the party or the specifics of his life in Detroit. Up to then, he had worked around the country in advertising for department stores and newspapers. In Detroit, he may have been employed by Hudson's, a large department store. That he lived in Detroit around that time I have confirmed through Social Security records, which show that he registered there in 1938.[6]

Harry was not above exaggerating the facts of his life. Given the circumstances when he told me about his ties with the Communist Party, I think he spoke the truth. It would have been very much in character for him to join a political party opposed to the dominant political and economic beliefs. He had been flinging himself against walls of this kind for most of his life.

Two central conditions, or facts of life, dominated Harry Davenport's boyhood and helped set his life's course. He was born the second son, behind a talented older brother, and his domineering father never let him forget it.

The father was John W. Davenport, who had come to the new town of Wilmerding in the early 1890s with, or shortly after, his older brother, Harry F. Davenport, the policeman who later was murdered. As a young man, John ran a restaurant and began promoting boxing bouts at the local YMCA. He married Margaret McNally, a second-generation Irish woman, who grew up on a farm north of Pittsburgh. Their first child was a son, Edward, born in 1899. Harry J. Davenport was born on August 22, 1902. Four more children, all girls, came along in the next half-dozen years.

In the meantime, John moved his family from Wilmerding to the much larger McKeesport. With a fast-growing population of mill workers and their families, McKeesport offered an expanding market for a restaurateur and sports promoter. John opened a restaurant and operated a small roller-skating rink. Not long after the Davenports settled in their new home, young Harry first demonstrated a precocious ability to attract attention. The May 27, 1907, edition of the McKeesport *Daily News* reported that four-year-old Harry was spotted riding on the front fender of a streetcar "going along at a high speed" on Fifth Avenue. Pedestrians shouted to the motorman, who halted the trolley car, forcing the boy to roll off into the street. Uninjured, he walked home. When his father asked what had happened, Harry replied that "the car was going too fast, and it just bumped me."

In about 1908, John Davenport left the restaurant business and concentrated on roller skating, a popular sport in those years. He installed a hardwood rink on the spacious second floor of a building known as the Palisades. Here he also staged boxing bouts and, eventually, dancing to big-band music. On boxing nights, John would set up a ring in the middle of the floor, and spectators, from a few dozen to a couple hundred, would encircle the ring. He attracted some first-class boxers, including Jim Jeffries and Frank Klaus. His "Majestic A.C." made McKeesport "one of the most prominent [cities], in a boxing sense, in this part of the country," said a Pittsburgh newspaper upon John's death in 1925.[7]

The Davenport children helped out at the Palisades and learned to skate at an early age. The two boys, Eddie and Harry, both excellent skaters, would whiz around the rink, assisting beginners and picking up fallen children. John Davenport, or Davvy, as he was known around town, developed his sons and other young men as speed skaters and staged racing events up and down the Monongahela Valley, matching skaters against bicyclists and even motorcyclists. Eddie became a champion speedster. At a national championship event in Detroit in 1920, he won the final race but lost first place by one point because of an accidental foul. He also outshone Harry as a student. Both had natural ability, but

Eddie, three years older, profited more from their father's attentions. Eddie, a generous and good brother, did not lord it over Harry, but their sisters knew that Ed was the preferred one in their father's eyes. And so did Harry.

Davvy Davenport was well known and respected outside the home. Inside, he was at best an unyielding disciplinarian, at worst a tyrannical father and husband. He himself had had a rough time as a boy. His father, an English physician who served in the Crimean War, came to America and made a fortune in a lucrative practice. He lost it all in financial speculations and died when John was eleven years old. By this time, Dr. William Davenport was "broken down in mind and money," according to a newspaper story at his death in 1885. His last years, possibly as an alcoholic, must have been harrowing for his children. John grew up to be a teetotaler of exemplary discipline. He even spurned a drink offered to him as he laying dying of pneumonia in 1925, a feat considered so awesome, even during Prohibition, that it was mentioned prominently in a local newspaper column on his death.[8]

This moralistic teetotaler was also a harsh, insensitive father. Decades later, my mother and her sisters remembered their father as a forbidding man. At the dinner table, he demanded that the children eat and remain silent unless addressed by him. He restricted his daughters' social activities and forbade them to learn how to drive a car. When they attended singles dances at the Palisades, he insisted on smelling the breath of any young man who asked them to dance. He forced one daughter, Kate, to stop dating a young doctor because he was Jewish.

Harry, however, was the prime target of John's mistreatment. His father constantly compared him unfavorably with his older brother and humiliated Harry in countless ways, according to tales later told by his sisters. Harry became a rebel, expressing his sense of injustice with keen humor. He had a talent for mimicking speech, and he mocked and made fun of his father when the latter was absent or not looking. Indeed, Harry mocked and parodied practically everything that others took seriously. Denied the attention of his father, Harry put himself on display, growing a brilliant plumage that could not fail to attract attention. My mother later told stories about Harry as a schoolboy. He was by turns an arrogant intellectual and an outrageous prankster. He loved to read, and he would dress up as Edgar Allan Poe with a string tie and cape and walk through the city with his nose in a book, reading poetry aloud. This would have been unusual behavior in any town, but it was especially so in a mill town like McKeesport. People were preoccupied with smoke and grime and making steel and making money. All the better for Harry. He was noticed. Whatever he did, he was always on display.

The Davenport sisters looked up to Eddie and laughed at Harry's antics and sympathized with him in his struggle against their father. But he became increasingly strange. His comedy acts obviously were meant to cover up a deep and bitter disappointment. Harry was a smart kid and a voracious reader and might have been a first-rate student but for his behavior. One concession that John, a nonreligious Protestant, made to Margaret was that the children be brought up as Catholics. The nuns who ran Catholic schools in those days had no tolerance for rebelliousness. Harry kept getting into trouble. During his senior year in high school, he pulled a particularly outrageous prank. If I remember correctly, it had to do with stuffing a cat in a drawer of a nun's desk. When she opened the drawer, a snarling cat sprang out, with easily imagined consequences for the nun, the cat, and ultimately Harry. Ousted from St. Peter's High School, he switched to the city's public high school. Harry must have gotten into trouble there as well because he never graduated.

Despite many tensions, the Davenports were not blasted apart by constant feuding among resentful brothers and sisters. Their mother Margaret, or Mae, rose above her own sorrows and acted as a stabilizing force. Eddie and Harry shrugged off the sibling rivalry promoted, consciously or not, by their father and remained friends until Eddie died. The four girls were particularly close as they grew up. They sang together and performed skits for family and friends. Forty years later they could still do an entertaining rendition of "When Papa Hung the Paper on the Wall." They would stand in a line with arms around each other's waists and dance an abbreviated can-can as they sang, with Sister Catherine's rosary beads clacking and her habit flying up naughtily over the instep of her black shoes. Sister Catherine was away for many years, but the other three sisters married and raised families in McKeesport and talked to each other practically every day.

In 1925, John Davenport contracted pneumonia during a flu epidemic and died at the age of fifty-one. The twins, Julia and Kate, both became nurses, and Julia soon entered a convent. Kate worked at a local hospital and married a pharmacist. Annamae, the brashest of the four, went to work as a secretary for a car dealer and married a shoe-store owner. Alyce, my mother, taught for a couple of years in a Catholic grade school and in 1929 married a McKeesport businessman, my father, John P. Hoerr.

A college degree was not necessary in those days for white-collar trades and many professions. Both Eddie and Harry were attracted to advertising; they liked to write and dream up promotional ideas. They took courses at the University of Pittsburgh and wrote advertising copy, promoting skating and boxing at the Palisades. Eddie became advertising manager of a local department store and quickly advanced to larger stores in Johnstown, Pennsylvania, and then Utica, New York. Harry followed his brother, practically walking in his footsteps from store to store, apparently getting jobs on Eddie's recommendation. He moved from Johnstown to Buffalo and to Utica. In 1927, the *Daily News* noted that Eddie Davenport was general manager and Harry advertising manager of Robert Fraser Inc., Utica's largest department store. Eddie soon switched to newspapers, serving as ad manager at various papers and coming to rest in 1929 in Seattle as merchandising counselor of all Hearst morning papers on the West Coast. Harry followed his brother there as well. This is where my relationship with Uncle Harry began.[9]

In the turbulent early days of the Great Depression, when people were migrating everywhere, looking for work, my father went to Seattle shortly after I was born. He and his father had been partners in a prosperous real estate and insurance business in McKeesport but lost practically everything in 1930. Ed Davenport, my father's best friend, got Dad a job in the circulation department of Hearst's *Seattle Post-Intelligencer*, where Harry also worked. When I was six weeks old, my mother took me to Seattle by train. Through most of 1931, my parents and I lived in a Seattle boardinghouse with Harry, Eddie, Grandmother Davenport, and Eddie's girlfriend Harriette, who later became his wife. My mother later remembered this as an almost idyllic interlude, though we had little money. When Dad and Harry were laid off, the entire group moved down the coast to Long Beach, California. But prospects were not much better there, and in the fall of 1932 my father and mother decided to return to McKeesport. Harry went with us.

For nearly two weeks, the three adults and a two-year-old toddler bumped and rattled across the United States in Dad's secondhand car, towing a small trailer loaded with luggage and personal possessions. As we drove across Death Valley in temperatures well over a hundred degrees, the car's thin-walled tires blew out repeatedly on the hot highways. The men would jack up the car under a broiling sun, remove and patch the tire, then set off again knowing there would be another blowout twenty or thirty miles down the road. Meanwhile, I would be bawling about one thing or another. In a dusty Oklahoma town, my mother, a fastidious woman, insisted that I had to be bathed. Uncle Harry found what he said was a small hotel that agreed to rent a room for an hour or so. When Mother returned to the car after bathing me, she spoke glowingly of a polite female proprietor, an exceptionally clean room, and a strangely shaped basin that made a perfect bathtub for a toddler. The men gave hearty laughs and poked one another in the ribs. Many years later, reminiscing about that stop in Oklahoma, Harry almost choked with laughter. He wiped his eyes and looked at me as if to see what had become of the brothel baby.

I do not know where Harry went or what he did after that cross-country trip. He always seemed able to get a job in advertising, and he probably worked in one or more cities before arriving in Detroit in the midthirties. Not much is known about his life during these wanderings. A strong swimmer, he probably would swim laps in a YMCA pool after work and eat dinner alone, poring over a book. Some evenings, during his Detroit years, he would attend a Communist cell meeting, I presume. Harry was introspective, secretive, possibly brimming with repressed desires. My sense is that he was preparing himself for something to come, a political career that as yet had no foundation.

Not long after I began my research into Uncle Harry's career I realized that he must have known Father Rice in the 1940s. Even if they never met in person, their paths crossed in a political sense—and apparently much to Harry's disadvantage. In the 1960s, when I talked often with Harry and occasionally with Rice, I did not know about the 1949 event that linked both men to Tom Quinn and, by extension, to one another. Perhaps I should have deduced a connection from a comment that Harry made one day when we were chatting about unions. I mentioned Father Rice, and added by way of identification, "the labor priest—"

"Labor priest, baloney!" Harry said, interrupting me. "Labor faker!"

I recall this conversation very clearly. I had invited my uncle to meet me for lunch at a tavern on Third Avenue in Pittsburgh. I can see the two of us sitting at the corner of the bar, Harry with a shot of Seagram's V.O. in front of him and I with a beer. Having no reason to think ill of Rice, I was startled by the harshness of the comment. But I attributed it to Harry's intellectual crankiness rather than to a personal grievance against the priest. Deaf to the clue, I did not inquire further. Our discussion immediately veered off on another subject. But I always remembered that explosive epithet.

By 2000, Harry was dead and Monsignor Rice was living in retirement at St. Anne's Church in the Pittsburgh suburb of Castle Shannon, where I interviewed him in June. Most elderly priests live in diocesan retirement homes, but the Church granted Rice special permission to stay at St. Anne's after serving his final pastorate there. His quarters were adjacent to parish offices in the rear of the church. At the age of ninety-one, he shuffled about energetically, obviously happy to have a visitor. Puffing on a black cigar that emitted thick, pungent smoke, he gave me a tour of his small but comfortable apartment and then led me down a corridor past a row of parish offices to his study. Inside were an armchair, a desk with a personal computer on which he still wrote a weekly column for the *Pittsburgh Catholic*, filing cabinets, and shelves crowded with books. The walls were covered with dozens of large and small photographs, mostly of famous people he had known and worked with in the civil-rights and peace movements of the 1960s. One of his favorites shows him walking arm in arm with Rev. Martin Luther King and Dr. Benjamin Spock at the head of a 1967 peace mobilization march in New York. King is in the middle and Rice and Spock on either side, closer to the sidewalks. "The cops placed me there," Rice said. "They were afraid King would be assassinated, and they didn't think Irish Catholics . . . well, they might be bigots, but they wouldn't kill a priest."[10]

We chatted amiably, and Rice attempted to respond to my questions. But many of his answers emerged as disassociated bits of memory, drifting from present to past and back again. I had been told by people close to Rice that his memory was fading. Although he could still write coherent essays on current political and social issues and give affecting performances as a reader of poetry, he could no longer focus comprehensively on past events. I managed to pick up a few things about Rice's involvement with the CIO in its early days and during the anti-Communist struggles of the late 1940s. His remembrance of Tom Quinn, however, was either purposely selective or honestly incomplete. As for Harry Davenport, Rice could recall only that he suffered some misfortune. After an hour or so of broken conversation, I was convinced that I would have to rely on other sources of information to give a useful account of Rice's background and his fight against Communists in the labor movement.

There is no shortage of other sources, which include several oral-history interviews recorded over the years, the substantial Rice Papers collection at the University of Pittsburgh, and many columns, radio talks, speeches, and letters in *Fighter with a Heart: Writings of Charles Owen Rice*, edited by Charles McCollester. The only Rice biography, *Rev. Charles Owen Rice: Apostle of Contradiction*, by Patrick J. McGeever, is unfriendly to Rice, but it provides a useful chronology and details of Rice's career. These sources provided enough material to sketch the outlines of an extraordinary life.[11]

In June 1937, when Harry Davenport was presumably attending Communist Party meetings in Detroit and Tom Quinn was working at the Aliquippa Works, the young Father Charles Owen Rice had his first encounter with organized labor. Accompanied by two fellow priests and four lay members of the newly formed Catholic Radical Alliance (CRA), Rice joined striking workers on a picket line at the H. J. Heinz Pickle Co. in North Side Pittsburgh to protest Heinz's refusal to recognize a union. The priests' appearance in support of a union—at a time when unionists were regarded by many as Socialists, Communists, or racketeers—caused a minor sensation in Pittsburgh. Nationally, *Time* magazine published a story under the alliterative headline "Priests, Pickets and Pickle Workers." Stung by the publicity, Heinz agreed to talk with the workers. Four more years and a decision by the U.S. Supreme Court intervened before Heinz signed a written contract, but Rice and his activists had helped get the process started.[12]

It was not unknown for priests to demonstrate publicly on the side of workers and against a powerful corporation. A well-known "labor priest" of the 1920s and early 1930s, Father James R. Cox, led a march of fifteen thousand unemployed workers to Washington in 1932. But Rice would soon eclipse Cox. Only three years out of the seminary, the twenty-nine-year-old Rice already demonstrated the bold assertiveness, self-confidence, and organizational ability of a much older and more experienced man. With two older priests and several laymen, he founded a discussion and action group, which they named (or misnamed, as McGeever argues in his biography) the Catholic Radical Alliance. The CRA did not really espouse radical political goals, McGeever contends, merely a reform of capitalism. It was modeled on the Catholic Worker Movement founded in the early 1930s by reformer Dorothy Day and her associate Peter Maurin in New York. Day and Maurin established two important institutions, *The Catholic Worker,* an influential monthly magazine, and St. Joseph's House of Hospitality, a hospice for the poor and center for spiritual and political discussion among workers and intellectuals.[13]

In Pittsburgh, the CRA also set up a St. Joseph's House of Hospitality, which fed up to nine hundred indigents every day and provided beds for several hundred every night. Rice became its director in 1940. But as early as 1937 he and his associates had veered away from Day's approach, which emphasized spiritual growth and renewal rather than political action. The CRA founders, especially Rice, preferred to follow a more activist path. He became involved on the side of many unions, including those representing paper workers, hotel workers, newspaper employees, and steelworkers. There were labor disputes all over western Pennsylvania and the industrial Midwest as workers sought union recognition under the authority of the 1935 Wagner Act. The Little Steel strike had broken out at mills in Johnstown and Sharon, Pennsylvania; Youngstown and Massillon, Ohio; and other steel communities. Appearing on picket lines and at union rallies in many towns, Rice soon became known as Pittsburgh's labor priest. He was selected to give the opening prayer at the first CIO convention, in 1938. But he was more than a "friendly cleric trotted out to bless union gatherings," historian Charles McCollester writes in an introduction to his collection of Rice's writings. "To workers and the general public, he [Rice] implicitly carried the Church's sanction for industrial union organizing which was being attacked from many sides as Communist inspired."[14]

This was the beginning of a long career during which Rice would come into conflict with corporations and conservative politicians, with Communist-led unions and the Communist Party, with bigots and racist institutions, with prowar policy makers during the Vietnam War, and occasionally with his Church superiors. Articulate and combative, he threw himself into moral and political causes with a religious zeal that earned him both admirers and enemies. He spoke out on controversial issues in columns written for the *Pittsburgh Catholic,* originally an independent paper, and other publications. For many years he commented on religion and topical issues in radio broadcasts that brought him into thousands of homes every Sunday night. Rice never deviated from Church dogma on matters such as contraception and abortion. But his writings and public activities in some areas of labor and politics offended many constituencies and occasionally tested the patience of Church leaders.

R ice was born in New York City on November 21, 1908, the second son of immigrant Irish parents, Michael and Anna. When Anna died in 1912, Michael sent Charles and his older brother, Pat, to live with relatives in the Irish town of Dundalk, north of Dublin. The local culture was steeped in Catholicism, writes McGeever. Charles and Pat attended church-run schools with a curriculum heavy in religious instruction as well as classical literature and history. When the boys returned to the United States in 1920, both had developed a love of English literature, as well as a priestly vocation. Charles also came back with an Irish lilt in his voice that he would nurture and later use to good effect in homilies, radio talks, and fiery speeches.

Michael Rice had remarried and moved to Pittsburgh, and this is where the Rice boys spent their teenage years. Both graduated from Duquesne University (Pat three years ahead of Charles); both entered the St. Vincent Seminary, a school run by Benedictine monks near Latrobe, about thirty miles east of Pittsburgh; and both became priests. Charles was only a middling scholar, but he displayed a talent for polemical writing well suited to what would become a lifelong series of forays into controversial issues.

Ordained in 1934, Rice was a curate in a Pittsburgh parish when he helped found the CRA. He apparently convinced his superiors that he could best serve the Church by engaging in social reform involving labor and working-class problems. Rice had had a liberal political upbringing under his father and naturally leaned toward the side of labor. Emerging Catholic doctrine supported this inclination. The Church was seeking a middle road between unfettered capitalism on the right and socialism or communism on the left. Since the late nineteenth century, the Church had looked with increasing favor on trade unions as a means by which workers could protect themselves from predatory managements. First spelled out in the papal encyclical *Rerum Novarum* in 1891, the approval of organized labor was emphasized and extended in an encyclical letter entitled *Quadragesimo Anno*, issued by Pope Pius XI in 1931. The emergence of this social philosophy, McGeever notes, helped create a new generation of labor priests, of which Rice became one of the best known.[15]

From the start of his public life Rice spoke out against Communism and Communists in debates and speeches. He regarded Communist unionists in some cases as allies but criticized others, though not with the vigor he would a few years later. He reluctantly accepted John L. Lewis's use of talented Communist organizers in the massive CIO recruiting drives of the mid-to-late thirties, in part because he wanted these drives to succeed. By then he had met the much older Philip Murray, founder of the United Steelworkers, who also tolerated Communists in his union in its early years. The developing relationship between priest and union leader assumed a special role when Murray was elected CIO president in November 1940, succeeding Lewis.

This was a critical adjustment for Murray, who had served as Lewis's lieutenant for more than twenty years and found it hard to escape his authority. There were few stranger moments in American political history. Lewis had risen to a position of extraordinary power as leader of the burgeoning labor movement. In 1940, he risked everything by opposing the election of Franklin D. Roosevelt to a third term and urging rank-and-file workers to vote for Republican Wendell Willkie. Instead they voted for Roosevelt in overwhelming numbers. Repudiated, Lewis resigned as president of the CIO at its November 1940 convention and named Murray as his successor—but under conditions that would enable Lewis to retain partial control. Murray turned to Rice "for a sympathetic ear," as Rice told his biographer, and gained the confidence needed to resist Lewis's demands and still be elected president. In this way, Rice became close friend and confessor to the new president of the CIO. The priest's influence with Murray would be a factor—how significant is not clear—in Murray's decision nearly a decade later to expel Communist-led unions from the CIO, a decision that would cause major disruptions in the lives of Harry Davenport and Tom Quinn.[16]

3

WORKING-CLASS POLITICS
IN ELECTRIC VALLEY

WITH Tom Quinn giving directions in the passenger seat, I drove up Centre Avenue in Pittsburgh's Hill District and turned left on Protectory Place. It was a cloudy, chilly day in early December 2000. We were setting out on a tour of important places in Quinn's past. He had submitted patiently to several hours of taped interviewing, but I wanted to understand more fully how the places where he had lived and worked, along with the social and political atmosphere of the 1930s and 1940s, had shaped his character and political outlook.

The Hill District had changed substantially since I last traveled through it thirty years before. From a distance, the Hill used to give the impression of buildings stacked upon buildings, which, closer up, swelled into wretched tenements, broken-down fences, brick streets, and dark alleys, any one section of which would resemble scenery designed for an August Wilson play set in the Hill District. But now, much of the old Hill seemed to have disappeared. Large portions of brick and mortar had been torn down and cleared out, leaving gaping holes and open spaces. An immense thinning out seemed to have occurred, as if someone had commanded, "Take every third structure and leave nothing in its place." Everything looked more open and clean, but sanitized and less interesting. Urban renewals often produce such desolate landscapes, yet it is foolish for an outsider to wish a neighborhood back to a colorful past that some inhabitants perhaps wanted to escape.

Protectory Place, in the thirties a narrow brick and cobblestone street, was now a ribbon of smooth concrete pitching slightly uphill to the north. Halfway up the block, Quinn said, "Here," nodding toward a large empty lot on the right side of the street. "This is where it was."

I parked at the curb and with him gazed across a field of weeds where St. Joseph's Protectory had stood in the 1930s. The orphanage consisted of three buildings. In the middle was a five-story main building, where the boys lived; a smaller structure to the south housed a bakery, gymnasium, and living quarters for staff members and two resident priests; a third building north of the dormitory contained a print shop, which handled all printing jobs for the Pittsburgh Diocese and employed many of the orphan boys as apprentices. The diocese then owned a considerable amount of property in this neighborhood, Quinn said, including twenty or so row houses across the street from the Protectory and a foundling hospital on Tannehill Street, one block down the hill to the west. The latter would be converted in the late thirties to the St. Joseph's House of Hospitality, directed by Father Rice.

Quinn recalled that there had been a vacant lot between the print shop and main building, where the Protectory residents and neighborhood boys played softball. He stared at the field with the kind of distant gaze that we fix on the past, trying to repopulate an empty space with the faces and figures of seventy years ago.

Later, reassembling that scene for myself, I visualized a black-and-white Depression-era photograph: in the smoke and dust of a low-bellying sky, hazy forms of the Protectory buildings sitting on high ground, surrounded by a metal fence . . . kids playing in the street, adults chatting in front of the row houses . . . teenage boys playing softball on the Protectory lot . . . younger boys in knickers peering through the fence . . . shouts, laughter, cheers, the clunk of a bat meeting a ratty old softball with ripped stitches . . . teenage girls strolling on the sidewalk, studiously ignoring the glances of the ball players. One of those girls could have been, almost certainly was at one time or another, the dark and pretty Irene Golding, who became the most important person in Tom Quinn's life.

"My future wife," he said softly, resuming his description of the neighborhood, "lived across the street in one of the row houses."

My future wife. It was a curious and revealing reference. Quinn had spent sixty-two years with Irene Golding Quinn, who died two months before our visit to Protectory Place. I had wanted to get a feeling of the old neighborhood where an Irish orphan could meet and fall in love with a Jewish girl. But the adjoining row houses of yesteryear had been supplanted by a row of adjoining town houses, built for people of moderate income. I was disappointed. No Protectory, no brick-and-cobblestone street, no row houses, no people, no neighborhood, not even a pile of rubble on which I could fix my imagination. (Within two years from the time of this visit, even the vacant field where the Protectory once stood had sprouted its own row of new town houses.)

Quinn was still ruminating on the past. "The row houses weren't tenements," he said. "They were pretty nice two-story houses, but there wasn't a lot of room for a large family like my future wife's. Four girls and three boys, plus their parents. There was a little yard behind each house." He spoke in a dry, formal tone, still struggling with his loss.

In our previous meetings, Quinn had told me about his courtship of Irene Golding and the very large obstacle that threatened their relationship. Irene's parents came out of a tradition utterly opposed to the marriage of Jews and gentiles. The young couple had to cling tenaciously to what they believed to be the right course, and in the end they did not overcome the obstacle so much as go around it.

Irene and Tom had seen one another many times on Protectory Place, walking to school, going on errands, loafing on the sidewalk outside the Protectory. They came to know each other by name. He played ball with her brothers. After moving to Aliquippa to work in the mill, Quinn thought more and more about Irene Golding. When J&L laid him off in the summer of 1937, he decided not to stay in Aliquippa and await a recall to the mill. He moved back to Pittsburgh to be closer to Irene. By that time, she was a dark-haired beauty of twenty-one, a high school graduate with a good job as a secretary for an auto-wrecking company. The two began dating in the fall when Tom worked briefly at Westinghouse Electric in East Pittsburgh. They had to conceal their romance from Irene's parents.

Levi and Lena Golding, both immigrants from Eastern Europe, were Conservative Jews who practiced a much less strict Judaism than did Orthodox Jews. Still, they "were very opposed to my mother having any relationship with my father," said Ron Quinn, Tom and Irene's second son. Levi was a dry-goods salesman who had lost his store early in the

Depression and in 1938 was selling fabrics out of his home. For many years he had served as a cantor in various synagogues, singing in a booming tenor. Irene and her brothers and sisters grew up with music. On Saturday afternoons Levi would play live radio broadcasts of the Metropolitan Opera, and everyone in the family knew not to disturb him.[1]

Tom liked everything about Irene. "She was pretty savvy, a stylish dresser, meticulous," he said in 2000. "Everything had to be just right and that appealed to me. She had a good head and a beautiful voice." Irene had inherited her father's musical talent and possessed perfect pitch, enabling her to sing naturally, without accompaniment. She particularly liked jazz and swing music and would have studied for a professional career as a pop singer if her parents had not objected. For the rest of her life, Irene would continue to sing as a talented amateur, breaking into song at all times of the day, especially while working in the kitchen. After Tom became a staff member of the United Electrical Workers, Irene often sang the national anthem on the opening day of the union's national conventions.

The winter of 1937–1938 was a difficult time for carrying on a serious courtship. Laid off by Westinghouse in December, Tom went back on the job-search trail. This bout of unemployment landed him in the middle of another historical development. Before now, in a society committed to unregulated free markets, even organized labor had opposed government intervention to aid the jobless. But with unemployment running above 20 percent in the 1930s, many political and social organizations—including the American Federation of Labor, which reversed course—lobbied for unemployment compensation. Quinn was among the first recipients of jobless pay in Pennsylvania, receiving fifteen dollars a week for thirteen weeks. The stipend helped Quinn through a bad time; he was out of work for most of 1938.

Tom spent most days looking for a job and many evenings on dates with Irene. Since he was not welcome at her home, they would meet at the homes of married friends or simply on a street corner. They would walk to downtown Pittsburgh and occasionally see a movie or window-shop at the city's several department stores. One of Quinn's most prized family snapshots shows him and Irene, a happy young couple despite their problems, striding along Fifth Avenue in 1938. After the unemployment pay ran out, Quinn applied for welfare to get a job with the WPA. The job never came through, but he received a four-dollar welfare check every Friday. "Friday evenings," he said, "with that four bucks in my pocket, I'd meet Irene and we'd walk down to the Fort Pitt Hotel, where they had a strolling musician in the lounge. We'd have a couple of glasses of beer while listening to the music."

For much of 1938 Quinn walked the streets, applying for jobs, picking up a day's wage here and there, getting laid off, making the required weekly visit to the unemployment office to testify about his job search. Thousands of others did the same. There was a great milling of workers in various stages of the cycle, either working or being laid off or looking for jobs or being recalled or quitting for a better job. Job seekers mingled with workers in a great confused mass, a chaotic version of a close-order military drill in which platoons, approaching from opposite directions, pass through each other in alternating files of soldiers. "Things were pretty fluid in those days," Quinn recalled with typical understatement.

Quinn and his friends were too busy foraging for a living to debate big issues such as, what is to be done? as Lenin famously put the question. One thing Quinn did know was that the poor, the uneducated, and people without connections got pushed around in America. His experience at Aliquippa had taught him that a union could give workers a feeling of gaining some control over their work lives. He had left J&L before he could determine whether that sense of power would be converted to real power, but it appeared to him that a union was the only kind of organization that might protect the interests of ordinary people. Corporations were not on the side of the workingman. Businessmen expected people to sit tight, have faith in America, and take wage cuts and layoffs without objection. As for the government, President Franklin D. Roosevelt often talked about helping the common man. But at the local level that help usually was personified by bureaucratic clerks telling you to fill out more forms. Government existed far above the fray, and perhaps it was better that way. Quinn was coming to believe that only workers knew what was good for workers and that they should take matters into their own hands.

As bleak as the economic future looked in 1938, Quinn felt contrarily buoyant, even ecstatic. He was a young man in love and wanted to get married. He needed money. When employers began hiring again late in the year, Tom took a job at a new U.S. Steel plant in West Mifflin, about fifteen miles up the Monongahela River from Pittsburgh. He usually had to work the night turn, 11 p.m. to 7 a.m. He traveled to and from work by streetcar, which took nearly two hours each day. Some weeks Tom and Irene saw each other only three or four times. But they were determined to be together. Finally, without informing the Goldings, they got married in a civil ceremony. They did not have enough money to rent an apartment, so Irene continued to live at home as if she were still single. She and Tom would meet whenever and wherever they could.

The Quinns talked openly about this difficult period with their sons when they were older. "When Mother became pregnant," Ron Quinn said, repeating her story, "she went to her parents and said, 'I'm married and I'm going to have a child.' Her mother slapped her. My mother knew then that she had to move out." The young couple rented a one-room apartment in the Hill District. In December 1939 Irene gave birth to their first son, Charles.

"My mother had backbone," Chuck said in a 2000 interview. "She left a Conservative Jewish family to elope with an orphan Catholic, and she was ostracized from her family. I don't remember grandparents till I was five or six years old. Our world was basically Jewish in culture, not religion." Eventually the Goldings' hostility abated, or at least Levi's did. "Grandfather felt he should have a part in raising his grandchildren," Steve Quinn said. "He was a compromising type. But Grandmother didn't get along with my mother for years."[2]

While Irene was still pregnant, Tom left U.S. Steel to try something different. Welding skills were coming into demand in other industries as the nation prepared for war. In those days, workers were not tied to one employer by health insurance and pension plans, which rarely existed. Young men with critical skills jumped from job to job, searching for the right blend of wages and working conditions. For the first time in his working life, Quinn felt that he could pick and choose among jobs. When a friend told him in 1939 about good pay at a Navy shipyard in Norfolk, Virginia, Tom went there and got a job welding gun mounts on freighters. Perhaps he wanted to escape Pittsburgh and his growing responsibilities. But after a few weeks he began feeling guilty about leaving Irene alone. He quit and returned to Pittsburgh.

When Chuck was born, Tom was still scrambling to make ends meet. He had traveled a tedious four-year journey through the smoke-drenched streets of industrial Pittsburgh, from the welding shop at Connelley's Trade School through a series of short-lived jobs interspersed with innumerable episodes of filling out forms and standing in line only to find, most often, disappointment at the end. He had made mistakes.

But he had tried to do the right thing according to his own standards. Now he had a family and it was no longer quite so easy to quit or say no when he disliked what was demanded of him. He was ready for a permanent job.

Of all the jobs he had had in the past four years, the most appealing was his brief stint at the East Pittsburgh works of Westinghouse Electric. It was cleaner than mill work and required top-level welding skills. He knew nothing about the union that represented Westinghouse workers, but it seemed to offer some protection. For more than two years Quinn had checked in at the plant every month to keep his name on the recall list. His diligence paid off when Westinghouse began expanding the workforce to fill defense-related orders.

In early 1940, Quinn went to work as a welder in the generator division at Westinghouse. For the next dozen years, this would be not only his place of work but also his school for labor relations, union leadership, and—in time—radical politics.

In the early forties, I knew East Pittsburgh and the Westinghouse plant only from an aerial perspective. On Sundays, when we drove from McKeesport to Pittsburgh to visit Grandmother Davenport and Uncle Harry, my father would take Route 30 across Turtle Creek and through Forest Hills and Wilkinsburg. Shortly after turning west on Route 30 outside McKeesport, we would descend a hill between halves of a bluff cleaved down the middle, blocking the view to either side. The road ahead appeared to float out into space, nothing above and nothing below, and just barely gain a precarious land hold on a distant hill. This was a wonderful illusion for a nine- or ten-year-old, this gravity-defying spatial causeway. My father referred to it as the Westinghouse Bridge, but I was dubious. In western Pennsylvania, where hundreds of bridges cross dozens of rivers and streams, you grow up with a paradigmatic silhouette of a bridge implanted in mind and memory, and this floating roadway had no superstructure of girders and suspension cables. It seemed suspended on a hope or dream. I awaited almost breathlessly each time we approached, knowing that it was a bridge because my father said so, but hoping it might turn out to be a magical crossing in the sky. As we drove onto the bridge, the cleaved bluff falling behind, a panorama opened on both sides, imparting a sensation of sailing over a bottomless chasm.

And what a chasm! On the left, nearly two hundred feet below, Turtle Creek was a barely visible sliver winding through a maze of railroad bridges and tracks with trains crisscrossing at different levels, small industrial buildings, transmission towers built on lumps of raw earth, steel storage, and junk yards. The creek vanished in this maze, winding the last half mile toward the Monongahela. At the mouth of the creek sat the open-hearth shop of U.S. Steel's Edgar Thomson Works, topped by a dozen or more tall, slim, open-hearth stacks that seemed to stretch across the narrow creek valley like a spiked gate. Reddish smoke pouring from these stacks was often thick enough to obscure high bluffs on the other side of the Monongahela.

Raw steel power lay on the left side of the bridge. Directly below, on the right side, were the silvery, triangular roofs of the Westinghouse Electric plant. Dozens of brick and metal-sheathed factory buildings, intermixed with taller office buildings, stood shoulder to shoulder in rows extending up the north bank of Turtle Creek until obscured by folds in the wooded terrain. From the bridge you could see a large section of the valley, with irregular clumps of houses splashed across the northern slopes in the towns of Turtle Creek and Chalfont and a few pioneer clapboards teetering on the steeper southern bluffs. The electric works lay in a canyon that had been cut through sandstone hills over many millennia by muddy little Turtle Creek. As the creek approached the Monongahela, the flanking hills pulled in tighter and tighter, practically choking it off where East Pittsburgh lies today. The stream found the shortest downhill pitch through these hills, creating a defile that must have offered a spectacular vista to early settlers, as well as to the Indians who had lived here for centuries.

In the deepest part of this canyon, George Westinghouse in the early 1890s built a factory to produce equipment that would generate electricity for a nation previously lit by candles and oil lamps. As an inventor, Westinghouse is usually overshadowed by his contemporary, Thomas A. Edison, whose electrical inventions became the foundation of General Electric's business. But it was Westinghouse who first recognized the efficacy of transmitting electricity by means of alternating current (AC) while Edison was pursuing the less-efficient direct-current system (DC). Westinghouse acquired the patents for AC from its discoverer, Nikola Tesla, and at East Pittsburgh began building the great turbogenerators that produced electricity in powerhouses around the world.

For many years, motorists on Route 30 had to descend into the valley and drive through choked traffic in East Pittsburgh before climbing out on the other side. In 1930–1932, Allegheny County built the George Westinghouse Memorial Bridge, spanning the valley at its narrowest point. The bridge roadway, nearly a third of a mile long, is supported by reinforced concrete arches. Viewed from the banks of the stream, the bridge sweeps across the valley on five muscular, parabolic arches, which themselves are strengthened by vertical columns in the spandrels (the areas between the exterior curves and perpendicular pillars). But for these airy spandrels, the bridge might have resembled a clunky Roman aqueduct. A dedication etched in a portal tower says that "in boldness of conception" the bridge "typifies the character and career of George Westinghouse" in whose honor it was dedicated on Sept. 10, 1932.

The greater part of East Pittsburgh lies beneath the bridge, and I must have passed over it hundreds of times as a boy and young man. Never in those days did I descend to the dank, narrow streets to view the plant or town from a closer perspective. With great steel mills providing fiery drama in a dozen mill towns along the Monongahela, East Pittsburgh might have seemed a pretty dull place. Yet the Westinghouse plant was one of the largest factory complexes in the country, employing twenty-two thousand men and women at its peak during World War II. Factory buildings continued up the creek from East Pittsburgh into the Borough of Turtle Creek. Wilmerding, with Westinghouse Air Brake, was farther upstream, and farther still the small towns of Pitcairn and Wall, each with large railroad yards where trains were made up to receive freight at WABCO and Westinghouse Electric, and farther yet the town of Trafford, where Westinghouse operated a foundry. The entire valley came to be called Electric Valley or Westinghouse Valley. People worked either at the Electric in East Pittsburgh or the Brake in Wilmerding. These were separate entities, as was a third company founded by George Westinghouse, Union Switch and Signal Company, or the Switch, located a few miles west of the valley in Swissvale.[3]

By the 1940s, this was just an ordinary industrial valley filled with factories and with people living ordinary, work-a-day lives—and yet it attracted an extraordinary amount of interest on the part of anti-Communist investigators. In assembling Uncle Harry's story, I asked why this small strip of geography, practically unknown outside (or even inside) the Pittsburgh region, merited so much attention. For these investigations changed the course of hundreds or even thousands of lives, including those of Uncle Harry and Tom Quinn. The United Electrical Workers, which became the most prominent union in the valley, was founded in part by workers with ties to the Communist Party. But the UE did not ride into the valley like a conquering army and impose radical politics on the inhabitants. It was the other way around: the UE, when formed, tapped into an existing vein of radicalism that flowed through the valley.

A great flood of skilled and unskilled workers had poured into the valley starting in the 1890s. By 1920, about twenty-one thousand people were packed into an area encompassing less than two square miles in East Pittsburgh, Turtle Creek, and Wilmerding. These communities were established almost overnight for one reason only—to house workers for the Westinghouse plants—and thus were heavily dominated by the working class. As in many turn-of-the-century factory towns and mining communities, Turtle Creek residents developed a class-conscious political philosophy that put socialist ideals above unfettered capitalism. Socialists ranged in ideology from revolutionaries to more temperate advocates of a larger government role in equalizing economic benefits and political power so that the social welfare would not be subordinated to markets and profits.

It is unclear which of these philosophies, or gradations in between, held sway among Turtle Creek residents. But the presidential election of 1912 demonstrated that socialism of some variety was, indeed, alluring (at least for male residents, since women were excluded from voting before 1920). Eugene V. Debs, running for president on the Socialist ticket for the fourth time, did very well in industrial communities around the country. Socialism was at its zenith in this period. Even so, support for Debs in the Turtle Creek Valley was astounding: he received 36 percent of the combined vote in Turtle Creek, East Pittsburgh, and Wilmerding, compared with only 7 percent across Pennsylvania.

Workers felt poorly served by the existing order in the Turtle Creek towns. Their willingness to rebel became apparent in major strikes at Westinghouse Electric in 1914 and 1916. George Westinghouse, the paternalistic owner who had the respect of his employees, died three months before the first strike began. But he had lost control of Westinghouse Electric years before, pushed aside by bankers following the economic panic of 1907. The new management, lacking the founder's rapport with employees, slashed the workforce, cut incentive pay, and instituted a production regime that substituted machine control for workers' skills. In June 1914, nearly ten thousand workers went on strike for three weeks, demanding that the company rescind its new policies and grant recognition of a union covering all employees. Led by workers committed to Socialist ideals, the strike amounted to a broad-scale revolt against management methods and control of the workforce. The strikers staged massive parades through valley towns, gaining much public support and good will with peaceful tactics. But Westinghouse Electric refused to negotiate on any issue. With the assistance of state police, the company eventually crushed this strike as well as the 1916 work stoppage, which ended in a riot with three deaths.[4]

The company's unconditional victories over the strikers of 1914 and 1916 may have seemed impressive to owners of that generation, but this success also sowed the seeds of an antimanagement animus that would last for decades. Coteries of radicals formed and remained active in Hungarian, German, Croatian, and Serbian fraternal lodges in the valley towns. The CPUSA, founded in 1920, gained a solid foothold in the valley. By the 1930s Communists were leading protest movements among the unemployed and schoolchildren. Economic conditions in the valley during the Depression underscored the message of groups on the left. In 2002, I interviewed a man named Alex Staber, who grew up in the town of Turtle Creek and later became an organizer for the UE. During the Depression, he recalled, "my father was out of work and we didn't have anything. They used to give out bags of food at the Turtle Creek Borough building on Wednesday and Saturday, and I went there for free food with my younger sister. My father was too proud, and so was my older sister. But she went with me once and saw that half of her class was there waiting for food. She lost her pride." Staber became politically active while still in his teens. In 1935, he and other youngsters passed out handbills at plant gates in a unionizing effort led by a professed Communist, Logan Burkhart. When the Depression and the Wagner Act created favorable conditions for unions, a core of workers eager to organize and join unions was already in place.

Labor historian Ronald W. Schatz interviewed many of the organizing pioneers of the Westinghouse local at East Pittsburgh for his 1983 book, *The Electrical Workers.* UE Local 601 was established soon after the national UE itself was founded in 1936. The founders of 601, Schatz notes, had first belonged to an independent union, the majority of whose members "were either Communists or sympathized with the party's political point of view." Westinghouse began dealing on a limited basis with the local after its certification in 1937. But the company took a hard line, refusing to sign a union contract until 1941, and union leaders apparently harangued management with anticapitalist rhetoric. This shaky beginning produced bad feelings that persisted for many years.

According to Schatz, Local 601 was divided politically into three general groups. Command of the local union swung back and forth between two small groups of politically committed unionists on the right and left, generally referred to as right-wingers and left-wingers. The former group, eventually known by the name Rank and File Group, was right wing only in a relative sense when compared with its enemies on the left. In the late 1940s, the Rank and File Group consisted primarily of semi-skilled workers (in their thirties and early forties), many of whom were anti-Communist. The left-wing coalition, which became known as the Progressive caucus, included generally older skilled tradesmen who tended to be Communists, Socialists, and other leftists who continued the militant, us-versus-them tradition of the local's founders. The third general group consisted of the vast majority of members, who, as is usually the case, stayed on the sidelines, rarely taking positions, voting for union leaders according to their record on specific workplace issues, often because of personal loyalties, and sometimes because of the candidates' stands on national political issues.[5]

When Tom Quinn went to work at Westinghouse in 1940, he immediately joined the union but stayed out of union politics, becoming by default a member of that amorphous majority group of workers. Although he had felt stirrings of leftist political sympathies, Quinn for the time being concentrated on learning his job and caring for his family. He and Irene and Chuck moved from their one-room apartment in the Hill District to a larger apartment in East Liberty, not far from a Pennsylvania Railroad station. Every workday Tom would board a train in East Liberty for a half-hour ride south and east through Pittsburgh and small towns lining the northern bank of the Monongahela and thence up the east side of Turtle Creek to a depot across the creek from the Westinghouse plant. Workers leaving the train would file across the creek on a walkway named Scab Bridge during the strikes of 1914 and 1916. On both occasions strikers massed on the creek bank and prevented scabs imported by the company from crossing the bridge, until the state police intervened on management's side.

Scabs! There's a hoary term coughed up from an industrial past that many Americans would prefer to forget or deny. This tale is very nearly a ghost story peopled by characters who used words like scabs and engaged in strange work rituals such as tossing rivets, tapping furnaces, and grieving (filing a personnel complaint) under the rubrics manufacturing and labor relations. They lived and worked in communities such as Wilmerding, McKeesport, and East Pittsburgh that once were vital, significant places and are now mere shadows of that era. My memory still populates these and other vanished mill towns with men and women stepping off streetcars, punching time cards at plant gates, strolling by shop windows filled with fancy hats, draining after-work mugs of Tube City draft before dashing for a bus, mowing patches of lawn outside small frame homes with paid-down mortgages, exulting in the tumult of high school football games, arguing politics in union halls and social clubs. Another shadow town is East Liberty, once a retail shopping center, which fell victim to a flawed redevelopment plan. In its heyday, East Liberty had a large population of mixed social, ethnic, and racial groups. So large that Tom Quinn would live in East Liberty for six years without ever meeting, by chance or otherwise, another newcomer who settled there at about the same time, another of my ghosts.

4

BUDDING POLITICIAN AND
LABOR PRIEST

DECADES before chroniclers of the baby boom generation appropriated the word boomers to refer to their cohort, the term had other slang meanings. In one of the most common usages, going back to the 1890s, boomers were drifters, hoboes, and migratory tradesmen such as railroad and construction workers, and even white-collar workers like telegraph operators and journalists, who moved from job to job, boom town to boom town, trading on their skills. My Uncle Harry Davenport might have been described as an advertising boomer. By 1938, he had been on the road for about fifteen years, practicing all the elements of his trade as he moved from city to city: Johnstown, Utica, Buffalo, Seattle, Long Beach, Detroit, and possibly other stops in between. He had sold ad space for newspapers, laid out pages, designed ad campaigns for department stores, and written copy touting every conceivable type and brand of consumer goods. For a good part of this time, especially in the thirties, he also had drifted politically to the left, finally joining the Communist Party in Detroit. Sometimes I think he must have wandered about in a perpetual state of inner contradiction, on the one hand despising bourgeois materialism but on the other hand promoting it with swift, sure strokes of his copy pencil. Ladies' undies, housewares, perfumes, shaving bowls and brushes, fake Persian carpets, rattans and hassocks, front-porch gliders, cut-rate cutlery, threads and needles, sewing patterns, new-fangled appliances such as washing machines with clothes wringers. Even in the Depression, manufacturers were constantly adding to the cornucopia of goods being offered to Mr. and Mrs. America, and brand names came and went on the waxing and waning winds of purchasing power.

Harry became adept at writing breezy lines for department-store sale items that lasted perhaps a season before fading into oblivion. A few examples from department-store ads in 1937 include the Rialto man's shirt, on sale for $1.28 apiece: "There really isn't any secret about this sale—we didn't turn magician, or pull these shirts out of thin air, even tho' selling Rialto shirts for $1.28 does sound like magic." Or Bodi-Kool slips with "shadow-proof panels," that were "as cool as cucumbers," and priced at 69 cents.

I once asked my uncle if he had specialized in promoting certain products as an ad man. "No," he said with a self-mocking grin, "whatever there was to sell, I sold it."

Nineteen thirty-eight, however, was a bad year for business, with the economy still mired in a recession within the Depression, and Harry either was laid off or quit his job. When he registered for Social Security that year in Detroit, he listed himself as unemployed. At the age of thirty-six, he was unemployed, unmarried, and unknown outside the advertising business and perhaps a small circle of acquaintances in radical political groups. But clandestine politics would not have satisfied the craving for attention that Harry had displayed in his early years. By the early forties, I believe, Harry desperately wanted to convert his book learning into action. He had made up his mind to be for the little man and against big business and for the victims of racial and ethnic discrimination and against racists and anti-Semites, and he wanted to fire up large masses of people with brilliant oratory on social equality. He also thirsted for the perquisites of public life, receiving the respect and admiration of others, being regarded as a hero by those who had no power.

Harry left Detroit in 1939 and eventually took a job with the chamber of commerce in East Liberty. The community had originated as a trading post on a road built in 1758 by English general John Forbes as he marched against the French in what is now Pittsburgh. The old Forbes Trail (today's Route 30) crossed Turtle Creek and passed through areas now occupied by East Pittsburgh, Forest Hills, and Wilkinsburg before arriving in East Liberty. Many thousands of settlers passed through the trading post as they headed west on the Forbes Trail, which eventually became Penn Avenue, the main street of a prosperous village. Situated on an unusually large area of flat land, it was a natural hub of streetcar, train, and automobile traffic, bringing shoppers from all over Pittsburgh and its northern and eastern suburbs. By the time the city annexed its smaller neighbor in the late 1800s, East Liberty's retail shopping center ranked behind only downtown Pittsburgh in sales volume. In the 1920s East Liberty had three department stores, several movie theaters, shoe stores, clothing stores, restaurants, and grocers.[1]

Although the 1940s would be East Liberty's peak as a retail shopping center, the chamber's own records about that period are sparse, and library collections contain few news clippings about the community from that decade. My search for documentation of Harry's arrival and work in East Liberty was stymied until I visited my sister Lynn in White Oak in 2002. She had kept a box filled with our mother's papers, and there we found several old clippings with news about Harry and other Davenports. One story, clipped from a *Pittsburgh Sun-Telegraph* of February 1942, has a photograph of him and his sister Julia, Sister Catherine, who had returned from China in December 1941. She appeared at a Lion's Club lunch in East Liberty, undoubtedly at Harry's instigation, to talk about her six years as a missionary. With a handkerchief flaring from a breast pocket of his dark suit, Harry is bending solicitously over his sister, clad in her habit, sitting at a table. She had arrived back in the States in December, two days before the Japanese attacked Pearl Harbor, and had fascinating stories to relate. Entering China in 1935 with the Sisters of St. Joseph order, she traveled a thousand miles to Chihkiang in Hunan Province by sampan and sedan chair. Her mission, which harbored orphans and wounded Chinese soldiers, was bombed more than once by the Japanese, who had invaded China in the mid-1930s. On one occasion she and other nuns worked through the night caring for people wounded in a bombing raid.

Her time in China was Sister Catherine's defining period, and she never stopped talking about the country and its people. My favorite story was about the bus trip she took from Chihkiang as she and other missionaries were being evacuated in 1941 a step or two ahead of a Japanese army. Bandits stopped and boarded the bus on a rural road and demanded money from the passengers. My aunt hid her purse under her habit and convinced the bandits that they would humiliate themselves by searching a woman's garments.[2]

In 1942, according to the *Sun-Telegraph* story, Uncle Harry was secretary of the East Liberty Chamber of Commerce, a position roughly equivalent to executive director. I still did not know when and how he arrived in East Liberty until 2004, when I received a copy of his FBI file through the Freedom of Information Act. FBI informants, it seems, began reporting on Harry's activities in 1942. For the next few years, Harry occasionally discussed politics with Max Weiss, the Communist Party chairman in western Pennsylvania, and traveled to Harrisburg and Washington to urge legislation to halt racial discrimination in employment. Not many white people were taking up that cause in the early forties, and twenty years would pass before Congress passed civil-rights measures. As it turned out, the FBI's interest in Harry was not deep and abiding: the agency concluded that although he occasionally met with known Communists he himself was not a party member. Harry's case file was closed in 1946. The file, however, notes that Harry worked as advertising manager for a retail furrier in Pittsburgh in 1939 and joined the East Liberty chamber in 1940.[3]

While at the chamber, Harry began editing and publishing the *East Liberty Shopping News*. This was a weekly owned by East Liberty merchants who composed the chamber's membership. The paper had no editorial content, only advertisements—page after page of retail ads. Although it was published for several years, no issues have survived that I am aware of. And why should they? Yesterday's advertisement is even more useless than yesterday's news. Fortunately, I did not have to rely on my memory for proof that the paper existed. I interviewed a man who not only worked for my uncle on the *Shopping News* but also served as an aide during his term in Congress.

When he first met Harry Davenport, John E. Connelly was in his twenties, an energetic young man who had started a small weekly paper in the Pittsburgh suburb of Etna. In about 1947 or 1948, Harry hired Connelly to assist with the *Shopping News*. This was the real beginning of Connelly's business career, he told me, because he learned much from Harry about advertising and marketing. He later started his own advertising firm, J. Edward Connelly Associates Inc., an incentive marketing company that in 2000 was grossing more than 100 million dollars a year. Connelly also owned and operated a fleet of excursion riverboats, Gateway Clipper Fleet, on the Monongahela and Ohio rivers.

"Harry was really a flamboyant man about town," Connelly said in a 2000 interview at his home in Fox Chapel, north of Pittsburgh. "People liked Harry tremendously, especially the store owners, and so they gave him the job of publishing the *Shopping News*. My job was to visit the stores, pick up their ads, book their space, and together Harry and I would go to the printers, which was the Braddock Free Press, where we would lay out the ads. The paper was full newspaper size, and it was a great medium because of the large distribution. Harry had a partner named Jack Kaufman whose brother owned a distributing company. They hired out-of-work people who would walk door to door with sacks of papers. But these people weren't allowed into the big apartment houses on Fifth Avenue [in and near East Liberty], so Harry hired me. I took my young sons with me, we were clean looking, and they let us into the apartment houses. We left a paper at every door. The overall distribution was tremendous, a hundred thousand or so every week, and the stores got fabulous results. Free distribution, no news columns, all advertising, but the people looked forward to it, let me tell you. It was an era when the stores knew that if they advertised good values in the *Shopping News*, they'd get results. And they did. The paper was always filled. Honest to God, we had to turn down advertising every week."[4]

When Connelly worked for my uncle, Harry no longer lived with my grandmother in the East Liberty apartment that I had visited so often with my family. In 1943, to the astonishment of everybody who knew him, Harry had gotten married at the age of forty-one and moved to another apartment with his new wife. Her name was Mary White. A divor-cée with two teenaged sons, Mary was a tall, attractive woman with a worldly sheen. Within the Davenport family, Harry's sudden betrothal and marriage produced shock waves of the kind generated by one of the outrageous pranks of his boyhood. In a photograph taken at the wedding reception, you can see a sort of numb disbelief etched on the faces of his sisters and brothers-in-law as they stand stiffly in a line, not quite sure whether to cheer or protest. While they all wished Harry well, they had for years regarded him as a strange loner more likely to live out his life in the company of books than of wife and children. For reasons that I was too young to understand (or care about) at the age of twelve, something about Mary White did not sit well with the Davenport women. In 1945 Mary gave birth to a daughter, Peggy Ann, who was baptized in the Catholic Church. She was a pretty, vivacious little girl, but the McKeesport Davenports seldom saw her because of the cool relations with Mary. In retrospect, Harry's sisters associated the beginnings of his personal decline with his marriage to Mary White. They seemed to regard her as a temptress who had appeared from nowhere and snatched up an eligible, and vulnerable, bachelor.

I cannot say whether there was any truth to their impression. Certainly, though, I never thought of my uncle as a man who would have attracted women through romantic appeal alone. Despite his considerable charm—which he turned on and off according to mood—Harry rarely projected the idea that he loved anyone or anything. Why this was so, I never understood, nor did anyone I knew. It is hard to imagine him as anything but a troublesome husband even if Mary had been the most understanding and truest of wives. But it appears that she was not. John Connelly, who saw her often during the years he worked for Harry, took a strong dislike to her. "It was not a good marriage," he said. "She was a volatile person." When Harry was running for Congress, Connelly would stop at their apartment every morning to pick him up. "Every morning it was, 'Oh, you don't love me, you don't care for me. All you're doing is working, running for Congress. You can't win. I need money to go shopping.' Harry would give her some money. One time, she took it and threw it in the fire. Man, I jumped up and got it out. It was burned, and I took it to the bank and exchanged it for Harry. But, oh God, it was a circus every day!"

As an avid newspaper reader, Harry undoubtedly knew of Father Rice long before he met him. The priest was often in the news, appearing on picket lines, or speaking on behalf of the unemployed and homeless as director of St. Joseph's House of Hospitality. By 1939 he was broadcasting a weekly fifteen-minute program on radio station WWSW, where he would continue as a commentator for more than ten years. He also wrote frequently for the *Pittsburgh Catholic.* In both forums, Rice delivered his thoughts on religion, politics, and social and economic issues. He urged compassion for the poor, expressed strong support for unions, and vigorously attacked racial prejudice. Uncle Harry must have felt stirrings of envy, thinking that Father Rice, by virtue of his clerical collar, had become what Harry himself longed to be, a celebrated hero of the oppressed.

In the late 1930s, the nation was hovering on a dividing line between two catastrophes, depression and world war, as if undecided which way to plunge. Viewed from sixty years on, this period seems fraught with doubt and fear. But Father Rice's activities evidenced none of this uncertainty. To get a sense of his bustling political life at this time, I turned to a collection of photographs selected by Charles McCollester for reproduction in his anthology of Rice's writings, *Fighter with a Heart.* My sampling starts with a photo taken at the 1938 CIO convention, showing the young, bespectacled priest sitting next to a brooding John L. Lewis in a row of union leaders, Rice obviously relishing this rubbing of shoulders as he contemplates the future of the labor movement amongst the powerful men who started it. In a scene at Hospitality House, we see Rice, cigar clenched between two fingers, in a group of men gathered around a large console radio, listening intently to some bit of news, just a bunch of pals. In an October 1940 photo, President Franklin D. Roosevelt is sitting in the rear seat of a convertible and making a typical expansive gesture to a crowd greeting him on his visit to a new housing project in Pittsburgh; in the middle of the picture, a father is holding up his small son to get a glimpse of the great man while, in the upper left, Father Rice in his clerical collar bestows a gaze of almost luminous approval on his political hero.

A fourth photograph is a close-up of Rice and the editor of the *Daily Worker* at the conclusion of their 1938 debate on Communism before a large Pittsburgh audience; each man is smirking with satisfaction at having bested his rival. This documents a role that Rice was beginning to take on, with a sort of grim enjoyment, as a scourge of American Communists. In the years just before World War II, the appeal of the Communist Party grew rapidly in the United States. CPUSA membership reached what would be its peak of eighty-two thousand members in 1938, and perhaps millions more people were influenced by Communist thinking. Especially troubling to Rice and other prounion priests was that 40 percent of CPUSA members belonged to unions. As historian Steve Russwurm notes, these priests worried that a militant, organized movement like Communism "appealed to the same instincts upon which

Catholicism ought to have been drawing." Catholicism and Communism both attracted absolutists and crusaders.[5]

In his early writings and debates, Rice assailed Communism as the Godless ideology of a totalitarian state, and on occasion he attacked Communists in the labor movement. Before 1939 he and the Communist Party occupied common ground on one issue: opposition to Fascist Germany. The party, however, reversed course twice between 1939 and 1941, first switching to an isolationist stance when Stalin signed the pact with Hitler and then urging all-out war against Fascist Germany after Hitler invaded the Soviet Union in June 1941. These flip-flops induced Rice to become more aggressive in his comments about union leaders he suspected of being Communists. "They have shown themselves to be utterly disloyal to the United States and loyal only to Communism and Soviet Russia," he wrote in a *Pittsburgh Catholic* column in June 1941. He added, "I solemnly warn the workers of the Pittsburgh district to have nothing to do with the Communists or their stooges."

It was not enough for Rice to vilify his suspects in print. He intended to run them out of office, and he had a vehicle suited to this purpose, the Association of Catholic Trade Unionists (ACTU). Founded in 1937 by priests and Catholic workers in New York City, the ACTU promoted the growth of non-Communist, corruption-free unions. Rice had formed a Pittsburgh chapter consisting of local priests, workers from several unions, and himself as chaplain. Acting in the ACTU's name, he challenged the left-wing officers of UE Local 601 in a series of skirmishes in 1940–1941. These leaders had loudly criticized President Roosevelt's military buildup and American support for England, which stood alone against Germany after the fall of France. In following the Soviet line, the left-wingers sometimes stumbled into foolish positions, such as the time they rejected a proposal to buy an ambulance with members' contributions and send it to England to aid the victims of Nazi bombing raids.

Under Rice's tutelage, a right-wing opposition group formed an election slate and devised a strategy to take over the local. Rice set up a labor school and trained activists in public speaking, parliamentary procedure, and labor history. He wrote leaflets and denounced the leftists from his church pulpit and in his radio broadcasts. In this battle, Rice was not a kindly pastor cheering feebly on the sidelines; he "gave no quarter," as Ronald Schatz writes, and encouraged the right-wing leaders to lash out at their adversaries. Aided by a welling up of patriotism after Pearl Harbor, the anti-Communist group won enough votes to oust key left-wing officers in December 1941. Among these were Charles Newell, the 601 business agent, and Margaret Darin, the local's first recording secretary, both of whom would become important in Tom Quinn's life.[6]

These early clashes between Rice and the leftists in Local 601 were merely warm-ups for what would come later in the decade, including the events that would engulf my uncle. But already UE leaders knew that they had in Rice a relentless opponent who was all the more dangerous for being a priest. By some estimates, up to half of all UE members were Catholics. Their loyalty to the union might be shaken by the accusations of a priest acting in the name of the Church. In 1940 and 1941, UE officials wrote indignant letters to Bishop Hugh Boyle of the Pittsburgh Diocese, urging him to halt Rice's "meddling" in union affairs. Their letters went unanswered. His diocesan superiors would admonish Rice for various activities during his long career, but never for fighting Communists.

The UE became Father Rice's favorite anti-Communist target for obvious reasons. It was the third largest union in the CIO (behind the Auto Workers and Steelworkers) and the bargaining agent for the great majority of workers in the critical electrical equipment industry, and it claimed the loyalty of more than twenty-five thousand workers in western Pennsylvania and West Virginia, right in his own backyard. At first he focused his attention on UE locals in the region. Ultimately, he took on no less a mission than purging the entire UE of Communist influence.[7]

Communists played a leading role in the UE from the beginning. Organizing in the electrical industry started in the early 1930s at General Electric, Westinghouse, and many smaller firms that manufactured turbines, generators, motors, and home appliances. At this time, before passage of the Wagner Act, only ideologically committed union activists were willing to endure employers' tough antiunion measures. When representatives from seventeen factories founded the UE at a convention in Buffalo on March 21, 1936, Communists, Socialists, and other left-wing radicals were among the most influential delegates, according to *Cold War in the Working Class,* an authoritative history of the UE by Ronald L. Filippelli and Mark D. McColloch. But there was a sizable contingent of non-Communist local leaders, a split that was reflected in the top leadership ranks.

The first president, James Carey, a semiskilled worker from a Philco radio factory in Philadelphia, was a Catholic and a liberal Democrat who Father Rice came to regard as a friend. Two other top-level officers were Julius Emspak, a worker-intellectual from a GE plant in Schenectady, New York, elected secretary-treasurer, and James Matles, who brought fifteen thousand machine shop workers into the UE in 1937 and became the union's director of organization. By 1941 nobody had presented proof that Matles and Emspak were Communists, although both had been identified by Communist defectors in congressional hearings. Both always denied the accusations. While researching this book, I came across irrefutable evidence that Matles, the more important of the two leaders, indeed served as a high-ranking official in CPUSA labor sections during the mid-1930s.[8]

The Carey-Emspak-Matles triumvirate worked well enough until the war in Europe widened the ideological gap between left and right in the United States. Disputes over union policy and politics broke out between Carey and, on the other side, Emspak and Matles. In 1941, forces led by Emspak and Matles rejected a proposal backed by Carey that would have barred Communists from holding union office. At about the same time, a key UE local in the GE chain rebelled against Carey, claiming he had proved inept in negotiations. One of the local officers, Albert Fitzgerald, ran against and defeated Carey for the UE presidency at the 1941 UE convention. Although Fitzgerald was not a Communist, he willingly followed Matles's and Emspak's lead on most issues. In the UE's political structure, the president had less power than the other two officers.

As for the rest of the UE staff, a rival union asserted that the UE employed two hundred Communists or former Communists in the late forties. Filippelli and McColloch treat this number with skepticism, contending that the number of open Communists on the staff was small. "Far more numerous," they say, "were the loyalists who lived in political limbo and did not participate in party matters, except on a semi-clandestine level, but openly supported the line." Schatz adds an arresting observation. In the 1940s, he writes, the UE was "the largest Communist-led institution of any kind in the United States." The UE's membership then numbered more than four hundred thousand while the Communist Party had only fifty-nine thousand members in 1948. Yet only a tiny percentage of ordinary UE members belonged to the Communist Party, less than 1 percent according to some calculations. Furthermore, a healthy portion of the UE's rank and file dissented from the leaders' politics while supporting their leadership on union matters.[9]

Today it may seem absurd to devote so much energy to determining who was and who was not a member of the Communist Party. But sixty years ago this mattered a great deal to people caught up in those struggles, people like Harry, Tom, and Father Rice. If the Communist Party had had its way, it may be supposed, the party would have imposed a stifling political conformity on American institutions as a possible first step toward their surrender to international Communism. As it turned out, the party barely inched one foot forward, and the CIO imposed conformity in the name of halting the spread of Communism. But in the late 1940s, many people believed that a hidden Communist conspiracy, which included or was led by unions such as the UE, was well on the way to a takeover of American institutions. Few held this belief as strongly as Father Rice. He summed up his feelings in a 1968 oral history interview conducted by Filippelli: "Oh, in those days [1940s]," Rice said, "we just thought Communism was going to conquer the world the day after tomorrow, and we weren't going to let them conquer the American labor movement."[10]

The right-wingers' takeover of Local 601 in December 1941 was short lived. A year later, the Progressives swept them from office. By this time, Hitler had broken his pact with Stalin and invaded Russia. For American Communists, what had recently been an imperialist war now became a great war for democracy. The UE realigned its policy, returned to the anti-Fascist side supported by most other unions, and urged the cooperation of government, labor, and business to defeat Hitler. There the political situation in Local 601 remained until the end of the war.

Rice, meanwhile, went on to other things. By 1942 the booming war economy had created an inflationary spiral that raised the price of everything, especially rental housing. When the federal government created the Office of Price Administration (OPA), the priest sought appointment as the OPA's rent-control director in Pittsburgh. He beat out several rivals and became Pittsburgh's "rent-control czar" in August 1942. At the end of the war, he would relinquish this post and resume his campaigns against Communists in labor unions. This time, the entire CIO would become engulfed in a Cold War of its own.[11]

5

THE MAKING OF A
UNION RADICAL

ABOUT twenty-five years after those boyhood days when I knew the Turtle Creek Valley only as an industry-stuffed gorge glimpsed from a car hurtling across the Westinghouse Bridge, I finally made my way down into East Pittsburgh. I had returned to western Pennsylvania in 1964 after a long absence and was embarrassed to find that my knowledge of the area was scanty. Here I was, a native of the region and a labor reporter who had never visited the East Pittsburgh Works of Westinghouse Electric—one of the nation's largest employers of labor and a center of historic union struggles. Despite the countless times I had viewed the plant from the bridge, I knew only slightly more about it and the people who worked there than a passenger on a transcontinental jetliner gazing serenely down at a pinpoint of light at dusk.

Over the next few years I found reasons to make several visits as a reporter to East Pittsburgh. On my first trip, I drove down a steep brick street from Ardmore Boulevard into the business center of East Pittsburgh. It was a marvelously cramped little town smashed up against the side of a hill and drenched in soot and smoke, most of it drifting up the valley from U.S. Steel's Edgar Thomson Works. Westinghouse Electric consisted of several rows of factory buildings extending from Braddock Avenue, a narrow brick street running along the valley floor, back to Turtle Creek. The plant occupied about three-fourths of the narrow bottomlands bordering the creek, squeezing the Borough of East Pittsburgh into little more than a few hundred yards at the narrowest point. Standing on Braddock Avenue with the Westinghouse Bridge soaring across the valley on the south, the west side of town hemmed in by a one-hundred-foot-high stone railroad bridge, and steep eastern bluffs hovering over the immense factory buildings, I felt as insignificant as I must have appeared to motorists on the bridge.

Across from the plant, Braddock Avenue was lined with shops and saloons huddled with their backs against the great stone railroad wall. In the saloons, men still wearing 1940s-style fedoras sat at bars that extended deep into gloomy interiors. They talked willingly enough about their lives, work, and union, but it is not what they said that I remember so vividly. Rather it is the feel and look of that dark and unpretty place under the Westinghouse bridge, the last frame in a strip of torn film documenting this nation's industrial era. I did not know then that that era was fading, that the East Pittsburgh Works had only twenty more years of life, that most of what had happened here—the manufacture of the turbines and generators that electrified America, decades of labor struggles against managerial and technological control of lives, and a battle over political beliefs and freedom of expression that destroyed a union and the lives of countless people—would largely be forgotten. I only had a sense that I was watching a torn frame of film fluttering in the projector's aperture.

For people who lived there, East Pittsburgh consisted of much more than a huge factory, a shadowy street under a bridge, and a dozen saloons. Hundreds of families lived in oddly shaped little houses running up from the valley bottom on steep, pinched streets named Electric, Cable, and Beech. At least one person in each house, sometimes two or three, worked at Westinghouse. They walked down the hill in the morning and back up in the evening. Steve Quinn remembered living with his parents and two brothers in an apartment over a bar on Beech Street in the early 1950s. "We had two bedrooms, a living room, and a kitchen," he said. "We were poor, like everybody else. But when I walked outside I saw all these friendly faces. You never met a stranger. It was like we were part of an extended family." It was a close-knit, blue-collar community of many ethnic groups but few black people; Westinghouse employed small numbers of African Americans, who tended to live in black communities such as the Hill District of Pittsburgh.[1]

Memories of my visits to East Pittsburgh came back to me at a crucial point as I was reconstructing the story of Uncle Harry's rise and fall. I realized that a vital piece of evidence was missing—not factual evidence but rather an insight into Tom Quinn's political motivation. I had a good idea why Harry and Father Rice took the political paths they did. From family tales and personal knowledge of Harry, I could imagine where his radical impulses came from and why he kept them mostly hidden. From interviews, biographical accounts, and archival research, I had learned something about the sources of Father Rice's fierce anti-Communism. As for Quinn, I had plenty of facts about his life—birth, marriage, jobs, firings, hirings, accusations, court cases, and so forth, provided mainly by Quinn and archived documents, supplemented by his FBI dossier. Even with this factual information, I did not fully comprehend what drove Quinn so far to the left that he would stand accused as a Communist.

It would have been easy to assume that coming of age as a penniless orphan at the bottom of the social scale in prewar Pittsburgh would be reason enough to rebel against the capitalist order. But millions of people of similar origins lived and died accepting the status quo. Most Americans have relied on social mobility to provide an economic and social lift during their lifetimes. Quinn chose the harder path of fighting for political reform. I asked him why and discussed it with his sons and people who knew him fifty to sixty years ago. Even with their answers, I still felt that a link was missing. And then I recalled one of my trips to East Pittsburgh in the sixties.

On this occasion a Westinghouse company man took me on a tour of one section of the plant, a large building where generators and turbines were assembled. Huge metal panels hung suspended from overhead cranes in the plant aisleways, like great slabs of meat, waiting to be fitted together and welded. Expecting to see a place dominated by machinery, I was stunned by the sight of hundreds of workers. Everywhere I looked there were people. I had worked briefly in a steel mill as a young man and had visited many coal mines, mills, and manufacturing plants as a reporter but had never seen anything quite like this. In a steel plant, you are overwhelmed by steelmaking technology and equipment: great ladles of molten metal soaring overhead, or red-hot ingots, slabs, and bars throwing off scalding chips as they emerge from a rolling mill. Much of the equipment is operated by one or two workers in a reinforced glass control room, or pulpit, with other workers sometimes clustered but usually scattered.

In the Westinghouse plant, massive numbers of people were laboring on many different operations—rigging, fitting, welding, drilling, grinding, and so forth—across a vast floor space. This remembered scene shed light on Quinn's political development. Every business requires organization, but the presence of so many people doing so many different things made strikingly obvious the need for a vast organizational or governance scheme, replete with rules for this and rules for that, to synchronize and coordinate the work. In preunion days, managers and supervisors had unbridled power over employees, power required for order in industrial production, but power that led to abuses ranging from favoritism in assigning jobs and promoting employees to disregard of safety hazards to the use of discriminatory pay systems and even to demands for sex with women workers. When unions came into factories, they forced management to modify plant governance to ensure fair and roughly equal treatment for workers. Although Westinghouse had halted the most egregious practices by the time the UE organized East Pittsburgh, the union demanded and won tough limitations on management's power to make personnel decisions. Someone had to enforce these new rules.

What originally turned Tom Quinn into a militant leftist had little to do with abstract political ideology and everything to do with the struggle between union and management over control of the shop floor. The UE's principal weapon was a grievance procedure that enabled workers to challenge management decisions involving disciplinary matters, job assignment and promotion, working conditions, hours of work, and disputes over pay. In today's union-free, postindustrial world, such restrictions on management power may seem a novelty, but in manufacturing's heyday they were more common than not in major corporations. About a third of all American employees worked in manufacturing industries by the late 1940s, and nearly 41 percent were covered by union contracts with a grievance procedure. The UE's grievance procedure at East Pittsburgh was enforced by a corps of union stewards that numbered more than three hundred in the 1940s. If the Westinghouse workforce had been a military division, the stewards would have composed an entire company dedicated to reviewing and contesting personnel decisions handed down by the division commander.[2]

When Quinn started his second stint at Westinghouse in 1940, he did not immediately become active, instead focusing on learning his job and surroundings. Although aware of union politics swirling around him, he stayed neutral and avoided taking sides in the campaign waged by Father Rice against Local 601 officers in 1940–1941. Even if he had wanted to become active, he saw that newcomers had trouble making themselves heard. "Most of the positions in the union at that time were held by the old-timers," he recalled. "So you had to take them on if you wanted to advance in the union." He was content to concentrate on his job.

He worked in a building like the one I visited many years later, perhaps the same one. Scores of crews were scattered across a wide floor area, assembling large and small generators and related equipment from steel and other metals. It was by no means as dangerous as a steel mill but hazardous enough, with overhead cranes always moving up and down aisles, carrying large stacks of steel or assembled units. From all sides came dazzling flashes of intense light accompanied by showers of sparks from welders' tools or reddish-blue bursts of flame and sparks where fitters cut steel with burning torches. Workers were lifting and hefting, measuring and fitting, unrolling blueprints, consulting with one another. There was a continuous rumble of large grinding machines, the whine and screech of overhead cranes, the intermittent sputtering of portable generators that powered electrical tools. Over this noise, occasionally, could be heard the shouts of mere men.

Quinn's welding crew used a technique called electric arc welding. Their tool was a metal rod encased in a heat-resistant holder. An electrical charge from a generator converted the rod into a metallic electrode that struck an arc when applied to steel members of various shapes. Both the steel and filler metal in the rod would melt in the intense heat, and molten globules of filler would flow into the gap between two workpieces. Quinn would guide the rod along the gap to create a continuous seam. He wore a hood with a glass visor to protect his face and eyes from the intense flash and heat. The job required a knowledge of good welding practice, a steady hand, and the ability to concentrate on a close task. "My personal satisfaction was, I did a good job on whatever I was doing," Quinn said. "Everybody knew who the better welders were, and I was one of them." Quinn showed so much aptitude that the company sent him to the University of Pittsburgh at one point during the war to learn how to diagnose weaknesses in steel castings using new metallurgical X rays. Finishing the course, he was sent to a company in Cincinnati to find and weld an internal crack in a Westinghouse turbine.

Long before the Cincinnati trip, however, a conflict over a divisive labor-management issue turned Quinn into an activist. It involved incentive pay. Like many manufacturers, Westinghouse was committed to the idea that people worked harder when they had a monetary incentive to produce more. The company paid a flat hourly rate based on skill and other factors, amounting to $1.10 to $1.15 an hour in the early 1940s for welders like Quinn. Workers could earn a bonus on top of the hourly rate by producing more than a minimum number of pieces in an allotted time. Using stopwatches, engineers would determine the minimum amount of time needed to perform each task and then establish a time value with a little give in it. Workers had to beat that time to receive a piecework bonus. If everything went right, incentive pay usually added 20 to 25 percent to the basic hourly rate, obviously constituting a significant part of a worker's paycheck. Even so, workers and unions had been fighting the incentive-pay concept ever since it was introduced in the 1880s, charging that it promoted greed and aroused conflict among different trades working on the same or related jobs. Quinn came up against a classic example of this problem in 1942.

His forty-member fabrication crew had worked for several months on assembling heavy steel frames for generators, or motors, that were installed on trolley cars. First, the fitters in his group would lay out the frame structure, according to blueprints, and put the parts together with temporary welds. In the second step, welders would permanently weld the members into a completed frame. The amount of their incentive bonus depended on how fast they finished welding, which in turn hinged on how well the fitters had laid out and aligned the frame. Before long, the welders were complaining that they were being penalized by the fitters' poor work.

Fitters, supposedly the more skilled tradesmen, already received about twenty-five cents an hour more in basic pay than welders. On top of this, the faster they assembled a frame, the higher their incentive pay. "The fitters did the job sloppily and made out because they did it quickly," Quinn told an interviewer in 1977. "We had to patch it up, fill all the holes, and we weren't making out." A flawed job by fitters forced welders to spend more time filling the gaps, limiting their incentive bonuses. Quinn and his co-workers complained to their group leader, a sort of subforeman who supervised incentive-pay arrangements but also was a union member and not part of management. The group leader, as well as Quinn's section steward, had come from the fitters' trade; neither man saw any reason to change things, and management was satisfied with the arrangement.

The injustice of the situation angered Quinn. "I didn't want anybody to misuse me," he recalled of that time. "I just wanted to be paid for what

I produced." The problem would not be fixed, he concluded, unless he became a steward and pursued the issue himself.[3]

Elected annually by union members, stewards were full-time employees empowered to press workers' complaints and challenges. On urgent problems, a steward could put down his tools, sign off company time (he would collect union pay for this period), and take up the problem with the immediate foreman, and go to higher levels if necessary. Section stewards, representing a half dozen to dozens of workers within one product division, were at the bottom of the steward structure. Other layers included subdivision stewards, division stewards, and at the top a chief steward.

It took nearly a year and one election defeat before Quinn could line up enough support among younger welders to overturn the old union order. In a 1943 election, he finally ousted the incumbent steward and began pleading his case to higher union officials. His solution was to have welders perform the entire job of rigging and welding the trolley frames. But management resisted. "They didn't want to change anything. 'Welders are dumb,' they said, 'They can't read a blueprint and wouldn't know what to weld.' I just kept at it, kept the pressure on, wouldn't let go of it, and finally we had this big meeting with the [plant] superintendent. He was bitter about it. Because of the pressure we put on the union leaders, they told him he had to do something. He agreed to a trial period, and we made it work. As a result, the welders' pay went up 15 percent to 20 percent in a couple of weeks."

As a section steward, meanwhile, Quinn represented the workers in his group on many other problems, though pay issues always topped the list. He pursued grievances with such doggedness and success that the workers in his section reelected him every year for the next four years.

Incentive pay must have seemed so simple to early industrial engineers like Frederick W. Taylor, the father of "scientific management." Attach a stuffed rabbit to a pole, make it revolve around a track, and the dogs will chase it until they drop. But the concept contained paradoxes and complexities. Workers enjoyed the extra income provided by piecework pay, but they hated being put on a stopwatch regimentation and constantly feared that management was manipulating them. They suspected, with good reason, that their reward for finding a faster way to produce something would be an even tighter time standard that would make them race faster to earn the same amount of money. It was only natural,

Quinn said, that workers used shortcuts unknown to engineers to undercut time values. No matter how tightly a time-study expert timed a job, a
longtime worker eventually could figure out how to do it faster but conceal the knowledge from management. Quinn saw this happening on
many jobs and did it himself when he could. "The time-study guys had to
know what was going on," Quinn said, "and even then the men could still
trick them."

From the point of view of Westinghouse management, union group
leaders bore much of the blame for incentive plans that paid too much.
"The group leaders were very clever at getting extra time allowances,
challenging time studies, and 'beating' the system," remembered Samuel
O. Lemon Jr., who worked as a labor-relations representative at several
Westinghouse plants in the 1950s. "This meant money in the pocket to
the group members." By the 1950s, he said, "the incentive pay system was
clearly out of control. Any resistance by management or the time-study
guys was fruitless."[4]

The UE went through a strange metamorphosis on incentive pay. In
its early days the union lashed out at the plans as immoral. But Westinghouse refused to give up a system that it believed produced good profits.
The UE's opposition abruptly ceased during World War II, as Ronald
Schatz points out, because the Communist Party threw its support
behind incentive pay as a means of increasing military production to
defeat the Fascist powers. What had been an immoral tool of management became a moral imperative for the union. Thereafter, the UE not
only defended incentive pay but also demanded more and more rules to
protect workers and prevent the company from slashing incentive times
and rates.

A battle of bureaucracies ensued. On the company's side, there developed a large department of time-study experts who timed the jobs and
developed pay formulas, industrial engineers who integrated pay plans
with the flow of work, labor-relations people who handled incentive
grievances, and clerks who dealt with the massive amounts of paperwork
and time cards generated by the Standard Time Incentive Plan. On the
union side, stewards spent an enormous amount of time filing and negotiating incentive grievances and aiding in the concealment of shortcuts.
When World War II ended, so did cost-plus contracts for government
work, and Westinghouse decided that the incentive bonuses received by
90 percent of some seventy-five thousand hourly workers were costing

more than they were worth. The monster it had created must be slain. But the tables had turned: now it was the UE that refused even to consider eliminating incentive pay from the Westinghouse contract.

Westinghouse, however, would have the last word. In 1950, when union members had to choose between staying with the UE or jumping to a rival, "non-Communist" union, the company would throw its considerable influence as employer against the UE. To justify the rare act of siding publicly with one union over another, the company would wrap itself in the flag of Cold War patriotism, citing the possibility of sabotage by Communist elements in the UE (though none had occurred or even been threatened). But there would be unspoken financial reasons as well. Most significantly, the company knew that ridding itself of the UE was the only possibility it would have of eradicating the abominable Standard Time Incentive Plan. No other union, the company felt, would take as hard a line on incentives as the UE. In this sense, the incentive-pay issue would play a large role in the eventual defeat of Tom Quinn and thousands of other UE loyalists.[5]

Through his battle over incentive pay, Quinn inevitably became involved in union politics. "I began to get more feelings about the importance of acting together in the union, the importance of the union itself," he recalled in a 2000 interview. "I read as much as I could about social issues, and I listened to other people. My cousin [in Youngstown] had introduced me to writers like Wells and Galsworthy and Shaw. So I had a feeling about socialism, about a better world. But it was all just theory. You know, 'Wouldn't it be better to have it this way?'" Now he saw evidence that a society based on notions of one for all and all for one could work in practice, at least in a manufacturing plant with a strong union. As a steward he often had to take hard-edged positions against the company, and this combative process itself strengthened his anticapitalist beliefs. He learned more about Marxist ideas by talking to other union activists and reading the *Daily Worker* and various socialist papers that circulated in the plant.

Quinn spent some part of every workday dealing with grievances. Eventually he allied himself with stewards in the left-wing Progressive caucus because they seemed more disciplined than their right-wing rivals in establishing a tight network of worker protections. In particular, he respected Tom Fitzpatrick, the man who headed the Progressives for much of the 1940s. Fitzpatrick, who was forty-three in 1945, was a veteran drill-press operator in the generator division. He served in several union offices during those years, including chief steward and president of District Council 6. In the late forties, he would be identified as a Communist by several sources, and while indisputable evidence of this does not exist, some people who admired him as a union leader (Tom Quinn for one) do not dispute that he likely was a party member.[6]

In his political analysis of Local 601, Schatz concludes that "a majority of the people active in the Progressive caucus in the late 1940s were loosely associated with the Communist Party." He names thirty people, including Quinn, who he says made up the core of the caucus. Quinn joined the Progressives in the midforties because Fitzpatrick and his allies were the most effective leaders on trade-union issues, not because of their political ideology. On ideological matters, the group was divided into smaller factions favoring specific ideologies, including Socialist Workers, Single Taxers, Trotskyites, and Communists, among others. The leftist rivalries could be so intense that some groups would form alliances with rightists at election time to deny office to other members of the Progressive caucus.

"These factions spent too much time arguing among themselves on what amounted to, as far as I was concerned, moot questions about strategy based on ideology," Quinn said in 2000. "All I wanted was to have a good union." Quinn's attitude was, as he told an interviewer in 1977, "I don't give a damn what these guys believe or what they want to peddle. As long as they work here and are active in the union, they have the same rights as myself. . . . [When] right wingers came to meetings, they'd say, 'So you're with the Communists?' I'd say, 'I am with the guys who I think are the best leaders of the union. I don't give a shit whether they are Communists or not.'"[7]

In 1953 a former Communist and Local 601 leader from 1942 to 1944, Francis Nestler, would testify before a congressional committee that he and a few other Progressives helped adapt party policy to Local 601 issues while attending CPUSA meetings. They would explain and discuss the "line" at caucus meetings to larger circles of Progressives who would later present a united front on the issues at sparsely attended union membership meetings. Nestler left the union movement in 1946. While many charges made before investigating committees should be treated with skepticism, Nestler's testimony and other evidence leaves little doubt that the Communist Party strongly influenced Local 601 when the Progressives were in power. But Nestler produced no evidence of subversive activity, and he specifically denied knowing Quinn as a Communist.

In the end, of course, Quinn could not draw a line in the dust at the plant gate between the Progressives' work as union representatives and their far-left positions on national political issues. If he was with them on the former, he at least sympathized with some of their political stands. He eventually became involved in one or two outside groups that were characterized as Communist-front organizations.[8]

The end of World War II in August 1945 brought a wonderful feeling of euphoria. On VJ (Victory over Japan) Day, when Japan surrendered aboard the USS Missouri in Tokyo Bay, ecstatic people howled and celebrated on Fifth Avenue in McKeesport as boisterously as in Times Square. The end of the war meant a future of unlimited hope. Horizons began to appear far beyond the National Tube Company for me and many of my friends as we entered sophomore year in high school, mill-town kids looking forward to college. All around us people were preparing either to jump aboard a streamliner to a wonderful new postwar economy or jump aside if the Depression Express returned. My father had our family lined up to catch that first streamliner, and I never doubted it would come.

A few miles away, in East Pittsburgh, Tom Quinn also was looking to the future, but not seeing any far-off horizons for welders. To know that you can weld two pieces of metal together as well as anybody is not the stuff the American dream is made of. He decided to make a career of union work. "I felt very strongly about the importance of the union and its future," he said, remembering that time. "The UE was a different kind of union, not as bureaucratic as other unions, and there was no doubt in my mind that the UE would fight harder for the ordinary worker."

From the perspective of the twenty-first century, Quinn's career decision might seem shortsighted. But in 1945 there were reasons to believe that unionism was just getting off the ground and would grow steadily in the years ahead, spreading from blue-collar occupations to professional and white-collar ranks. We know now that the percentage of the workforce belonging to unions was still growing and would reach its peak in 1953. At the time, few people anticipated that jobs in manufacturing, the largest union sector, would shrink by several million over the next two decades. Corporations had barely begun to avoid unions by moving production to southern states and to foil organizers by exploiting weaknesses in the Wagner Act, the revelation of corruption in the Teamsters and a few other unions was still a decade away, and the postwar boom was only beginning to lure people from collective action to an ethic of economic individualism. From 1945 to the end of the decade, the unions' ability to mount nationwide strikes, raise workers' standard of living, and influence national politics would argue persuasively that organized labor was the most powerful social and political institution in the nation.[9]

To aspire to a career as a union leader or staff member was to attach oneself to the future of an idea in somewhat the same way that enthusiasts of computer technology hooked themselves to new-technology businesses in the 1990s. While the latter grabbed at the ring for a profitable, entrepreneurial joyride, the former hoped to realize political and social ideals or carve out a niche of personal power. But you did not join a union staff to make money, especially not the UE staff. Reflecting its rank-and-file origins, the UE had a constitutional provision that limited the pay of top officers to the highest hourly rate in any UE shop, and staff members with positions like those Quinn would fill made considerably less than the officers.

The great strike wave of early 1946 unexpectedly gave Quinn a chance to advance in the UE. Union members had begun suffering from the loss of overtime pay and jobs as production slowed in 1945. Businesses were clamoring for an end to wartime price controls, presaging a rise in consumer prices that would further reduce real wage income. CIO president Phil Murray tried to coordinate a collective-bargaining assault by unions in mass-production industries, intending to set a wage pattern for most industries through the combined strength of several million union members in the CIO.

Undercut by interunion rivalries, Murray's plan succeeded only in part. Still, more than a million workers went on strike in the auto, steel, and electrical industries between November 1945 and the following January. Eventually they all settled for a wage increase of 18½ cents per hour (roughly 15 percent)—all but the UE at Westinghouse. Testifying to their volatile relations, the UE and Westinghouse remained deadlocked from January to May 1946. The strike ended only when Westinghouse agreed to an above-pattern increase of 19 cents per hour. The additional half cent (amounting to millions of dollars calculated on man-hours worked) would be used to eliminate pay disparities between men and women workers. It was the first time a union had addressed this difficult issue.[10]

During the four-month strike, Quinn volunteered to work in the Local 601 office, handling paperwork and administering union welfare programs for members who ran out of money to buy food and pay rent. He prepared strike updates for daily radio broadcasts and often served as the on-air newsreader. "There was always something that had to be done, and so I did it," Quinn said. "That brought me to the attention of not only the rank and file, but also the leadership."

The leadership included three influential persons in the Pittsburgh headquarters of UE District Council 6, which oversaw all UE locals in western Pennsylvania and West Virginia. One was Tom Fitzpatrick, who then was serving as the district president. The other two were Charles Newell and Margaret Darin, former Local 601 officers accused of (but never legally charged with) having Communist ties. After their defeat in Father Rice's 1941 campaign, these two UE loyalists were appointed to posts in District 6. Darin became the office manager. Newell saw war service as a pilot and returned to Pittsburgh as a representative of the UE national office, sharing district leadership with Fitzpatrick. All three took a liking to Quinn and began grooming him for more responsibilities in the UE.

By the end of the strike in May 1946, the Quinns had exhausted their savings and were struggling to meet expenses. They now had three children to feed and clothe; Irene had given birth to their third son, Steve, in 1945. To eliminate the cost of Tom's daily train trip to and from work, they moved from East Liberty to the apartment over a tavern on Beech Street in East Pittsburgh. Now Quinn had only to walk a block to get to work. It would still be touch and go for a quite a while, but Irene never complained, never questioned his commitment to the union. Quinn's growing reputation as a dedicated, competent union man and a leader in the Progressive caucus had filtered up to top UE officials in New York. His friends and even newspaper reporters began referring to him as Tommy Quinn, friendly and well liked, but defiant of management and not afraid to stand up for what was right regardless of the consequences.

Quinn had become interested in national and state politics during the war years, widening his knowledge of world affairs by extensive reading of newspapers and political journals. Although a man of the left, he was not blindly partisan and generally got along with most people, whether they were left-wingers, right-wingers, or in-betweeners. With the backing of Progressives and other factions, he was elected legislative chairman of Local 601. Quinn took up these duties in the summer, too late to organize for the congressional elections of 1946. Meanwhile, Harry Davenport, fulfilling a long-held ambition, also took a political path, one that would intersect with Quinn's.

6

A PROMISING BID
FOR CONGRESS

IF the war was a time of coming together, of linking arms across national and political boundaries to fight a common enemy, the immediate postwar period was a time of flying apart. There was a great clamor of flapping wings and clashing swords. Uncrossable divides opened up on all sides: on the international scene, between the Soviet Union and its former allies in the West; in the United States, between business and labor, Democrats and Republicans, foreign affairs hard-liners and soft-liners, and anti-Communists and Communists. Political rifts extended from the Cold War back into the United States and widened everywhere, but especially in the CIO and particularly in the United Electrical Workers. In this atmosphere, my Uncle Harry Davenport launched his political career.

In all my conversations with Harry, I never asked why he decided to run for Congress in the first place. I must have assumed that politics was in his nature, and I saw no contradiction in the idea of adman and politician being fused inside one skin. Being political, however, was one thing and getting elected to public office quite another. When Harry made his first bid for office, in 1946, he had never been elected to anything; he had no voting record, no list of accomplishments, and no constituency of political jobholders who owed him allegiance. He was forty-four years old and a chamber of commerce executive who professed to be, of all things, a liberal Democrat seeking election in a solid Republican district.

Serving in Congress, I believe, had been a dream of Harry's for several years. By the midforties he was getting rather old to jump into political combat, but he probably was encouraged by his brother Eddie's experience. After operating a public relations–advertising–real estate firm in Los Angeles for about fifteen years, Eddie won a seat on the Los Angeles City Council in 1945 at the age of forty-six. He and Harry had remained close over the years, and Eddie had always been the one who raised the bar, hauled himself up, and then reached down to grasp Harry's hand. Eddie undoubtedly gave him political advice and urged him to seize an opportunity when one became available.

That opportunity finally presented itself in 1945. The officeholder in Allegheny County's Twenty-ninth Congressional District, which encompassed Harry's home base of East Liberty, announced that he would not seek reelection in 1946, leaving the door partially open to a newcomer. The Twenty-ninth was a relatively new district, having been carved out of two older ones in 1943 by the Pennsylvania legislature. The Republicans in control had structured the district so that it would remain in the GOP column no matter who ran on the Democratic side. In the 1944 presidential election, Franklin D. Roosevelt carried Allegheny County by 90,000 votes but lost in the Twenty-ninth by 494 votes. Given these odds, there were no Democrats clamoring to get on the ballot for the 1946 election.[1]

Harry set about acquiring political friends, setting his sights in particular on David L. Lawrence, the most powerful Democrat in Pittsburgh and probably all of Pennsylvania. Starting in 1920, when he was appointed chairman of the Allegheny County Democratic Committee, Lawrence had built a party machine based on a patronage system so extensive that he could, in effect, determine the outcome of votes among Democratic candidates in every city ward. If he did not like a candidate, he would issue a "cut" order, and the candidate almost invariably would lose. Lawrence also gained control of federal patronage throughout Pennsylvania in the 1930s, became chairman of the state Democratic Party, and served as a Democratic national committeeman from 1940 until the end of his life. Before 1945 he had preferred to wield his substantial power behind the scenes, but in that year he ran for mayor of Pittsburgh. Harry formed an independent committee to campaign for Lawrence. This was probably more symbolic than effective, but it linked Harry politically with the man who not only would be the next mayor but also commanded all entry points to the Democratic political system.

Lawrence had promised, among other things, to rebuild Pittsburgh's deteriorating business district. To publicize this issue, he went to New York in August 1945 to meet with Mayor Fiorello LaGuardia, who had led a vast renewal program planned by urban expert Robert Moses. Lawrence's visit to New York earned what is known today as a photo opportunity with the highly popular "Little Flower." A photograph published in the *Pittsburgh Press* shows Lawrence and LaGuardia bending thoughtfully over a table covered with blueprints. A third man in the photograph, Harry Davenport, had accompanied Lawrence on the trip as a chamber of commerce representative. Whether Uncle Harry had much interest in urban renewal is beside the point; he definitely wanted to obtain Lawrence's approval to run for Congress. In November 1945, Lawrence decisively won the mayoral election. He would prove to be probably the most effective mayor in Pittsburgh history. As the co-leader of an unusual Democratic-business alliance, he helped bring about one of the most thoroughgoing city renewals in American urban history, the so-called Pittsburgh Renaissance. Lawrence won two more terms as mayor, graduated to the Pennsylvania governorship for one term, and remained a prominent figure in national politics until his death in 1966.[2]

Harry's strategy apparently worked. In early 1946 he was endorsed by the county Democratic Party to seek the nomination for Congress in the Twenty-ninth. This would not have happened without Lawrence's backing, although John Connelly—who became Harry's assistant about a year later—retained the impression that Lawrence was less than enthusiastic. "I think Dave gave it to him because, you know, nobody wanted to make that run," Connelly told me. A victory by Harry was considered so unlikely that the party provided only minimal financial help. Still, he got the most important thing, Dave's nod, as some politicos called it. That famous nod, Harry would learn to his regret, also created a debt that might come due at an inopportune time.[3]

With the Democratic endorsement, Harry resigned from the chamber of commerce to campaign for the nomination (he continued to publish the *Shopping News*). Winning the Democratic primary in May 1946, Harry moved on to challenge a well-known Republican in a district posted with Democrats Not Wanted signs. Covering six wards in the north-eastern corner of Pittsburgh, the Twenty-ninth stretched eastward to take in several Republican suburbs, including Wilkinsburg, Forest Hills, and Edgewood. At the eastern edge of Forest Hills, the boundary line took a Republican jog to the northeast, crossed the Turtle Creek Valley north of Democratic territory, and hooked around to take in more GOP suburbs. By this gerrymandering, Republican legislators had excluded the Democratic blue-collar factory towns of East Pittsburgh, Turtle Creek, and Wilmerding. Crafty as they were, the planners may have wrongly assumed that all the people who worked at Westinghouse Electric and WABCO lived only in those towns. But many workers had moved out of the shadow of the plants, and by the 1940s the homes of some ten thousand UE members were scattered across the Twenty-ninth. Harry saw that if he could win UE backing and convince the union to mount a major effort among its members, it might be possible to assemble a Democratic vote large enough to overcome an enormous deficit in voter registration and a Republican opponent with several advantages.[4]

John McDowell had an established name in political circles by virtue of having served one term in the House of Representatives, in 1939–1940, when the districts were configured differently. As editor, publisher, and front-page columnist of the weekly *Wilkinsburg Gazette*, McDowell had an excellent publicity platform. Considered by everybody, including himself, as unbeatable, he condescended to give my uncle a gracious nod in the *Gazette* when he won the Democratic nomination. Harry, McDowell wrote, was "a pretty good fellow . . . probably the best secretary the East Liberty Chamber of Commerce ever had." In a few months, McDowell would wish he had never given that generous assessment.[5]

Harry had some points in his favor. He was well known to East Liberty businesspeople and civic leaders and had kept his name in the news with a busy schedule of lunch speeches and other appearances. Every December, for example, he had played the role of Santa Claus during East Liberty's popular Christmas parade. He was no longer that oddest of creatures, a middle-aged intellectual bachelor who spent his off time poking around in library stacks. Harry was now a family man, married (happily, as far as the outside world knew) and the father of an infant daughter, Peggy Ann, who was born in 1945. He was a good speaker who could disarm people with wit and charm. Pronouncing himself a New Deal liberal who championed the union cause, he won the endorsement of the UE and the CIO.

Even so, Pittsburgh newspapers paid little attention to Harry during the early months of his campaign. It was a foregone conclusion that he had no chance of beating McDowell in a gerrymandered district that had shown its distaste for Franklin D. Roosevelt and the New Deal. But Harry intended to bring more to the party than liberal views and the support of a few unions.

Uncle Harry passed his last years in such dreary circumstances that a tendency arose in our family, the Davenports, to view the final third of his life as a mirror image of previous decades of failure. I might have carried that judgment to my grave if I had not set out to unravel the mystery of his fall. There was a time, I discovered, when a good many people invested large hopes in Harry as a fighter against ethnic bias and racial hatred. John McDowell gave him a rare opportunity to assert these virtues.

McDowell, forty-four, a small-town reporter and editor most of his life, had acquired the *Wilkinsburg Gazette* in the 1930s. Winning election to the House in 1938, he showed himself to be an anti–New Dealer and isolationist who voted against conscription and FDR's war-preparedness plans. A darker aspect of McDowell's character emerged in 1940 when a county judge named Samuel ("Sammy") A. Weiss challenged his bid for reelection. Speaking of Weiss, McDowell declared that "no Russian is going to take my seat in Congress." To many Jews, this was blatant anti-Semitism. As the editor of a Jewish newspaper pointed out, Weiss had emigrated to the United States from Poland, not Russia. McDowell implied that "his opponent was a Jewish upstart and a 'foreigner' who was trying to muscle in on a 'pure American.'" Judge Weiss, who proved to be popular with all ethnic groups, defeated McDowell and went on to serve a second term.[6]

During his out years, McDowell continued to wage political fights in his weekly column, which he called "Country Editor," though there was nothing rustic about Wilkinsburg. The *Gazette* typically ran McDowell's column on the left side of the front page and one local news story in the far-right column; the rest of the front page and three or four other pages would contain social notes about weddings and parties, municipal news, obituaries, other typical weekly fare. McDowell's columns were breezy, sometimes amusing, often contemptuous. If writing could talk, McDowell's would be a scratchy echo of the colorful style employed by Westbrook Pegler, the syndicated national columnist of the thirties, forties, and fifties who also indulged in anti-Semitic diatribes.

The McDowell-Davenport race in 1946 was all but ignored by Pittsburgh dailies until late October, when the *Pittsburgh Post-Gazette* took surprised notice of the "sharp, angry and confused contest" in the Twenty-ninth. McDowell is pictured as still battling against the New Deal programs put in place by FDR, who had died in 1945, and scornful of what he called the "European influence" on the United States. Harry, in contrast, declares with pride, "I'm a Roosevelt New Dealer," adding that he is "probably the only secretary of a chamber of commerce in the United States who was for Roosevelt." I could picture his lips curling in a wry grin. The allusion to "sharp, angry, and confused" seems to refer to charges of bias and bigotry that are not explained in this story or by any of the daily papers. What began as a sleepy campaign had erupted into a sharp and angry debate all right—and not particularly confused. I stumbled on it while scanning microfilm copies of McDowell's columns in the *Gazette*. A few days before the election in November, McDowell bitterly criticized the editor of another weekly, the *Jewish Criterion*, for unleashing "a dastardly racial attack against me." The *Criterion*, I learned, was a prominent Jewish weekly published in Pittsburgh for more than sixty years before it ceased publication in 1960 and was succeeded by another weekly.[7]

In October 2002, I visited Rodef Shalom Congregation on Fifth Avenue in the Oakland section of Pittsburgh to read old *Criterions* in the synagogue library, one of the main repositories of information about the history of the Jewish community in western Pennsylvania. Jews began moving into Pittsburgh in substantial numbers in the middle of the nineteenth century. By 1948, according to one estimate, about fifty-four thousand Jews lived in the Pittsburgh area, with the largest concentration in the Squirrel Hill section of the city. In the 1940s, Squirrel Hill was part of Harry Davenport's congressional district, and I knew from having lived there twenty years later that the community was highly politicized and could be counted on to turn out a large vote in every election. I was eager to find out what the connection was between Uncle Harry and the *Jewish Criterion*.[8]

The Rodef Shalom librarian, Martha Berg, directed me to a stack of well-preserved bound volumes containing practically every *Criterion* published between 1902 and 1959. In 1946, the weekly consisted of about thirty tabloid-size pages devoted to news about Pittsburgh's Jewish community, with sections on international and national news relating especially to the establishment of a fledgling state that, in 1948, would become Israel. Every week, a column called "As I See It" by editor Milton K. Susman appeared on page 3 opposite the editorial page. A facile writer, Susman wasted little space on gossip, addressing instead the great humanitarian issues of the day, such as racial hatred in the South and continuing discoveries about the Holocaust. Susman's column was as liberal and open minded as McDowell's was insular and close-minded.

In the middle of August 1946, Susman tossed a grenade into the somnolent congressional race in the Twenty-ninth, endorsing Harry Davenport over John McDowell. This column was the first in a series of withering attacks on McDowell as an anti-Semitic racist. Quoting excerpts from McDowell's *Gazette* columns and comments in political debates, Susman compiled a series of poisonous remarks about Jews, Eastern European immigrants, and African Americans. In a 1946 column, McDowell seemed to support the migration of Jews from Europe to Palestine but in the same breath pictured them as "climbing, like flies, out of the carnal pit of Middle Europe." In another instance, he used code words to heap ridicule on Jewish writers, referring to them as "professional propagandists [who] seem to breed like rabbits on Manhattan Island; and after getting a heavy dose of good Russian ideology there, they sell their vocabulary of invectives to any organ of the oppressed . . .[and] write books on how rotten everything in America is from the viewpoint of the ghetto refugee."

Susman had never before endorsed a congressional candidate. But over the next three months, he made an extraordinary effort in Harry's behalf, devoting all or part of eight columns to the election contest in the Twenty-ninth. In a final column before the election, he declared that voters faced a choice between Davenport, who "believes in a government for all peoples regardless of class, religion or ancestry," and McDowell, "whose voting record and published sentiments reflect a passion for the high walls of factionalism and group hatred."

McDowell seems to have been caught off guard by the vehemence of Susman's attack. Not until early November did he reply in the *Gazette*. "Mr. Davenport," he wrote, "is campaigning with, and, at the expense of, a group of people who have been whipped into a mental dismay by a cold lobbyist and a publicity man, with the taint of Communist direction behind them." Leaving the Communist connection unexplained, McDowell continues: "Davenport is campaigning on a platform of being against bigotry and intolerance. This man has charged into place after place announcing he was the candidate running against the G—D— Kluxer from Wilkinsburg." McDowell took out a half-page ad in his own paper to declare that "I am not a member of the Ku Klux Klan, and I don't believe there has been any Ku Klux Klan in Pennsylvania for more than twenty years."[9]

If McDowell truly believed this, he did not live in the Pennsylvania I was growing up in. In about 1938 or 1939, when I was eight or nine years old, the Klan burned a huge cross atop Auld's Knob, the most prominent hill in White Oak. I recall viewing it from the back porch of my Aunt Annamae's home, with my father standing silently beside me in the warm night air. It was a chilling sight, and my father's grim, forbidding look gave me to understand that I had witnessed something ugly and hateful. Years later, my mother told me that her uncle, Harry F. Davenport, the murdered constable in Wilmerding, was reputed to have been a notable Ku Kluxer.

Recalling the cross burning as I read McDowell's disclaimer, I decided to see how the Davenport-McDowell race was viewed by African Americans (usually called Negroes or coloreds in 1946, they are referred to here with the more modern terms blacks or African Americans). In the 1940s, blacks in the segregated South were still being lynched and denied the right to vote, and the situation was only marginally better in the North. Many public accommodations in Pennsylvania might as well have been segregated by local ordinance, as in the South; blacks were excluded from most white-operated restaurants, taverns, and swimming pools. Whites and blacks worked together in the steel mills and coal mines, but went their separate ways after work. Hill District residents could find only menial jobs in downtown Pittsburgh as shoeshine boys, street cleaners, and drivers and helpers on garbage trucks. As late as the 1960s, when I worked in the Gateway Center office complex, I rarely saw black faces among the professionals and businesspeople. Of the several hundred clerks and secretaries employed in the five office buildings that made up Gateway Center, very few, if any, were black. Department stores hired only a small complement of black clerks and rarely promoted them.

I was reminded of that racist climate when I looked over a file of news clippings from 1946 issues of the *Pittsburgh Courier*, the well-known national weekly published by and for African Americans. Practically every issue in the fall of 1946 had stories about discrimination in jobs, housing, and public accommodations. The November 2 issue, for example, contained one front-page story about Pittsburgh department stores balking at proposals on "integration of Negroes into their sales forces," another about eight black high school students who were denied admittance to a skating rink in East Liberty, and a third about the actress Ingrid Bergman, who was appalled to learn that "Negroes would be barred from the theatre where she was to perform" [in Washington, DC].

Facing hatred, discrimination, and neglect on all sides, the *Courier* adopted a curious, though understandable, editorial policy on the congressional elections of 1946. Believing with good reason that "reactionary and backwoods Democrats of the South" controlled the Democratic Party, the editors declared that "the fortunes of the Negro people" could best be served by electing a Republican Congress. The paper therefore urged its readers to vote the Republican slate. One exception was Harry Davenport, "a fighting, progressive Democrat," as the *Courier* described him in a house advertisement urging Harry's election. He would challenge racists in his own party such as Representative John E. Rankin, a notorious segregationist from Mississippi.

It is difficult after a half century to assess the extent of John McDowell's racial and ethnic bias on the basis of fewer than a dozen published comments. Perhaps the *Courier* expressed it most judiciously. It did not appear that McDowell was "a violent anti-Semite or Negrophobe," the paper concluded. But, it added, "we are sure from what he has said and because of his natural conservatism, that in Congress he would become a dangerous tool of reaction." Davenport, in contrast, would work to "end discrimination" and would fight for antilynching, anti-poll-tax, and fair-housing laws.[10]

The leaders of UE District 6 endorsed Harry in the district newspaper, *Progress*, as a candidate who stood "squarely for the policies of Roosevelt and the New Deal." The paper also noted that Harry, unlike other Democrats, did not engage in Red baiting. The electrical union was initially drawn to Harry because McDowell for years had waged a fierce, noisy fight in the *Gazette* against what he called the "puppets of Moscow" who ran the UE in western Pennsylvania.[11]

By Election Day 1946 Harry Davenport had become the candidate of choice of two major ethnic groups, African Americans and Jews, and of the largest union organizations in western Pennsylvania. Not a bad accomplishment for a non-Jewish white man who had never belonged to a union and was a political newcomer.

Political trends, however, were running against all Democratic candidates. A tide of anger and dismay over Harry Truman's handling of the Cold War and the domestic economy gathered through the summer and fall of 1946. From the political right he was accused of not standing up to Soviet expansionism in Europe, while critics on the left charged that he was overreacting to the Russians. At home, a dramatic rise in the cost of living and a series of labor disputes and nationwide strikes were damaging the postwar recovery. Republicans were building massive support for legislation to reduce union power, a drive that would culminate in passage of the Taft-Hartley Act in 1947. The anti-Truman tide built into a wave that broke over the nation on election day, November 5. Although 1946 was not a presidential-election year, the election results were taken as a repudiation of Truman's policies and leadership. Republicans won control of both houses of Congress for the first time since 1928.

Raised by the GOP tide, McDowell defeated Davenport with 53 percent of the vote, 55,329 to 48,091. Although disappointed, Harry recognized that he had performed far better than anybody had expected, except he himself. McDowell finished significantly behind the Republican ticket throughout the district. Harry's campaign against McDowell's racial and ethnic bias had a significant effect in Pittsburgh's Fourteenth Ward, comprising Squirrel Hill and Homewood-Brushton, a large black community. Aided by a turnout of more than 70 percent (astounding for a non-presidential-election year), Harry won the ward by nearly five hundred votes, while the Democratic candidate for governor lost by fifty-eight hundred.

Harry concluded that he had been right to focus on McDowell's penchant for allowing his tongue and typewriter to reveal his essential bigotry. Given a bit of luck, McDowell could be counted on to engage in some foolish activity in Congress, which would make him even more beatable. Harry also saw that he did well in places where unions made an effort to get out the labor vote. A prime example was the town of Swissvale, the home of Union Switch and Signal Company. The Republicans had a large registration lead here, but UE Local 610, which represented the Switch workers, mounted an aggressive voter drive, enabling Harry to edge McDowell by 63 votes out of 5,757 cast. Commenting on the election results, the UE's *Progress* noted that Davenport had "succeeded in rallying a great progressive vote" where organized labor prepared for the election. With a larger turnout in the presidential election year of 1948, the paper said, "a campaign like Davenport's will have every probability of success."[12]

But Harry had lost a hard, grinding, personally expensive campaign. Doing it all over again would be a daunting prospect to some. As John Connelly told me in 2000, "Harry was the kind who would never say die." He had to display some humility in defeat, but secretly Harry was elated. People now could say of him, this stuffed-shirt chamber of commerce guy is real! The best display of all was when you emerged from nowhere, regarded as a nobody or as a cold, shallow businessman, and showed yourself to be instead a very liberal, perhaps even radical, Democrat who just happened to wear a starched shirt over a compassionate heart. He liked the epiphany that occurred in other people when they saw the real Harry Davenport.

L ocal 601's political organizing had been sidelined in 1946 because of the long Westinghouse strike. But Tom Quinn, as legislative chairman, was laying plans to wage a strong campaign for favored congressional candidates in 1948. Meanwhile, he continued to rise in his union. The UE employed staff members on two levels. Like many American unions with members in Canada, the UE referred to itself as an international union; people hired by top officials in New York City were called international representatives. In 1947, Quinn took a leave of absence from Westinghouse to work as district representative for UE District 6. Under the UE-Westinghouse contract, employees could take a leave of absence for three years to serve on the district staff and return to the plant without losing seniority. This enabled the union to rotate workers in and out of staff positions as one means of infusing the union bureaucracy with a rank-and-file point of view. Quinn gladly accepted the promotion, even though he had to take a substantial pay cut. His UE salary was equivalent to his hourly rate in the plant (about $1.50 an hour in 1947), but it did not include incentive or overtime pay. Still, he said, "I didn't hesitate much when they asked me to take the job. I told Irene what was going to happen, that I wouldn't make as much money. She said, 'Whatever you want to do.' We had to adjust to the change."

He became one of three staff representatives working out of the District 6 office in Pittsburgh. Two performed administrative work in the office. Quinn drew what was called the Pennsylvania Railroad assignment. The UE did not provide cars for its reps, so he traveled on the Pennsy to Latrobe, Johnstown, Altoona, and other outlying towns, handling grievances and negotiating contracts for small local unions. In this job he gained invaluable experience as a negotiator and organizer. The plants produced all kinds of products, with workforces ranging in size from a couple dozen to several hundred. Too small to have full-time officers, they were "serviced" by District 6 representatives. In those years, most labor contracts were short term, lasting only one or two years. "You were almost constantly engaged in negotiations," Quinn recalled. At each company he first had to absorb basic information about the business: how the products were produced and sold, the skills involved, the types of occupations; he had to assess the personalities of managers and union leaders in each firm and draw conclusions about the existing relationships between management and workers, or what today is called the culture of the workplace. "There was a lot to learn," Quinn said. "A different set of things in each company, different products. Electronics was just coming in, and circuit boards. New occupations, salaried people. There was always conflict between skilled workers and the unskilled, and you had to deal with that."

The international union's research department provided economic data to assist negotiators, and more experienced district officials occasionally gave Quinn advice. For the most part, though, he had to figure out by himself how to translate workers' needs and wishes into bargaining demands, how to work politically with the local union and negotiate with more experienced management officials, and how to decide when to reach agreement or call a strike. "When I first went on the staff," he said, "there wasn't a whole lot of direction from the union. The fact is, I learned a lot of things from my opponents, especially the lawyers who represented the companies. I watched what they did."

During World War II the UE, like most unions, observed a no-strike pledge. After the war, the UE negotiated so aggressively that it earned a reputation among some management people as a "strike-happy" union. In fact, though, Quinn spent much of his time trying to avoid walkouts. He knew from his experience in the 1946 strike at Westinghouse how devastating a long work stoppage can be for workers and the community as well as the company. "I knew what it meant personally, about the stress and what happens to the community and the people when you have a long strike," he said. "Quite often the determination of whether there would or would not be a strike would lie in my hands, and I had many difficult nights on the day before we had to make a decision, thinking about the workers and their families and the community." Sometimes a hard-line management forced the union to strike. In a few cases, militant local unionists were more intent on punishing the company than settling a dispute. In one small firm, Quinn remembered, such a faction resisted his attempts to reach a settlement. "We [UE officials] couldn't do anything with them," Quinn said. Realizing that the local committee would not vote to end the strike, "I finally had to go in and tell them that the strike was over. I just wrapped it up."

In taking the staff job, Quinn realized he was associating himself politically with district and national union leaders who had been branded as Communists. Some UE critics contended that the union hired only card-carrying Communists for staff positions, but Quinn said he was not asked to join the party as a precondition for promotion. As long as UE officers ran an honest, effective union, he would give them his loyalty. For their part, UE district leaders undoubtedly felt that they knew their man, that he could be trusted not to turn against the union or its policies. On foreign policy, Quinn believed that the United States was just as guilty as, if not more so than, the Soviet Union in provoking Cold War aggression. On domestic issues, the UE's efforts to broaden union power appealed to him, as did the union's opposition to anti-Semitism and racism and its fight against poverty.

In 1947, Quinn was becoming known to a wider circle of labor and political people in Pittsburgh—as well as to the many enemies of the UE, including anti-Communist union groups, FBI agents and informants, and the man who would become the UE's main antagonist. At about the time Quinn joined the union staff, Father Charles Owen Rice—freed from his wartime duties as rent-control czar—embarked on his second anti-Communist foray in the labor movement. This time, focusing on the UE, he intended to mount a crusade that would stop at nothing less than removing Communist leaders from power through a rank-and-file insurgency.

7

TAKING ON THE UE

F ATHER Rice emerged from the war years still breathing fire and
eager to finish the fight he had started a half-dozen years earlier.
Two developments drove him back into the left-right struggle in
the labor movement. One was the revival of ideological battles in the
CIO between pro-Soviet and anti-Soviet unions at the outset of the Cold
War. Rice also saw himself as representing Catholic workers with roots in
Eastern Europe who were outraged by the Soviet Union's repression of
the Church in Hungary, Czechoslovakia, Poland, and other countries.
Rice jumped into the fray with several weapons at hand. He still had his
weekly radio show and his column in the *Pittsburgh Catholic*. Duquesne
University, his alma mater, had provided him with a new center of operations, the Institute of Management-Labor Relations, established in 1945
with Rice as director. He taught evening courses on labor economics and
collective bargaining for local union officials and lectured to under-
graduates during the day. The students provided invaluable assistance as
researchers and typists. They collected evidence of Communist activity in
unions, maintained a filing system, and helped Rice conduct a volumi-
nous correspondence with unionists around the country.[1]

One of Rice's first actions in this new campaign was to write an article for *Our Sunday Visitor*, the most widely read Catholic newspaper in the

United States. Available in Catholic churches every Sunday, the *Sunday Visitor* had a conservative editorial policy that welcomed anti-Communist diatribes. Years later, Rice would speak of it as "a very lousy right-wing McCarthyite [newspaper] before McCarthy's day." In his 1947 article, he painted a scary picture of Communist activity in organized labor and offered to help union members rid their union of Reds. More than a thousand readers replied, giving Rice a nationwide base of information. A year later, in May 1948, he offered to all readers of the *Sunday Visitor* a twelve-page pamphlet titled *How to Decontrol Your Union of Communists.* A section describing how to disrupt a left-wing meeting might have been ripped from a Communist book of tactics: disrupters should hurl such time-honored abuses as "'sell out,' 'double cross,' 'ineffective,' 'stumble bum,' etc." at the leaders. The pamphlet was a big success. Rice estimated that thirty thousand to forty thousand copies of *How to Decontrol* were printed and mailed.[2]

In March 1947, Rice reactivated the Pittsburgh chapter of the Association of Catholic Trade Unionists. He also worked with a number of anti-Communist factions within the UE, the largest of which was called the UE Members for Democratic Action. It was headed by the former UE president, Jim Carey, now serving as secretary-treasurer of the CIO, who intended to return to the UE if the anti-Communist faction ousted the incumbent officers. By 1947 Rice was "almost a full-time functionary in the UE opposition," as Catholic writer Michael Harrington described him in a 1960 article. Rice took on an assistant named John Duffy, an officer of a UE local and a dedicated anti-Communist. The two men visited UE locals throughout western Pennsylvania, urging members to revolt against Communists where they held power. Rice and Duffy were not welcome everywhere. In Wilmerding, for example, WABCO Local 610, whose leadership was composed of both Communists and anti-Communists, told Rice to stay out of their affairs. With the help of Duffy and his student researchers, and with intelligence obtained from hundreds of correspondents all over the country, Rice compiled information on Communist activity in the UE and more than forty other national unions. He once claimed to have assembled "a dossier on every communist union in the United States, a bigger anti-Communist file than anybody had."[3]

When I interviewed Rice in 2000, he could not remember many details of his battles against the UE in the 1940s. He readily acknowl-

edged that he pursued the union with excessive zeal but at the same time
expressed pride in having done so. Twice he interrupted questions to
make this point, saying, first, that he "pushed" Phil Murray to expel the
UE and other pro-Soviet unions from the CIO and, second, that he "engi-
neered" the formation of a new union to replace the UE once it was
expelled. The rival union, the International Union of Electrical, Radio
and Machine Workers (IUE), created in late 1949, eventually would supplant the UE as the dominant electrical union. Rice's ambivalent attitude—"I'm sorry I did it, but wasn't it a wonderful accomplishment?"—
was not new. It had colored most of the "confessions" about his role in
the Communist purges that he began making some fifteen years after the
event. The Rice I visited on that day in 2000 was a ninety-one-year-old
man whose fiery convictions and self-serving notions of right and wrong
were only muted, not gone. I had seen him do some admirable things in
the 1960s civil-rights movement, and now I confirmed for myself that he
also had helped set in motion an event that would lead directly to a crisis in Tom Quinn's life and indirectly to a pivotal point in Harry Davenport's career.[4]

But that event occurred in 1949, toward the end of Rice's second
anti-Communist crusade. During the previous three years, Murray had
resisted the demands of Rice and others to act against the Communists.
The loss of nearly a dozen left-wing unions would cost the CIO about 1
million members, more than a quarter of its total membership. Murray
also was reluctant to punish individual unionists because of their political beliefs. And yet, for two years ending in 1950, he channeled one
thousand dollars a month in clandestine payments to Rice for use in his
ACTU activities. Rice disclosed the payments in a 1968 oral history interview, saying that the money came directly from the Steelworkers' treasury. As president, Murray could easily have arranged this secret transfer
of funds. Even he, one of the most esteemed labor leaders of the time,
played a double game in those years of political intrigue.[5]

Murray's resistance gradually broke down. From 1946 to 1949, a
growing fear of Communist infiltration focused mostly on the federal
government and labor unions. Newspaper columnists on the far right
declared flatly that many CIO unions were awash in Communists. Spies
and saboteurs were said to be using unions as fronts for subversive activities in industrial plants and defense industries. There was no hard evidence to back up these suspicions, but the fear of industrial subversion

fitted nicely into the mosaic of fears, half truths, and lies that settled over the United States. Most workers, war veterans in particular, disliked being tainted as Communists merely because they belonged to a union. Under these pressures, the CIO shifted gradually to the right, starting with the 1946 convention, which passed a resolution warning the Communist Party to stay out of CIO affairs.[6]

The UE, meanwhile, came under siege by Congress and various federal agencies. The Atomic Energy Commission ordered GE to withdraw recognition from the UE as the representative of workers at atomic power laboratories. Between 1947 and 1950, congressional committees conducted three separate investigations of the UE, in each case focusing on alleged Communist Party membership of national, district, and local officers. These hearings usually ended inconclusively, but they generated damaging publicity that aided the UE's right-wing insurgents. Obviously, this was an intended outcome. The government attacks on the UE, Ronald Schatz writes, were "a feature of the McCarthy era at least as important as the much-better-remembered attacks on radicals in Hollywood and liberals in the State Department."[7]

In 1947 the Republican-controlled Congress injected an inflammatory issue into the left-right fight in the CIO. Making good on their promise to reduce union power, Republicans enacted the Taft-Hartley Act over President Harry Truman's veto. The law amended the Wagner Act by imposing severe restrictions on union tactics and organizing ability. It also required union officials to swear an oath that they were not members of the Communist Party. Union leaders bitterly resented having to affirm their loyalty when corporate chiefs were spared the same humiliation. But if officers refused to sign an affidavit, their union would lose its certification under the National Labor Relations Board and would be excluded from the ballot in NLRB representation elections. Most unions quickly complied, but officers of the Steelworkers (led by Phil Murray) and the UE rejected the oath on constitutional grounds. With its hundreds of small shops, the UE immediately became vulnerable to raiding by other unions. Rivals would send organizers to UE-represented shops, sign up enough workers to petition for an NLRB election, and win the election by default. Rice later compared the raiders to "vultures tearing a corpse apart." In the first two years after Taft-Hartley went into effect, the UAW and other rival unions conducted more than five hundred raids on UE locals and stole thousands of members from the electrical union.

Eventually, in 1949, Murray abandoned his court test of the provision and signed an affidavit. The beleaguered UE officers followed a few months later; they had no choice if they wished to prevent predatory rivals from gorging on the UE, plant by plant.[8]

Although weakened by these many assaults, the UE's left-wing leadership was far from toppling. The two most powerful officers, Jim Matles and Julius Emspak, supported by President Albert Fitzgerald and a majority of the national executive board, retained tight control over the union. At each annual convention from 1946 through 1949, local delegates reelected the incumbent officers over anti-Communist slates. Big locals like 601 in East Pittsburgh, with large voting power, were the key to convention elections. But anti-Communist forces failed to permanently oust Progressive leaders in Local 601, despite winning control of the local in 1946 and 1948. In each case, Progressives held on to one or two important posts and sent proadministration slates of delegates to conventions. Rice complained about the tricks left-wingers would use to elect their adherents, such as flooding nominating meetings with friends—tricks that entrenched officeholders have employed since humans first started forming social groups. Both sides played rough in the UE struggle.[9]

With the Matles-Emspak faction still controlling the UE as 1948 drew to a close, Rice adopted more aggressive tactics. He already had exchanged information with FBI agents about Communists in unions before the war. It was never clear how much information he gave or received, or whether the information consisted of loose talk and suppositions or documented evidence of Communist Party membership. In his critical biography, Patrick McGeever contends that Rice actually acted as an FBI informant, a characterization that Rice rejected when the biography appeared in 1989. Yet he admitted to another historian that his cooperation with the FBI was "a grave error."[10]

In 1949, Rice would go further down that slippery path. He would collaborate with congressional-committee investigators in setting up a plan to ensnare Local 601's left-wing leaders in a web of accusations. His ultimate aim was to weaken local support for the national UE administration so that Carey's forces might overthrow the Matles-Emspak regime in the next union election. It must have seemed a clever thing to do. But like many bold moves in politics, this scheme would result in far more harm to several people, including Tom Quinn and Harry Davenport, than Rice ever intended.

The person who had the most lasting impact on the policies and direction of the United Electrical Workers was Jim Matles, who served as a principal officer for more than thirty years. I came to know Matles in the 1970s and from then on always thought of him as personifying this most idiosyncratic of unions on the national level as Tom Quinn did locally. Both men held minority views and refused to back down in the face of accusations, mud slinging, or appropriate criticism of political actions. Both were hard nuts who could not be broken by any hammer, on any anvil.

In the early seventies, I interviewed Matles several times and heard many stories about him from management negotiators and other unionists. Disregarding for the moment his political beliefs and associations, people who knew and worked with him ranked Matles among the most honest, knowledgeable, and effective union leaders of his time. His origins explain much about the man he became.

Born in Romania in 1909 to Jewish parents, Matles witnessed the oppressive spread of Fascism and virulent anti-Semitism in his native country. After completing a machinists' apprentice program in 1929, he immigrated to the United States. He worked in machine shops in Brooklyn and New York and became a union organizer. Within a few years he headed a metal workers' union, which merged with the UE in 1937. Matles learned to speak English with an unusual accent, mixing the Eastern European pronunciation of *w*'s as *v*'s with a sort of Brooklynese that made *working class* come out as *voiking class* and *concern* as *consoin*. Both as a young and middle-aged man, Matles was lean and dark visaged, with a narrow face and pencil mustache. A casting director would search for just this face in selecting an actor to play the agent of a foreign power in an American movie of the 1940s era.[11]

In 1973 I saw Matles for the first time as he addressed a UE convention in Pittsburgh. In most unions, top-level officers usually delegated the nitty-gritty regulation of local union conduct to staff subordinates. Not Matles. In remarks on union finances, he delivered an impromptu scolding to local officers who had engaged in dubious financial practices. It was an impassioned speech that revealed much about Matles's view of ethics in a capitalist society. After describing various ways that a few locals had misused dues money, he broadened his comments. "Our society is a corrupt society," he said. "It starts [with] the corporations set up in America and it permeates every single branch of our society, whether it is government, medical or the legal profession, whether educational, whether it is the labor movement . . . corruption permeates every single area of life." Unless local union members fought to preserve "the purity and integrity of our organization," Matles told the delegates, "it's [corruption] going to swamp us." Several hundred delegates remained resoundingly quiet as he spoke, reflecting their respect. He addressed them directly and honestly, radiating acuity and probity. I later learned that he brought these same qualities to interviews. On one matter, though, Matles never was completely open: his relationship with the Communist Party.[12]

At this time, I knew only a little of Matles's background and the struggle between left and right in the CIO. Despite growing up in the Pittsburgh area, I had paid little attention to the Communist issue in unions as a teenager in the 1940s, and I spent most of the 1950s away from the Pittsburgh area. I started writing about labor relations in the early 1960s, covering the UAW and the auto industry in Detroit. I occasionally ran across an old-time Communist or a reporter for the *Daily Worker*. But Communism in unions was a dead issue by then. When I met Tom Quinn after returning to Pittsburgh in the midsixties, I was not aware of his decade-long battle with investigating committees.

In 1973 I was working for WQED, the Pittsburgh public television station, as a reporter and commentator on an experimental nightly news program. After witnessing Matles's convention speech, I invited him to come to our studio and be interviewed on our program. He and his publicity man were taken aback. The UE received few such invitations; it had never fully escaped the old Communist taint and was still a pariah in the labor movement. That past did not seem relevant to me. I wanted to interview Matles because the UE soon would be negotiating with Westinghouse, one of Pittsburgh's largest employers. He came to the station that evening, accompanied by Quinn, and we did a live interview lasting about eight to ten minutes in our half-hour program. Matles spoke in coolly analytic terms about the national economy and wage negotiations. I do not recall that we received any phone calls or letters from shocked viewers who remembered Matles from the old days. Perhaps that past really was dead, but then our program only had a nightly audience of about ten thousand to twenty thousand viewers.

Some months later, Matles sent me a copy of *Them and Us*, a history of the UE written by Matles and a coauthor, James Higgins. Matles refers to himself in the third person, gives few personal details, and avoids the Communist issue except to attack those who brought it up. I wrote a review for a small magazine, focusing on Matles's story of the UE's negotiating rivalry with the UAW and the Steelworkers in 1946. I mentioned but did not examine the Communist accusations against him and the UE, though I probably should have questioned his avoidance of the issue. A short time later, I left television to become labor editor of *Business Week* in New York. Labor news commanded a lot of attention in those days because large unions in the steel, auto, coal, trucking, electrical, and railroad industries still had the capacity to mount nationwide strikes. Union wage settlements influenced pay and benefit levels throughout the economy, as well as corporate profits. For these reasons, *Business Week* considered labor reporting a major part of its economic and business coverage. In 1975, as the UE, IUE, and other electrical unions prepared for a major round of bargaining at GE and Westinghouse, I interviewed Matles two or three times.

The UE headquarters building was located in Cornelius Vanderbilt's old townhouse on West Fifty-first Street across the street from St. Patrick's Cathedral. It was a musty old place, boasting none of the jazzy adornments or expensive decor that could be found in most corporate and many union offices. Riding in a tiny elevator with clacking cagelike doors and a crusty old operator was like time traveling back to the thirties. Everybody was very polite. Matles's secretary would lead me into his office on the third or fourth floor. Matles liked to place his visitors (at least in my case) in a chair beside his desk, rather than in front of it, so that we faced each other from a distance of a few feet. I was not stared down on by an imperial personage. The UE may have gone out of its way to project its image as a rank-and-file union, but I felt more comfortable with Matles than with some other union leaders. We always talked about economic and labor relations issues and touched only rarely on politics. I never asked about the Communist purge in the CIO or the accusations made against him and his union. I was writing journalism, not history.

On one occasion he referred obliquely to that period, saying that he respected *Business Week*'s labor coverage partly because the previous labor editor "never Red-baited me." I think also I brought with me a sort of unintended innocence that may have passed as tolerance.[13]

My last interview with Matles occurred in August of 1975. He suggested that I bring a tape recorder. For nearly two hours he discussed the state of the economy, multinational corporations, economic trends, and union strategies in a monologue interrupted by occasional questions. It was an astonishing performance. He did not engage in empty rhetorical flourishes using adjectives such as *greedy* or *oppressive* to describe his corporate adversaries. As Matles saw it, corporations were doing what they always do, trying to take more and more out of the economy in profits by shifting the burden to the workers. But he did not talk of "striking the bastards" or "hitting the bricks"—typical inflated threats of romantic roughnecks. Nor did he talk of revolution. "Working people," Matles said, "are not interested in making a revolution. They are not ideologists. They are interested in improving their lives. This is what the labor movement has to address itself to—how to compel the system to spread some of the fat among the people." He thought unions should form a political opposition group of working-class people strong enough to force corporations to "pay their dues to the people." In other words, a labor party driven by a Marxist worldview and organized, not to elect the next president but to wage a long-term campaign for fundamental changes in social policy. Matles was not sanguine about this happening.

When the time was up, Matles suggested that we might have more such taped conversations after he attended the UE's convention in San Francisco in September. I got the impression that he wanted to create a record. But he did not spell out what he had in mind, and I put off asking until our next meeting. In mid-September, news came from San Francisco that Matles had announced he would retire at the end of October. Obviously he had not mentioned this to me because the members of his union should hear it first.[14]

Management negotiators had no use for Matles's political philosophy, but they had a high regard for his abilities. One Westinghouse negotiator, Sam Lemon, was a friend of mine from college days. We lived in the same fraternity house for three academic years at Penn State, where both of us finished our undergraduate work in 1953. Sam was no stranger to unions. He grew up in the coal-mining community of Brownsville, Pennsylvania, where many people idolized John L. Lewis and where Sam's father, a local officer in a railroad union, lost a leg in a train accident. After graduation, Lemon joined Westinghouse as a management trainee and served in industrial-relations posts at several plants over the next decade. He began participating in top-level bargaining meetings with the UE in 1969 and twice served as the company's chief negotiator with the union. By this time the UE had only about fifteen thousand members at Westinghouse and was third in size to the IUE and the International Brotherhood of Electrical Workers in a bargaining coalition. But Matles, with his long experience and knowledge of the industry's economics, exercised a disproportionate influence over the coalition's tactical decisions. I asked Lemon to relate some of his experiences with Matles for use in this book, and he did so in a letter.

Skilled labor negotiators usually are excellent storytellers. They tell jokes and anecdotes to disarm the other side, they tell some stories with strong economic lessons to support demands, and they tell others as a means of tactical filibustering. Matles, according to Lemon, "was quite a story-teller. When he got going, it could last a while, and he usually injected a little humor." He talked often about growing up in Romania when Fascist groups were strong. "I heard Matles talk about his days in the Young Communist League of Romania and his mistreatment at the hands of fascists," Lemon said. "I never heard him utter that word [fascism] without an emotional tone in his voice. He was powerfully opposed to fascism. So if communism opposed fascism, communism had to be okay. Despite his knowhow in costs and business finance, etc., Matles never accepted the legitimacy of the profit motive. He may have conceded that lots of us were okay guys, but we were captive to an evil system. He told his people that if Westinghouse sold a product for $100 and spent $70 in employment costs, the Company was stealing the other $30 out of the pockets of the workers. He never liked to talk about the overhead or staff expenses of running a business. In his mind, everything started and stopped with the 'workers.' Once you get past hating fascism and hating the Company, communism is about all that was left. He just sneered at socialism as being useless and helpless. He even overlooked communist excesses as the failures of misguided individuals, but never questioned the aims, goals and benefits that communism would bring. As time wore on, and the public image of the union changed, he spent more and more time on 'shop' items and less and less on political philosophy."

Many bargaining rounds extended over several weeks, and some days there would be long breaks between sessions. The negotiators would step outside their adversary roles and talk about other things. "Matles was a lover of classical music," Lemon wrote, "and frequently attended concerts at Lincoln Center [in New York]. I like that kind of music also, and on a couple of occasions we chatted at length about Beethoven, Mozart, Brahms, etc. When it came to sports, I don't think he knew the difference between a first down and a double play." Matles also was an accomplished flutist who played for his own amusement or that of a few friends, according to Tom Quinn.[15]

Another Westinghouse negotiator, Robert McCoy, told me about negotiating with Matles and local union officials to resolve a strike at a Philadelphia-area plant. They met in a motel conference room rented by the company. When the meeting adjourned late at night, Matles—who had come down from New York—asked if he could sleep on a couch in the conference room. It was an unusual request from a union that rarely asked for help from the company, but McCoy readily assented. "He slept on that doggone couch," McCoy recalled with astonishment. The incident verified for him that UE officers, in fact, did not make much money or travel on lavish expense accounts.[16]

Tom Quinn, who worked under Matles for two decades as a UE representative, remembered most vividly how, at union conventions, Matles would toss off extemporaneous talks on complex policy matters, using only notes on index cards. He would insert jabbing thrusts of humor. One such speech Quinn would never forget. It came at a UE convention in Pittsburgh in the 1960s. Staff members were unusually cantankerous at this meeting, complaining that the union was scanting them on pension benefits, which were lower than those of long-serving Westinghouse and GE retirees. As Quinn told me the story, fondly mocking Matles's way of speaking, Matles replied bluntly to the complainants. "If you voik the vay you should, you von't live to get a pension."

Matles here led by example. After announcing at the San Francisco convention in 1975 that he would soon retire, Matles did not immediately return to his home in New York. Instead he went to Santa Barbara over the weekend to help a local union in an organizing campaign. On

Monday he passed out leaflets at the plant gates, then returned to his hotel to rest. He died of a massive heart attack that afternoon, a little more than a month before his retirement date. He was sixty-six.[17]

Jim Matles had been dead a quarter of a century when I began my search for what happened to Uncle Harry. After all those years historians still could not say with certainty whether Matles had ever been a member of the CPUSA. There was plenty of circumstantial evidence, including his association with party organizations and the pro-Soviet positions taken by the UE on foreign-policy matters. Beginning in 1938, several former Communists testified at various hearings that they had known Matles as a party member in the early thirties. On the combined weight of this evidence, many historians have asserted flatly that Matles was a Communist. Others have refused to go that far. Ronald Filippelli and Mark McColloch, for example, point out that it has "never been conclusively proven" that Matles was a party member, though it would be "straining credibility" to think that he was not. Their conclusion was accurate as of 1995 when *Cold War in the Working Class* was published, but since then a major new source of information about the American Communist Party has become available.[18]

For decades it was assumed that records of the CPUSA's secret meetings and internal affairs had been destroyed. When the Cold War ended, however, a historian at the Library of Congress, John Earl Haynes, learned that CPUSA records from 1919 to about 1937 had been shipped to the Soviet Union and stored in Communist Party archives. The Library of Congress obtained a microfilm copy in 1998 and opened it to researchers in 2000. If this had happened ten or twenty years earlier, I think, labor historians would have lined up to view these files. But the history of the UE already had been treated exhaustively, though not completely, by the early twenty-first century, and no new work based on the CPUSA collection appeared. In November 2003, I made several trips to New York University's Tamiment Library, which had acquired a microfilm copy of the CPUSA records from the Library of Congress. Scrolling through documents dating back to 1930, I found conclusive evidence that early in his career Jim Matles had been a high-ranking leader in the trade-union section of the CPUSA.[19]

The highlights of Matles's activities in the early thirties were already known to historians. As a working machinist, he helped organize, and became a leader of, the Metal Workers Industrial Union, affiliated with a Communist organization, the Trade Union Unity League (TUUL). The party established TUUL in 1929 with the mission of forming "revolutionary" unions outside the American Federation of Labor. Except for two unions, including Matles's Metal Workers, the TUUL efforts were unsuccessful. The party abandoned this dual-union approach and dissolved TUUL in March 1935. Under a new policy, Communist union leaders were to take their members into existing AFL unions and "bore from within." In March 1936, Matles led eight thousand metal workers into the International Association of Machinists (IAM). But the IAM, an old-line craft union, failed to follow through on promises to Matles, and the newly formed CIO was beckoning. In 1937, Matles resigned from the IAM and took his union, now fifteen thousand strong, into the UE-CIO. These activities strongly suggest but do not prove that Matles was a CPUSA member. Only a small percentage of workers affiliated with TUUL belonged to the party.

The CPUSA files provide that proof. I found Matles first mentioned in 1934 in minutes of weekly meetings held by the TUUL Buro, a board of union leaders and party officials that directed the activities of TUUL unions. Organizing and strike reports were presented and discussed, and the current party line was handed down by one of the top officials. Each set of minutes begins with a list of people present, usually ten to fifteen names, starting with the top leaders and including a group under the heading "also present," indicating a lower status. The name Matles first occurs in the second group of attendees for July 23, 1934. Halfway down the first page appears this notation: "Brief report made by Comrade Matles who was present at last board meeting of NTWIU [Needle Trades Workers International Union]." Matles attended four other meetings of the TUUL Buro before the end of 1934, always in the also present category.

After the CPUSA disbanded the Trade Union Unity League in early 1935, it formed another body to direct labor activities, the Trade Union Commission (TUC). Matles appeared at several TUC meetings toward the end of the year (minutes of earlier meetings are missing) and was listed on the same line as Communist notables such as William Z. Foster, Jack Stachel, and Roy Hudson. The minutes of December 2, 1935, include a two-page report by Matles on his negotiations with the president of the IAM for a merger of the two unions. The TUC apparently was satisfied with Matles's efforts, stating: "We approve the report of Comrade Matles and the general line of policy as carried through." There also appears in the record a November 2, 1935, letter to a party superior that Matles signed "Comradely, Matles." He appears at several other TUC meetings in 1935 and early 1936. By the latter date the records are thinning out, and only a few scattered files are available for 1937.[20]

While it is beyond dispute that Matles belonged to the CPUSA and followed the party line in his union activities from 1934 to 1936, the nature of his association with the party after that period can only be guessed at. Was Matles merely a channel through which the party dictated policies to the UE in the late 1940s when he and his union were in the crosshairs of Red baiters and spy hunters? Father Rice and other critics believed so, but documentary evidence is lacking. Indeed, the UE acted contrary to party policy on important occasions. Moreover, the CPUSA records reveal that the party viewed unions as the potential core of a political movement, not as vehicles of espionage and sabotage. In the early thirties the TUUL leadership was obsessed with creating mass movements through "revolutionary" strikes, most of which were dismal failures. After 1935, the CPUSA concentrated on organizing workers for existing unions (while trying, much less successfully, to recruit the workers as party members) and gaining influence in those unions. The Communists succeeded to some degree in about a dozen unions, including the UE. But even under Communist influence the UE remained a trade union instead of converting itself into a tool of subversion.

The FBI began interviewing people about Matles in the 1930s and later compiled a dossier of his activities. It contains many notes of Matles sightings outside party meeting places and reports from informants (their names blacked out) who claim to have been associated with Matles in Communist affairs. Aside from one vague reference to an allegation by an informer, Matles is not linked in bureau reports with any spying. Historians have sifted through investigative and criminal records during the decades when left-wing unions were at peak strength. Not a single act of sabotage or espionage has ever been attributed to a member of the UE. Ellen Schrecker, a noted historian of the American Communist movement, found only one job-related action by a Communist-controlled union that had to do with international affairs: the refusal of West Coast longshoremen led by Harry Bridges to load scrap metal for Japan before the Second World War. Three strikes in 1940–1941 involved

Communists in local unions (none affiliated with the UE), including a notorious strike at North American Aviation that halted production of U.S. warplanes. But historical accounts leave in doubt whether these stoppages were brought about by the Soviets' antiwar stance or conditions in the plants.[21]

Although government agencies and congressional committees investigated and prosecuted UE officials and members on an unprecedented scale for more than ten years, from the midforties to the late fifties, no one was charged with traitorous or subversive activity. Several officials were tried on charges of contempt of Congress for refusing to answer questions relating to their political beliefs and associations, but most of these convictions would be overturned on appeal. One UE district leader, a professed Communist, was convicted of violating the Smith Act (urging overthrow of the government). There were no charges that the UE committed wholesale acts of violence or deliberately harmed employers or cheated its members of money or routinely demanded kickbacks from employers or conspired with mobsters.[22]

It might be supposed that the UE could cause economic damage by striking and extracting exorbitant pay increases from employers. The UE did conduct long strikes at GE and Westinghouse in 1946 (as did the steel and auto unions in their industries), but these corporations were far too large and economically strong to be put out of business by a single union acting under the restrictions of American labor laws. Furthermore, no union would participate in the destruction of its members' jobs. This is not to say that the UE made it easy for employers to change work processes, introduce new technology, or reduce incentive pay unilaterally. The UE also infuriated employers by conducting local strikes over unresolved grievances instead of submitting to arbitration. But these were matters of protecting workers' immediate interests, not of wrecking the capitalist system.

Unable to unearth any overt actions of a traitorous nature, the UE's critics could only point to its political pronouncements indicating sympathy with the Soviet Union, especially on foreign-policy issues. Of this the union was guilty, particularly in the 1940s up to 1949. The *UE News,* a bimonthly newspaper, frequently carried slanted news stories reflecting support for Soviet, and opposition to American, policies. Pro-Soviet positions also were embodied in resolutions passed by a handful of members at local union meetings or by hundreds of delegates at national conventions. For the most part, these resolutions reflected the thinking of local or national leaders who (as in every union, and every corporation, for that matter) controlled the content of policy statements adopted by the organization. In convention resolutions and editorials in the *UE News*, the union lashed out at U.S. policies such as the Marshall Plan. The UE muted these attacks after it was branded as Communist dominated and expelled by the CIO in 1949. In subsequent years, the union took a softer line of advocating world peace. Occasionally, the *UE News* would suggest that the United States started the Cold War, avoiding any mention of aggressive moves by the Soviet Union. Indeed, the paper rarely mentioned the Soviet Union at all, and certainly not in 1956 when Premier Nikita Khrushchev revealed some of the horrific crimes committed by the late Josef Stalin against his own people.[23]

Up to the 1949 split in the CIO, however, the UE's positions on foreign policy came not from independent thought but from an unswerving devotion to one line of thought, the Soviet line. The Soviets could do no wrong. An egregious example involved Josef Cardinal Mindszenty in Soviet-occupied Hungary. An outspoken Catholic prelate, he refused to secularize Catholic schools. The Soviets arrested him in 1948, put him on trial and convicted him of treason, and sentenced him to life imprisonment. This caused an uproar around the world, not least among Americans with roots in Eastern Europe. When the UE supported the Soviet action, many members were outraged. In February 1949 about eight hundred members attended a Local 601 meeting at which right-wing leaders introduced a resolution condemning Mindszenty's trial. When Tom Fitzpatrick and other left-wingers spoke against the proposal, they were "booed off the floor," according to a newspaper account. The resolution passed. Mindszenty was set free during the Hungarian uprising of 1956 and later spent fifteen years in voluntary confinement in the U.S. embassy in Budapest.

Quinn remembered that local meeting. Although he generally sided with Fitzpatrick on foreign-policy matters, Quinn regarded the stand on Mindszenty as "ridiculous." He added, "It seemed our leadership was kind of baited into that [position] by Father Rice and the ACTU. They would find issues to raise at membership meetings of that kind of controversial nature which would give the parish priests something to raise at Mass on Sundays before the meeting." Quinn's good friend, Margaret Darin Stasik, one of the founding officers of Local 601, expressed regret about the Progressives' pro-Soviet positions in a 1977 interview. "Hell of a lot of difference it [the Mindszenty resolution] made to us. What did that have to do with the price of milk? It meant nothing. But they [some UE leaders] felt as if, 'Oh boy, the world would come to an end.'"[24]

It is uncertain what the UE leaders hoped to accomplish by hewing to the Soviet line. Perhaps they wanted to build a political juggernaut that, in time, would be able to elect pro-Soviet legislators who, over more time, would gradually pull back American forces abroad and dismantle the Marshall Plan and NATO, enabling the Soviet Union to expand at will. Such a plan depended on the voting power of the rank and file. But while many members accepted the UE's leadership on trade-union matters, it is doubtful that they could ever have been molded into a solid block of support for the union's pro-Soviet line. Following this line damaged the union's credibility in the eyes of many members and certainly of the public. It is fair to ask why Matles and his associates never came to understand this, or if they understood, to do anything about it. In concealing their Communist affiliations, Matles and other UE leaders corroborated the party's image as an undemocratic conspiracy, thereby seeming to justify its repression, as Ellen Schrecker writes. My impression is that Matles had wound himself up so tightly in his worldview of the exploiting and exploited classes that he could not renounce generic, small *c* communism and remain true to his principles. At some point, probably in the early fifties, he finally detached himself from the party. To what degree he faithfully followed the party line before then remains clouded.[25]

Even if Matles and other UE stalwarts were merely ideological communists, America in the late forties was not a place in which the difference could be appreciated. A communist was a Communist, a foreign intriguer, and so were those who associated with communists. Rice propounded this view, Quinn would suffer from it, and Harry avoided the issue when he ran for Congress in 1948.

8

THE HARRY-TOM
CONNECTION

Perhaps most Pittsburghers know Fox Chapel as an upper-income
enclave of fine homes peering at one another through dense
foliage on hillsides running up from the Allegheny River across
from Pittsburgh. Farther to the north, though, the hills level out in farm
country, where long meadows sweep up from a two-lane road and horses
graze in spring pastures enclosed by rambling white fences. In April
2000 I visited John Connelly, who for more than fifty years had lived and
raised horses on a farm in this area. His home sat at the top of a mead-
ow, in the middle of a circular drive. I knocked on a door at the lower
end of the drive and was admitted to a large den comfortably furnished
with couches, chairs, and, off to one side, a dining area where Connelly
often took his meals so he would not have to climb stairs. At the age of
seventy-five, suffering from various ailments, he looked somewhat pale
under a flying shock of white hair. This was the man who was present at
both the creation and the fall of Congressman Harry Davenport.

By the time I set out to discover how Uncle Harry achieved his ultimate political triumph in 1948, decades of overgrowth had obliterated
his trail. I had one possible lead. Someone (my sister Lynn, I believe) had
sent me a 1990 newspaper profile of a Pittsburgh marketing entrepre-
neur named John Connelly, who mentioned that he had served as a con-

gressional aide to Harry Davenport. I introduced myself to Connelly by letter and asked for an interview. He responded enthusiastically in a follow-up phone conversation. "Harry was a great guy," he said. "He was a genius, but nobody recognized it."

Uncle Harry, a genius? I came to understand that in Connelly's business world great value was attached to a marketing idea or scheme that makes people want to buy something or vote for somebody. Translated from advertising lingo, "genius" meant that Harry could run a flashier flag up a flagpole than most people in the trade—or in politics. For that matter, so could Connelly. As a teenager he made his first score ($102) by persuading a savings and loan institution that customers could be lured to a new branch office by passing out free key chains and ballpoint pens. Connelly bought the trinkets wholesale and sold them at a profit to the bank. Expanding on this idea, he mounted innumerable promotions, buying brand-name merchandise at bulk-purchase discounts and reselling it to corporations, banks, and other institutions to pass out to employees and customers as incentives to save more. The institutions also paid sizeable fees to Connelly for devising incentive plans to justify the purchase of his merchandise. J. Edward Connelly Associates became one of the largest financial-promotions firms in America—and Connelly became a millionaire many times over. In one inspired deal, he became a sort of exclusive franchise holder for the sale of reproductions of Vatican Museum treasures. There followed many other side businesses and real estate deals, including the founding of the Gateway Clipper Fleet.[1]

On the day I visited him, Connelly had stayed home from his office because of poor health. But he wanted to talk about my uncle because "I really liked him and learned a lot from him." Sitting with his legs outstretched on a reclining couch, he spoke in a low, husky voice. He had started working for Harry in about 1947 and vividly remembered Harry's campaign for Congress in 1948 against John McDowell. According to one report, the Democratic Party endorsed Harry for the second time, in 1948, only because Local 601 leaders promised they would throw the union's weight behind him rather than divide Democrats by supporting a third-party candidate. But the Democrats put little money into Harry's campaign. "To the party, Harry was a maverick," Connelly said. "They didn't think he could win. They didn't see his marketing genius. I was a marketing man also. We didn't have the money it took to win, so we had to devise a clever way to do it."[2]

After defeating a rival for the Democratic nomination, Harry set out to draw attention to himself. He selected an issue, inflation, that affected everybody and especially working people who lived payday to payday. Consumer prices had soared more than 15 percent in 1946 and nearly 10 percent in 1947. Harry came up with a plan to dramatize the issue, using a truck owned by Connelly as the stage. They installed sound equipment and a microphone on the truck bed and painted VOTE DEMOCRATIC. VOTE FOR HARRY J. DAVENPORT on each side of the truck. Every evening during the campaign, Harry would give Connelly one hundred dollars, and Connelly would buy that much worth of groceries—mostly staples like bacon, eggs, bread, beans—and women's stockings. The two men would set out in the truck at five o'clock the next morning, first to catch the shift change at mill gates and then to accost people on street corners near shopping areas.[3]

Harry would stand in the rear of the truck at the microphone. "He was a dynamic speaker," Connelly recalled. "When a crowd gathered, he would say, 'Under the Democratic Congress and the OPA, eggs were 22 cents a dozen, now they're 42 cents under the Republicans. Bacon was 15 cents a pound, now it's 35 a pound. Think about this inflation, think what the Republicans have done to you by taking away the OPA.' And then he'd hand out a pound of bacon to some millworker, hand out a carton of eggs to another, hand out the stockings to some girl. Well, it got around. Harry Davenport was handing out groceries. People loved to get the free groceries."

Free groceries and a promise from Harry that, if elected, he would push for a resumption of price controls on many consumer products. If his antidote for inflation was questionable economically, Harry's showmanship enabled him to draw a sharp distinction between liberal Democrats like himself and Republicans, like McDowell, whose control of Congress had tilted economic policy toward the interests of big business. Democrats wanted to expand Social Security benefits, raise the minimum wage, and initiate new social-welfare programs such as national medical insurance and low-cost housing. Since union members made up a large part of the Democratic base, the liberal wing of the party generally favored prolabor legislation and pledged in particular to repeal the "slave-labor" Taft-Hartley Act. A fight with Republicans over this issue loomed large for the next session of Congress.

For most of the 1948 campaign, it appeared that President Harry Truman, running for reelection, was dragging down the entire Democratic ticket. A new third party, the Progressive Party, had formed under Henry A. Wallace, a former Democratic vice president and cabinet member, who was expected to draw millions of votes away from Truman. Pollsters and political pundits, almost without exception, pictured Truman as running far behind Republican Thomas E. Dewey, even up to election day. Harry had cast himself as a Truman man, but I suspect that his views on labor, foreign policy, and civil rights were closer to Wallace's than to Truman's. Harry, of course, did not criticize the president, but he staked out some positions to the left of Truman's, especially on civil rights. As in 1946, he attacked racism and anti-Semitism, calling McDowell to account on these issues.

Harry left no papers at his death, not even a scrap of a campaign speech. The only speech that survives, as far as I know, is the text of a radio talk given in early 1948 and filed in the UE Archives at the University of Pittsburgh. In this address, Harry spoke passionately in favor of creating independent Jewish and Palestinian states in Palestine. He criticized Great Britain and the United States for not following through on a plan to partition warring Palestine, though the United States later in 1948 recognized the new state of Israel. Unfortunately, my research did not turn up public comments by Harry on racial issues, but his endorsement by the editors of the *Pittsburgh Courier* indicates that they found him convincing. Milton Susman, editor of the *Jewish Criterion*, again endorsed Harry and apparently opened doors for the candidate in the Jewish community. John Connelly recalled accompanying Harry on many occasions to Jewish homes in Squirrel Hill. My uncle could be very persuasive when speaking to small groups. He and Connelly would play a tape recording of a radio interview in which McDowell, years before, had made anti-Semitic references to the popular Judge Sammy Weiss when McDowell ran against him for a congressional seat. "We'd hold a meeting, play that tape, and then collect money so I could do the shopping for the groceries that we handed out," Connelly said.[4]

In the spring of 1948, Local 601's legislative chairman, Tom Quinn, gave Harry's campaign a shot of energy and enthusiasm from the crucial labor sector. Quinn later could not recall when they first met, but he retained a vivid memory of Harry standing on his campaign truck and tossing women's stockings and bacon into a crowd. Like many in the crowd, Quinn was hooked by Harry's theatrics. By now he knew something about organizing political support. He convinced the union officers to assign a full-time secretary to his legislative committee and embarked on an ambitious voter registration program, the first ever mounted by the local. With precinct captains and assistants in every voting district, he managed to add many hundreds if not thousands of names to voter rolls. Meanwhile, Local 610 at WABCO in Wilmerding was conducting a similar campaign. These two locals had a total of about twenty thousand members in 1948, about half of whom lived in the Twenty-ninth District. Other unions, especially the Teamsters, also worked hard for Davenport. On election day, more than a thousand union members were distributing literature at polling sites, phoning voters, and driving them to the polls.

Quinn spent much time with Harry, taking him to and from rallies and meetings, listening to his impromptu speeches, making sure he got home late at night after setting up drinks at various saloons. The two advanced beyond a political relationship and became friends, the middle-aged, one-time chamber of commerce official and the young labor organizer. The pairing was not as odd as it might seem. Harry would have been flattered that someone in the working class enjoyed his company. He and Quinn had similar political beliefs, and both enjoyed free-flowing discussions, analyzing trends and devising tactics to exploit various ideas. "I thought he was a pretty decent guy in every way," Quinn recalled. "We got along well, and I liked him a lot. I had a very strong feeling how important it was to get him elected. I thought Harry could become the leader of the Democratic congressional caucus for western Pennsylvania. He had that kind of ability." Of the five men who served as U.S. representatives from Allegheny County in 1948, two were Democrats. "They were good on labor issues," Quinn said, "but I thought Harry would be far more progressive, especially on issues like anti-Semitism and racism. Everybody who knew Harry felt that he would make a difference. He *was* different."

John Connelly viewed Harry from a different perspective, that of a young salesman eager to learn from the master. "We got along so well because our marketing minds coincided," Connelly said. "I just loved working with him. I was on time every morning to pick him up and go out and work the mill gates. Then we'd work street corners and evenings we'd work the mill gates again, then we'd work the crowds." He enjoyed

Harry's wit. One day they were attending a rally, sitting on the platform as Harry waited to speak. "I said to Harry, 'See that blonde in the front row. Boy, is she hot!' Harry said, 'Yes, but is she registered?'"

Connelly also had to contend with Uncle Harry's peculiarities, including "a horrible fetish for cleanliness," as Connelly put it. "He would wash his hands a hundred times a day. He would take steam baths three or four times a day." Connelly laughed as he recalled those days. "Many a time I went with him to a bathhouse in the Hill District, and we would sit in the steam and plan what we'd do next. I was cleaner that year than I'd ever been."

As the campaign went into the final months, Harry seemed to be running neck and neck with McDowell, possibly a nose ahead. He could still be dragged down if Truman did as poorly as practically everyone forecast. And Truman's prospects depended in large part on how he responded to problems abroad and to the threat posed by Henry Wallace.

M uch of Europe remained a rubble pile from the war. The Soviet Union had established control over Eastern Europe. The national economies of Western European nations were stalled, and Communist insurgents were exploiting political unrest and poverty in Greece, Italy, and other places. On all sides, it seemed, Communists were winning the hearts and minds of hungry people. The Truman administration had responded, first, by embracing a policy of containment, the so-called Truman Doctrine, intended to halt the spread of Soviet-sponsored Communism. Second, by the summer of 1948, under the Marshall Plan, the United States was dispensing billions of dollars in food and economic aid to European allies and nations threatened by insurgencies. The Russians viewed the Marshall Plan as part of an American expansionist policy. Along thousands of miles of border separating Eastern and Western Europe, hostilities threatened to break out between the two superpowers at any time. In huge and unwieldy China, meanwhile, Communist leader Mao Zedong was on the verge of overthrowing Chiang Kai-shek's feckless Nationalist government. From the political right Truman was accused of not standing up to Soviet expansionism and the Communist takeover of China, and from the left came charges that he was overreacting to the Russians and propping up the corrupt Nationalists.

The most prominent critic on the left was Henry Wallace, whose third-party movement, ironically, would do more harm to his nominal friends on the left—especially the CIO—than to his enemies on the far right. A world-famous agronomist, he had served as agriculture secretary and later vice president under Franklin Roosevelt and secretary of commerce under Truman. He described himself as a progressive capitalist, sided with unions on labor issues, and argued for racial integration. He publicly criticized Truman's "get-tough" containment policy and the Marshall Plan. After one such speech, in September 1946, Truman forced Wallace to resign from the cabinet. From then on, Wallace served as a lightning rod for Americans on the liberal left. The Communist Party USA threw its support behind Wallace for president. This turned out to be a deadly embrace. The Red baiting began immediately. Wallace refused to repudiate the Communists. By the spring of 1948, according to a biography of Wallace, *American Dreamer*, a majority of the American public regarded Wallace as a dupe of the Communist Party. Brushing aside such concerns, Wallace accepted the nomination of the new Progressive Party of America.

Wallace was an exceptional man in many ways, but his foreign-policy ideas were at odds with the dominant American perception of the Soviet Union. Although he opposed the spread of Communism, he contended that the Truman Doctrine bred "hatred and hysteria." If the United States would take the first step in defusing tensions, he argued, Russia would take the next step, and so on. It was a classic confrontation between the hopeful approach and the realistic. Some historians are still debating today whether adopting the hopeful path might have ended the Cold War forty years sooner. But this was by no means a popular sentiment in 1948, and loud anti-Communists like McDowell found it convenient to smear their enemies by associating them with Wallace. Speaking sarcastically of his Democratic opponent, "the gifted Harry Davenport," McDowell declared in October 1948 that "he has placed his hopes in the gentle hands of the strange association of Communists, dupes, bamboozled patriots and frustrati known as the Henry Wallace followers."[5]

Wallace's run for the presidency ended badly. But unlike many failed third-party adventures, his had a lasting, adverse impact, though not one of his making. It would hit the CIO with explosive force, creating an unbridgeable fissure between anti-Communist and left-wing unions. More immediately, fears about Communist influence in the Progressive Party fed a growing hysteria in Pittsburgh, with its large union presence. The *Pittsburgh Press* in April 1948 published a list of all citizens in

Allegheny County who signed nominating petitions to get Wallace's name on the presidential ballot. This was equivalent to painting a red star on the forehead of anyone who merely expressed support for a presidential candidate.[6]

Quinn not only signed the petition but also ran for the Pennsylvania legislature on the Progressive ticket. This was more of a declaration of principles than an active campaign for office, and predictably he collected only thirty-six hundred votes. Quinn agreed with many of Wallace's views, especially on labor, civil rights, and foreign policy. "He wanted to get away from warmongering, all that talk about the [atomic] bomb, and try to get some agreement with the Soviet Union," Quinn said. "I didn't like Truman. He intervened in some important strikes in 1946." But, I asked, did Truman not veto Taft-Hartley and promise to lead a drive to repeal it? "Yeah," Quinn said. "But when he vetoed the bill, he had a responsibility to round up support for his veto and prevent the Republicans from overriding it. He didn't do that." In Quinn's view, which is substantiated by accounts of men who were close to Truman, the president vetoed Taft-Hartley to win labor's backing for other measures. When Congress overrode the veto, Truman abandoned the fight against the law.[7]

In 1948 the search for Communist spies and saboteurs became something of a national preoccupation. The FBI was screening more than 3 million federal employees under a program set up by Truman in 1947. Nearly 3,000 of these workers would be arraigned before Loyalty Review Boards and 378 fired on evidence, or merely suspicion, of belonging to the CPUSA or any of dozens of organizations designated by the attorney general as Communist-front organizations. The Justice Department began assembling cases against top Communist Party leaders. Several congressional committees sprang into action, holding public hearings and calling witnesses to testify about Communist activity. The most active of these committees was the House Un-American Activities Committee, and in 1947–1948 one of its most active members was Representative John McDowell.[8]

Starting as a temporary committee in 1938, HUAC achieved permanent status in 1945. It was authorized to investigate un-American activities and propaganda and to recommend remedial legislation. Unions were major targets from the first, with the CIO and the UE being accused in 1938 and 1941 of harboring Communists. But from its early days

HUAC itself harbored its share of right-wing zealots, racists, and down-right criminals. One influential member was John E. Rankin, a Democratic representative from Mississippi and an inveterate anti-Semite and racist. Among many anti-Semitic statements, he once asserted that 75 percent of Communist Party members were Jews. J. Parnell Thomas, Republican of New Jersey, who headed the committee in 1947, was later convicted on charges of receiving kickbacks from employees in his congressional office.

The elections of 1946 brought new members to HUAC, including McDowell and a representative from California named Richard M. Nixon, whose adroit handling of the investigation of Alger Hiss drew the nation's attention. In 1947–1948, the committee cut a wide swath through political and cultural America with its highly publicized hearings. On its best days, the committee exposed the secret world of American Communism through testimony by former party members. But on too many other days, subpoenaed witnesses were confronted with charges by nameless, unknown accusers. Hearings on Communists in the film industry received enormous publicity, with dozens of famous actors, directors, and screenwriters appearing before the committee. Some identified colleagues as CPUSA members; others refused to answer questions, citing First Amendment free-speech rights or the Fifth Amendment protection against self-incrimination. Eventually, ten writers and directors—the so-called Hollywood Ten—were charged with contempt of Congress for refusing to testify and were ultimately found guilty. Most were sentenced to a year in prison and later blacklisted for many years.[9]

McDowell, remembered by one historian for calling Karl Marx "a bum," served as temporary HUAC chairman for several months in 1948. On his watch, a well-known scientist, Dr. Edward U. Condon, chief of the National Bureau of Standards in the Commerce Department, was accused of associating with Communists. Although finally cleared, he had been indelibly tainted and ended a broken man. Another episode involved HUAC allegations against Steve Nelson, a well-known Communist who headed party activities in western Pennsylvania. McDowell demanded that the Justice Department prosecute Nelson and four other people on treason charges stemming from an investigation of the alleged theft of atomic secrets in California in 1945. The department refused, saying it would not engage in "witch hunts" on the basis of HUAC's "hearsay testimony." Publicly embarrassed, McDowell backed down. Although HUAC called Nelson to give additional testimony, the case collapsed for lack of evidence.[10]

McDowell's HUAC record gave Harry Davenport a broad target to shoot at. According to Connelly and Quinn, Harry did not raise the HUAC issue before general audiences, recognizing that many people applauded the committee's broad-brush approach. Speaking to more liberal voter groups, Harry made it very clear that he thought HUAC an abomination and would seek to abolish it. Even if Harry's anti-HUAC attack was low-key, it apparently caught the attention of many, including the *Pittsburgh Post-Gazette*. The paper ran two editorials critical of McDowell's role "as one of the star performers of" HUAC. The second editorial, published on election day, urged voters of the Twenty-ninth to defeat McDowell to protect the nation from his "irresponsible conduct."[11]

Although more anti-McDowell than pro-Davenport, the *Post-Gazette* editorials nonetheless invigorated Harry in the late days of the race. He was much more wary of support from another newspaper, the Communist Party's *Daily Worker*, which lost few opportunities to blast the "reactionary" McDowell. Harry knew that Communists were playing a strong hand in his campaign, and certainly he was aware of a close relationship between the party and UE District 6. Fortunately for him, his Communist support drew little outside attention in 1948.[12]

As election day approached, Harry seemed to have a reasonable chance of winning. But he would have to overcome the huge liability of public dissatisfaction with Truman. The final, preelection Gallup poll in late October showed that Truman, with only 44 percent of the popular vote, still lagged well behind Dewey, with 52 percent.[13]

On the morning of November 3, 1948, the day after election day, I walked into my eight thirty German class at Bethany College without knowing the outcome of the elections. Television had not yet made it to the West Virginia panhandle, and few of us had radios in our dormitory rooms. My German professor, a heavy, mustached man, was a strict disciplinarian with regard to German grammar and had never talked to us about anything else. That morning, however, as we settled sleepily at our desks, he held up the front page of the *Pittsburgh Post-Gazette* showing a three-line banner: "Truman Leading; Democrats Take House and Senate." Truman had scored such an astonishing, come-from-behind victory, the professor said, that we scholars and future voters should draw a lesson from the accomplishment. Not only had he defeated Dewey but he also had pulled with him dozens of Democratic congressional candidates. For example, the professor said, pointing to another front-page story, a relatively unknown Democrat named—and he glanced at the story for confirmation—Harry Davenport had beaten a Republican incumbent in a district thought to be locked up by the GOP. If ever clinging to a president's coattails meant something, this was it.

The news startled me, and I felt a warm glow rising in my chest, as if the professor had singled me out for giving just the right *eu* sound to nouns with an umlaut *o*. When he finished his civics lesson, he acknowledged my tentatively raised hand. "Harry Davenport," I said with a mixture of pride and humility, "is my uncle." I waited expectantly for a word of thanks for having made flesh and blood of an abstract statistical example. A few students half-turned to see who had spoken up.

"Ah, yes," the professor said, barely acknowledging me. He seemed to regard my contribution as an intrusion on his story. Resuming the role of disciplinarian, he brusquely ordered us to open our textbooks.

For many years, indeed most of my life, I accepted the professor's assumption that Uncle Harry rode into Congress on the Truman wave. When I finally looked into the matter, I found that the opposite actually occurred. Davenport amassed 63,454 votes and McDowell 53,609, a margin for Harry of 9,843. But Truman lost Harry's district by 5,526 votes. Harry outdrew Truman in every ward and borough and won by 2,900 votes in the key Fourteenth Ward, which Truman lost by 2,700. Harry's attacks on bigotry, racism, anti-Semitism, and McDowell's participation in HUAC's Red witch hunt had had some effect after all. His defeat of a HUAC member won special, if brief, mention in the *New York Times*.[14]

In the closing two weeks of the campaign, later analysis would show, millions of undecided voters chose Truman, helped not a little by get-out-the-vote campaigns waged by unions. Truman received 24 million votes, Dewey 22 million; Wallace and a candidate on the segregationist Dixiecrat ticket, Strom Thurmond, each received a little more than 1 million votes. Instead of producing a debacle for Democrats, voters had given them full control of the White House and both congressional chambers.[15]

The election changed nothing for my family, nor did we expect that it would. I remained at school until the Christmas holidays, and by then Uncle Harry had gone to Washington to stake his claim. Harry's wife, Mary, and daughter, Peggy Ann, probably went to Washington for his swearing-in ceremonies early in the new year. Mary, however, had decided not to live in Washington, possibly because she had two teenage sons by a previous marriage back in Pittsburgh. Whatever her reasons were, they seemed insufficient in light of what later happened. In January 1949, Harry may not have been particularly concerned about his marital problems, given the excitement of his new life. I can imagine him, exuberant, chest puffed out, attending cocktail parties, making friends among other freshmen representatives, laying plans for a quick strike against bigotry in the opening days of the Eighty-first Congress, and making himself known to all the little people—clerks, pages, secretaries, and Capitol shoeshine boys. "The little people loved him," John Connelly said.

The man of words goes to Washington. Harry had lived in a world of catchy phrases and marketing schemes, and he had mastered the art of self-display at a time when society was just beginning to reward those who could package and sell themselves like a product in an ad campaign. Harry really believed in the brotherhood of man that he so rapturously preached. This I know. I do not know whether he understood what would be required to carry his beliefs into action and then to withstand the reaction. He was a natural politician, as John Connelly said, but not yet an experienced one. Harry would be tested on his ability to compromise on the periphery while keeping the core of his principles intact. In a constant world, perhaps he could have managed that. But as he set off on his biggest adventure, shifting perceptions of the Communist threat already were undercutting the near-left political positions he had staked out.

9

BLONDE SPY QUEEN
TELLS ALL

WHILE searching for clues about my uncle in history's forgotten corners, I stumbled on some unexpected links between people and places. Among other discoveries I found that my hometown, McKeesport, might have been the seedbed in which sprouted one of the most important Soviet agents of the thirties and forties. I say might because the woman known as the Red Spy Queen grossly overstated the case when she claimed that the "dirt, filth and squalor" of McKeesport drove her into the arms of the Communist Party. She was Elizabeth Bentley, a CPUSA member who turned against the party in 1945 and helped the FBI expose some of the most important Soviet spies of World War II. Bentley spent part of her girlhood in McKeesport, just up the street from where Harry Davenport lived as a teenager and not far from where I grew up fifteen years later. The amusing part is that there was nothing dirty, filthy, or squalid about the neighborhood where she lived as the daughter of a well-paid department-store executive. People invent all kinds of stories to account for taking the wrong path in life.

A graduate of Vassar College, Bentley joined the Communist Party in New York in 1935 and fell into a long affair with Jacob Golos, a high-ranking Communist Party official and Soviet agent who directed several networks of spies employed in the federal government. These included

Gregory Silvermaster, Harry Dexter White, William Remington, Victor Perlo, and Lauchlin Currie, former advisor to President Franklin Roosevelt. Bentley, who served as Golos's courier, continued his work when he died in 1943. Two years later, fearing exposure, she voluntarily went to the FBI, told of her role, and identified more than eighty Soviet spies, including twenty-seven employed in government agencies. Only two of those exposed were convicted of crimes because of evidentiary problems, but the spying came to an abrupt end for all.

Bentley's cooperation with the FBI remained secret until 1948, when the Un-American Activities Committee learned about her confession and subpoenaed Bentley to appear at a public hearing in July. Now seeking publicity, praise, and money for turning the tables on her Russian spy-masters, Bentley testified eagerly and with verve. She publicly identified the agents she had named (by this time they had been discharged from government) and exposed a world of intrigue and betrayal that opened many eyes. For the first time the American people heard evidence that seemed to back up long-running rumors of widespread Russian espionage. The press gorged on the details of her story, dubbing her the Red Spy Queen and, against physical evidence to the contrary, describing her as a "striking blonde" and "beautiful young blonde."[1]

Elizabeth Bentley was of no special interest to me until one day in 2002 when I came across a headline in a Pittsburgh newspaper published a few days after her testimony: "Red Spy Spent Early Years of Her Life in McKeesport." According to this story, she told congressional investigators that "her leftish tendencies may have sprung from the 'dirt, filth and squalor'" of McKeesport, where she had lived as a girl. The quote, it turned out, came from one man, HUAC member John McDowell, who told the reporter of having lunch with Bentley during her visit to Washington. In her testimony, she had spoken of her dislike for McKeesport, but apparently she employed stronger language in her talk with McDowell.[2]

Could my poor, little, sadly decaying hometown really have been the cause of such high-level subversion? I consulted Bentley's self-serving memoirs, *Out of Bondage*, as well as two critical biographies. What I found not only satisfied my curiosity about Bentley but also provided perspective for my own story about the Red hysteria. Born in Connecticut in 1908, Bentley lived in McKeesport for a few (or several) years when her father, Charles F. Bentley, worked as a buyer and department manager for a large McKeesport department store. Two newspaper stories, both based on reporting in McKeesport, say the family resided in that city from 1914 to 1921. In her memoirs, Bentley says the years were 1920 to 1923. In either case, if Bentley's contention is believed, she observed such horrific conditions in McKeesport as a young girl that she later fled to Communism. She also was influenced by descriptions of tenement life that her mother encountered as a volunteer relief worker.[3]

Like all mill towns, McKeesport had plenty of dust and dirt, and squalor, too, but not from one end of town to the other. The city's small black population and the families of recent immigrant millworkers lived in tenements and ramshackle frame houses near the mills in downtown McKeesport. These were impoverished neighborhoods, to be sure, but I doubt that young Miss Bentley saw much of them. The Bentleys lived a half mile from downtown, at the corner of Jenny Lind Street and Beech Street. Jenny Lind ran along the crest of a hill high above the Youghiogheny River. That neighborhood, populated by working-class to middle-class families, had no squalid tenements. Bentley would not have seen much squalor unless her father went out of his way to take her through the downtown sections. During Bentley's years in McKeesport, the Davenport family lived only a few blocks farther west on Jenny Lind. Uncle Harry, about six years older than Elizabeth, might have seen her in the neighborhood. My mother, who was born in the same year and month as Elizabeth (January 1908), might have played hopscotch with her, if Elizabeth indulged in such childish games. According to people who knew the family, she was a "gangling kid who was smart but sometimes peculiar."[4]

However much filth and dirt Bentley saw in McKeesport, she turned it to her advantage in recounting her life. According to a biographer, Kathryn S. Olmsted, Bentley had a mostly unhappy life and throughout her adult years tended to embellish or even falsify her personal story when she deemed it useful. In the congressional testimony, she "emphasized her own naïveté," Olmsted writes. "She maintained that as an idealistic liberal she had been propagandized by subversive teachers and seduced by an older ideologue. The implication was clear: she should not be held responsible for her actions." Bentley, still unhappy, died in 1963 at the age of fifty-five.[5]

None of this detracts from the value of Bentley's confessions. In the 1990s, new research resulting from the so-called Venona Project con-

firmed that the people named by Bentley were, indeed, Soviet agents.
Venona was the code name of a National Security Agency project involving the decryption of thousands of cablegrams transmitted between
agents in the United States and Moscow during World War II. On the
basis of these documents scholars compiled a comprehensive record of
Soviet espionage activities before 1945. Among other things, the record
revealed that the Communist Party USA, long regarded by many historians as merely a political organization, actually had provided spies for the
Soviet KGB. No longer could the toughest of party critics be dismissed as
fearmongers.

The Venona record also put Soviet spying in chronological perspective.
In 1945, the year that Bentley first told her story to the FBI, Igor
Gouzenko, a code clerk at the Soviet embassy in Canada, defected and
helped the FBI locate other Soviet agents. The defections of Gouzenko
and Bentley, concludes an authoritative study of the Venona documents,
"combined to end most of the spying that had provided the USSR's leaders with a cornucopia of policy and technical secrets from the United
States during the war." Although Red hunters such as Joe McCarthy and
members of HUAC would continue shouting allegations about Communist agents in the federal government well into the 1950s, the government
networks had been cleaned out by the midforties. Spies who emerged
decades later, in the 1980s and 1990s, were recruited solely by Soviet intelligence agencies, long after the demise of the American Communist Party.[6]

The Venona Project provides abundant evidence of spying in government but so far has produced little evidence of espionage elsewhere
(though only a small fraction of all cablegrams have been decoded).
Recent research in the newly available files of the Communist Party USA
also has not so far documented a determined use of the party to steal
industrial secrets or commit espionage. Just as we now know that Soviet
spying on the U.S. government up to 1945 was more pervasive than
some liberal commentators allowed, we also know that espionage in
other sectors of American life, such as heavy industry, was much less pervasive than conservative alarmists contended. Bentley's sensational testimony, however, fostered the notion that subversive Reds lurked
everywhere in American society. Commies were no longer merely malev-
olent foreigners with mustaches and insinuating ways; now they included
an unhappy middle-aged woman who had spent an awkward childhood

in dirty old McKeesport. If she could be involved in stealing state secrets, anybody could.

Bentley leaped into public view at a time when Americans were becoming truly worried about Stalin's maneuvers in Eastern Europe and the Communist takeover of China. Her confessions, as one biographer puts it, "would form the foundation of the post–World War II Red Scare." Now it became easier to believe allegations about Commies inserting propaganda into movies (the Hollywood Ten), taking over the factories (unions such as the UE), subverting politics (Henry Wallace's Progressives), brainwashing college students (Red professors), raising money in Communist-front organizations (fellow travelers), and doing who knew what else in all other institutions. As other insiders, including FBI undercover agents, began emerging from the depths of the party to expose subversive persons and activities, both real and invented, it became nearly impossible to cleave cleanly between tangible threat and baseless suspicion. Illusions rose up like dust clouds, and in the darkness bad was confused with good and vice versa. The real story was obscured not only by the secrecy of Communist spy operatives but also by elements of hysteria drifting around like shreds of fog at dawn. Some things you could see and some you could not see. Many Americans imagined what they could not see.[7]

Father Rice is an example. By 1948 he knew with relative certainty that Communists held upper-echelon posts in the United Electrical Workers, but he did not know for a fact that the leaders were intent on carrying out espionage on orders from CPUSA officials (the evidence is that they were not). Politically passionate, he believed fervently in the labor movement as a vehicle for attacking economic and racial inequality and extending power to ordinary people. He genuinely worried that if Communist influence grew unchecked in the CIO, the federation and its unions could be destroyed. "If the CIO were to go down," he wrote in a 1946 letter to a friend, "a lot of freshness, honesty and good Liberalism will go out of the Labor movement and out of American life. The Labor gangster would be strengthened." Like most zealots, Rice believed that his interpretation of political events and movements trumped all others and that his duty lay in protecting his special flock (workers and their families, Catholic and otherwise) from the false god of Communism. Many workers were grateful for his efforts. The Rice Papers archived at the University of Pittsburgh contain letters from many union members seeking advice on ridding their locals of Communist influence.[8]

The growing frenzy drove Quinn further to the left. In 1948 he was attending meetings of leftist organizations, reading the *Daily Worker*, and drawing ideas from radical political journals. In his political views, union work, friendships, and loyalty to the UE, Quinn had found a substitute for the father he had never had as a child. He was influenced by older people in the Progressive caucus, including Charles Newell, Margaret Darin, and Tom Fitzpatrick. Quinn assumed that Fitzpatrick was a Communist Party member, but he did not know for sure. "I didn't go around saying, 'Well, Tom, are you a Communist?' You didn't do that," Quinn said. Fitzpatrick's political affiliation was irrelevant, Quinn thought, when set beside his ability as a labor negotiator, and he never asked Quinn to join the Communist Party. Other UE members did, but Quinn held back. "I never joined anything that I had to renounce," he told me during a discussion of the matter in 2000. He was about as close to the party as one could be without becoming a member. But collaborating with Communists on gritty union issues in East Pittsburgh, Quinn felt, was not equivalent to taking orders from Joe Stalin to overthrow the U.S. government.

Jim Matles and other UE officials may have been Communists, Quinn said, but "I didn't see any reason for me to change my feeling about them and my relationship with them." Furthermore, "I didn't have any basis for believing" that the CPUSA actually controlled the UE—that is, dictated policy decisions on union issues. Hard-line critics of American Communists would say that Quinn deceived himself, citing the UE's support of Soviet foreign policy. Quinn acknowledged that the UE often sided with the Soviet Union on policy conflicts in the forties, but the union did not engage in overt acts against the United States. "I never saw any, and it would have concerned me if I did," Quinn said. "I didn't have any allegiance to Stalin at any time. I thought what he did in his own country was bad, terrible. But I never talked to anybody about it." For Quinn, the UE's record on asserting and protecting workers' rights overshadowed the negative consequences of its pro-Soviet stance.

"If I found out my father belonged to the Communist Party at some time in his life," Ron Quinn told me in a 2001 interview, "it wouldn't change my opinion of him. But I think he wasn't a Communist for the same reason he wasn't a Catholic. It wasn't belonging to something that was important. It was putting together an organization that made life better for working-class people."[9]

Quinn made friends across the political spectrum. One of these was John Vento, a UE steward at Westinghouse who differed with Quinn on the Communist issue but regarded him as a friend and ally on labor-relations matters. A few years younger than Quinn, Vento joined Westinghouse in 1946 after World War II service in the Pacific. In 1950, when the CIO created the IUE to replace the UE, Vento became a leader in the new union and eventually joined the staff of the Pennsylvania AFL-CIO. He retired as secretary-treasurer of the state body in 1994 but was still working part time when I interviewed him in Pittsburgh in 2002. He remembered Tom Fitzpatrick as a "very bright man" and a "strong, hands-on leader" as well as an "admitted Communist." While Quinn was "very much involved in that movement" (the UE-Communist alliance), Vento said, "I thought he was one of the moderates. Tom would sit down and try to reason why you should be with him on the issues. Some of these other guys would want to fight you. Tom was a bit to the right of those guys. I never thought he was a member of the Communist Party."[10]

Early in 1948, an acquaintance asked Quinn as a favor to chair a meeting of the Civil Rights Congress (CRC). Within a short time he was elected chairman of the CRC's western Pennsylvania chapter and immediately came under FBI surveillance. The CRC, founded in 1946 to protect the constitutional rights of persons accused of subversive activity, had itself been designated as a subversive organization by the U.S. attorney general. Led by Communists and sponsored by notable fellow travelers such as Paul Robeson, the CRC filed suits, mobilized public support, and provided bail money for defendants in civil-liberties cases. The most notable were twelve party officials who went on trial in 1949, charged with conspiracy to advocate the violent overthrow of the government. Quinn reasoned that party membership should not cancel one's constitutional rights. He rationalized his role in the CRC as doing nothing more than presiding over meetings of "a handful of people talking about civil rights." Quinn left the CRC in 1950.[11]

The only Communist meeting that Quinn attended was a public rally in April 1949 at Carnegie Hall in North Side Pittsburgh. A crowd estimated in the thousands gathered outside to protest the rally. American Legion members and anti-Communists from several unions, including

Local 601, set up a picket line blocking the entrance. Quinn accompanied Fitzpatrick to the rally, and the two had to break through the picket line to enter the hall. Thereafter they were reviled by the 601 right wing for crossing a picket line, as if they had busted through to take strikers' jobs. Father Rice addressed the demonstrators from a sound truck, attacking the Communists but urging the crowd to be calm (his detractors contended that he actually incited the mob). In any case, when the rally ended, the protesters broke through police lines and rushed people leaving the building. There was scuffling and jostling, but nobody was seriously injured.[12]

There were many such incidents, most less violent, in Pittsburgh during the late forties. Within the UE, the issue of communism, like all civil wars, came between good friends and turned brother against brother. Tom Fitzpatrick's older brother Mike also worked at Westinghouse in East Pittsburgh, and the two were on the same political side for several years before a break occurred in 1945. Mike Fitzpatrick switched allegiances and became a leader of the anti-Communist faction. So bitter became their split that they refused to talk. When they had to communicate, Mike's son, also named Tom, served as an intermediary. One photograph shows him standing between the two as they glare in opposite directions, their bodies stiff and defensive. In 1949, when Mike and Tom ran against each other for chief steward in Local 601, Mike denounced his brother as "a mouthpiece for the Communist Party." Tom won that contest, but Mike's side was the ultimate winner.[13]

In his acclaimed history of the United States after 1945, James T. Patterson devotes a chapter to what he calls the postwar Red Scare and says that it was an "undercurrent" in American life before 1949. This may have been true nationally, but it was more like a riptide in Pittsburgh from 1946 on. Since 1920, the Communist Party had focused recruiting efforts on western Pennsylvania, among a few other heavily industrialized areas, in the absurdly inflated hope of creating mass movements of workers that eventually would take control of key industries such as steel, coal, and electrical equipment. It would never come remotely close to that goal. When the Communist functionary Steve Nelson took command of the party's western Pennsylvania district in 1948, he says in a 1981 autobiography (written long after he resigned from the party), the CPUSA had only about three hundred members in and around the city, most of whom worked in the steel and electrical industries. They had gained influence in fraternal organizations such as the American Slav Congress, and they also controlled a few of the hundreds of local unions in the Pittsburgh area.[14]

After Elizabeth Bentley testified in late July 1948, newspaper coverage of Red-hunting activities accelerated. On thirteen of the first fifteen days of August, the *Pittsburgh Press* gave banner-headline treatment to stories about Red spies and other Soviet threats in the United States. Naturally enough, unions came under increased scrutiny. Local 601 became a frequent target of the press, and the phrase Communist infiltrators was often used, implying that party members had filtered into East Pittsburgh from some faraway place and tricked Westinghouse into hiring them and union members into electing them. In fact, as historians such as Ronald Schatz have pointed out, most of the 601 radicals were homegrown. But blaming outsiders for criminal or social activity that threatens traditional beliefs is a hallowed tradition in America.[15]

In a book aptly titled *The Great Fear*, a leftward-tilted but comprehensive history of America's Communist purge, David Caute describes Pittsburgh, in a much-quoted phrase, as "the violent epicenter of the anti-Communist eruption in postwar America." Caute is not referring here so much to physical violence as to the violence done to justice when common sense and fair play give way to paranoid actions based on scare-mongering by demagogues. This is what happened in Pittsburgh at the height of its purge activity, starting in 1950. Although separated by nearly two years from Bentley's emergence, the events of 1950 flowed directly out of her testimony and the Cold War battles that had been taking place in Pittsburgh since 1946.[16]

In February 1950, an FBI informer named Matthew Cvetic, who had been planted in the Communist Party in Pittsburgh in 1943, stepped out of the shadows and began talking. Appearing before HUAC, he named more than three hundred people in western Pennsylvania as either Communists or Communist sympathizers. Many of these were members of unions, particularly the UE, and ethnic organizations. Pittsburgh newspapers printed their names, places of employment, and a brief summary of Cvetic's testimony about them, as if they had been found guilty in a jury trial. Nearly one hundred persons lost their jobs as a result. Many other workers "were ostracized, were refused credit at local stores, saw their kids abused or attacked at school, were denied state welfare benefits, or were threatened with denaturalization or deportation." Several men named by Cvetic were expelled by their unions. A young war veteran was forced to resign his position with the AFL because Cvetic identified his father as a Communist. Schoolteachers were fired. A member of the Pittsburgh Symphony Orchestra not only lost his job but also was expelled by his union. Cvetic's testimony, so dramatic and apparently authoritative, seemed to neutralize the skeptical instincts of newspaper editors. "There has been no room for doubt at any time about the veracity of Matt Cvetic," declared the *Pittsburgh Press* on February 28. But there should have been room, as later revelations about Cvetic would show.[17]

I remember the uproar that accompanied Cvetic's disclosures. I also remember the 1951 film, *I Was a Communist for the FBI*, based loosely on Cvetic's life as an undercover agent. When I first watched the movie some years later on television, I found it to be an improbable, stupid melodrama. The movie depicted Cvetic, in real life a "little mousy guy," according to Quinn, who knew him, as a fictitious action hero who fought bare knuckled against evil Communist bosses. I did not realize until many more years passed that Cvetic surfaced, perhaps not accidentally, in the middle of the Local 601 Progressives' last struggle to keep their union affiliated with the UE rather than with a new anti-Communist union.

Reverberations from Cvetic's allegations would continue for years. Some of the more outrageous incidents involved a Pittsburgh judge, Michael A. Musmanno. Less than a month after Cvetic came to the surface, Musmanno recognized a woman sitting on a grand jury panel as a person named as a Communist by Cvetic. Musmanno not only dismissed her but also denounced her from the bench. The woman lost her job and was not reinstated after the Pennsylvania Supreme Court condemned Musmanno for his arbitrary and illegal action. But this was only the beginning of Musmanno's trampling of civil rights. He was a flamboyant, bizarre, and dangerous man who declared himself a friend of labor, championed the cause of Sacco and Vanzetti, spoke favorably of Fascism in Italy, and belonged to a vigilante organization called Americans Battling Communism. Although this was an advocacy organization, Musmanno and two other judges were prominent members who sat in judgment on defendants with opposite views.[18]

Cvetic's naming of Steve Nelson came as no revelation since Nelson operated openly as the CPUSA leader in western Pennsylvania. But Cvetic's testimony added inflammatory and unproven details about Nelson's activities. In August 1950, Judge Musmanno put on a sheriff's hat and led a posse, including Cvetic, in a raid on Nelson's office. He seized papers and documents and persuaded a county judge to issue a warrant for Nelson's arrest under the state's rarely used sedition law, which banned incitement of rebellion against the government. When Nelson and two associates went on trial in December 1951, Musmanno appeared as a witness with the books and magazines he had taken from Nelson's office. "I regard these books as more dangerous than any firearms," Musmanno testified.[19]

The trial was held in Pittsburgh despite the massive publicity that had attended the premier showing of *I Was a Communist for the FBI* in Pittsburgh only seven months previously. The city had staged a parade in Cvetic's honor on April 19, designated by Mayor David Lawrence as Matt Cvetic Day. In the movie, a villain identified in reviews as a character representing Nelson, commits a fictitious murder. Nonetheless, the Nelson trial went forward. Nelson had been severed from the case because of illness, but his two codefendants, whose convictions could have been influenced by the movie, were sentenced to twenty years in prison. Nelson's postponed trial was held in December 1951, and he also received a twenty-year prison term. In 1956, the U.S. Supreme Court invalidated the sedition convictions on the grounds that the federal Smith Act took precedence over the state law. In the same year, the court also reversed Smith Act convictions of Nelson and other top Communists when the government admitted that one of its key witnesses was a perjurer.[20]

All of the above must give the impression that the Red Scare of the 1940s had descended like a plague on every living creature. Actually, it touched Americans in a highly selective way, even in western Pennsylvania, one of the real hot spots of Communist activity. Although anti-Communist fervor was building generally in the spring of 1948 when I was a senior in high school, it had no effect on me and my circle of friends. We now and then talked about the Cold War and the Soviet Union, but never about a Communist conspiracy at home. My mother and father never uttered the word Communist that I recall, and so I did not have a fear of the beast implanted in me at an early age. I did not know any party members in McKeesport, but that was not unusual. Only 10 percent of Americans surveyed in 1954 said they knew someone who might be a Communist.[21]

Some would argue that we had our heads in the sand, which may be true. But they would not have been there if we had sensed danger. A fear of Communist subversion did not impinge on my life at any time during the late 1940s and first couple of years of the 1950s. Nor, I must admit, was I overly concerned about violations of the privacy and constitutional rights of people who were wrongly harassed. I did not know anybody in that situation. My abhorrence of Soviet-style Communism came not from life but from books, such as *Darkness at Noon*, Arthur Koestler's novel of the Soviet purge trials, which I read in about 1950; *The God That Failed*, a collection of essays by disillusioned Communists; various writings of George Orwell; and, a bit later, *Conversations with Stalin* by the Yugoslav Communist Milovan Djilas.

For much of Joe McCarthy's tenure in the early 1950s, I was sequestered in places where news of world events seemed remote, first at school in State College, Pennsylvania, and then in the army, at Camp Gordon, Georgia. Television watching was not a daily, or even weekly, event at either place. But on one day during my senior year at Penn State in 1953 I come face to face with the Red Scare. I was taking a political science course on individual rights and civil liberties. Our professor was a highly regarded expert on these issues. One day, entering the class-room, he appeared downcast and flustered, dropping his books with a sigh on a desk. He stepped in front of the lectern without his usual notes and said that he would begin the day's lecture with a personal story. In a halting, emotional voice, he told the class that he recently had signed a loyalty oath required of professors under a new state law, the so-called Pechan Law. A teacher who refused to sign could lose his or her job. The idea of having to prove one's loyalty by swearing an oath violated his deepest beliefs about academic freedom. But he had signed in order to keep working. As he spoke, the professor broke down and wept before the class.[22]

The irony is that I had already had much more intimate contact with a man deeply bruised by the Red Scare, though I did not realize it at the time. Harry Davenport had won election to Congress by a wide margin in 1948 without being unduly affected by growing concerns about Com-munist subversion. But the political atmosphere was drifting swiftly toward a danger zone at the beginning of 1949 when Harry began his first and last term in Congress.

10

HARRY'S BID FOR GLORY

UNCLE Harry had finally scrambled onto a national stage where he could display his passion and courage as an enemy of injustice and bigotry. On January 3, 1949, the opening day of the Eighty-first Congress, he spoke his first lines with a flourish that caught many an ear. He rose on the floor of the House, this intrepid freshman from Pittsburgh, and tried to offer a resolution to abolish the House Un-American Activities Committee. He was greeted, I can imagine, by incredulous gasps, excited snorts, and derisive gestures of dismissal. It is certain that people sat up and took notice. Jay Walz, a reporter for the *New York Times*, described what happened. "Mr. Davenport tried in vain to present his resolution on the floor, but was ruled out of order. So, as scores of his colleagues did with other measures, he filed his proposal with the House clerk and let it go at that." The Associated Press reported that the House parliamentarian "informed him [Harry] his move would be out of order, and so he dropped the proposal in the hopper along with all the other first-day bills and resolutions."

It was a brazen act of a freshman legislator not yet broken to the saddle of party discipline. Abolishing HUAC was not on a list of priorities for House Democratic leaders, though they could have forced the issue with the party's dominating 262–171 vote margin over Republicans. But the

137

leaders preferred not to pin that target on their rumps for the tabloids
to take aim at: "Pinko Democrats Attack Commie-Hunting HUAC." John
Connelly, who accompanied Harry to Washington as his congressional
aide, remembered the incident when I interviewed him in 2000.
"Harry," Connelly said, laughing, "had big brass balls, he certainly did.
He didn't care what the leadership said. Although down there, boy, you
learn to follow leadership!" Harry would learn.

Democratic leaders engaged in one battle on the opening day of the
Eighty-first Congress that pleased reform-minded freshmen like Harry.
For more than a decade, a coalition of Republicans and Southern
Democrats on the House Rules Committee had prevented liberal and
progressive legislation from reaching the floor for a vote. Now, Speaker
Sam Rayburn summoned the strength of the huge Democratic majority
and stripped the Rules Committee of that power on a roll-call vote of 275
to 142. Harry voted yes on the rules reform and several days later was
allowed to introduce his HUAC resolution.

In its ten years of existence, HUAC had often been challenged by liberal House members aghast at its willful destruction of reputations and
lives. The challenges usually took the form of unsuccessful efforts to
defeat bills authorizing the committee's operating expenses. No one had
actually tried to abolish HUAC until Harry's Resolution 36, which proposed that the Judiciary Committee assume HUAC's duties. The *Congressional Record* for January 13, 1949, presents Harry's brief speech in
support of his motion. "The people of the whole country are sick and
tired of the silly antics of that committee," he said, noting that "scores of
prominent educators, scientists, writers, and liberals have been smeared,
maligned, slandered, and scored by the head-line hunting committee."
HUAC had been "directly responsible for either murder or suicide . . . to
blame for broken homes, broken lives, and shattered reputations." For
all of its investigations into un-American activities since 1938, Harry continued, the committee had failed "to uncover and publicize the hordes
of anti-Semitic, anti-Catholic, antilabor, anti-Negro, anti-foreign-born
groups that infest many sections of our country."

Resolution 36 was never discussed in committee or brought to a vote.
The chances of its passage were so slim that it barely drew a nod even
from liberal journals. The *New Republic*, for example, dismissed the issue
in these words: "The Administration maintained that a counting of noses
had indicated that it did not have the votes to abolish the group

[HUAC], and discouraged attempts by a group of new and ardent members to kill the committee." A few weeks later, the House voted 353–29 to continue HUAC with an authorization of two hundred thousand dollars. Harry was not present for the vote because his flight from Pittsburgh had been delayed by bad weather. But he inserted in the record that, if present, he would have voted against the committee.[1]

Back at Bethany, I did not realize that Uncle Harry was establishing a reputation as one of those "new and ardent members" of the House. My German professor never mentioned Harry again, or politics either, for that matter. In weekly phone chats with Mother and Dad, they wanted to know about my studies and I wanted to know when my next box of laundered socks and underwear would arrive from home. They seldom, if ever, speculated about Harry's life in Washington. Mother did not wonder aloud, for example, why Mary Davenport had not moved to Washington with Harry. That was curious. Harry had reached the pinnacle of his career, of his life, and his wife was not with him. Perhaps their marriage was in trouble by then, as John Connelly told me. Perhaps Mary wanted to stay with her teenage sons. Maybe Harry did not want her in Washington for his own reasons. I don't know what the truth is. But Mary occasionally took Peggy Ann to visit her father in the capital, I later learned. Both were present in the visitor's gallery in February 1949 when House leaders chose Harry to read Washington's Farewell Address to Congress in commemoration of the first president's birthday. A newspaper photograph shows him posing with four-year-old Peggy Ann in his arms. Curiously, a fellow congressman is in the picture, but not Mrs. Davenport.[2]

In May 1949, my father suffered a massive heart attack early one morning at home and died within hours. He was only fifty-one, but he had put himself under extreme pressure in renovating the McKeesporter Hotel. Death cut short his effort to pay off the remodeling debt with operating profits, and the hotel owed a large amount of money to suppliers and contractors. Instead of selling the business, my mother decided to run it with the assistance of her sister Annamae, who had been Dad's office manager, and pay off the debt. Although they had to reduce expenses, there was never a question that Grandmother Davenport, who had lived rent-free in an apartment in the McKeesporter since Dad took it over, would stay in the hotel. An unintended consequence of Mother's decision was that Uncle Harry would have a place to live when things went badly for him.

Because of the financial squeeze, I dropped out of school after finishing my first year at Bethany and went to work at National Tube for a large construction company that was building a boiler house inside the plant. I would return to college in the fall of 1950, transferring to Penn State. In the meantime, I saw Uncle Harry only two or three times and made no effort to find out what he was doing in Washington. The crisis in my own life pushed everything else aside. I knew that Harry was a liberal Democrat, but I had no idea what issues concerned him, what bills he was championing or fighting against. Most of Harry's experiences in Congress remained unknown to me until long after he died. When I began research on his career in 2000, I compiled a partial record from his speeches and remarks in the *Congressional Record* together with a few mentions in newspaper stories. Harry, I found, was among the most active of all first-year representatives in the House. He spoke and voted consistently on the liberal, or progressive, side of major social and political issues.

Harry attacked bigotry and discrimination and in general lived up to the promises he had made to his most liberal supporters, especially organized labor and the Jewish and African American communities. He vigorously supported repeal of Taft-Hartley (the effort failed), advocated a continuation of federal rent controls, and urged public housing for low-income people; he spoke for the expansion of Social Security benefits, for better treatment of displaced persons who had settled in the United States after the war, for raising the minimum wage, and for extending unemployment compensation for jobless veterans. He gave especially strong support to a Fair Employment Practices Bill (forerunner of the Equal Employment Opportunity Act of the 1960s) and joined other House members in demanding an investigation of charges that five railroad unions banned Negroes, Mexican Americans, and Japanese Americans from membership. Whenever he had a chance, he spoke (or inserted in the record) stirring words in support of home rule for Ireland. Bowing in the direction of his Jewish constituents, Harry introduced a bill to "suppress anti-Semitism." His sentiments, as they say, might have been on the side of right, but the bill died without consideration, possibly because its aims would be hard to achieve without violating the freedom to say foolish and hurtful things guaranteed by the First Amendment.

Harry's one side trip out of the liberal track came on a proposal to ban a specific kind of pricing mechanism used for decades by the steel industry, one that equalized freight costs on steel shipments across the country so that Pittsburgh-area mills could compete with newer mills in the Midwest and West that were closer to markets. "I told you that I was a small-businessman," Harry said in this debate. "I am also a liberal. I am for the repeal of the Taft-Hartley Act. I voted for an extension of rent controls. I voted for the housing bill and for the elimination of slums. I will vote for the expansion of the Social Security benefits. I will vote for a 75-cents-per-hour minimum wage law. Yes, I am a small-businessman and a liberal, but I am not such a liberal as to vote against a bill which will maintain a high level of steel production in the Pittsburgh area." At least he was honest. The so-called basis-point pricing practice, or "Pittsburgh-plus," really was indefensible, and Congress banned the practice in 1949. This action was a significant factor in Pittsburgh's decline as a steel center.[3]

One of Harry's more notable attacks on racism occurred in a debate over a proposal to ban the discriminatory poll tax. In 1949, seven southern states still levied such a tax as a prerequisite for voting. In some states, it amounted to only $1.50 a head (though in many places it progressed with age), but in poverty-stricken areas the tax was high enough to disenfranchise large numbers of poor blacks and many whites. It originated in the 1890s as a method of denying the vote to blacks, and in poll-tax states, typically fewer than a third of the voting-age citizens would cast ballots. Southern congressmen had managed to defeat five previous attempts to halt the practice, and several of them spoke virulently against the latest bill when it came to the floor on July 26. John Rankin, for example, described the bill as the beginning of "a communistic drive" to enact other legislation such as an antilynching bill ("which ought to be called a bill to encourage rape"), fair employment practices ("that bill that Stalin wrote"), a bill to end segregation in public schools ("that would mean race riots and mob violence"). "We have the most peaceful relations between the races in the South that has ever been known, living side by side in such great numbers," Rankin said.

Harry took the floor next and accused Rankin of speaking "unadulterated balderdash." He then pointed out acidly that when the Mississippi Democrat was elected to Congress in 1946 only 2 percent of eligible voters in his district cast ballots. At this point, another member, apparently intending to defend Rankin, asked Davenport to yield the floor, a routine request that is usually honored. "No!" Harry said. "I have been waiting twenty years to say what I have got to say." He went on, defining the issue as "whether a narrow group of bigoted men will continue to control the political destiny of their states by restricting the suffrage of those who support them. . . . No state has the right to deny to any American the right to vote because he is poor or because of his race."

Next morning the *New York Times*, reporting that the bill passed by a vote of 273 to 116, singled out Harry's remarks. He ridiculed the insistence of Southern congressmen that only individual states—not the federal government—had the right to set election requirements. This was, he said, "nothing but a ruse, a trick by which they hope to perpetuate the poll tax." Noting Harry's attack on Rankin, the *Times* reported that when Rankin was recognized again for a brief comment, he archly complimented Harry "for putting in twenty years accumulating so much ignorance." If Harry's floor time had not expired, he undoubtedly would have responded in kind. I can picture him laughing at Rankin's comment, for Harry had a self-deprecating sense of humor. He also knew that on moral and factual grounds, he had gotten the better of the exchange.

The poll-tax ban died in the Senate that year, as it had previously. Predicting that this would happen, Harry in September proposed creation of a committee to investigate voting restrictions and recommend penalties for states that denied the vote on account of race, color, or previous condition of servitude. This effort also failed. Fifteen years would pass before passage of the Twenty-fourth Amendment to the Constitution finally disallowed the poll tax as a prerequisite for voting in federal elections. Two years later, in 1966, the Supreme Court extended the prohibition to state and local elections.[4]

B y the end of July 1949, Harry had compiled a respectable record as a first-year congressman. But even as he exulted in his role as a fighter against bigotry and repression, he must have sensed approaching danger. The Red Scare was intensifying. In Washington, investigations, accusations, and denials added fuel to the fire almost daily. The names of famous accusers and deniers filled newspapers: Whittaker Chambers and Alger Hiss, Elizabeth Bentley and Gregory Silvermaster, Harry Dexter White, and many more. And floating unfurled above these proceedings, as if written in huge, black gothic letters on a banner tied to a spire atop the Capitol, the questioning mantra of the day, "Are you now or have you ever been . . . ?" It was not that Harry feared being exposed as a one-time party member: he had obscured that past. He could not as easily hide from unpredictable dust storms rising out of the sharpest of all battles in the domestic war against Communism, the struggle in the CIO. In the summer of 1949 that battle was heading toward a climax.

In the two years before 1948, Phil Murray had held the CIO together as a split widened between hard-line anti-Communist leaders like Walter Reuther and those who followed a pro-Soviet line on foreign-policy issues, including the UE officers. Murray's patience came to an end when the Communist Party USA, in late 1947, backed the third-party movement that drafted Henry Wallace. Intending to make labor the backbone of the movement, party leaders ordered Communist unionists to support the third party "even if the cost was a break with Murray and other centrist CIO leaders," as a definitive history puts it. This move jeopardized the CIO's goals of reelecting Harry Truman in 1948, repealing Taft-Hartley, and enacting other prolabor legislation. With Henry Wallace taking votes away from Truman, Republicans stood a good chance of winning the presidency and rejecting labor's legislative program. The CPUSA's decision to jump headfirst into politics exposed a fundamental conflict that had been obscured by cooperation between the party and the CIO on some labor issues. The party's political goals, partly determined by allegiance to a foreign power, would never be compatible with the CIO's homegrown political and trade-union goals.

In January 1948, the CIO executive board voted to oppose Wallace's third party, and Murray took steps to eliminate Communists from all CIO offices at the national, state, and local levels. CIO affiliates, employees, and officers were bound by federation policies to oppose the third party and support the Marshall Plan, the Murray forces said. The UE and other left-wing unions took the opposite view, that as autonomous bodies they had a right to choose their own political course. The underlying irony of this struggle was that the determination of pro-Soviet unions to support Soviet policies drove the CIO toward subordinating its economic interests to the foreign and domestic policies of the U.S. government.

Through the 1948 political campaigns, the UE was squeezed between the CIO, which wanted all unions to disavow Wallace, and the Communist Party, which insisted that its members back Wallace. The UE top officers—Jim Matles, Julius Emspak, and Albert Fitzgerald—took a middle course at the union convention in September. Realizing that the rank and file favored Truman, they did not try to force through a vote endorsing Wallace. On this issue the UE did not abjectly follow CPUSA policy, nor did it take the course demanded by the CIO. By this time, though, the Wallace movement had faded, and Wallace won only 2.3 percent of the total vote. As Harvey Klehr and John Earl Haynes conclude in *The American Communist Movement*, "The 1948 election broke the back of communism in America. What followed was a long dying."[5]

Even with Wallace out of the way, the UE's relations with the CIO were stretched to the breaking point in the first half of 1949. Dominant anti-Communist forces in the CIO kept pressing demands for political conformity, and the UE continued to resist. Meanwhile, union raids on UE locals increased in tempo; by the middle of 1949 the UE had lost about thirty-four thousand members as a result of the union's refusal to sign the non-Communist affidavit. The UE was further besieged by its own anti-Communist rebels. Jim Carey's dissident group, with the help of Father Rice, had grown in strength at every UE convention since 1946 and was trying to amass enough voting power to oust Matles, Emspak, and Fitzgerald at a convention in September 1949.[6]

In Washington, Uncle Harry was aware of these developments. He frequently talked with CIO and UE representatives and undoubtedly heard, with increasing frequency, predictions of an approaching split; either the CIO would expel the UE, or the UE would withdraw from the federation, or both. He must have felt trapped. No matter how courageously he fought for union rights and civil rights and against bigotry and for the common man—all stands that would give him a 100 percent voting record on both the CIO and UE scorecards—he could win the everlasting displeasure of one side or the other if he had to choose between them. He desperately hoped to stay out of the line of fire. But the political climate made this difficult. The Red Scare was expanding day by day, depositing a residue of fear on everything and everyone it touched. This was especially true in Pittsburgh.

All of the fears and concerns generated by a barrage of sensational news landed on Harry's desk in the form of phone calls and letters from constituents, visits by lobbyists arguing for and against anti-Communist activity, and the daily papers with their scary headlines. He probably was responding to this pressure on July 1, 1949, when, granted permission to address the House for one minute, he lashed out at Communists abroad. He denounced the Russians for silencing Roman Catholic archbishop Josef Beran in Czechoslovakia and declared that the United States must not recognize a Communist Chinese government. America had contained Communists in Europe, Harry said, "but in the Orient we have steadily practiced the policies of Henry Wallace." He added, "The one overriding doctrine of communism is world conquest. The Reds fix no limits on their aims. They want the world. The time to stop them is now." Only a few years before, Harry had said he liked Wallace's ideas on foreign policy, but now he was speaking derisively of him. This kind of turn-around was typical of liberal politicians who desperately sought to avoid being stigmatized as "soft on Commies." It was getting harder to be an anti-Communist liberal and almost impossible to be an anti-Communist radical on the left.[7]

Harry put himself at arm's length from Russian and Chinese Communists, but Americans now were worried about Communist infiltration in their own backyard, particularly in unions. There was not much Harry could say about domestic Communism without angering one side or the other among his strongest supporters in the labor movement. He might have sensed that something dreadful was likely to happen but could do nothing to forestall it.

And then it happened.

The first hint of trouble for Quinn and his friends in Local 601 came in the *Post-Gazette* of Sunday, July 31, 1949. The paper's Washington correspondent, Ingrid Jewell, reported that HUAC intended to subpoena witnesses to answer questions about Communist activity in Local 601. Representative Francis Walter, a Democratic member of the committee from eastern Pennsylvania, had told Jewell that a "Pittsburgh clergyman" came to him with a warning that Local 601 "is being 'converted' to Communism by . . . out-of-town Communist leaders." This should be of concern to HUAC, the unnamed clergyman said, because Westinghouse had a contract to manufacture secret radar devices in East Pittsburgh. UE partisans knew immediately that the unidentified clergyman could be none other than Father Rice. He obviously was accelerating his campaign against left-wingers in Local 601, enlisting the aid of a congressional committee. Within a few days, federal marshals tracked down and handed subpoenas to four Progressives, including Quinn. The other three were Tom Fitzpatrick, then serving as the Local 601 chief steward; Frank Panzino, a former local business agent, and Robert Whisner, a subdivision steward. In addition, four members of the right-wing Rank and File Group, who had been advised by Father Rice, were called to testify before HUAC in hearings starting on August 9.[8]

The purpose behind the hearings was evident to Quinn and his friends. It was an attempt on the part of Rice and his allies to wrest con-

trol of the UE from Matles, Emspak, and Fitzgerald when they ran for
reelection at the national convention in mid-September. Local 601, the
union's second-largest local, was allocated ten delegate seats, with a total
of 152 votes, possibly enough to swing a close election at the convention.
The local would elect convention delegates on August 14, when headlines generated by the HUAC hearings of a few days earlier might influence members to vote against Progressive candidates and send a
right-wing delegation to the convention.

If HUAC's intention was to inquire into Communist activity in Local
601, a glaring question was why none of the open, admitted Communists
in the local were subpoenaed. "If they were looking only for people who
might have some relation to the Communist Party, they could have found
other people," Quinn said. "But they picked popular leaders. The whole
purpose was to interfere in the election." Quinn was not running for convention delegate but instead was seeking a seat on the District 6 Council
in a concurrent election on August 14. But he had achieved some prominence as a district staff man, and to brand him as a Communist would
help indict the Progressive caucus. Fitzpatrick and Panzino, both candidates for convention delegate, had been leaders of the caucus for years.
The choice of Whisner, who also sought a convention seat, was somewhat
odd. Although well known in the plant, he could not be characterized as
a Progressive leader. But something in his past made him especially
attractive to HUAC investigators—and would be Whisner's undoing.[9]

Father Rice already had begun a publicity campaign urging the election of right-wing delegates. Writing in his *Pittsburgh Catholic* column,
Rice termed the Local 601 election, with more than a little exaggeration,
"probably the most important election ever held in a labor union in the
Pittsburgh district." He did not disclose his own involvement in arranging the hearings, but Congressman Walter did—to Rice's acute embarrassment. In her second story on the situation, Ingrid Jewell reported
Walter's disclosure that Rice and two right-wing UE members visited him
(Walter) in Washington and sought the Local 601 investigation. But this
was only part of the story. A full accounting of the unusual efforts to set
up the hearings would not emerge for several years. Rice may not have
initiated the plan, but he played a major role in making the final
arrangements.[10]

Jewell's second story would turn out to be painfully prescient for
Harry Davenport. Speculating on how the HUAC hearings might affect

Democratic congressmen from six Pittsburgh-area districts, she pointed out that, while UE members lived in all six districts, the UE vote "is decisive in the Twenty-ninth Pennsylvania district, now represented by Harry Davenport." Given this insight, it is especially curious that Harry's political vulnerability was promptly forgotten by Jewell's newspaper. At many papers, an editor would have filed her story in a "futures" file with a reminder to look into the political consequences for Harry if the UE investigation went forward. But the *Post-Gazette* never followed up on its own lead, not even when Harry sought reelection in 1950. If it had, I might have understood decades ago what happened to my uncle.

I can imagine Harry ruefully agreeing with Jewell's assessment. He was honest in that way. The political life of a congressman must have seemed particularly unfair to him at this point. Whatever he felt for Father Rice before the Walter story broke, Harry now harbored something close to the contempt that would burst out years later when, in a conversation with me, he referred to the "labor priest" as a "labor faker."

On August 8, the day before the hearings were to start, Quinn, Fitzpatrick, Panzino, and Whisner took a train to Washington and checked into a hotel. That afternoon they met with the UE's general counsel, David Scribner, who had been assigned to represent them during the hearings. The UE leaders might be legitimately accused of putting political ideology ahead of the welfare of the union, but they did not abandon union activists and ordinary workers who came under attack by government investigators. Over the next several years, the UE would stand by relatively defenseless members caught up in many such investigations. The union provided lawyers and paid all expenses incurred in the defense of their members at hearings and in court if it came to that— as it would for Quinn.

Believing that the committee had no right to inquire into their political beliefs and associations, Quinn and his friends wanted to know how they could avoid answering such questions without going to jail or losing their jobs or both. Scribner suggested that the four men present a united front in the face of hostile, Red-baiting questions by HUAC members. The famed Hollywood Ten, the screenwriters and directors who defied HUAC in the 1947 hearings, had refused to answer whether they were or had been members of the Communist Party, citing the freedom of speech and association guaranteed by the First Amendment. But all ten were convicted of contempt of Congress; both the trial and appeals judges took the position that HUAC's right to ask the question in defending the nation against international Communism superseded the Ten's free-speech rights. Since the Supreme Court was still considering whether to review that case, Scribner told the Local 601 men, the legal status of unfriendly witnesses at congressional hearings remained unsettled. (Three months later, the Supreme Court refused to take the case, and the Ten began serving prison sentences of six months to one year in the summer of 1950.)[11]

There was no harm in raising the free-speech issue, Scribner said, but the witnesses might receive better protection under the Fifth Amendment's guarantee against self-incrimination. This strategy had its own pitfalls. Merely citing the Fifth created the impression that the witness had indeed been engaged in criminal activity. Furthermore, if the committee granted immunity from prosecution under the Fifth, a witness either would have to answer all questions, including questions seeking to implicate others, or face a contempt charge. To make the best of a dangerous predicament, Scribner advised the four men to prepare a joint statement to be read by whoever testified first, probably Tom Fitzpatrick. The statement would say that all four witnesses claimed the protection of the Fifth Amendment, as well as the First (for good measure), and that all would refuse to answer questions about political affiliations. Quinn, Fitzpatrick, and Panzino readily agreed. Bob Whisner seemed to hold back.

A half century later, Quinn remembered Whisner with affection and sorrow. A forty-seven-year-old skilled toolmaker, he was a large man, standing six feet three and weighing well over two hundred pounds. He had helped found Local 601 and had served as a steward and executive board member. "Bob was just a guy in the local," Quinn said regretfully, "an effective steward and a very decent guy with principles." Never shy about his leftist political beliefs, Whisner was a core member of the Progressive caucus but not a leader on a par with Fitzpatrick, Panzino, and Quinn. In response to Scribner's advice, Whisner said he had nothing to hide. He would claim the constitutional protections like the other three. But he intended to tell the committee anything they wanted to know. What harm could come to him if he replied honestly?

11

HUAC HEARINGS

O N Tuesday, August 9, 1949, Quinn and his friends had front-row seats as spectators to their own political lynchings. It was the first day of hearings entitled *Regarding Communist Infiltration of Labor Unions—Part 1*, convened by HUAC in room 226 of the Old House Office Building in Washington. Four committee members, impaneled as a subcommittee, sat on a dais with the HUAC counsel, Frank S. Tavenner Jr., and directed questions at witnesses sitting at a table in front of the dais. According to HUAC's usual format, friendly witnesses—in this case four members of the right-wing Rank and File Group from Local 601— led off the testimony with unchallenged charges to which unfriendly witnesses—in this case, Quinn and three other members of the Progressive caucus—would be asked to respond later in the hearings. Meanwhile, the latter four sat in a spectator section at the rear of the room, listening to accusations that could (and ultimately would for three of the accused) ruin what remained of their lives. They did not have the right under committee rules to cross-examine their enemies to test their truthfulness or bring out contrary or exculpatory evidence. After all, as HUAC members frequently said in defense of their procedures, hostile witnesses could not expect those legal niceties because they were not "on trial in a court of law." No, but they were on trial.

A crowd jammed the small hearing room, according to one newspaper account, with spectators probably numbering three or four dozen, including Communist haters, Communist lovers, union and company officials, newspaper reporters, and all kinds of people curious about the state of Communist subversion in the United States. Quinn noticed that Father Rice was not present, nor was any of the congressional delegation from Allegheny County. He had had a flicker of hope that his friend Harry Davenport might stick his head in to offer support, or even stride in like a movie hero and denounce the hearings and the committee and all it stood for. He could imagine Harry wanting to do that. "I thought that he of all people would feel that he had to speak up in some way," Quinn said, remembering that day.[1]

The pretense that HUAC needed to explore Communist infiltration of Local 601 because of Westinghouse's work on secret defense projects evaporated in the first minutes of the hearings. In introductory comments, counsel Tavenner noted that a bill had been proposed to make it a crime for Communists to be "employed in connection with the performance of any national defense contract." So far so good: it was well-established law that congressional committees had the right to conduct investigations related to existing or proposed legislation. But a HUAC investigator, when asked whether Westinghouse was engaged in defense projects, replied "not at the present time," though it had been in the past. The secret radar project mentioned by Representative Francis Walter and Father Rice as urgent justification to investigate Local 601 seemed to have vanished.

After these preliminaries, the hearings moved into the prosecution phase, so to speak, with testimony from the Rank and File Group members. First off was Charles E. Copeland, the current business agent of Local 601 and a right-wing leader for several years. Thirty-nine years old, Copeland had served in various UE local offices since the 1930s and later would become a district officer in the rival IUE, created to replace the UE. Quinn, who typically got along with most of his political adversaries in and out of the union, uncharacteristically had a strong dislike for Copeland. "Charlie was a blowhard, always shooting his mouth off," Quinn told me. "I never cared much for him." Under questioning by Tavenner, Copeland admitted having belonged to the Communist Party from 1943 to 1945. During this time he saw three of the Progressive caucus witnesses—Tom Fitzpatrick, Frank Panzino, and Bob Whisner—at party meetings, and he believed that Fitzpatrick and Panzino in particular were CPUSA members. Asked about Communist strength in Local 601, Copeland avoided using "Communist" but estimated that 200 to 300 of the local's 13,500 members were "active supporters of the left-wing element." He contended that Communists did not currently control the local.

If HUAC was seeking proof of party membership, Copeland's testimony was the strongest they would get this day. Indeed, he would be the only witness positively identified as a current or former member of the party. The next witness, William H. Peeler, a division steward and executive board member, named Fitzpatrick and Panzino as possible Communists, though his only evidence was a sort of indirect hearsay. Peeler, who was a black man, said he had never joined the party despite several invitations. One recruiter, he testified, tried to convince him that Communists "were the only ones doing anything for your race." Fitzpatrick and Panzino, he was told, "had done a terrific job in getting Negro girls in the plant." Tom Quinn also "had done something for them [Negro girls]," Peeler said he was told. In Red-hunting circles, it was taken for granted that people who fought against racial discrimination were most likely Communists or fellow travelers. Curiously, the one man that Peeler named with certainty as a Communist, the man who tried to recruit him and who openly sold the *Daily Worker* in the plant, aroused no interest on the part of the HUAC interrogators. Their goal obviously was to associate Progressive leaders with the CPUSA, thus promoting the idea of a hidden Communist conspiracy that could result in sabotage. The committee saw no value in hauling into the hearing room a man who operated openly as a Communist, who was not a leader in the Progressive caucus, and who was not running for convention delegate. Smearing such a person had little value in HUAC's strategy.

The next two right-wing witnesses both testified that Fitzpatrick had told them he was a Communist. They presented no specific information about Quinn, Panzino, or Whisner but said that all Progressives followed the Communist line. Curiously, when asked their opinion of the proposed law banning employment of Communists in defense work, both expressed skepticism about whether such a law could be fairly applied. "A lot of the people who are members of the Communist Party are innocent workers," said Stanley Glass, the anti-Communist recording secretary of Local 601.[2]

By the time committee chairman John S. Wood adjourned the hearing in late afternoon, Quinn and his friends realized that the term *setup* was too mild to describe what they had walked into. Tavenner had known precisely which question to ask each witness to elicit damaging testimony against one or more of the Progressives. The witnesses, for their part, clearly knew which questions were coming their way. The committee had loaded the cannon with anti-Communist grapeshot and fired an initial salvo that would incapacitate the victims, in the public eye, before they had a chance to defend themselves. Quinn did not think of himself as naive, but he later remembered feeling surprised as he listened to this testimony by men he had known for some years. "They were framing guys that worked with them," he said, "and there was nothing we could do about it." Still, no one had presented evidence of subversive acts. And the testimony against Whisner and Quinn was especially dubious. Whisner had been seen at one CPUSA meeting, and the sole reference to Quinn in any of the testimony was that he had "done something" to help "Negro girls" at Westinghouse. On the basis of this flimsy evidence, Whisner and Quinn would be paraded into the national spotlight and forced to respond to the question, "Are you now or have you ever been . . . ?"

The setup had been much more elaborate than Quinn and the others suspected. Three years after the August 1949 hearings, one of the friendly witnesses, Bill Peeler, disclosed what he knew about the origins of the hearings. In 1952, he became disaffected with Copeland's leadership in the IUE after it replaced the UE in East Pittsburgh. Switching his allegiance back to the UE, Peeler issued a nineteen-page notarized statement detailing his involvement in 1949 with Father Rice and other anti-UE leaders. In February 1949, Peeler said, a HUAC investigator came to Pittsburgh and interviewed him about Communist activity in Local 601. Some months later, after Rice talked to HUAC officials in Washington, final preparations were begun for hearings in August. Peeler, Copeland, John Duffy, Stanley Glass, and other Rank and File members met in a Pittsburgh hotel with HUAC investigators and selected local UE leaders to be subpoenaed. Fitzpatrick, Panzino, and Quinn were picked because they "would be the biggest threat to us in the election." As for Whisner, Peeler said, he "wasn't really any threat," but he was chosen anyway, because one of the Rank and File men remembered a possibly compromising episode in his background.

Peeler and his group arrived in Washington the day before the hearings were to begin. Meeting with HUAC staff members, they were given a list of questions that would be asked during the hearings. "After study-ing the questions, we were asked how we would answer them and pro-ceeded to a 'trial run.' When our answers were not satisfactory, we were told just how to give the 'right' answer and how to emphasize the points the committee needed. We were well rehearsed." Because of this prepa-ration, questioning of the right-wingers had proceeded smoothly and efficiently on August 9.[3]

On the second day of the hearings, August 10, HUAC interrogators shifted their attention to the unfriendly witnesses from Local 601. The cli-mate in the hearing room changed from polite and rambling to hostile and brusque. The Progressives, as Peeler noted in his 1952 statement, "were interrupted, harassed and otherwise treated like small children who didn't know what they were talking about." They, in turn, acted with defiance, lectured the committee on their constitutional rights, and refused to answer certain questions. August 10 happened to be Quinn's thirty-second birthday, and he spent much of it choking down anger.

Tom Fitzpatrick testified first. Forty-six years old, he had worked as a drill-press operator at Westinghouse since 1926. Many people regarded him as the most effective local leader on strictly trade-union matters—grievance handling and negotiating—in Local 601. After answering questions about his personal history, Fitzpatrick delivered a defiant and belligerent statement, claiming among other things that the hearings had been "rigged" by Rice and two right-wing unionists, who persuaded Francis Walter to start the investigation. But the committee had failed to show that secret defense work was at risk of subversion. Fitzpatrick point-ed out that the right-wing witnesses had denied that the local was domi-nated by Communists. Furthermore, although the UE often had been smeared, "you will find that not one case of sabotage or disloyalty has been brought forth and proven." He then uttered the words that he and the other Progressives had agreed on as a general defense. He would answer "all honest questions put to me," but the Constitution gave citi-zens the privilege to hold "opinions or beliefs that may be unpopular" and to keep these opinions secret. "This is a protection of the First Amendment, supplemented by the Fifth Amendment."

Fitzpatrick had no sooner spoken these words than Frank Tavenner asked, "Mr. Fitzpatrick, are you now or have you ever been a member of the Communist Party?"

"I say that this committee has no right to pry into my mind."

"We are not concerned with your opinion of the committee," Wood interjected. "We have asked you a simple question. Do you want to answer it or not?" He demanded a yes or no answer.

Fitzpatrick replied that "being just a common workingman, I will answer it in my own words." He continued: "The Constitution guarantees the right to me and every other citizen to have beliefs, whether they are popular or unpopular, and to keep them to themselves if they see fit, and I have no intention of being a party to weakening or destroying that protection in the Constitution."

Try as they might, Wood and Tavenner could not budge Fitzpatrick from this position, and he sparred with them about as effectively as one could given a difference in power. He was reminded that he had been named as a Communist by Charles Copeland. Did he deny that accusation? "I have no intention," he replied, "of permitting this committee to abridge my constitutional rights on political opinions, associations, who I work with, who I meet with, what I read or think, or anything of that kind." Later he said that the committee had the right to ask questions about his loyalty and that he would answer them. But nobody took him up on this challenge.[4]

Frank Panzino, testifying next, also refused to answer questions relating to political beliefs or associations. He claimed the protection cited by Fitzpatrick: "I support the basic position Tom Fitzpatrick took in his preliminary discussion," he said. Having experienced Fitzpatrick's defiant retorts, the committee decided after a few of the same from Panzino to excuse him and move on to a witness who—the committee knew from its investigatory work and cooperation by the right-wing witnesses—offered a tasty vulnerability.[5]

Bob Whisner had worked twenty-seven years at Westinghouse and had served in a variety of union offices since the local's inception in 1937. In an opening statement, he spoke of first hearing that he had been subpoenaed on the radio in early August. "This thing," he said, referring to the publicity, "set us back on our heels. My kids and wife and friends have been kind of disgraced by this smear campaign." He held up a newspaper with the words "Ex-Red leader" in a headline. A HUAC member asked, "Does that 'Ex-Red leader' refer to you?" Whisner replied impulsively, "I guess I am one of them." A moment later he rashly volunteered that in the plant where he worked, "I am known as a left-winger. I have been fighting on the side of the working class."

Whisner then declared that he took "the same position the other boys took. I consider I am protected by the Constitution of the United States under the First and Fifth Amendments." Tavenner began to bore in, abruptly changing the subject to a trip that Whisner had made to Europe in 1934. He wanted to know which countries Whisner had visited. "I have nothing to hide," Whisner said. "I consider myself a pretty good American."

But it turned out he did have something to hide, and he walked into the committee's trap. He testified that workers at East Pittsburgh "elected" him to serve on a trade-union delegation to the Soviet Union in 1934. At the first mention of Russia, one reporter wrote, "the crowd which jammed the hearing room responded audibly." Whisner tried to explain. He had four small children at the time. "There was a depression on . . . I was out of work, my electricity was cut off, they took my washing machine, and they wanted to take the linoleum off the floor. They [a different they] said: 'How would you like a trip to Europe?' And I said I wouldn't mind, I wasn't doing anything anyway." Westinghouse workers collected about $250 to pay for his trip.

Tavenner began to close the trap. Whisner's passport application showed that he had stated only that he was traveling to England and France to visit friends. "You knew before you signed that application that you were going to the Soviet Union, didn't you?" Without hesitation, Whisner replied, "That is right, and everybody in Westinghouse knew I was going to Russia." Why, then, did he lie on the visa application? He personally did not lie, Whisner replied, because an official of the Friends of the Soviet Union obtained the passport for him. This was a Communist-front group, listed as a subversive organization by the U.S. attorney general in 1946.

Fortunately for Whisner, Chairman Wood interrupted the hearing at this point so panel members could respond to a quorum call in the House. During the four-hour recess, Whisner consulted the UE attorney, David Scribner, who for some reason was absent earlier. When the proceedings resumed, Whisner said his lawyer had advised him not to say anything more about the trip to Russia "because it looks like you fellows are going to try to do a job on me on the passport business, and this thing is fifteen years old." Tavenner assured him that the statute of limitations on the passport violation had expired. Scribner still advised Whisner to refuse to answer on Fifth Amendment grounds. But, Whisner told the committee, "my conscience is clear on it. I have nothing to hide." He did have more to hide, however.

Now Tavenner and several members of the committee began firing questions at Whisner, one after another, quick and low and accusatory. Why had he lied on the visa application? What "friends" did he have in

England and France? If he did not type false information on the form, who did? Would he verify his signature on the form? (He did.) And so on. The proceeding began to take on the attributes of a criminal trial with four or five prosecutors hammering away at a bewildered defendant testifying in his own defense without benefit of counsel. Under committee rules, a witness's lawyer could not object to any question or line of questioning; he could only advise the witness whether or not to answer. Fitzpatrick and Panzino's refusal to answer political questions had robbed the committee of an opportunity to create sensational headlines. When they had a patsy like Whisner on the stand, a man guilty of a visa offense so old that it was beyond reach of the law, the panel punished him for their inability to make hay with the previous witnesses.

Any one of dozens of men like Whisner would have taken the trip to Russia in 1934 if "elected." (Obviously, Whisner had been selected for the trip by the front organization rather than elected by workers.) But Whisner it was, and with the tip from the Rank and File Group, committee investigators had an easy time documenting the trip and its aftermath. One thing led to another. Whisner kept answering questions, participating in his own lynching. The committee gave him every opportunity to kick the crate out from under his feet.

HUAC investigators had obtained Whisner's falsified passport application along with evidence that a representative of the Friends of the Soviet Union had filled it out for him. But they conducted the questioning as if catching Whisner in a major criminal act. They produced other documents, including a 1935 magazine article with Whisner's byline, saying, "I am now convinced that it is the duty of every worker in the U.S.A. to defend the U.S.S.R. in every way possible, for the Soviet workers have shown us the way out." Whisner said he no longer subscribed to that opinion. "We had sixteen million people unemployed at the time I was over there, and I felt the workers over there were better off than here, but now things are better here."

Whisner was excused a few minutes later, not because the committee took mercy on him, rather because it had wrung him dry and had nothing further to gain. Once again they had proved their worth through the passion and skill they exhibited in setting up an overconfident witness and then proceeding to flay him alive with biting questions exposing the grand fact that he had been conned by his tour guides in Russia. In this, he joined the many leading writers, politicians, and industrialists, including George Bernard Shaw and Henry Ford I (who even invested in Stalin's Russia), who also were taken in by the Russians. One of America's greatest heroes, Charles Lindbergh, visited Nazi Germany in the 1930s and was gulled into defending Hitler's march toward war. The reputations of these false prophets suffered to some degree, but none lost his livelihood for promoting rosy-hued views of totalitarian societies.[6]

When the furious barrage of questioning was finished, not one allegation of wrongdoing was made against Whisner that was less than fifteen years old. No evidence was submitted suggesting that he had ever thought of committing an act of sabotage, much less participated in one. He was, of course, just one of hundreds if not thousands of witnesses who were victimized during the Red Scare years by HUAC, Joe McCarthy's Senate subcommittee, the Senate Internal Affairs Committee, President Harry Truman's Loyalty Review Boards, and any number of state and local agencies and commissions. Over the years, I had read many stories about people, some Communists or fellow travelers and some neither, who had been abused far beyond any offense they had committed by associating with the wrong people or thinking the wrong thoughts. But I could not merely cluck my tongue over Bob Whisner; he was not a remote victim but one who entered my life when I began to write about his experiences. A few months after I read the transcript, I mentioned it to Quinn during an interview in December 2000. I told him I could not picture Whisner as a dangerous man. Quinn laughed and shook his head. "No," he said sadly. He paraphrased Whisner's testimony: "'I don't have anything to hide. I just believe in workers' rights.' That's the way Bob always talked. He talked all the time. He was a steward for tool and die makers, who in terms of intelligence and skill were a cut above the ordinary factory worker. They had faith in Bob. He was just a big, bearlike guy who stood up for the workers."

If Whisner had suffered only minor consequences as a result of his appearance before HUAC, there would be little reason to cite his example. But the "boys" down in Washington, as Whisner called them, really had done a "job" on him. The Pittsburgh papers reported extensively on his trip to Russia, his falsifying of the visa application, the same thing over and over. Later he would lose his job and much more as a direct result of the HUAC exercise at his expense. By the end of the August

1949 hearings, the committee had not finished with Fitzpatrick, Panzino, and Quinn. But it had finished with Whisner. It had emptied him out and tossed him aside.

The committee's session with Whisner took longer than expected. When it was over, Wood adjourned the hearings for the day. Quinn was ordered to return the following morning. He might as well have had an appointment to be executed.

A s I reviewed news coverage of the August 1949 HUAC hearings, I gradually became aware of what was not being said by people who surely regarded the proceedings with repugnance. The more outrageous the inquisitorial methods of the committee, the louder resounded the silence of journalists and political leaders. It was a silence pregnant with unspoken protests. As far as I could determine through a search of newspaper and magazine coverage, no member of Congress uttered a critical word about HUAC, nor even posed a question about its methods, as the committee solemnly trampled underfoot the free-speech rights of the Local 601 Progressives. Where were the outspoken reformers who had so bravely talked of abolishing HUAC, or at least curtailing its freewheeling investigations, at the start of the Eighty-first Congress? As the poet Oliver Goldsmith wrote two hundred years ago, "Silence gives consent."

Uncle Harry was not prepared for the moral agony of making difficult political decisions. This was the man who half a year earlier had stood on the floor of the House of Representatives and spoken of the "broken homes, broken lives, and shattered reputations" that had resulted from HUAC investigations of innocent people. Now, following newspaper coverage and daily congressional summaries, he saw that the Local 601 hearings were a perfect example of what he had railed against. Yet he went about his business of legislating, as did the dozens of other congressmen who found HUAC's tactics distasteful, if not horrifying. To say nothing seemed the better part of prudence and would offend nobody except UE leaders and civil-liberties groups, who commanded few votes. But what about anti-HUAC representatives whose own constituents were put on trial before the committee? Did these congressmen have a duty to protest the smearing of people they represented?

This was the dilemma confronting Harry Davenport and Frank Buchanan, another Democratic congressman from Allegheny County. Buchanan's district, the Thirty-third, abutted Harry's on the east and south and included the Westinghouse factory towns of East Pittsburgh, Turtle Creek, and Wilmerding. It also encompassed steel towns in the Mononga-hela Valley such as Homestead, Munhall, Duquesne, McKeesport, and Clairton, with tens of thousands of steelworkers who provided an over-whelming voter registration margin for Democrats. It was one of the safest Democratic districts in Pennsylvania, and Buchanan had glided to a second-term victory in 1948 by a two-to-one vote. He was a particular friend of UE Local 601, but as a former mayor of McKeesport, Buchanan also had ties with the Steelworkers and CIO that extended back into the 1930s. He and my uncle were the same age, in their late forties, and probably had known each other as young men in McKeesport. Buchanan lacked Harry's color and flair, but he was staunchly prolabor and had been one of the twenty-nine representatives who voted against funding HUAC operations in 1949. Quinn remembered him as a "very good congress-man, a good guy." Like Harry, though, Buchanan remained silent during the HUAC hearings.[7]

Since most of the subpoenaed witnesses lived in the districts repre-sented by Buchanan and Davenport, the HUAC investigation of Local 601 put these two men to the sharp edge of the sword. Both could take refuge in the argument that to condemn the proceedings would be to favor one group of constituents over another, the left faction over the right faction. In normal times, a congressman should be able to distin-guish between people who make unfair, undocumented accusations and those who are the victims. But these were not normal times; they were morally murky times discolored by the Red Scare. Most important, the struggle between left and right in the CIO had produced political under-currents that exerted a powerful drag on all congressmen elected with labor support. They were faced with the simple but unpalatable choice of siding with Phil Murray and the anti-Communist CIO unions or against them.

By the middle of 1949, everyone familiar with the CIO knew that a showdown between Murray's forces and left-wing unions probably would occur at the federation's convention in November. But if right-wing forces defeated Jim Matles and his running mates at the UE convention in Sep-tember, Murray would not have to expel the UE. Under new leadership the UE would have no reason to pull out. This was the dynamic that Buchanan and Davenport had to consider in responding to the HUAC hearings. It is highly unlikely that Murray personally approved the plotting by his friend Father Rice to smear the Progressives. But once the hearings were scheduled, it would be very much in Murray's interest to see them go forward. Democratic congressmen, for their part, would not want to land on the wrong side of Murray: the well-funded CIO Political Action Committee could make or break congressmen running for reelection in industrial states. Over and above these concerns, the growing national furor over the Communist threat at home and abroad had intimidated HUAC's liberal critics, leaving the committee free to do as it pleased.

Many times during the three days of the hearings Harry must have resolved to charge out of his office on a white horse, slay the dragon, and rescue his friends. He probably thought it was unfair that he should be presented with such a dilemma so early in his career. Instead of slaying the HUAC dragon, he would most likely kill his own chances for reelection, and he had to be reelected if he were to continue his bold course against injustice and ignorance. Harry's idealism, I discovered years later when I came to know him better, was tempered by a pragmatic sense of self-preservation.

So stood the situation early on the morning of August 11. Quinn had slept poorly and awoke feeling apprehensive. He wondered why Harry had not come to the hearings or made any effort to get in touch with him. Quinn had sized him up as one of those rare politicians who would do what was right, regardless of consequences. Maybe he needed some prodding. After breakfast, Quinn gave in to an impulse he had repressed since coming to Washington. The hearings would not resume until ten thirty, and he had ample time to confront Congressman Davenport.

Consulting a House directory, Quinn located Harry's offices in room 334 in the Old House Office Building, one floor above the HUAC hearing room. A receptionist admitted him to an inner office, where he found the congressman sitting behind a large desk covered with books, papers, and photographs. Harry reluctantly shook hands, displaying a forbidding demeanor. He sat back in his chair, saying nothing, signaling that he was not pleased to see Quinn. His look clearly said, "I know why you have come, and I have nothing to say to you." Nothing to say to a man who had helped get him elected, a man who had pushed him up the stairs of his apartment building after many a night of drinking, a man whom he had called a friend!

Harry's unfriendliness startled Quinn, but he pressed on. "Harry," he said, "don't you think you have an obligation to say something? I know you have a difficult problem. There are two [opposing] union groups involved and both are in your district. But this is outrageous, to use a congressional committee to engage in this kind of interference in the local union. I think you ought to say something about that.'"

Harry listened without comment. And then a bell rang for a House vote. He got up from his desk, took his Panama hat from a rack, and started out the door. He stopped and said, "You fellows have to clear yourselves."[8]

W Then Quinn took his seat at the witness table, he had never felt more alone. Less than an hour ago, he had followed Harry out of his office, half-expecting him to turn and apologize. But the congressman had departed without a goodbye, swinging his Panama hat as he strode down the corridor. Quinn later remembered that he said to himself, "Well, that's the end of a friendship, and if I have anything to do about it, the end of Harry's sojourn in Washington." That was the last cogent thought he had as he walked in a dazed state from the congressional offices to hearing room 226. Now, sitting alone in front of the dais, he tried to control his anger. There was not a friendly face in sight. Four committee members were settling into their chairs on the dais, throwing glances his way with casual hostility. Staff members shuffled papers. Tom Fitzpatrick, Frank Panzino, and Bob Whisner had stayed overnight in Washington to see Quinn through his ordeal, but they were seated in the audience behind him. Ordinarily, the lawyer, David Scribner, would be sitting beside him at the witness table, but not today. Quinn later could not remember why he was absent, but the U.S. Supreme Court would note that Quinn was "unaccompanied by counsel."[9]

Chairman John S. Wood finally convened the hearing, twenty minutes late. After Quinn swore the oath, Frank Tavenner commenced a series of questions about his personal history. Two minutes into the questioning, counsel abruptly took another tack, asking whether Quinn held any position in the Civil Rights Congress. Yes, Quinn said, he was chairman of the western Pennsylvania Civil Rights Congress.

"Do you hold any position in the East Pittsburgh section of the Communist Party?" Tavenner asked.

"No, I don't," Quinn replied, wondering what had inspired that question. None of the right-wing witnesses had connected him to the party. (Most likely, HUAC investigators had misread an FBI file reporting that Quinn was chairman of the East Pittsburgh chapter of the Progressive Party.)

Tavenner continued. "Are you now or have you ever been a member of the Communist Party?"

Quinn later would not deny that the thought of saying no had crossed his mind. He could save himself and his family much grief and unwelcome publicity by simply denying party membership. Let the committee attempt to prove that he was a member. Of course they would cite his close association with Tom Fitzpatrick and other leftists in Local 601 who had been identified by co-workers as CPUSA members; they could demonstrate that Quinn had run on the Progressive Party ticket, supported Henry Wallace, and received the *Daily Worker* at his home every morning. All this they undoubtedly knew; all this and more. The thought that someone had compiled a dossier on the life and beliefs of Tom Quinn sharpened his anger.

Tavenner was glaring down at him from the dais. The four committee members looked alternately bored and predatory.

"I would like to make a statement along the lines that Mr. Fitzpatrick made yesterday in regard to a question of that nature," Quinn said. "I feel that the political beliefs, opinions, and associations of the American people can be held secret if they so desire."

Wood broke in. "And for these reasons do you decline to answer that question?"

"I didn't say I was declining to answer the question. Before I do answer the question, I should like to say that I support the position taken by Brother Fitzpatrick yesterday."

"Do you support it in its entirety?"

"In its entirety," Quinn said.

He may have been rattled; certainly he was nervous. If Scribner had been sitting at his side, whispering in his ear, Quinn might have mentioned specifically the First and Fifth Amendments as his justification for refusing to answer. He simply forgot to do so. A minute or so later, he added, "I don't feel I am hiding behind the Constitution, but in this case I am standing before it, defending it, as small as I am."

The only activity ascribed to Quinn by the right-wing witnesses was that he had "helped Negro girls." Nobody on the committee asked him about that. What Tavenner now asked, again, was, "Have you ever been . . ." Again Quinn declined to answer. A few minutes later the committee was finished with him. But Quinn spoke out on his own. He pointed out that one of the committee members yesterday had said that the hearings gave Quinn and his friends "the opportunity to clear themselves." Instead, Quinn continued, "I feel the opportunity I am given here is a choice of clearing myself at the price of assisting this committee and destroying the Constitution, and I could not join the committee in doing that."[10]

Wood excused the witness. Quinn joined Fitzpatrick, Panzino, and Whisner, and the four took a train back to Pittsburgh. Quinn realized that a profound new thing had entered his life, but he could not identify it or see where it would take him. His visit to Washington had been the most miserable three days in his life. But of all the nasty things that happened on the record—the behavior of the committee, the accusatory words of the right-wing witnesses, the ordeal of his fifteen minutes under fire—none shocked him as much as the incident that was never mentioned in newspaper accounts or labor histories, his private meeting with Harry Davenport.

The name calling, whispering behind the back, and shunning began the day the four returned from Washington. It would continue intermittently for ten years, intensifying for a few days or weeks after each new publicized accusation, fading away for a while, then flaring again. They were called Reds, Commies, Stalinists, Soviet stooges, traitors, Stalin's henchmen, Commie goons, and a variety of other derogatory names. Many people took their opinions from newspaper headlines, and the HUAC hearings had produced exactly the kind of headlines that Rice and the right-wing leaders of Local 601 had hoped for. All three Pittsburgh dailies ran front-page stories about the proceedings, featuring accusations by the Rank and File Group witnesses and denials by the Progressives. A sampling of headlines on August 10: "Fitzpatrick Silent on Reds in UE" (*Pittsburgh Press*), "Fitzpatrick at UE Probe Won't Say If He's Red" (*Sun-Telegraph*), "UE District Called Red" (*Post-Gazette*). The newspapers could not be faulted for playing the initial story on the front pages. It was what they failed to do later that was worrisome. Journalism has an obligation, first, to describe an event as it occurs and, second, to follow up quickly with an investigation of injurious political accusations and allegations, especially if they are prominently displayed.

The Pittsburgh dailies flunked the second part of their obligation. None of the papers attempted to find out if there had been incidents of sabotage at Westinghouse; none attempted an analysis of the free-speech constitutional issue presented by the left-wing witnesses; none examined charges that the government had no right to interfere in the affairs of a private organization; none questioned why Tom Quinn had even been subpoenaed, given that the right-wing witnesses did not name him as a Communist. Indeed, his testimony resulted in only a one-paragraph mention in each of the three papers, although his name had been listed over and over again in rundowns of the left-wingers who had been subpoenaed. None of the papers objected editorially to the stringing up of Bob Whisner for traveling to Russia with an organization that had not yet been put on an attorney general's list of subversive groups because no such list existed in 1934.

Ingrid Jewell of the *Post-Gazette* made a serious attempt to be fair. She reported that even the right-wingers denied that Local 601 was currently controlled by Communists and that Fitzpatrick, Panzino, and Whisner professed loyalty to the United States. She also gave the fullest description of Whisner's trip to Russia and his reasons for making it. But she was a Washington correspondent, and the story soon passed out of her hands. Back in Pittsburgh, reporters and editors swallowed the line that the left-wing witnesses were guilty of . . . something.

Three days before the election for convention delegates, Quinn and his friends set about defending themselves and attacking right-wing "stool pigeons," Father Rice, and the Un-American Activities Committee. In East Pittsburgh's time-honored tradition, they held impromptu meetings on street corners and drew small crowds from the many people walking up and down Braddock Avenue. UE president Albert Fitzgerald came in from New York and addressed a large rally. Organizers dispatched from other union districts helped the Progressives turn out sympathetic voters.

The first time a fellow unionist made a derogatory remark about Quinn and his friends, the accuser probably wished he had not. The incident occurred at a meeting of the Local 601 Stewards Council a day before the elections. As chief steward, Tom Fitzpatrick called the meeting to present the Progressives' side of the case. Debate continued for hours over a left-wing proposal to condemn HUAC. A man named Tom Sullivan led the right-wing defense of the hearings. Speaking from a podium, he declared that Fitzpatrick, Panzino, Whisner, and Quinn were "Commies" and "Reds" who deserved the rough treatment they received at the hands of the committee. As Sullivan stepped down from the podium, Quinn rose from his front-row seat in the audience and punched him in the face. Before more fists could fly, other men jumped up and restrained the two. "I didn't like what he said about us," Quinn told me. Rice heard about the incident and reported on it a few days later in his column for the *Pittsburgh Catholic.* "Tommy Sullivan," he wrote "was assaulted by a Communist bully boy." This was the closest that Rice ever came to referring to Quinn in any of his writings.[11]

On Sunday morning, several Catholic churches in the valley called on Catholic workers to vote against the left-wing candidates, framing the issue in religious terms. "It is your duty, your Moral duty to vote against those who uphold communism," declared a typical church bulletin. "The people behind the Iron Curtain cannot vote against Communism. YOU CAN—YOU MUST." Some churches also provided cars to haul members to and from the polling place, as did the Progressives on the other side. Voting began in the afternoon at East Pittsburgh High School and drew considerable press attention. A reporter and photographer showed up from *Life* magazine, one of the best-selling weekly magazines in America. About three thousand voters actually cast ballots, nearly twice as many as usually turned out to vote for convention delegates, and many more apparently wanted to vote. Some found no place to park or disliked waiting in line and simply gave up. The *Life* story would attribute these problems to dirty tricks by the Progressives, although the right wing controlled Local 601's election machinery. The chances of vote tampering were considered so high that the ballots were stored overnight in a "triple-locked" vault guarded by two men from each faction.[12]

The ballot count on Monday morning produced a partial victory for each side. Seven of the nine men elected to serve as convention delegates were on the right-wing slate. But despite everything that HUAC had thrown at them, Tom Fitzpatrick and Frank Panzino were elected. Whisner, however, was defeated. The Rank and File Group thus would send eight delegates to the UE convention (the local president automatically had a seat) with a total of 122 votes, to 30 votes for the Progressives. Tom Quinn also beat the Red-baiting attack and won election to the District 6 Council. This was some vindication, though hardly enough to allay his concerns about his family, his job, and his union. Now he was a marked man—and he no longer had a friend named Harry Davenport.[13]

In one of my conversations with Harry, he alluded to a conflict between him and the UE during the final struggle for control of Local

601 several months after the HUAC hearings. But he never mentioned his fateful meeting with Quinn on the morning of August 11. Some actions, after all, are too painful to confess. It was Quinn who first related that incident to me, in the December 1999 letter that set me on my search for Harry's story. The revelation startled me, and I asked Quinn in subsequent interviews to repeat the story. Now and then he added a minor point, but the basic story always had the same memorable details: Harry sitting sullenly behind his large congressional desk, the bell signaling a vote, Harry taking his Panama hat and saying, "You fellows have to clear yourselves."

Harry's behavior that day, Quinn said in one of our discussions, "was so out of character. Here was a guy who had gone around day after day with me during the campaign. I thought he had a knowledge of Red-baiting and how it was used." It was not that Quinn expected Harry to persuade HUAC to excuse Quinn from testifying. It was too late for that, if it had ever been possible. Quinn did think, however, that Harry might have issued a public statement condemning the committee's interference in union affairs. Even that would have been difficult, Quinn acknowledged, in the climate of the times. But Harry could have, and should have, expressed concern about Quinn's situation, if only in private. "I thought the kind of relationship we had was, I should be able to walk into his office and sit down and get a hearing," Quinn said. "What I got was a dismissal."

Something had happened to the freshman congressman with the "big brass balls," as John Connelly described Harry, who only seven months earlier had proposed abolishing HUAC. Something or someone had caused Harry's manhood to shrivel. Political fright, I imagine. He knew that public opinion had crossed the line of mere annoyance on the subject of domestic Communism and was rising like a feverish man's temperature. After failing to gain his father's love and respect, Harry had chosen the road to political power, with its accompanying adulation by adoring masses, as a path to redemption in his own eyes. He liked what he had become, and he enjoyed the perquisites of being what he had become. It would be foolish to squander all that, sticking his neck out in a futile protest that could only serve to isolate him and reduce his effectiveness. None of this excuses Harry's behavior. He was the one who wanted to confront bigotry and injustice on its doorstep. Here it was, big and ugly, grinning in his face. He remained silent and passive.

In my first interview with Quinn for this book in March 2000, as we drank after-dinner coffee at the home of his son Ron, I asked why he refused to answer the membership question before the committee. "Because," he said, "we didn't think the committee had any right to ask that question." So you were taking a principled stand, I said. "Right," he said, and he repeated word for word one remark he made in the hearing: "I'm not hiding behind the Constitution, I'm standing in front of it, defending it."

"Did you have any inkling what the outcome of the hearings would be?" I asked.

"No. I simply assumed that . . ." His voice trailed off, and he shrugged.

"That this is America, that kind of thing?"

"Yeah," Quinn said, and laughed.

"So you were surprised when it [his post-hearings life] turned out as it did?"

"You bet. Everything!"

H arry later would contend that he came under unusual political pressures as the Red Scare grew in intensity. So did many liberal and left-leaning politicians and bureaucrats in that repressive era. But the pressures emanating from a hydra-headed anti-Communist lobby were moderate compared with the coercive force of a monolithic political machine under the command of Pittsburgh mayor David Lawrence. As the boss of the Allegheny County Democratic Party, Lawrence ruthlessly enforced party discipline when his or the party's interests came under threat. Such an instance came in the last half of 1949. It would put Harry at odds with Lawrence and further undercut the congressman's ability to act according to his principles. Once again the issue was friendship. Friendships, Harry was discovering, could be as dangerous a liability in old-fashioned ward politics as in the Cold War politics of 1949.

During his years in East Liberty, Harry had formed a personal friendship with a local Plasterers' Union leader named Eddie Leonard. A centrist Democrat, Leonard had served several terms on the Pittsburgh City Council, mostly supporting but sometimes criticizing Lawrence's leadership. As the end of his first mayoral term approached in 1949, Lawrence began campaigning for reelection, confidently expecting to receive the Democratic nomination without opposition. But several unions affiliated with the American Federation of Labor, unhappy with Lawrence over local issues, pushed Leonard to run against Lawrence in the Democratic primary elections in November. Leonard's candidacy seemed only a moderate challenge for an exceptionally popular and successful mayor. But an affronted Lawrence took it seriously. To bolster his standing, he demanded that all elected Democratic officials, including congressmen, publicly endorse him. Harry felt that this demand unfairly stretched him on the rack. It was true enough that he could not have run for Congress without Lawrence's assent, but he also had received strong support from his friend Leonard and other AFL leaders. Contending that Lawrence did not really need his backing, Harry stayed neutral in the primary despite a personal call from the mayor. John Connelly remembered the episode. "The Democrats didn't realize that Harry would turn into a maverick," Connelly told me. "But he wouldn't endorse Lawrence. He said, 'You're putting me in the middle, against the union [AFL] and a friend,' and he wouldn't do it. And for that, Lawrence cut his balls off, really."

The castration would come later, in Harry's second confrontation with the UE. Meanwhile, still seeking high-level support for his campaign, Lawrence forged an alliance that, as it turned out, would further limit Harry's freedom of action. The mayor sought and obtained an endorsement from Phil Murray as a means of influencing the powerful vote of steelworkers who lived in the city. If Lawrence demanded loyalty, he also repaid people who responded, punished those who did not, and lived up to the terms of his alliances. Thereafter, if Murray got into a scramble with leftist elements in the CIO and needed political assistance, Lawrence would rush to his side. By sticking to his friendship with Leonard, Harry had put himself in an extremely vulnerable position should the threatened CIO split occur. As it would. A postscript to this complicated business was that David Lawrence beat Eddie Leonard in the primary with 58 percent of the vote (75,800 to 53,200) and easily defeated a Republican in the general election.[14]

Harry may not have shown it at the time, but I believe from the evidence of later events that he deeply regretted the way he had acted toward Quinn. It pricked at him forever after. During the period when I knew him best, after I had blundered into and out of moral quandaries of my own, I felt occasionally that I could see right through his skin into a tormented soul. Most professional politicians develop ways of disguising and refusing to acknowledge errors of judgment and behavior. By this definition Harry was not a pro. He may not have voluntarily confessed his mistakes, but they were etched in his behavior, screaming to be let out and atoned for. But he kept them inside and punished himself over and over by alienating family and friends.

Father Rice's involvement with HUAC in August 1949 was only one in a long series of episodes in which he battled Communists in the UE and other unions. Many people would applaud his entire campaign, but in this one instance, at least, he allowed his zeal to carry him too far, as he himself later admitted. But, blessed with a hardier psyche than Uncle Harry's, he repressed his remorse for long periods and then expressed it in words rather than destructive behavior. More than thirty years elapsed before the priest talked publicly about that specific episode in his anti-Communist crusade. In the mid-1980s, he told his biographer that he had allowed himself to be "suckered in" to meeting with Representative Francis Walter to plan the hearings. A few years later, in a film interview with a BBC reporter, Rice said he was ashamed of his role in arranging the hearings.

When I interviewed him in 2000, Rice's memory of the affair was spotty. "I remember Walter," he said. "He promised me that he would not use my name. But as soon as the heat was on, of course he did. I will tell you this. I did not denounce anybody as a Communist who wasn't one, or very close to the party. I did not denounce any innocent person." On what basis, then, I asked, were Quinn and Bob Whisner selected to be subpoenaed? He could not remember, but at the mention of Quinn's name Rice became animated. "I remember Tommy Quinn. Did he survive?" I took the question to mean, did Quinn survive the smear campaign. I told him that alone among the four left-wing witnesses Tom Quinn had survived without disastrous personal consequences. Quinn, I added, was still perturbed about that incident and about Rice's entire campaign against the UE. "Oh, sure," Rice acknowledged. He lowered his voice. "I don't blame him for being angry."[15]

In the weeks immediately after the 1949 hearings, though, Rice carried on unapologetically, still hoping to unseat the top UE officers at their convention in September. But all the elaborate planning and conspiring came to naught. As it turned out, Local 601 could have sent fifty antiadministration delegates to the UE convention in Cleveland and still not defeated Jim Matles, Julius Emspak, and Albert Fitzgerald. Although the forces led by Jim Carey had tripled their voting strength, each of the three incumbent officers beat his opponent by more than eight hundred votes out of about thirty-nine hundred cast, a three-to-two margin. After all the turmoil and effort, after the lives of Quinn and his fellow witnesses had been turned upside down and indelibly marked, the political status quo in the parent UE remained unchanged. Misreading the strength of antiadministration forces in the locals, Father Rice and his allies had exaggerated the closeness of the election race from the beginning. What they did achieve was what HUAC excelled in: exposure, or illuminating in a public glow people accused of having Communist ties, according to political opponents who had an axe to grind.[16]

In his weekly *Pittsburgh Catholic* columns in late 1949, Rice never explained how the right-wing forces had miscalculated so badly. Nor did he apologize. But even then he must have had misgivings about his role in the HUAC affair. Reporting on the convention, he slid into a sort of rueful humor in describing the proceedings as he watched from the visitors' gallery. The *UE News*, he wrote, "got over-excited" about his presence and in its story on the convention "credits me with directing operations from the gallery." Rice continued, "I did not do very well. That is the day the right wing was beaten in the elections." In another column at about this time, he indicated sympathy for a man not linked with a union who had been wrongly accused by HUAC investigators. "We have to be very careful in our fight against Communism lest good liberals and friends of the people be victimized by vicious reactionaries anxious to use any stick to beat a dog," Rice wrote. If this is where his heart lay, Rice surely had a sense of doing wrong to Quinn and his friends. But in 1949 his concerns about the spread of Soviet-led Communism, especially in the American labor movement, blinded him to his own inherent belief in the need to protect civil liberties. As if undergirding his concerns, it was announced in September that the Soviet Union had tested its first atomic bomb.[17]

Carey's right-wing forces put up a strong fight at the UE convention, but the incumbent officers pushed through a new policy governing relations with the CIO. It authorized them to stop paying per capita dues to the CIO (amounting to about forty thousand dollars a month) unless Phil Murray accepted the terms of an ultimatum. Among other things, he must stop CIO affiliates from raiding the UE and force those unions to return captured shops to the UE. The ultimatum also demanded Murray's assurance that UE members could "run their union in accordance with their own wishes." In other words, the UE would be free to oppose a Marshall Plan or support a third-party candidate despite a majority vote of the CIO executive board.[18]

To shore up the union's defense against raiding, the UE leaders decided to give up their struggle against the hated anti-Communist affidavits required under Taft-Hartley. With the delegates' approval, the three top officers and ten vice presidents would sign the oath a few weeks after the convention. Almost immediately the FBI would swing into action, setting up a network to monitor the activities of Matles, Emspak, and other UE officials, hoping to find evidence of Communist activity, in which case they could be prosecuted on perjury charges. This monitoring would continue for at least ten years. Rice predicted that "some" of the UE leaders "will eventually wind up in the penitentiary on the head of it [signing the affidavits]." He was wrong. But the highlight of the convention was the decision to defy Murray and the CIO rather than to seek a compromise, unlikely as that may have been. As much as he wanted to maintain unity, Murray could not accept the onerous demands contained in the UE ultimatum. "The UE administration," said the *New York Times*, "can expect an almost certain expulsion" at the CIO convention in November.[19]

In Washington, Congressman Davenport undoubtedly read that prediction, and every other bit of news he could find about the UE convention. Each development must have seemed more alarming than the last, carrying the threat that he would again be forced to choose sides. As the UE delegates departed Cleveland in late September, the eye of the storm in the CIO drifted back to Pittsburgh, where Murray and his Steelworkers entered an epochal battle with the steel industry.

12

CIO SPLIT

FOR six months, starting in the fall of 1949, western Pennsylvania whirled furiously in a vortex of interrelated labor events ranging from a coal-mine shutdown to a national steel strike to the splitting apart of the CIO. These were massive economic and political struggles, the working class against the owning class in the coal and steel disputes and working class against working class in the CIO division. Practically everybody in the region was affected in one way or another, either swirled around the periphery of the whirlpool or flung up on a fortuitous wave of economic gain or dashed to the bottom in the churning within the labor movement. As fissures from the CIO eruption raced across the country, politicians like Uncle Harry, who depended on labor support, had to decide which way to jump to avoid tumbling into the abyss.

On October 1, Phil Murray ordered nearly a half-million workers in the basic steel industry to shut down the nation's mills. Since summer he had been trying to negotiate a new industry-wide agreement with twelve large steel companies. The industry leader, U.S. Steel, had rejected the union's demand for a noncontributory pension plan—that is, one that would be entirely funded by the corporation. Few wage workers in any industry could retire with a pension, and Murray wanted to establish a precedent that would sweep through industrial America. But U.S. Steel opposed the noncontributory concept as socialistic and contrary to the American ethic of self-reliance. After innumerable hearings, fact-finding reports, and government mediation efforts, the corporation continued to say no, and the Steelworkers went on strike.

In the Monongahela Valley, more than sixty thousand steelworkers shut down a dozen mills, putting thousands of supervisors and white-collar workers out of work. Imagine a fleet of huge, unwieldy dreadnoughts suddenly going dead in the water, clogging the valley with great piles of inert metal and reducing commerce to a trickle. Meanwhile, coal mines in western Pennsylvania were producing coal only three days a week under a slowdown ordered by John L. Lewis to put pressure on coal producers in wage negotiations. The industry employed thousands of men in large and small mines throughout the region. On the Monongahela, string after string of barges heaped with coal and coke normally traveled downstream every day, some dropping off loads at mills and power plants along the river and others continuing down the Ohio. With the flow of coal partially choked off, Lewis's tactics affected not just the coal industry but the entire regional economy.[1]

In McKeesport, my mother, sister, and I, like most people not directly involved in the strike, were spun round and round in the middle of the whirlpool but sustained no lasting damage. The strike eventually reduced our hotel's bar and restaurant business. Fewer steelworkers stopped in after work for a quick shot and a beer before catching a bus. But everybody who lived in a steel town adjusted her or his life and expectations to the rhythms of work, layoff, recall, boom times, strike, back to work, and so forth. We were all in it together, though the strikers and their families suffered most. By the end of four weeks, however, a settlement seemed imminent, and we never worried about the possibility of catastrophic economic loss. But I remember the tension that came from the threat of almost continuous labor conflict.

Since 1946, large strikes (or threats of strikes) had lashed western Pennsylvania almost continuously, month after month, year after year, in the coal, steel, or electrical industries, as well as railroads, utilities, breweries, public transportation, and other businesses. There seemed no end to these epic battles, just brief pauses while labor and management took a cigarette break. When John L. Lewis threatened to escalate the mine slowdown into a national coal strike, I made a note in an early journal entry: "It is extremely dangerous for one man to have enough power to control the production of coal so vital to our nation's industries." Years later, when I covered mine disasters; observed miners at work in damp, dark places under creaking timbers; and interviewed men still in their thirties gasping for breath because of airways plugged with coal dust, I revised my opinion about the use of union power to reform such a world.

I had been working since June as an engineering clerk for Stone and Webster, a large national construction company retained by U.S. Steel to erect a boiler house at the National Tube Works in McKeesport. Every day I would walk a quarter mile or so from the plant's main gate to the construction site where the Stone and Webster field and office staff operated out of a mill office building. I folded and filed blueprints that arrived by the dozens every day from the home office in Boston, assembled a daily report on construction progress, and did a little drafting. No special knowledge was required, merely dexterous fingers and a supply of Band-Aids to cover paper cuts. For this sort of work I earned $1.10 an hour, somewhat less than an unskilled mill laborer.

The building tradesmen, of course, refused to cross the steelworker picket lines, and so the office staff was laid off for the duration of the strike. Luckier than most, I went to work immediately as a desk clerk at the McKeesporter Hotel, filling in for a regular clerk who obligingly took a vacation. It took me a day or so to learn how to check people in and out and operate the telephone switchboard. After that, the job was routine and often boring, especially on the midnight-to-eight a.m. shift, when the switchboard stopped buzzing and guests stopped arriving. The four-to-midnight shift sometimes provided entertainment in the form of a free-flowing debate about the strike by retired railroaders and out-of-work construction men who lounged in the lobby.

For all the labor conflict in the mills and mines, I remember that fall as being exceptionally quiet and slow moving. No street riots or chanting marchers. Few if any incidents of violence on the picket lines, largely because U.S. Steel did not attempt to run strikebreakers into the mills. Looking down Locust Street from Fifth Avenue, I could see pickets massed at National Tube's main gate, occasionally marching in a circle, but more often standing around fires blazing in metal drums. The silence was deadening. Something essential seemed to have gone out of our lives when the background noise disappeared: the continuous low-key roaring and rumbling of blast furnaces, the intermittent pealing of crane sirens from within the plant, the clang of pipe knocking against pipe in the shipping bays, the dreadful moaning of National Tube's steam whistle, which for generations had sounded three times a day at shift change. Looking back, I see our valley of mills and mines and people who served them isolated in our own small universe, impervious to innovation and new ideas, gazing inward instead of outward. The steelworkers and coal miners were battling, justifiably, for better wages and benefits on an economic battlefield that within a couple of decades would slip into the past.

Uncle Harry was caught up in this industrial conflict no less than any of us in the Monongahela Valley. He had linked himself to the labor movement, and more specifically to one union, because he believed in the labor cause, but also because unions could get voters to the polls. It had not occurred to him that the movement itself could break apart and that the link would become a manacle, restraining him politically. As the Eighty-first Congress moved toward adjournment in October, Harry anxiously followed news of the labor troubles back home, probably hoping for a miraculous rapprochement between the UE and the CIO. In New York, Jim Matles and his colleagues were marshalling arguments to buttress the ultimatum they would hand to Murray at the CIO convention in November. Murray, meanwhile, was alternating between negotiations with steel executives and meetings with CIO aides on the threatened UE insurgency.

The three labor events in fall 1949 were interconnected in several ways. The main issue in the coal conflict was Lewis's demand that operators pay more money into a welfare and retirement fund that provided health benefits and pensions. Negotiations had been stalled for months, largely because U.S. Steel and other big steelmakers, which operated their own coal mines, were not eager to negotiate seriously with Lewis until they saw how the pension dispute with the Steelworkers would turn out. Eventually a series of wildcat strikes broke out in coal, leading to President Truman's threat to seize the mines. The two sides would finally reach agreement in March 1950. The Mine Workers had led the labor movement in negotiating health and retirement benefits, giving rise to the then novel idea that employers could, and should, provide a pension as an additional payment for work performed. Murray picked up the idea and pursued it in steel, as Walter Reuther did in the auto industry. Victories in steel and autos would encourage other unions to demand noncontributory pension plans. The 1949 steel strike was a watershed event.[2]

Looking back from the perspective of fifty years, I see compelling reasons for the strikes that once seemed merely inconvenient to people not directly involved. The coal and steel disputes pitted the working class against corporate owners in the final round of a postwar struggle over the principles that would guide industrial wage bargains between employers and unions over the next thirty to forty years. Included were periodic wage increases (eventually with cost-of-living raises), incentive pay, pensions, medical benefits, vacations, and job-protection measures. These were large matters to workers who had been beaten into poverty during the Depression. The war in a sense had rescued them, providing steady jobs for the first time in a decade, and they had begun a slow climb toward economic security. But at the end of the forties, the Quinns, like many blue-collar families, were only beginning to think about leaving cramped apartments and putting money down on their first home or buying their first refrigerator and automatic washing machine. The postwar economy was buoying up everybody, but unions gave workers the extra thrust needed to deal with powerful employers. With so much at stake, it was only natural that workers caught in the CIO split, such as the members of UE Local 601, would fight ferociously among themselves to determine which union would represent them in the future. And this is where the third major event of fall 1949 entered the picture.

On October 31, Bethlehem Steel Corporation, the nation's second-largest producer, broke ranks with U.S. Steel after four weeks of strike and granted the Steelworkers' pension demand. This move broke the back of the industry's united front, though U.S. Steel and other companies would hold out for two more weeks. And now the CIO fight overlapped the steel dispute. On the same day that Murray signed a tentative agreement with Bethlehem, he also opened the CIO convention in Cleveland. Meeting privately with UE officers, he rejected their demands for autonomy on political and foreign-policy matters. The UE officers responded by boycotting the convention and withholding dues payments.

At the same time, the Communist press and some UE locals, including 601, published vicious personal attacks on Murray, accusing him of selling out steelworkers in the pension negotiations. Yet Murray's willingness to strike over pensions may have been intended in part to demonstrate that anti-Communists could be just as militant as Communists. And so the sellout charges "were likely the last straw" for Murray, one historian says. In his opening convention report, Murray replied angrily that the "carping, unjustified criticism" constituted "the most flagrant approach to union strikebreaking" he had ever seen. The convention immediately began expulsion proceedings against the UE and ten other unions on grounds they had followed policies "directed toward the achievement of the program or the purposes of the Communist Party." The UE, having stopped paying dues, thereafter would insist that it could not be thrown out because it had already pulled out. As Quinn and many others put it, "We said you can't fire us, we quit."[3]

The other ten unions would be tried by panels of CIO officials in what turned out to be kangaroo courts over the next several months. All were found guilty and expelled. Chief among these unions were Harry Bridges's longshoremen's union on the West Coast; the Mine, Mill and Smelter Workers; Office and Professional Workers; Fur and Leather Workers; and Food and Tobacco Workers. These unions, together with the UE, represented about 1 million members, or a quarter of the federation's total membership. Many would be recruited by other CIO and AFL unions, but many also slipped into a nonunion zone, never to be recovered. It was a crippling blow that sent the CIO hobbling toward its end in a 1955 merger with the AFL.[4]

The indictment against the UE included the charge that it amounted to little more than "the Communist Party masquerading as a labor union." The UE, indeed, had flipped and flopped on foreign-policy issues in sync with the CPUSA and the Soviet Union. But no one could seriously argue that it had failed to represent its members on trade-union issues. Furthermore, UE leaders had ignored the urgings of party officials to stay in the CIO and fight from within. "We are against splits, against secessions, and against expulsions," declared an editorial in the Sunday edition of the *Daily Worker*, the party's mouthpiece, in early October. But Matles and his fellow officers refused to surrender their demands for political autonomy within the CIO either to avoid expulsion or to follow the party line.[5]

While striking the UE from its rolls, the CIO created a new union, the IUE, to replace it, and named Jim Carey as president. Father Rice celebrated this action with joyful hurrahs. Never before, he wrote in a column, had a new union been created "out of the body of an existing one." But this was not the outcome that Rice had wanted. Privately, said Charles McCollester, who talked with Rice about the event in about 1987 while collecting material for *Fighter with a Heart*, Rice was dismayed at the turn of events. "He had built his strategy around taking control of the UE by slugging it out at the grassroots and beating the UE officers in an electoral struggle. Complete victory, not a split, was what he wanted. He supported formation of the IUE with feigned enthusiasm when it became clear that the UE was pulling out."

Although Rice had been pressing Murray for some time to take forceful action against Communists in the CIO, it is unclear how much his influence counted in Murray's decision. Rice's *Pittsburgh Catholic* columns from the final weeks of the internal fight in the CIO exude a sense of its author observing wistfully from the outside rather than reporting from the inside. They exhibit a shoot-from-the-hip quality that could be expected from one of today's Web site commentators, and Rice's rhetoric ran away with him. He constantly heaped praise on Phil Murray ("that great man") and, with considerably less reason, on Jim Carey.[6]

Quinn thought the split was unavoidable. In addition to other differences separating Murray and the UE, the CIO had amended its constitution to bar Communists or those who "consistently pursue policies" of the CPUSA from membership on the CIO executive board. In accepting this ban, the UE would have denied itself a voice in CIO affairs and overthrown its long-standing opposition to exclusion rules relating to race, religion, ethnicity, or creed. "The UE position was that everybody has equal rights, and I saw no reason to abandon that," Quinn said. But he refused to join some UE loyalists in branding Murray "an enemy of working people" and a "lackey" of capitalists. "I don't think Murray had his heart on going down that road [expulsion]," Quinn said. "He had a difficult decision, and he was dealing with hysteria."[7]

In McKeesport, many of us were oblivious to the upheaval in the CIO. There were no large UE-represented shops in our town, and the steel strike cast a long shadow over most other news. U.S. Steel had been put on the defensive by the Bethlehem settlement and a recent Ford Motor Company decision to grant a pension to its UAW hourly workers. In the middle of November, U.S. Steel capitulated and accepted the noncontributory concept. The first recipients would receive a minimum monthly pension of one hundred dollars, including a small Social Security stipend. And so began what came to be known as the defined-benefit pension plan: the company committed itself to provide a specified monthly pension to qualified retirees by paying actuarially determined amounts into a fund that would dispense benefits upon retirement. The Steelworkers would build on the original plan in subsequent bargaining rounds. By 2004, about three hundred thousand steelworkers at U.S. Steel alone had retired on a pension, and the total for the entire steel industry probably exceeded nine hundred thousand.[8]

The noncontributory, defined-benefit pension eventually became the standard not only for union employees but also for nonunion white-collar workers in most large industries. By 2004, 44 million Americans were still covered by defined-benefit plans. But this pension system had run into enormous problems because of poor actuarial assumptions and underfunding by employers, the liquidation of huge swaths of heavy industry beginning in the 1980s, and the deunionization of a large part of America, enabling employers to cut back on pension promises to their employees. Finally, the decline of air travel after the terrorist attacks of September 11, 2001, forced major airlines into bankruptcy. But those are other stories.[9]

Sometime during his first year in Congress—I am unsure whether it was before or after the HUAC hearings in August—Harry began drinking heavily. The attachment to drink was not unfamiliar among Davenports. Alcoholism was a snake coiling around the staff of life in our family, sinking its fangs into Harry and his brother Eddie and spitting venom in the direction of other family members, including me. The brothers in particular were conjoined, both politically and addictively, at a deep and crucial site in their psyches. There was a constant pulling and tugging, influencing and being influenced. You could know them separately but only really know them as a twinned pair, though they were not twins.

In his four years on the Los Angeles City Council, Eddie had become, as the *Los Angeles Times* once described him, "one of the most colorful figures in city legislative history." A rightist Democrat as opposed to Harry's leftist variety, Eddie made the council chambers shake when he attacked pornographic comic books, vivisectionists, Los Angeles smog, and Communists. He promoted loyalty oaths for government employees and led a successful fight against a massive, government-subsidized public-housing program. Outside of politics, Eddie and his wife Harriette promoted cultural causes and often crossed paths with the elite of the movie industry. Every month Eddie sent Grandmother Davenport a check covering a large part of her living expenses.[10]

But Eddie was a notable binge drinker. To avoid the possibility of scandal, he rarely drank in Los Angeles. He would remain sober for months at a time and then, usually on trips, he would not merely fall but jump off the wagon for a week or two before returning to sobriety and Los Angeles. As distressed as my mother and her sisters were about Uncle Eddie's alcoholism, they forgave and loved him. Harry had a much harder time gaining the love and respect of his sisters and thus of his nephews and nieces. Where Eddie was kind and loving, Harry hid his feelings behind standoffishness and sarcasm. Remembering my uncles, I wonder about the early family life in McKeesport that produced such talented brothers with similar styles, proclivities, and weaknesses. Alcoholism is a physical disease, abetted probably by upbringing. The brothers, I think, were in part reacting in some way to their unreasonably harsh, teetotaling father, who himself was reacting to his alcoholic father. The damage that fathers can do!

Compared with Eddie, Harry was a steadier boozer. He had reduced his intake while learning how to be a congressman. But after some months on the job, Harry began drinking on a regular basis. John Connelly saw the change occur in Harry's behavior during that first year in Washington. There were plenty of people in the capital to drink with, including perennial political hangers-on and influence peddlers who knew how to rope in a vulnerable congressmen with praises, liquor, and women. It was not as if Harry abandoned his duties or missed a lot of roll calls or swayed drunkenly when he rose on the House floor to make a speech. He was one of those people who could function well enough on a diet of booze. But a steady, heavy reliance on alcohol affects behavior. You lose a certain edge, and your mind creates a new executive subbranch dedicated to planning where and when to obtain the next drink and anticipating the next stimulation. Harry's marital problems probably helped push him over the edge. "If he had a good wife, it could have made a tremendous difference," Connelly said. "He had no family life, no stability in his political life."[11]

Harry probably deserved a large share of the blame for his marriage difficulties. Whatever the problem was, it pushed him into other relationships. Sometime before the end of his first year in Washington, he began an affair with a woman in his office. Winning a desirable woman can make a man feel very good about himself, for a while. Harry pursued his affair vigorously and openly, according to Connelly. Rumors about his behavior eventually reached Pittsburgh. Tom Quinn remembered hearing about the drinking and an affair, probably from UE representatives in Washington.

Toward the end of 1949, Harry asked Connelly to move back to Pittsburgh to run Harry's office in the district and work on the *East Liberty Shopping News*. With Connelly gone, Harry could promote his mistress to administrative assistant with higher pay. Connelly did not feel slighted because he missed his wife and children and wanted to go back. "I don't want to throw rocks at Harry because I think he was a great guy," Connelly said. "But he was unstable."

Harry was a complex man who always had multiple forces working on or against him. Being elected and sent to Washington, instantly elevated into an official position with a little power, given command of the loyalties and fealties of hundreds of people—especially secretaries, clerks, shoeshine boys, security guards, and so forth—had such a liberating effect on him that he went on a two-year spree even while serving more or less conscientiously. Or perhaps less and less conscientiously and more and more politically. For once he got there he wanted to stay. Connelly was saddened by Harry's decline. "You couldn't talk to him. He became a big shot. He was a big man down there in Washington among the peons, but not among the other congressmen."

While Harry was creating problems for himself, an ominous threat to his political future was developing as a result of the CIO rupture. The IUE and CIO began moves to supplant the UE as bargaining agent for workers in the electrical manufacturing industry. In November and December, Westinghouse, GE, and several other companies, complying with personal pleas from Murray, petitioned the National Labor Relations Board to hold representation elections. With production workers deeply divided over which union should represent them, the companies rightly argued, they could not conduct labor relations on an orderly basis. But Westinghouse and GE also eased the way for the IUE, relieving the union of the need to show support at many plants where it had no presence. The board eventually ruled that elections should be held at dozens of Westinghouse plants in the first half of 1950.[12]

From the day that the NLRB received the petitions, Harry had premonitions of being caught in the middle. It was a foregone conclusion that an election would be held at East Pittsburgh, where the anti-Communist rank and file and leftist factions had been fighting bitterly for a decade or more, and that he would come under pressure from both unions to take sides in what would be a highly partisan campaign. Harry probably sensed that it was too late to make amends with Quinn and his friends for not speaking up during the HUAC hearings. There would be a campaign battle in East Pittsburgh, and when that happened, two organizations that composed a large part of his political strength, the IUE-CIO and the UE, would be running full tilt at one another. Harry could win nothing in this fight, and he might lose everything. His only practicable position was to squat silently in neutral territory and hope he would be forgotten.

That clash was a few months in the future when we saw Uncle Harry on Thanksgiving Day in 1949. He and Eddie, visiting from Los Angeles, both came to the McKeesporter Hotel to have dinner with the Davenport family. About fifteen family members gathered for the event, including Grandmother Davenport, her two sons, four daughters, two sons-in-law, and six grandchildren. We ate heavily and told family stories. This turned out to be the last time I would see Uncle Harry before he lost his bid for reelection and the last time I would ever see Uncle Eddie.

No one in the family seemed surprised that Harry was not accompanied by his wife and daughter. We had not seen Mary and Peggy Ann for more than a year, and my mother and aunts probably had concluded long since that his marriage was in grave trouble. But he was not one to sit ruminating moodily while others around him gabbed away. In a group of people he always grabbed the microphone. I seem to recall him telling a hilarious anecdote, complete with mimicry, about a self-important congressman making a bloated speech before an empty House. One would never have guessed that Harry had anything to be worried about.

In retrospect, I think of Harry's performance that day like that of a brilliantly colored bird that flares all the brighter and sings all the louder when it senses danger. Looking ahead he could not see, through the gathering murk of illiberalism fostered by the worldwide march of Communism (Chinese Communists were on the verge of pushing Chiang Kai-shek's Nationalist forces off the mainland to Taiwan) precisely where and when the attack would come. Nor could he have known that the entire nation was soon to enter a crazy, irrational period in which a demagogue named Joe McCarthy would hold the nation in ugly thrall.

O n January 21, 1950, Alger Hiss, the man whose spy case had come to symbolize treachery in high places, was convicted of lying to congressional investigators and sentenced to five years in prison. Six days later, physicist Klaus Fuchs, who had worked in the American atomic-bomb project, was arrested in England on charges of transmitting atomic secrets to the Soviet Union (he later was convicted and imprisoned). These two events heightened Americans' suspicions that a vast Communist conspiracy remained embedded in the U.S. government and prepared the way for the most notorious of all Red hunters. Less than a month later, Senator Joseph McCarthy unleashed the devil in America's soul.

In a speech before the Ohio County Women's Club in Wheeling, West Virginia, on February 9, McCarthy said he had in his possession the names of 205 Communist Party members who worked in the State Department. His notorious list proved to be written in invisible ink, for he never produced a single name. Thus began one of the great hoaxes in American political history. Even though built on baseless allegations and outright lies, McCarthy's campaign met the approval of enough government leaders, officeholders, rightist interest groups, and ordinary citizens—and intimidated enough liberals and conservatives of otherwise high principle—to keep his fraud going for nearly five years. McCarthy himself came late to the practices that came to be regarded as features of McCarthyism: making false charges of disloyalty, insinuating guilt by association, forcing people to inform on one another, and encouraging blacklisting of workers because of their beliefs and associations. But the senator from Wisconsin engaged in these practices with fewer scruples and more audacity than his predecessors. The Wheeling speech initiated a furor that continued with increasing intensity through the spring of 1950, highlighted by press conferences, congressional hearings, investigations, and exhaustive newspaper coverage.[13]

In this supercharged atmosphere, Tom Quinn, Jim Matles, and thousands of other loyalists in the UE would mount the fight of their lives to keep their union alive. NLRB elections were scheduled in the first eight months of 1950 at hundreds of plants owned by General Electric, Westinghouse, General Motors, RCA, Sylvania, and other companies. More than 250,000 UE members would be put on a sort of self-service auction block, open to bids by other unions. The workers had a choice of sticking with the UE or replacing it with the brand new IUE or another interested union; or they could vote for "no union." In the process, many thousands of workers conceivably might shift from one union to another in a single day, and the companies just as swiftly could benefit immensely from the resulting union fragmentation. Nothing remotely like it had happened before nor has since.[14]

Nowhere were these interunion contests more intense than at Westinghouse in East Pittsburgh, with more than thirteen thousand workers eligible to vote. A group of right-wingers formed IUE Local 601 and begun weaning members away from UE Local 601. Only the UE was certified to deal with management, but labor relations were at a standstill anyway as the two locals feuded and fought. It was a different kind of labor struggle from the old shooting wars between striking workers and company guards or police, but it was every bit as intense in its own way. The stakes were very large for those workers—a vast majority as it turned out—who believed a union made a big difference in their lives in at least two ways. First, a strong union could protect its members from unilateral and arbitrary management actions on the shop floor, as well as negotiate good wages and benefits. Second, a union could influence political decisions in the wider community, and many workers objected to their union promoting policies that appeared to be dictated by a foreign country.

For the better part of seven months, starting at about the time of the CIO split and ending with a runoff election in June, continuous warfare between the two groups roiled the entire Turtle Creek Valley. Day or night, the valley's narrow streets often throbbed to the sounds of rallies, parades, street-corner harangues, loudspeakers. A blizzard of leaflets, pamphlets, campaign buttons, and letters greeted workers in the plant, on the street, at home. They were subjected to propaganda of every type, distributed by every conceivable means, including radio broadcasts (both unions had daily programs), billboards (the CIO spent $150,000 on billboard ads plugging the IUE), posters in store windows and on telephone poles, loudspeakers mounted on sound trucks, and occasionally even banners towed overhead by airplanes. Both unions played dirty tricks, and fights occasionally broke out in the streets and saloons. Engaged in a bitter propaganda war, the two sides indulged in flagrant exaggerations and falsehoods. The UE kept referring to the IUE as the imitation UE or the dual union or the CIO company union, formed to help the company gut its contracts with the union. On the other side, the IUE associated UE leaders with Reds beholden to Joe Stalin. The new union tried to create the impression that all UE members who worked in plants with federal contracts were in jeopardy. On the day of the election sound trucks drove up and down Braddock Avenue blaring out a false report that President Truman would withdraw federal contracts from all UE-organized plants.[15]

Tom Quinn's two-year stint as a district staff representative had ended, but the international union had promoted him to its staff for the third and last year of his leave of absence. Now he spent an increasing amount of time in East Pittsburgh, organizing support against the IUE. "It would have been best for me in some ways, I suppose, to simply join the IUE," Quinn recalled. "I had more credibility than those guys [the right-wingers] did. I could sell anti-Communism as good as they could, or better." But he was contemptuous of his old right-wing foes who had served him up to HUAC. Realizing that he could not possibly work under them, Quinn decided to stick it out with the UE.

The campaign had barely begun before external events helped the IUE cause. Ten days after McCarthy's Wheeling speech, Matt Cvetic emerged from seven years as an FBI plant in the Communist Party and testified for several days before the House Un-American Activities Committee in February and March. He named three hundred western Pennsylvanians as Communists or Communist sympathizers, including Quinn and several other UE members. Portraying himself as a heroic undercover agent (the FBI said he was merely a confidential informant), Cvetic became an instant celebrity. Not known at the time was that he had been dropped from the FBI payroll for excessive drinking and other problems. But the FBI kept Cvetic's unsavory past a secret, and he would testify many times at committee hearings and in deportation cases before a federal appeals court in 1955 rejected him as a credible witness.[16]

In early 1950, however, the IUE could not have hired a better propagandist. Testifying before HUAC, Cvetic gave useful information about the internal workings of the CPUSA and how it extended its influence into various organizations, particularly ethnic fraternal societies such as the American Slav Congress. The questionable part of his testimony involved the scores of people he identified as party members with no documentation other than his claims to have seen them at CPUSA meetings. Many probably were Communists, but Cvetic provided no dates for the meetings or other evidence to support his allegations. For example, he placed Quinn and Tom Fitzpatrick at Communist district committee meetings "on many occasions."

"I never did that," Quinn told me in 2003. "I didn't go to any meetings with Tom Fitzpatrick, except the one public rally in North Side Pittsburgh." Quinn's FBI file supports this contention. The main entries linking him with the party involve his activities in the Civil Rights Congress and his attendance at the public rally sponsored by the Communists in April 1949 and a picnic the same year. Nowhere in the 230-page file are there references to his attendance at district committee meetings. It is inconceivable that Cvetic would tell the FBI of Quinn's involvement in the Civil Rights Congress, which operated mostly in the open, but not report on his attendance at secret party conclaves where the real work of the party was done.[17]

Quinn had known Cvetic from his visits to the UE's District 6 office to have documents copied. "I never thought much of him. He seemed kind of a mousy guy, always sort of creeping around. And then there was that movie, *I Was a Communist for the FBI*," Quinn added sarcastically. "Spies running through the plants, and people chasing them. The guy who played Cvetic in the movie [Frank Lovejoy] was six-two, a big handsome guy." Quinn laughed. "Cvetic was a little mousy guy." Even so, people listened to him in 1950. On March 19, Cvetic spoke to more than twelve hundred Westinghouse employees at East Pittsburgh High School in an event set up by the IUE. On a tape recording of the meeting, one can hear enthusiastic applause when Cvetic is introduced by a CIO official. Many Westinghouse workers wanted to get out from under what they felt was the UE's Communist yoke.[18]

Father Rice, hovering on the sidelines throughout the election campaign, gave advice to the IUE when asked and commented on the contest in his weekly column. In one column he charged that "the old bankrupt and Communist-ridden UE has served the workers in the electrical industry poorly indeed and allowed them to slip below other workers in average hourly earnings, pensions, and other benefits." This was not true, but Rice seemed almost desperate to dip his oar in the water.

His relationship with Local 601 had changed since the days when he formulated strategy for a disorganized band of anti-Communists. Some of the old right-wing leaders, including Charles Copeland, Mike Fitzpatrick (Tom's brother), and Rice's assistant, John Duffy, still commanded the local effort. Bill Peeler, the man who testified against Quinn and other Progressives in August 1949, had become publicity director for IUE Local 601 and would play a key role in what happened to Harry Davenport. But the right-left fight in East Pittsburgh had risen far above a merely local affair. Second in size only to an eighteen-thousand-member local at GE's Schenectady, New York, plant, UE Local 601 was a prize that the IUE and the CIO needed to win. Both poured money and organizers into the race. Phil Murray assigned David J. McDonald, the Steelworkers secretary-treasurer, to raise money and round up organizers for the IUE effort across the country. He, too, would become involved in Harry's story.[19]

If Rice no longer operated on the inside of the anti-UE campaign, he continued to promote opposition within the Catholic Church. Pastors at parishes in East Pittsburgh, East Liberty, Turtle Creek, Braddock, and Pitcairn criticized the UE in sermons and church bulletins. At St. Joseph's in Braddock, a priest told parishioners, "Don't believe these punks who tell you Albert Fitzgerald [UE president] is a good Catholic—he is no more a Catholic than I am a Jewish rabbi." On the Sunday before the election, St. William's Church in East Pittsburgh, spiritual home of hundreds of Westinghouse workers, distributed a mimeographed attack on the UE as a "Godless conspiracy" and declared that "it is not lawful for Catholics to support a Communist enterprise, even if it appears a temporary good will thereby be procured."[20]

Up to April, Harry Davenport had managed to stay clear of the conflict, viewing it from a distance as he carried out his congressional duties in Washington. But things were about to change. With the election slated for April 27, the two unions appeared to be running neck and neck. Scrambling for every possible advantage, they turned to endorsements from public officials. These were of dubious value because union members did not like to be told by outsiders which union they should choose to represent them. In a close race, however, a big name might nudge a few undecided votes into the endorsee's column. The IUE had an overwhelming edge in this game. Because of Murray's influence, President Truman, secretary of labor Dan Tobin, and air force secretary W. Stuart

Symington voiced support for the IUE. The UE could not put up matching endorsements. No politician of sound mind would attach his or her
name to the UE's cause with Joe McCarthy scouring the news for names
of prominent Commie lovers to investigate. Understanding this very
well, the UE actually urged prolabor congressmen in western Pennsylvania to remain neutral. They themselves would soon face tough election
contests, said a UE newsletter, "and we do not want them to weaken their
chances by taking a partisan position in the NLRB election, even though
there is plenty of reason for UE to rightfully claim their full support."[21]

The UE was offering congressmen a free pass to avoid taking an
action that would be of dubious value to begin with. It was doubly ironic, then, that Uncle Harry, despite all his efforts, suddenly found himself
on dangerous ground.

From the time Cvetic first told his story to the *Pittsburgh Press,* Harry
could feel a noose tightening around his political hopes and ambitions. Buried deep in the story is a disclosure by Cvetic that in 1948 the
Communist Party had organized a "smear attack" on John McDowell
when Harry sought his congressional seat. CPUSA officials felt "that if
nothing else was accomplished in western Pennsylvania, we had done a
good job if we could defeat McDowell," Cvetic is quoted as saying.
Harry's name is not mentioned, but the implication that he benefited
from the CPUSA campaign was the stuff out of which classic guilt-by-asso-
ciation cases were woven. To make matters worse, a well-known Pittsburgh Communist confirmed the story in a *Daily Worker* column,
declaring, "The Communist Party is indeed proud to declare that we contributed our modest share in achieving McDowell's defeat."[22]

The possibility that all hell could break loose made Harry skittish and
more determined to stay as far away from the UE-IUE fight as possible.
But in April came a call that he had dreaded. A UE official asked Harry
to meet with a committee regarding the NLRB campaign. Harry reluctantly invited the group, named the Defend UE Committee, to his Pittsburgh office. It would do no good to antagonize them by refusing to
meet. A group including Tom Quinn arrived at the appointed time.
Harry greeted them in a businesslike manner, not offering to shake
hands with his one-time friend. But as far as Quinn was concerned,
Harry had terminated their friendship anyway. Once they had cam-

paigned together and talked far into the night about many things; now they had nothing to say to each other. A UE spokesman asked Harry to pledge that he would remain neutral in the election. He assured the committee that he would not get involved. The group departed believing they had his word on the matter.

As the campaign entered its final weeks, the Defend UE Committee visited Harry again on April 13. This time they showed him a leaflet distributed by the IUE, listing his name among a number of prominent people who had agreed to appear on an IUE radio program. The leaflet bore the name of the IUE's publicity director, Bill Peeler. Expressing surprise and anger, Harry immediately telephoned the IUE and, with the UE delegation sitting in his office, "bawled out Peeler," as the committee later reported in a bulletin to members, for using his name. Harry also put out a news release declaring his neutrality. He was interested, he said, "solely in supporting progressive legislation for the welfare of all the people, including all the trade union members of my district." The response satisfied UE leaders. That was the Harry Davenport they had helped put in office.[23]

Three days later, UE leaders tuned into the IUE's evening radio broadcast and were startled to hear Harry denouncing the UE and endorsing the rival union. I searched newspaper coverage of the 1950 NLRB campaign but came up with nothing to shed light on why he did it. Harry's story had been lost in the general hubbub. Memos distributed by the Defend UE Committee, now on file in the UE Archives, report on Harry's endorsement of the IUE. But they do not explain his change of mind. There seemed no rational reason why he would break his word, knowing that such an action would sever all chances of retaining any UE support for his reelection campaign. Finally, I remembered the provocative comment of John Connelly regarding Harry's refusal to endorse David Lawrence as the Democratic nominee for mayor over Harry's friend Eddie Leonard and Lawrence's retribution. Interviewing Connelly again by phone, I confirmed that he was referring to what happened during the Westinghouse election campaign in 1950. Lawrence was at the center of it.

There is no evidence that Lawrence was a rabid anti-Communist. In 1951 he would show considerable courage in appearing at a public hearing on behalf of an assistant district attorney, Marjorie Matson, who was accused by Cvetic and the Pennsylvania attorney general of having "Communistic associations." Lawrence's testimony would help clear her of charges and prevent her dismissal. But if Lawrence had no deep interest in the union rivalry at Westinghouse, he knew that it was of great importance to his friends Murray and Father Rice. Further, ever since Murray had gone to Lawrence's aid in 1949 during the primary battle with Leonard, Lawrence had taken care to maintain his alliance with Murray and the CIO.[24]

As Connelly remembered it, Lawrence called Harry in April 1950 and told him to endorse the IUE. The implicit threat was that if Harry refused, he would lose Lawrence's backing for reelection in 1950. Harry would have trouble winning in his Republican district even with the help of the Democratic Party, and he would certainly lose if the party quietly opposed him. "Lawrence was the absolute power," Connelly said. "If he told ward chairmen to cut Harry, they wouldn't get the votes out. He told Harry what to do and Harry had to do it." That is, if he wanted to remain a congressman, as Harry did.

According to Connelly, Murray and Lawrence "forced Harry to get in the middle" of the UE-IUE battle. "If he'd been allowed to sit on the sidelines and let the unions fight it out, he may not have been affected so badly. But Phil Murray and Dave Lawrence pushed him right to the front because the union was in his district. The man was torn terribly. They burnt his bridges." Connelly did not necessarily mean that Murray personally descended into the political pits to put pressure on one relatively unimportant congressman. But someone must have approached Lawrence, and Uncle Harry thought he knew who it was.[25]

In 1967, more than thirty years before I started on this book, I had my one and only conversation with Harry about his failed reelection bid in 1950. He was in a talkative mood that day, and he told me the following story, sardonic and dipped in bitterness. In the spring of 1950, the Steelworkers' Dave McDonald called Harry's office in Washington and told a secretary that he wanted to recommend a woman for a job on Harry's staff. Without consulting Harry but speaking for him, the secretary said there was no job. McDonald, known for his vindictiveness, was in a position to retaliate. Acting as Murray's surrogate on political matters and as his deputy in the IUE campaign, McDonald told Lawrence that Davenport should be driven into the fold. Lawrence assumed the demand came from Murray and complied.

"Lawrence told me to issue a public statement denouncing the UE," Harry said in our 1967 conversation. "I argued with him, but . . ." Harry made a helpless gesture. "If I wanted Democratic organization support, I had no choice. So I appeared at an IUE rally and said, 'The UE is controlled by the puppets of Moscow.'" He added, with a bitter grin, "And all because McDonald wanted to place a friend on my staff." Harry forgot to mention his part in the radio broadcast, but a newspaper story confirmed his presence at the IUE rally on April 16.[26]

A partially confirming account is given by Bill Peeler, the IUE publicity chairman, who lined up speakers for IUE rallies and radio programs. In a 1977 oral history interview, Peeler recalled asking Davenport to appear in support of the IUE. When Harry refused, Peeler insisted. "I said, 'You'll speak.' He said, 'No, I won't.' We called Davey Lawrence and Davey Lawrence called somebody, I don't know who he was . . . and poor Davenport come and beg for time to speak. Well, I'd made out the program. I said, 'How long you want to speak?' He said, 'I'll speak about fifty.' I said, 'I'll give you five minutes, period.' And he got up and said, 'Any red-blooded American should speak out against Communism, and so on.' So then he lost the election, the next election. He got wiped out."[27]

Both stories could contain elements of truth, and Lawrence could have heard from both Peeler and McDonald. Whatever the case, Harry Davenport reversed course and stabbed in the back the very people who had done most to get him elected. The UE committee that had asked Harry to remain neutral reported his reversal in a daily briefing. "After assuring two UE delegations of his complete neutrality, Congressman Harry Davenport has come out for the company union," the memo says. The memo writer apparently spoke with Harry and reports him as saying, "Those Republicans are right-wing fakers, but me—I'm a left-wing faker."[28]

The quote sounds authentic. In later years, I occasionally heard Harry utter similar self-deprecatory remarks. He did not delude himself that he had acted appropriately. He had set out to be independent but found himself enmeshed in organization politics. In the end, Harry became the ultimate organization man. And yet his endorsement of the IUE was such a minor development that no newspaper mentioned it except the *Daily Worker*. In a sense Harry was used up and thrown away by the Democratic organization in the same way that HUAC dealt with Bob Whisner.

On April 27, 11,743 men and women voted in the NLRB election at East Pittsburgh: a 90 percent turnout of 13,035 eligible workers. And in the end, despite four months of histrionics, hyperbole, character assassinations, false charges, and appeals to patriotism, Local 601 was still hewn down the middle as near to perfectly as a democratic vote can be. Only 100 votes separated the two unions, the IUE emerging with 5,763 votes; the UE, 5,663; and "no union," 170. An examination of 147 challenged ballots still failed to produce an absolute majority for either union. In a runoff election on June 1, the IUE increased its margin of victory to 258, amassing 51 percent of the total vote.

A detailed analysis of voting patterns by Ronald Schatz indicates several general trends. Catholic workers and the less skilled and lower paid were more likely to vote for the IUE; the more skilled and highly paid workers tended to choose the UE. The IUE vote was helped by the statements of Turtle Creek Valley priests, the CIO's expulsion of the UE, and the "general public antipathy toward Communism." The company's preference for the IUE and the support of the Truman administration may also have swayed some votes. As Quinn saw it, given the Cvetic allegations, the general Red-baiting atmosphere, and the resources committed to the campaign by the CIO, it was surprising that the IUE won by so few votes. However it happened, thirteen years after the UE came to East Pittsburgh it was ousted as the bargaining agent for Westinghouse workers.[29]

In all NLRB elections at Westinghouse plants in the first half of 1950, the IUE and other unions took forty thousand members away from the UE, leaving the latter with about fifteen thousand. By the end of the 1950s, after further union raids, only 20 percent of Westinghouse's production workers would belong to the UE. A three-way split among the IUE, UE, and International Brotherhood of Electrical Workers had severely weakened union bargaining leverage, a result that Westinghouse, acting alone and setting up nonunion plants in the South, might not have achieved for another decade. The UE was not pushed completely out of the Turtle Creek Valley. In June, UE loyalists managed to beat off an election challenge at Local 610, representing workers at the Air Brake plant in Wilmerding and Union Switch and Signal in Swissvale. But by late 1950, the national UE was in deep trouble, having lost about 152,000 members throughout the electrical industry to the IUE and other rivals.[30]

Historians have found all parties at fault for the CIO purge, election battles, and loss of bargaining power. The larger effects would not become visible for several years. But it was already clear in 1950 that the CIO unions and the UE had injured themselves in the public eye. By banging each other around the two sides had aided their antiunion enemies enormously and contributed to a growing public suspicion that unions were irrelevant in a capitalist society that from the beginning had merely tolerated unions in the same way the body tolerates a carbuncle.

The threat now facing Congressman Davenport contained a vicious irony. Of all the factors that influenced the union election in East Pittsburgh, his denunciation of the UE probably came nearest to having no effect. Yet it may have ended his congressional career.

13

DEATH OF A CONGRESSMAN

HEN it was all over and Uncle Harry had returned to Mc-Keesport a defeated man, he began writing a book about his experiences in Washington. He was living with Grandmother Davenport at the McKeesporter Hotel when I first saw him after his election loss in November 1950. Home from college for a weekend, I found Harry working at a small coffee table in the apartment he shared with his mother. Wearing a crisp white shirt with cufflinks and tie, he might have been awaiting a bell summoning him to the House chamber for a vote. Papers, magazines, and books were scattered across the couch, and sheets of paper filled with his handwriting lay on the coffee table. As we shook hands, he made a bemused inspection of this college student he had known as a wailing toddler on a cross-country drive in 1932. We exchanged a few words. I had no idea what to say to a man who had just fallen to earth after a dizzying flirtation with prominence. Uncle Harry probably sensed my awkwardness. Sitting down, he picked up his papers and stacked them carefully, this side, that side, and informed me breezily that he was writing a book.

Death of a Congressman was the name Harry had given to his work in progress, obviously borrowing the idea from Arthur Miller's acclaimed *Death of a Salesman*, first produced on Broadway in 1949. Harry's choice reflected more than a desire to hitch a ride on Miller's fame. The title carried echoes of the bitterness and failure of a Willy Loman, Miller's aging salesman so contemptuously discarded by a materialistic society. But I got the impression that Harry had more in mind than blaming his downfall on America's warped political values. He thought he had the goods on specific people and would bring them to account in a drama alternately scorching and comedic. All memoirs and autobiographies are self-serving to some degree, and so Harry's would have been. But if he had written honestly, he might have set down a powerful, even tragic, story of a left-liberal congressman so intimidated by the anti-Communist ethos that he was driven to the political center, if not beyond, causing him to abandon friends, supporters, and principles. There were many others like him in the Eighty-first Congress, but Harry stands out in this respect because he retreated farther and faster than most on a very slippery track.

To follow Harry's voting record in his second year in Congress is to watch a man far out in front of the pack suddenly reverse field and race toward the opposite goal line. At the beginning of 1949 he had been one among a bumptious crop of freshmen representatives, sometimes referred to as the Fair Deal congressmen because they generally supported President Harry Truman's economic and social-welfare programs. Like so many other freshmen classes they entered Congress with what they believed was a mandate, in their case to pull the nation moderately to the left. The agenda included repeal of the poll tax and the Taft-Hartley Act, establishment of a fair employment practices commission to attack racial discrimination in hiring, passage of an antilynching law, a cutback in the power and free-wheeling authority of investigative committees such as HUAC, and reform of House legislative practices that enabled high-seniority Southern Democrats to control important committees. Initial successes on legislative reform were quickly followed by close defeats on issues such as the poll tax and Taft-Hartley repeal. Around the middle of 1949, Republicans and conservative Democrats regained the upper hand, bashing Truman and his followers over Soviet aggression, the Communist takeover of China, and the perceived threat of Communist spying and sabotage in the United States. The Red Scare intensified in the 1950 session with the emergence of Joe McCarthy and the outbreak of the Korean War in June.

In the face of these developments all but a very few liberal Democrats in the Eighty-first Congress retreated on a wide front, abandoning even the civil-liberties bastion that Harry and others had occupied in early 1949. Harry signaled his 1950 turnabout in a debate over authorizing $150,000 in expenditures for the Un-American Activities Committee. In 1949, he not only introduced a resolution to abolish HUAC, he was among thirty House members who opposed paying the committee's annual expenses. By March 1950, eighteen of that number had changed their minds, including Harry, who deliberately drew attention to his new support for HUAC in a speech on the floor. "Today," he said, "I believe it [HUAC] is serving a worthy function." He had spoken against the previous committee, he said, because it was led by men "who wanted to use their authority to sow fear and prejudice among the American people." In contrast, the current committee "is constituted of high-caliber men— persons of integrity, who are concerned with the national well-being." Such a dramatic change in the character of committee members has not been remarked by historians. The appropriations resolution passed, 348 to 12. Harry's western Pennsylvania colleague Frank Buchanan also shifted from opposition to support for the committee.[1]

In August, Tom Quinn came back into Harry's life, though not by Tom's choosing. HUAC asked the House to vote contempt citations against fifty-six persons who in 1949 had refused to testify regarding political associations or beliefs, citing the Fifth and First Amendments. Quinn was in this group, as were Tom Fitzpatrick, Frank Panzino, Jim Matles, and Julius Emspak of the UE. If cited by the House, the witnesses would be tried in a federal district court for contempt of Congress. The legal questions involved were whether witnesses could plead possible self-incrimination before legislative committees and, if so, what form the claim must take. The issue in these cases was not whether the witnesses were Communists but whether they had correctly asserted their constitutional rights. But such distinctions were lost at a time when GIs were dying in Korea.

Harry and most other members were mute during the opening debate. Only one representative, Vito Marcantonio, a member of the American Labor Party in New York and a perennial supporter of leftist causes, spoke in opposition to the committee's request. On the first case presented, the House voted, 373–1, in favor of contempt, Marcantonio dissenting. Thereafter, all other cases were decided by unrecorded voice votes. Harry did not have to register a vote against his former friends.

The proceedings took hours, and he probably left the floor of the House and tried to forget. When all cases had been disposed of, one exuberant Republican member could not restrain his glee. Referring to former HUAC critics (like Harry), the congressman chortled, "I saw them turn and like frightened children run away." The citations were forwarded to the Justice Department for prosecution.[2]

A final major challenge was thrust upon liberal Democrats in September. At least thirty-eight anti-Communist bills were introduced in the Eighty-first Congress, but the one that passed was among the toughest— and most unworkable. This was the Internal Security Act of 1950, known as the McCarran Act. It required the Communist Party and other organizations designated as subversive to register with the new Subversive Activities Control Board (SACB) and provide information about their activities and membership. It also restricted entry of suspected individuals into the United States and provided for the detention of potential spies and saboteurs in times of emergency. The bill passed by large margins, 51 to 7 in the Senate and 312 to 20 in the House, with Harry one of the majority. Truman vetoed the bill, noting that the registration requirement was like "requiring thieves to register with the sheriff." His action "flushed a little courage out of a handful of liberals," as one writer puts it. But still only 48 House members voted to uphold the veto. Harry, drained of political passion, lined up with 265 others who voted to override. "Though the liberals were obviously trying to protect themselves from appearing soft on Communism, their support for such a repressive piece of legislation gave additional legitimacy to Joe McCarthy and his cause," remarks historian Ellen Schrecker.

The McCarran Act was irreparably flawed. Whoever dared to come forward and register the Communist Party could be prosecuted under the Smith Act's provisions against advocating overthrow of the government. To register would be coerced self-incrimination. Government and party lawyers fought over the issue for years before the Supreme Court settled the matter in 1964, letting stand a lower-court ruling that nobody could be required to commit a self-incriminatory act. Neither the Communist Party nor any other organization was ever registered with the SACB, but it nonetheless would pose a severe threat to the UE before being abolished in 1973. In the meantime, national-security concerns were placed above the Constitution. The McCarran Act, as one historian says, "reflected a war mentality that equated dissent with treason."[3]

As the remains of the congressional session drained into the election season, Harry Davenport was a shrunken political figure. He had turned himself inside out in accommodating to the political climate, compromising deeply held beliefs, including freedom of speech and association, that he had once held inviolate. He could cite few positive accomplishments and would have a hard time running on credible and hopeful programs of social equality and labor reform.

When I began searching for newspaper coverage of Harry's election campaign in 1950, I discovered why he had vanished so completely from the history of that time. In the fall of 1950, all three Pittsburgh dailies were shut down for forty-seven days by a strike extending from early October to mid-November. The mailers union, representing workers who bundled papers coming off the presses, rejected a wage offer made by an association negotiating for the three publishers. The papers then halted all operations, idling workers represented by nine other unions. Except for a small substitute paper published during part of this period by the unions, news was blacked out in Pittsburgh for a month and a half, covering the most critical time of a political campaign, as well as the election itself. Local television news had not yet appeared, and the interim union paper published little more than headlines and news highlights. The daily papers, resuming publication on November 18, chose not to recapitulate the two-week-old election news. As a result, the public never knew why Harry was turned out of Congress.[4]

On November 7, a Republican named Harmar Denny Jr. beat Harry Davenport by nearly 5,900 votes, 54,076 to 48,198, according to the official tabulation. Unable to follow the campaign in news accounts, I must rely on a mixture of conjecture and the recollections of Quinn and others to infer what happened. Harry's opponent, Harmar Denny, was no John McDowell. Much to Harry's benefit, McDowell had stirred up anger and resentment in the Jewish, African American, labor, and liberal communities. Denny, a sixty-four-year-old lawyer, was a moderate Republican who aroused little passion. His name may have been his biggest asset: he had served as the city's director of public safety, and his great-grandfather had been the first mayor of Pittsburgh.[5]

Several factors contributed to Harry's defeat. Perhaps most important, the UE's formidable political apparatus in the Twenty-ninth Congressional District stopped functioning when the IUE took over Local 601. In the fall of 1950 the IUE was focused inward, with local officials busily running against one another in the local's first election of officers. It did not have a Tom Quinn organizing a get-out-the-vote effort. The UE endorsed neither Davenport nor Denny. Quinn and his friends, however, regarded Harry as something akin to a traitor, and they did their best to make good on Quinn's vow to turn him out of office. They conducted a word-of-mouth campaign among loyal UE members, urging them to switch their vote from Davenport to Denny. "It wasn't hard to beat Harry in 1950," Quinn told me. All it took was for the UE to actively do nothing while the IUE passively did nothing. "They didn't have a campaign structure to help him, if that's what their intention was," Quinn said.

David Lawrence may have had a hand in Harry's defeat, if only by withdrawing organization support. According to John Connelly, Lawrence was annoyed by Harry's independent streak. Moreover, a rumor has circulated in the Davenport family for years that Lawrence turned against Harry because of his "behavior" in Washington. If Quinn had heard tales of Harry's drinking, Lawrence undoubtedly did as well. He detested excessive drinking; his wife had turned to alcohol for solace after two of the Lawrences' sons died in a car accident in 1942. The relationship between the Lawrences never recovered. "He thought liquor was the curse of politics," said James Knox, a longtime Democratic office-holder in Allegheny County who served with Lawrence on the county Democratic Committee. When I talked to Knox in 2000, he retained a vivid memory of Harry Davenport, but he had forgotten the specifics of Harry's election loss in 1950. "I knew he liked a drink," Knox said, "but I never saw him drunk or out of control. If he had been out of control, Lawrence would have been after him."[6]

Whether Lawrence deliberately withdrew Democratic backing from Harry could not be determined a half century after the elections. County Democratic records were destroyed in a fire. The vote results show that Harry lost support in every quarter but one, the African American community, or more precisely the newspaper that served that community. The *Pittsburgh Courier* again endorsed Harry. "Davenport has been one of the greatest fighters in Congress for the minorities," the paper said a few days before the election. "As an example, he fought hard for the Fair Employment Practices Bill, fought against the poll tax and battled for the

anti-lynching law." Furthermore, Harry had "personally called on president Truman and told him that 'the war in Korea makes the enactment
of civil rights laws urgent'" because "Negro boys" were serving in Korea.
Harry also promised to appoint a "Pittsburgh Negro boy" to Annapolis if
he was reelected.[7]

Given Harry's ability to publicize himself, the news blackout probably
hurt him more than Denny. How the campaign progressed is not known.
Whether Denny branded Harry a fellow traveler for proposing to abolish
HUAC or how Harry explained his shift to the right or what new promises he made to the voters—none of this is part of recorded history. Without the UE's efforts to get members to the polls, voter turnout in the
Twenty-ninth dropped from the 71 percent of 1948 to 59 percent. The
decline in Harry's labor support shows up starkly in vote results for Swissvale, the home of Union Switch and Signal and of many UE members.
He won the town by an eleven-hundred-vote plurality in 1948, but 11
percent fewer residents went to the polls in 1950 and gave Harry only a
one-hundred-vote edge. In Pittsburgh's key Fourteenth Ward, where liberal and Jewish backing lifted Harry to a twenty-nine-hundred-vote win
over McDowell in 1948, residents rejected Harry's reelection by nearly
sixteen hundred votes.

The 1950 elections exacted a large toll on Democrats nationwide.
The party lost twenty-eight seats in the House of Representatives and five
in the Senate. Effective control of both houses passed to a conservative
coalition made up of Republicans and Southern Democrats. And so
ended all chances of passing anti-poll-tax, nondiscrimination, and other
civil-rights and social-welfare legislation and of repealing the worst provisions of the Taft-Hartley Act. Harry Truman's Fair Deal had fallen victim to an irrational fear of domestic Communism as portrayed by HUAC.
That fear was manifested in several congressional races; two stand out.
Richard Nixon in California employed Red-baiting tactics to defeat
Helen Gahagan Douglas for a Senate seat (both had been in the House).
As Walter Goodman points out, she had been one of HUAC's most persistent critics. Vito Marcantonio, "the *most* persistent critic," was beaten
by an alliance of Democrats and Republicans in the East Harlem district
he had represented for eight terms. Republican leaders ascribed their
party's victory to Truman's "coddling of Communists at home and
appeasement of Russia and Communist China abroad." The Communist
issue had gutted Truman's legislative agenda, just as it had pushed the

CIO to wound itself mortally by expelling unions representing a fifth of its membership.[8]

So ended Uncle Harry's cruelest year. He had waited twenty years to get onstage, and he had leaped high—but oh so briefly—before tumbling back to earth under political gravity's unforgiving pull. He would blame his downfall in part on David Lawrence, but Lawrence did not force him to endorse the IUE after he had pledged neutrality or to vote for the contempt citations and the Internal Security Act. Harry would try unsuccessfully over the years to make a comeback. But no matter how he turned, twisted, weaved, and stumbled around the stage, he would never again find the spotlight.

Harry, Tom, and Father Rice had collided at a political crossing backlit with flashes from clashing ideologies and demagogic comets. Each wounded in his own way, the three went limping down different paths. The rest of their lives would turn on the pivotal events of those Cold War battles at the end of the 1940s. Time, after all, does not heal all wounds.

When Quinn's three-year leave of absence from Westinghouse expired in the summer, he left the UE staff and returned to his old welding job in the plant. He had little hope now of moving up in the union. With the loss of thousands of members, the UE reduced staff in the Pittsburgh region. The IUE had far more members, dealt with more employers, and by the strength of numbers took over the lead union role in labor relations on a company-wide basis at Westinghouse. Back in the plant, Quinn found himself in a distinctly unfriendly environment. Company officials and local IUE leaders viewed him as a hard-core UE loyalist and therefore an unwelcome troublemaker. Nonetheless, Quinn and scores of other UE activists refused to pay dues to the IUE. Having poured much of their lives into UE Local 601, they felt that disbanding it would be to repudiate everything they and their predecessors had accomplished since 1937. So Quinn, Tom Fitzpatrick, and other Progressives kept UE Local 601 intact. It had no official standing with Westinghouse but continued to exist as a shadow union, holding regular meetings, electing officers, and laying plans to seek another representation election in a year or two.

Through the fall of 1950, Quinn held onto that hope even as his personal situation grew worse. In November, he was indicted by a federal grand jury in Washington for contempt of Congress, and a trial date was set for early 1951. By the end of 1950, Quinn's life was in turmoil. His local union existed only as a shell, the parent UE was in deep distress and threatened by more congressional investigations, and Quinn would go on trial for refusing to answer questions that he felt never should have been asked.

Father Rice, meanwhile, was withdrawing gradually from the anti-Communist battles that had consumed him for four years. In his columns and radio broadcasts, he continued to inveigh against Communists and to cheer on government investigators and prosecutors who bore down on the Communist Party and leftist unions from all sides. But his life changed in significant ways. Because of disagreements with a new administration at Duquesne University, Rice resigned as director of the Management-Labor Institute. Bishop Hugh C. Boyle, who had allowed Rice such latitude in carrying out his political and labor activities, died in 1950 and was succeeded by John Dearden. Rice requested a transfer from the House of Hospitality, where he had served since 1940, and in 1951 Dearden moved Rice to a parish in the Hill District. In 1952, he would be reassigned again as pastor of a parish in Natrona, Pennsylvania, a small town on the Allegheny River north of Pittsburgh. His column in the *Pittsburgh Catholic* would be discontinued when the diocese acquired the paper in 1954. None of these changes necessarily implied that Rice had fallen into disfavor with the Church hierarchy, although he sometimes talked (perhaps boasted) of being "exiled." He wrote articles occasionally, continued his weekly radio program, and remained a union advocate.[9]

After a life swirling with activity and controversy, Rice entered a strange, quiet period, metaphorically akin to hibernation. In 1958 he would be transferred to a larger parish in Washington, Pennsylvania, or Little Washington, as it is called, about thirty miles south of Pittsburgh. It would be another half decade before he reinvigorated his political life in another arena. Then it would become clear that although he had finished his anti-Communist crusading in the early fifties, that period of his life had not finished with him.

The 1950 term of the Eighty-first Congress stretched out longer than usual, keeping Harry and his defeated Democratic colleagues employed as sitting lame ducks through the end of the year, as if providing a soft transition to early retirement. But there came a time when Harry had to wrap up his affairs, pack up his books, and say goodbye to all the little people, as John Connelly referred to them, who had served his drinks and shined his shoes and opened doors for him and who were sorry to see him leave. Connelly recalled Harry telling them, "Don't worry, I'll be back. I'll be back." And then, to the surprise of the Davenport family, Harry did not return to his wife and daughter in their elegant Fifth Avenue apartment in Pittsburgh but instead threaded his way back to his dusty hometown and settled in with Grandmother Davenport in her third-story apartment in the McKeesporter Hotel, with a view of the bus depot on Ringgold Street where mill workers lined up after shift change (and perhaps a shot and a beer) to catch a bus going up the hill to their homes on Sumac, Jenny Lind, and scores of other streets.

We soon learned that Harry had no loving wife waiting for him in Pittsburgh and had run out of money when his congressional salary ended. He had sold his interest in the *East Liberty Shopping News* while still in Congress and probably had disposed of other assets to cover the expenses of his last campaign and to support Mary and Peggy Ann in the apartment that Mary no longer wanted to share with him. In November 1950, shortly after Harry was voted out of office, she swore out a divorce complaint. Reading the complaint in 2003, I saw that their marriage had turned sour as early as 1946 when, according to Mary, Harry deserted her. The charge of desertion in a divorce petition apparently can be stretched to cover many situations. But if he did actually leave her, he had apparently returned by 1948, when he ran for Congress as a happily married family man. But there was no family life during his sojourn in Washington. In her divorce filing, Mary based her request on ritualized phraseology well known to Pennsylvania divorce courts. Harry, she said, had made "conditions intolerable and life burdensome" for her, causing her to suffer "indignities." The court documents do not specify details, nor do they contain any evidence that Harry contested either the divorce itself or Mary's claim of custody of their daughter. A judge would grant the divorce in August 1951. Mary and Peggy Ann moved away from Pittsburgh, and it is doubtful that Harry ever saw either again.[10]

I never dared ask Harry how a man could give up a five-year-old daughter, knowing he might never see her again. It was not natural. If my mother and her sisters knew the reason, they never told the rest of us. Harry was not a lovable or loving man, but he was not so cold hearted that he could dismiss the loss of his daughter with a shrug of his shoulders. Perhaps he expected to reenter her life after making a comeback of heroic proportions, which would wipe away the many mistakes he had made. Or, it may be that those ruinous two years in Washington, stumbling from pothole to pothole, events never letting up on him, a streak of bad luck and worse decisions, had mentally unhinged him. Connelly, who saw Harry on many occasions in later years, believed that he became "unstable" after leaving Washington. "He couldn't put together the fact [understand how it happened] that he had climbed to the top of the mountain and then slid right off."[11]

When he first returned to McKeesport, though, Harry acted like a normal guy who had experienced a personal catastrophe and was trying to get his life back on track. Grandmother Davenport's apartment was a convenient port, not least because he did not have to pay rent. My father and mother had invited Grandmother to live at the hotel rent-free because she had no income except the monthly checks that Uncle Eddie sent from Los Angeles for food and clothing. She was well into her seventies then, and Mother likely thought that Uncle Harry, while hardly a companion one would choose to assuage loneliness, could be of some help in looking after her. The apartment had a kitchen, living room, bedroom, and small dining area, where Harry stored his personal effects and slept on a daybed. In the summer of 1951, when I worked as a vacation replacement in National Tube's coupling shop, I spent a lot of time at the hotel, only a few minutes' walk from the mill's main gate. I would stop at the McKeesporter before and after each turn in the mill to do odd jobs for Mother or eat in the coffee shop or visit Grandmother and Harry. Thus I first came to know him as an adult.

Harry, along with Uncle Eddie, already had given me an important piece of advice about college. Having worked around newspapers most of their lives, both advised against majoring in journalism. If I could write, I could write, and I should not waste my time with courses on news and headline writing. It was more important to read extensively and steep myself in history, political science, philosophy, and literature. That was before I started my freshman year. When I told Harry I had followed his advice, he nodded approvingly and from then on talked frequently about books. He usually asked what I was reading on any given day and then he would suggest what I should be reading, mostly in the areas of political theory and history. "It's essential that you read so-and-so," he would say. "You must ground yourself in such and such." I would listen carefully and nod. But a young man who works rotating shifts in a steel mill in summertime has little appetite for reading *The Rise and Fall of the Roman Empire* on his days off. Besides, I was in a fiction-reading phase that year.

I was grateful for Harry's attention. He also helped another nephew, Ben Bast, the son of Mother's older sister Kate and two years younger than I. Ben had developed a keen interest in politics at McKeesport High School, and as a star member of the debating team had learned how to rip opponents' arguments to shreds. He was not shy about using this ability to ridicule other kids, including me, who bent their minds only to sports. Uncle Harry recognized Ben's interests and in 1950 obtained an appointment for him as a congressional page while Ben attended Georgetown University on a scholarship. It was a marvelous opportunity for Ben, and he returned to McKeesport with even more authority to criticize us apolitical Davenports. I never saw much of Ben after about 1953. He and his wife, Doreen, went to Guam to study and teach at the University of Guam. Ben become a specialist in Russian history and wrote for scholarly journals. He probably could have given me insights about Harry's last year in Congress, but he died shortly after I started research for this book.

For quite a while Harry worked on *Death of a Congressman.* Another of my cousins, Mary Kate (Bast) Gillespie, Ben's older sister, recalled seeing Harry clad in a silk robe, scribbling away at the kitchen table in Grandmother's apartment. Either from shyness or lack of interest, no one questioned the McKeesporter's writer in residence about his progress. I got up enough nerve to ask how it was going only once. Harry avoided a direct answer. Instead, with a wry smile he said he had decided who should play the lead male character when Hollywood adapted his book for the screen. His choice was Edward Everett Horton, a well-known character actor in film comedies of the thirties and forties who often played well-intentioned, droll, and ineffective gentlemen caught in sticky situations. Horton was marvelous at portraying a misunderstood man of principle, Harry said, and looked to me for comment. I was stuck in that awkward place between belief and disbelief and could only gulp in agreement. Even if Harry was joking, the choice of actors revealed something of his state of mind. He could have picked Gregory Peck, say, as his alter ego but instead had reached far down in the ranks of supporting actors to come up with Edward Everett Horton, who, as Harry saw himself, displayed wit and good grace when he stumbled innocently and comically into bad places.[12]

On the whole Harry behaved very well while living at the McKeesporter. He only occasionally loafed in the two hotel bars, preferring instead to do his drinking in the numerous other taverns and saloons that lined Fifth Avenue and other downtown streets of McKeesport in those days. He enjoyed spending time in workingmen's saloons, engaging honest-to-God soft-cap workers in political conversations. One of my oldest grade school friends, Ruth Ann (Baird) Molloy, recalled that her father, Howard "Red" Baird, an electrician at National Tube who loved to talk politics over a beer or two, would bring home an impressive-looking man late at night, and they would sit around the kitchen table, drinking and talking. Her father always addressed the visitor as Senator. That was my uncle. He and Red Baird had probably known each other as young men in the McKeesport of thirty years before.[13]

Harry would stroll around town, always dressed in a suit and tie, his nose in a book, making people flow around him on busy sidewalks, just as he had as a teenager. Occasionally, my sister would encounter him as she window-shopped on Fifth Avenue with high school friends. Suddenly Uncle Harry would be looming in front of her. He must have seen her coming around the edges of his book. He would come to a sudden stop, give a deep formal bow, and sweep his hat across his waist. "How do you do, Miss Hoerr," he would say with a mocking grin. "My friends thought he was a little crazy, and I was embarrassed," Lynn recalled.[14]

Harry was forty-eight years old when he moved in with Grandmother at the McKeesporter. I am sure he told her and my mother that he intended to stay only long enough to begin the next phase of his life. This seemed perfectly reasonable, especially since he was writing a book, or so it seemed. After a while the temporary stay lengthened into weeks, then months, then years. After he arrived at the hotel, I finished two more years of schooling, worked through two summers, graduated from college, went into the army—and still Uncle Harry was staying at the McKeesporter. My sister and I never heard Mother complain about him getting a free ride. But the longer he stayed, the more Mother's and her sisters' respect for him diminished. In their world it was not common for a grown man to give up working simply because a job or a business disappeared. Their own husbands each had lost jobs or suffered business failures during the Depression, and each had taken whatever work he could get and hauled himself back up the ladder.

Although Uncle Harry was not a young man, he possessed skills that could be used by many employers. He knew everything there was to know about the ad business, he could write, he could advise municipalities on the care and handling of retail business; under the sobriquet "former Congressman Davenport" he might have worked as a front man or lobbyist for any number of companies. Or, he could have sold shoes or suits or clerked in a confectionary store or worked as an adjunct lecturer on politics and political science. He did none of these things; as far as I know, he never applied for a "regular job," as we ordinary mortals called earning a living. He was writing his book, he said. Every now and then he would travel to Pittsburgh or Washington, probably on money borrowed from his brother, to establish or retain political contacts. Occasionally he earned a bit of money as a political publicist or consultant. For a few months one year he ran a campaign (a losing one, as it turned out) for a Republican running for mayor of McKeesport. What Harry was really trying to do was position himself for a comeback, probably one in which he could contend with the man he viewed as responsible for his downfall, David Lawrence. But Harry had come to think of himself as a politician of national stature and had no interest in becoming, say, a city councilman doubling as sewage commissioner. It would have been hard to rise above that level as a Democrat in western Pennsylvania with Lawrence controlling the party organization. Harry's dreams were never more than dreams.

And so Harry stayed on at the hotel, reading as always. After a while it became clear that the writing of *Death of a Congressman* had come to a halt. I have no idea when or why he stopped working on it. Or maybe he never did. Perhaps he was still scribbling passages on scraps of paper and in the flyleaves of books up to the day he died in Ulrich's Hotel in Millvale. If so, the housekeeper discarded the manuscript, or whatever he was writing on. There were no papers found after his death.

In August 1953 I was inducted into the army. Before boarding the bus on Fifth Avenue for a long ride with other draftees to Fort Meade, Maryland, I ran upstairs in the hotel to say goodbye to Grandmother and Uncle Harry. Apparently she had gone out because Harry opened the

door, spiffy as usual in a shirt and tie, carrying a book with a finger mark-
ing the page he had been reading. He seemed impatient with my intrusion. Softening a little when I said goodbye, he wished me good luck and
said, dryly, "I suppose you'll turn out to be a nice guy like your father."

What a strange thing to say. Words like that one does not forget.
Knowing that Uncle Harry had liked and respected my father, I took his
comment partly as a compliment. But the way he said it implied that he
did not see much intellectual value or profit in simply being a nice guy.
Later I would hear Harry make other double-edged remarks. I am not
sure he himself knew what he meant to convey. He was an intellectualized man who could not bring himself to display sincere affection. This
is the mark of someone who has been hurt deeply by someone or some
thing.

I t is a sad thing when a man betrays himself as Harry did. I believe he
was deeply committed to labor rights, civil liberties, and racial and
social equality. But he acted contrary to his own beliefs. Mulling over this
contradiction as I assembled his story, I remembered an incident that
occurred sometime in 1949, either in the summer or fall, when Congressman Harry Davenport came to McKeesport to visit his mother and
sisters.

Harry drove up from Washington in a rented limousine. I happened
to be at the McKeesporter Hotel when the long, black car pulled up at
the rear entrance on Ringgold Street, across from a bus stop where
dozens of people stood watching. The front door opened and out of the
driver's seat sprang a young African American chauffeur in a brown uni-
form with a high-necked jacket, britches, and knee-high boots. He put on
his peaked cap and opened the rear door. The congressman emerged
resplendent in a double-breasted tan suit, Panama hat, and two-tone
white and brown shoes. He twirled slowly, taking in the crowd at the bus
stop, then swept into the hotel. This scene taught me all I needed to
know, though I would not have phrased it this way then, about the minor
perquisites of minor power.

He was to have dinner at the hotel with several Davenport family members, including my mother, two of her sisters, Grandmother Davenport,
and a few nieces and nephews. While the chauffeur parked the limousine
in a nearby garage, the family greeted Harry with a flurry of hellos and

kisses. After a while we all went downstairs to the basement cocktail lounge where dinner would be served. Ralph, the head bartender, looking crisp and authoritative in a white shirt, bow tie, and bar apron, came out from behind the bar to greet the celebrity. When the black driver joined us, Ralph stiffened. "Not him!" he said, definitively shaking his head. "He's not eating in my lounge." An experienced, no-nonsense man in his fifties, he knew his turf and considered it his kingdom.

There was a conference in the doorway: Ralph, Mother, Aunt Annamae, Uncle Harry, assorted other family members. Uncle Harry did not have much to say, possibly because he did not want to create a scene. My mother, the hotel owner, and Aunt Annamae, the manager, did not put up much of a fight. Annamae was a pragmatist who would do what was necessary. Mother had never been confronted with such a decision. She was a good woman, but men had always ruled her world. She feared that Ralph would walk out and take the rest of the bartenders and waitresses with him. And she had never quite made up her mind about the race issue because she had never had to. The only black people she had ever known were housemaids. With a relatively small African American community in the 1940s, McKeesport was not a center of racial protests. I had never known of any black people who tried to rent a room or buy a meal at the hotel.

When I had a chance to speak, I argued that the driver should eat with us. But I was not assertive at the age of eighteen. Even as the son of the owner, I was unable to take command of the situation. Ralph turned away from me and said to Mother, "Absolutely not!"

The decision was made: the limousine driver would eat in the kitchen. I made a decision, too. I ate in the kitchen with him. The driver, a handsome guy in his midtwenties, urged me to go back to the family. "Don't let it worry you," he said. But he seemed to appreciate my presence. We talked about the weather, his drive up from Washington, baseball. The cook, an elderly white woman, served us herself, and we ate at a wooden table that she used as a chopping block, with butcher knives and meat cleavers dangling from hooks above us.

This is a painful memory. My family and I did not measure up to the test, and Harry, the fiery liberal congressman, would always seem something of a hypocrite to me after that. This may be unfair; it is possible that he did not object too strenuously because he did not want to cause trouble for my mother. If he had walked out with the driver, they might have gone hungry. No other white-owned McKeesport restaurant would have served a black man. As late as the 1960s, long after I left town, black people still could not eat in many McKeesport restaurants or drink in the bars. At the least Harry should have anticipated the problem and avoided subjecting the driver to this humiliation. Here was a man who had fought for racial equality at least since the early forties. But too often when his deepest beliefs came into conflict with the even more basic urge to put himself on display, the latter won out.

◄ Portrait of Harry
Davenport, ca. 1946–1949.
Credit: Harris and Ewing
(Hoerr family files).

▼ In September 1932, Harry Davenport (right) accompanied his sister Alyce
Hoerr; her two-year-old son, John; and her husband, John (taking the picture), on
a cross-country automobile trip from Long Beach, California, to McKeesport,
Pennsylvania. Hoerr family files.

▲ The George Westinghouse Bridge in the 1930s, looking up the Turtle Creek Valley (right). Beyond the bridge is the Westinghouse Electric plant. East Pittsburgh lies on the hillside behind the plant and atop the hill (left). The creek runs under the second arch from left. Carnegie Library of Pittsburgh.

▶ David Lawrence (left), candidate for mayor of Pittsburgh, and Harry Davenport (right) meet with New York Mayor Fiorello LaGuardia to look over New York's rebuilding plans in August 1945. Copyright *Pittsburgh Post-Gazette*, all rights reserved. Reprinted with permission.

WESTINGHOUSE MEMORIAL BRIDGE

▼ The Davenport family at Harry's wedding reception, 1943. Left to right, Harry's sisters and brothers-in-law: John and Alyce Hoerr, Ben and Kate Bast, Harry and Annamae Osterman. At extreme right is Margaret Davenport, Harry's mother. Harry is second from right, and his wife, Mary, is on his right. The two couples in the middle of the picture were family friends. Hoerr family files.

▲ Harry and his brother, Eddie, a Los Angeles councilman, pose for a picture with Hollywood celebrities, ca. 1945–1949. Eddie Davenport, third from left, has his hand in his pocket; Dan Dailey, a singer and dancer, is next to Eddie; Harry Davenport is on the far right; and the others are unknown. Hoerr family files.

▶ Irene and Tom Quinn, walking on Fifth Avenue, Pittsburgh, 1938. Quinn family files.

▲ President Harry Truman (front, center) with Democratic congressional candidates, September 17, 1946. Harry Davenport is the second from the right in the third row. Immediately in front of Harry is Congressman Frank Buchanan of McKeesport (white hair). From the files of James W. Knox and used with his permission.

▲ John L. Lewis (left), first president of the CIO and head of the United Mine Workers, and Father Rice at the first CIO convention in 1938. Rice Collection.

▼ Left to right: Tom Quinn, Frank Panzino, Bob Whisner, and Tom Fitzpatrick pose on the steps of the Old House Office Building in Washington in August 1949 during hearings held by the House Un-American Activities Committee. *UE News* Photograph Collection.

▲ Father Rice addressing a radio audience in 1946. Rice Collection.

▲ In December 1945, thousands of UE Local 601 members attended a mass rally at Turtle Creek High School stadium and voted to go on strike unless Westinghouse

met their demands for a two-dollar-a-day wage increase. When negotiations failed, the union conducted a four-month national strike against Westinghouse. *UE News* Photograph Collection.

▲ A rally outside Westinghouse Electric, East Pittsburgh, during the 1946 strike. *UE News* Photograph Collection.

▼ Strikers parade past the Westinghouse Electric plant (left) on Braddock Avenue in East Pittsburgh in 1946. *UE News* Photograph Collection.

▲ Harry Davenport (right) campaigning for Congress in 1948. Francis J. Myers, Democratic senator from Pennsylvania, is speaking as Harry awaits his turn. Hoerr family files.

▶ Tom Quinn standing outside his home in East Pittsburgh in the mid-to-late 1940s when he worked at Westinghouse Electric. Quinn family files.

▼ Quinn family at a swimming pool in the Pittsburgh area, ca. 1952. From left on bench: Tom, Steve, Irene, Chuck. Ron is in front. Quinn family files.

▲ Left to right: Pittsburgh mayor David L. Lawrence (profile); Father Benjamin Masse; Phil Murray, president of the CIO and the United Steelworkers; and Father Rice at a communion breakfast in 1952. Rice Collection.

◀ Father Rice (right) and Byrd Brown, president of the Pittsburgh NAACP, appearing at a rally in the 1960s. Rice Collection.

▲ Left to right: Dr. Benjamin Spock, Rev. Martin Luther King Jr., and Msgr. Charles Owen Rice leading an antiwar march to the United Nations (the Spring Mobilization March) in New York, 1967. Rice Collection.

▲Irene Quinn singing the national anthem at a UE convention in 1969. Standing at left is Jim Matles, UE secretary-treasurer. To the right of Irene is Daniel Marguerite, president, UE District 6, Western Pennsylvania. Quinn family files.

◄Tom Quinn speaking at the 1969 UE convention. For several years he served as chairman of the convention resolutions committee. At this time he was still business agent of UE Local 610 in Wilmerding. *UE News* Photograph Collection.

▲ Tom and Irene Quinn with Lifetime Achievement Award plaque, presented to Quinn by the Department of Industrial and Labor Relations at Indiana University of Pennsylvania, 1987. Quinn family files.

14

FREE SPEECH AND FAMILY SOLIDARITY

AMERICA'S attention was riveted on the war in Korea in the first months of 1951. American and United Nations forces had come perilously close to being swept off the Korean peninsula when massive Chinese and North Korean armies drove south from the Yalu River in December 1950. In February, the U.S. Eighth Army halted the advance and began a counteroffensive that would retake the South Korean capital of Seoul and eventually push the invaders north of the thirty-eighth parallel. But the entrance of Chinese Communists into the war inflamed anti-Communist passions in the United States and strengthened the popular appeal of Joe McCarthy and other Red hunters. McCarthy had become, in fact, "the most famous figure" in the Republican Party, writes one historian. It was a dangerous time for people who had to defend themselves against charges related to Communist activity.[1]

Nonetheless, Tom Quinn had reason to be hopeful when he went on trial in Washington on February 26 on the contempt-of-Congress charge. It seemed a simple case, turning on whether he did or did not invoke the Fifth Amendment when he testified before HUAC in August 1949. A mere reading of the hearings transcript, Quinn thought, would reveal that the facts were on his side. For this reason he had waived a jury trial, empowering the federal district judge who heard the case to consider the evidence and render a verdict. Since no witnesses would be called, Quinn and his lawyer expected the trial to take no more than a few hours. He told Irene and the children that he would take an evening train back to Pittsburgh.

The proceedings, in fact, were short. The government prosecutor argued that Quinn's claim of protection was insufficient; he did not actually say the words Fifth Amendment while testifying but instead linked himself to a statement previously made by Tom Fitzpatrick. Quinn's lawyer took the opposite view, of course. But Judge James R. Kirkland agreed with the government, declaring that one could not refer to a claim of protection made by somebody else. He therefore pronounced Quinn guilty of contempt of Congress in refusing to answer whether he had ever been a member of the Communist Party. Quinn was stunned. But worse was to come.

After pronouncing the verdict, the judge immediately handed down the sentence, infusing his announcement with an infuriating note of patriotic self-righteousness. While American soldiers were fighting in Korea, Kirkland opined, Quinn represented an "imminent danger to our republic and democratic form of life." He ordered that Quinn serve four months to a year in prison and pay a one-thousand-dollar fine (later changed to six months and five hundred dollars). Adding to Quinn's humiliation, the judge refused to set him free on bail that he had already posted (an unusual move for such a conviction). Forced to stay overnight in jail, Quinn was not allowed to call home and explain the situation to Irene and set her mind at ease. She learned the bad news in a call from his attorney.[2]

The Quinns' oldest son, Chuck, who was eleven at the time, recalled that evening. "I remember breaking down and crying," he said. "I didn't understand what had happened, but I was very angry." His mother undoubtedly was distraught, he said, but she did not swoon or weep. "She was a very warm and soft woman, but there was a tough resolve about her. She was pretty together." That evening, several of Quinn's union friends, came to the Quinn apartment in East Pittsburgh and consoled Irene. "Our lives revolved around the union, and Dad had a lot of close friends," Chuck said. "But I remember being taunted by schoolmates because of all the publicity surrounding my father." Ron Quinn, who was eight at the time, recalled that people started calling on the phone. "They said, 'Why don't you go back to Russia where you came from?' To a young boy! I said, 'We were born here.' I didn't understand the point they were making."[3]

The Quinns would live through many difficult experiences in those years. But Quinn remembered this one in particular. It was the only time he went to jail and the only time that Irene suggested he might try another line of work. "She wasn't happy about this," Quinn said. "But she never asked me to get out of the UE. I told her I wanted to work for the union, and she accepted it."

Of the fifty-six people cited by the House for contempt of Congress, only three actually were convicted of the offense and two of these were from the UE—Quinn and Julius Emspak, the UE secretary-treasurer, who was convicted by another judge on the day of Quinn's trial. In the ensuing weeks, Tom Fitzpatrick and Frank Panzino were found not guilty; they had actually used the words Fifth Amendment. For Quinn there now began a long appeals process that would last for years. In December 1952, a nine-member federal appeals panel would rule that the trial court erred in finding Quinn guilty and would order a new trial.[4]

The possibility of serving a long prison term would hang over Quinn for four years. He and Irene decided not to dwell on the possibility, but to put it aside and focus on more immediate things. At her insistence in 1952 the family moved from East Pittsburgh to Pitcairn, farther up Turtle Creek. They rented a larger apartment on the outskirts of town, away from the heavy traffic moving up and down the valley. Instead of playing on a busy street with streetcars rattling by, the three Quinn boys now could roam in nearby woods. Since there was no bus or trolley line from here to East Pittsburgh, Tom bought the family's first car, a second- or thirdhand 1939 Dodge, for thirty-nine dollars. The family also acquired its first electric washing machine. Irene still had to use a hand-operated wringer to squeeze water out of the clean clothes before hanging them out to dry. But the Quinns were progressing. Gradually they were realizing the part of the American dream that had to do with acquiring material things that would make daily living more comfortable. As pleased as he was about that, Tom felt there had been too little progress on the more important parts of his dream—obtaining equal economic and social rights for all Americans and protecting his right to speak his mind freely on political issues without fear of persecution.[5]

The Quinns' home life was going better than his work life. Back at his welding job, he faced the same routine hour after hour, day after day. No longer did a workday promise the variety and sense of purpose, even excitement, that the steward's job had provided him in years past. The union, Quinn realized, had been more than a helpful adjunct to his work life; it had become the center of that life. He longed to be involved again in that kind of activity, pushing management and the union to improve conditions on the job. But that was out of the question, he knew, unless he joined the IUE and ran for election. He was sure he could find plenty of support among his co-workers, but he would have to play up to IUE local leaders—many of whom he detested—and pretend that he really had had a change of heart. The very thought of doing this was nauseating. "I just didn't want to join the IUE," Quinn said. He saw only one course open to him, and that was to bring back the UE.

Quinn and other people from the old Progressive caucus continued to meet during off hours, periodically electing officers in UE Local 601 and pressing the NLRB to conduct another election. They contended that the IUE had fallen short on promises and accepted compromises that weakened the incentive-pay system and steward structure. But by the time the NLRB finally conducted an election, in August 1952, memories of the union battles of the 1940s had begun fading. Many ordinary workers apparently felt that the IUE performed well enough. Even so, the UE lost by only about 2,000 votes out of 11,600 cast. The local remained split almost down the middle. Since many former UE members, like Quinn, refused to join the IUE, some of the most talented and experienced unionists in the plant could only play the role of powerless critic. The same was true in many other Westinghouse and GE plants. Instead of one union, several unions now represented electrical workers, and both companies took advantage of the split in bargaining. Over the next several years, electrical-company wage rates, once on a par with those in the steel and auto industries, would fall far behind.[6]

The same dynamic was occurring on a broader scale throughout industries where unionism had been weakened by the CIO expulsions. The CIO itself grew weaker through the loss of the few unions that had been organizing new workers. And then, on November 13, 1952, Phil Murray died of a heart attack while attending a Steelworkers convention in California. That evening Father Rice delivered a eulogy of sorts in a broadcast over station WWSW in Pittsburgh. "Not often have we the opportunity to observe the great ones of the earth as they go about their daily tasks, not often do we observe great, human, humble figures so close to us. Not often do we see those who 'can walk with kings, nor lose the common touch.'" The Steelworkers executive board named Dave McDonald to succeed Murray. A blustery leader, always on the defensive, jealous of Walter Reuther, who was elected CIO president, McDonald turned his union away from Murray's political and social activism.[7]

Since the mid-1930s, the Communist Party had favored unified union movements over independent party-controlled unions. Fearing a loss of influence following the CIO rupture, the party ordered Communist union leaders not to go it alone but to move their unions back into the mainstream of the labor movement. In the UE's case, this would have meant merging with the IUE—on the IUE's terms. According to labor historian Bert Cochran, who interviewed former party officials in the 1970s, the UE flatly rejected this plan. In 1950, he writes, a CPUSA official accused UE leaders of "blind factionalism" in resisting merger with the IUE. In a "stormy session" with CPUSA officials over this issue in early 1951, Jim Matles rejected the policy and said he had no confidence in the party leadership. He and other UE leaders, Cochran continues, had followed the party line on many issues. "But the instruction to liquidate the union to which they had devoted their adult lives was beyond the pale of contemplation." This ended the UE's "close relations" with the party.

The CPUSA policy, however, apparently did influence leaders in several UE locals who, in the early 1950s, pulled their locals out of the UE and joined the rival union. A similar movement in UE Local 601 would leave Tom Quinn isolated from his old political associates. This began in early 1953 when Tom Fitzpatrick and several other men in the Progressives' left wing decided that it was time for the UE and IUE locals at East Pittsburgh to forge a united front in negotiating with Westinghouse. Only by becoming a member could Fitzpatrick and others like him run for office in the IUE. A group of militants in the IUE, including Quinn's friend John Vento, were eager to take in the UE people, believing they would strengthen the union. The IUE, however, insisted that former UE officers would have to swear a non-Communist oath before a justice of the peace.[8]

Fitzpatrick and three other UE members submitted their affidavits and became IUE members; Frank Panzino had joined the new union some time before. Quinn refused to go along. As the current president of UE Local 601, he already had signed a non-Communist affidavit to comply with the law governing union officers, but he would not demean himself by signing another one merely to be admitted to a union he despised. He did not trust and would not serve under leaders such as Jim Carey and Charles Copeland, the current IUE Local 601 president, who had helped arrange the HUAC hearings in 1949. He lined up openly with Matles in opposing merger at any level of the union. Fitzpatrick's idea of uniting with Vento's group in the IUE to get rid of that union's "sell-out leaders" would not succeed, Quinn wrote in a memo, adding, "I am reminded of childhood fairy tales where the forces of good triumph over evil merely because they were good." He and Fitzpatrick took different paths but remained friendly.

Quinn's distrust would prove to be well placed. In early 1954, Fitzpatrick would seek election as an IUE delegate to the state CIO convention, viewing this as a first step in building a new union career. "Even though people thought he was a Red, he was still regarded as the most effective union leader in the plant," Quinn recalled. "So he ran for an office—for whatever it was worth, I didn't think it was worth much—as a delegate to the state CIO convention, and he got elected. The convention was in Pittsburgh that year. IUE President Jim Carey came to town and went before the credentials committee of the state CIO and asked them not to seat Fitzpatrick. And they didn't. The guy signed a non-Communist affidavit, and he was elected by the members of this local. But they wouldn't seat him." A few months before this run-in with Carey occurred, however, Fitzpatrick and Quinn, among others, were put to the fire by another congressional committee.[9]

The number of congressional committees claiming responsibility for investigating the "Communist conspiracy" was increasing as the political clamor rose in volume. In addition to HUAC, Joe McCarthy carried out his helter-skelter attacks from the dais of the Senate's Permanent Subcommittee on Investigations; in both houses, committees dealing with labor relations occasionally held hearings on Communism in unions; and a new committee, the Senate Internal Security Subcommittee, had been formed under the Internal Security Act of 1950. The subcommittee was a subsidiary of the Senate Judiciary Committee headed by Pat McCarran, author of the new law. Among the senators he chose to serve on the subcommittee was John Marshall Butler, Republican of Maryland. Butler was known mainly for having defeated Democrat

Millard Tydings in 1952 with the help of Joe McCarthy and his infamous composite picture. During the campaign, McCarthy's staff had prepared and distributed a composite with two separate photos, one of Tydings and one of Communist Party chief Earl Browder, set side by side as if the two were friends. The trick helped ensure Butler's victory.[10]

On November 9, 1953, Butler and a subcommittee task force opened hearings in Pittsburgh for the purpose of investigating subversive influence in UE locals of Pittsburgh and Erie, Pennsylvania. There was no more evidence of sabotage, or planning for subversive activity, than there had been in 1949. But the cycle started that year had not yet played to its end. Butler intended to document the need for a bill outlawing Communist infiltration of unions. Quinn, Fitzpatrick, Panzino, and several other current and former members of the UE were trotted before this committee and linked to the Communist Party by informants and former party members.

Quinn went up against a familiar adversary in Matt Cvetic, who declared that he had met Quinn on "a hundred or more occasions where we had discussed Communist strategy." A hundred meetings? When another witness referred to "hundreds" of meetings with Tom Fitzpatrick, the latter interrupted the testimony to observe, "We must have been to meetings all the time. When did you work?"[11]

This time Cvetic's testimony about Quinn was supplemented by other witnesses. One was a lawyer named Harry Allen Sherman, chairman of the right-wing Americans Battling Communism, who had acted as Cvetic's agent in introducing him to HUAC in 1950. Sherman produced no personal knowledge that Quinn was a Communist, merely that he had "known him to be [read rumored to be] very active" in the party. The committee accepted this statement as if it were real evidence. A third witness against Quinn was Joseph Mazzei, who served as an FBI plant in the CPUSA from 1941 to 1953. He testified that he had attended closed party meetings with Quinn. Refusing to answer any of the accusations, Quinn claimed the Fifth Amendment protection. His contempt conviction was still moving through the appeals process, and he did not want to endanger a possible reversal by saying anything that might be used against him.

A former Communist and UE member named Francis Nestler gave what appeared to be truthful information. A Westinghouse employee at East Pittsburgh, he joined the Communist Party and became one of the

leading Progressives in Local 601 before joining the Marines in 1944.
After the war, he quit the party and became a commercial photographer.
He remembered Quinn as a young steward and member of the Progressive caucus in 1944 but not as a party member, although "the Progressives were working on him." He added, "I mean the Communists were
working on him [Quinn] to become a Communist" but had not succeeded by 1944.[12]

During a 2000 interview, Quinn looked back with wry amusement,
recalling how new witnesses kept appearing to link him with the Communists. Every time an investigating committee knocked on wood, ter-
mites came crawling out. Of the four who testified against him in 1953,
Quinn knew only two, Cvetic and Nestler. He had read about Sherman
in newspaper stories. But Joseph Mazzei was a puzzle. Quinn had never
met or heard of him. Both the FBI and Justice Department would wish
they had never heard of him either. A movie-theater manager in Pittsburgh, he pleaded guilty to adultery and bastardy in Allegheny County
Criminal Court in 1952 and later was arrested for molesting a young boy.
Yet the Butler subcommittee took him on, and he testified with strong
self-confidence. Like Cvetic, Mazzei became a favorite government witness until he was caught in one perjury too many.[13]

For the second time, Quinn's loyalty as an American citizen had been
impugned in public testimony before a congressional committee. He was
not an innocent victim, in the sense that a child is innocent of crimes it
cannot comprehend. Quinn was, indeed, guilty of associating and working with Communists on union matters, of belonging to a union with
Communist leaders, of expressing support for some of the political goals
espoused by Communists (as well as members of many other parties)
such as racial and ethnic equality, redistribution of income, price controls, removal of restrictions on union behavior, and halting the worldwide arms race. These political associations and opinions were never
linked to any actions aimed at committing sabotage or subverting the
government. Quinn and hundreds like him in the early 1950s were per-
secuted, not for illegal conduct, but for voicing anticapitalist opinions
and associating with Communists—behavior that, however unpopular,
was presumably protected by the First Amendment guarantee of free
speech.

But the American judiciary, led by the U.S. Supreme Court, had created a legal climate that was hostile to free-speech rights where Commu-

nists were involved. The high court's 1951 decision in *Dennis v. United States* upheld the convictions of eleven Communist Party leaders accused of violating the Smith Act. Government prosecutors were unable to show that the defendants committed acts aimed at overthrowing the government, or conspired to overthrow, only that they conspired to advocate overthrow by urging the teaching of Communist doctrine. They "were prosecuted for their speech because they could not have been successfully prosecuted for their actions, or for any danger they actually presented to the United States," concludes Geoffrey R. Stone in a history of First Amendment trends. One of the two dissenters in *Dennis*, Justice William O. Douglas, scoffed at the notion that American Communists, who were "miserable merchants of unwanted ideas," posed any threat to the U.S. government.

With the *Dennis* decision, the court "placed the full weight of its authority behind the aggressive anti-Communist prosecutions, programs, policies, investigations, and exclusions that marked the first decade of the Cold War," Stone writes. From 1951 to 1957, while congressional committees such as HUAC operated with few restrictions, the government arrested and prosecuted 145 members and leaders of the Communist Party under the Smith Act. A reconstituted Supreme Court reversed course in 1957, ruling in *Yates v. United States* that advocacy of doctrines that include overthrow can be a crime only if "those to whom the advocacy is addressed must be urged to *do* something, now or in the future, rather than merely to *believe* in something." No further Smith Act prosecutions were filed after this decision.[14]

Senator Butler's bill to exclude Communists from union membership did not pass. But some of its provisions found their way into the 1954 Communist Control Act. Under this law, the Subversive Activities Control Board could designate a union as a communist-infiltrated organization, in which case the union would be denied legal privileges such as proceedings before the National Labor Relations Board. This law, like the Internal Security Act, eventually was declared unconstitutional. Before that would happen, though, even such a famous liberal Democrat as Senator Hubert H. Humphrey would advocate its passage. Three years after Harry Davenport turned against everything he had stood for, other liberals were still taking that path.[15]

The Butler hearings added another notch to Quinn's growing reputation as a radical malcontent. He had appeared before two congressional committees, been convicted of contempt of Congress, and served on the UE staff. He had supported Henry Wallace, run as a candidate for office on the Progressive Party ticket, and associated with the most prominent left-wing leaders in UE Local 601. As president of the local in 1953, Quinn was a rallying point at Westinghouse for the dwindling band of recalcitrant UE members. He went to work every day, did whatever welding the foremen told him to do, and tried to stay out of trouble. The bosses rarely said anything to him, but he had a feeling his days at Westinghouse were numbered. The IUE was more direct. "Charlie Copeland was calling on the company to fire me. He said the only thing I was welding was better relations with Russia."

Quinn was working the night shift with another man on December 31, 1953, New Year's Eve. When they finished a job in the evening, they left the plant some hours before their shift ended. It was not difficult. People were always going in and out. It was not unusual for welders to leave the plant when they had finished their assigned jobs before the end of a shift. "In fact," Quinn said, "on New Year's and Christmas and the day before, people often had parties in the plant. Everybody else was partying that night, and so we left." He laughed.

A few days later, the company fired him and his co-worker, claiming they had falsified time cards. "Technically I guess that's true," Quinn said. "But you know, what the hell, they were going to fire me one way or another." John Vento remembered the circumstances of Quinn's firing. "The ironic part is, Westinghouse set him up and fired him on a phony issue. Tom did the same thing every day, and so did I. But somebody was out to get him." Quinn had to find work quickly, but he wanted to avoid returning to Westinghouse if possible. He reported his firing to UE officials, and within a few days the union hired him as an international staff representative.[16]

Working for the UE, of course, would not take Quinn out of the line of fire. Once a person appeared before an investigating committee, his or her name would come up each time that committee, or any other, decided to revisit the subject. Escape was almost impossible, unless one confessed something or recanted or agreed to testify against friends and acquaintances. Quinn might have thrown the hunters off track by turning to another trade. But he enjoyed representing people, negotiating contracts, and engaging in political activity, and he would not think of pursuing this work with any other union. The UE, however, was still under attack by the government, and anyone who worked for the union was at risk.

He had been a marked man, Quinn realized, ever since his encounter with HUAC in 1949. For four and a half years that record had followed and almost destroyed him. The same was true of the other three men who appeared as unfriendly witnesses in hearing room 226 on those hot August days of 1949, with one notable difference. Tom Fitzpatrick, Frank Panzino, and Bob Whisner would suffer far more than Quinn.

In December 1953, General Electric issued what became known as the Cordiner Policy (after Chairman Ralph J. Cordiner), giving notice that the corporation would suspend employees who exercised their Fifth Amendment rights before an investigating committee. It was as if the company had repealed the Fifth Amendment. GE defended the policy under the rationale that employees who refused to testify might subject the company "to serious embarrassment." Westinghouse adopted a similar policy and first applied it, acting on a cue from the IUE, to Tom Fitzpatrick and Frank Panzino.[17]

On March 29, 1954, the day after Fitzpatrick was denied a convention seat on Jim Carey's say-so, Westinghouse fired him. He was, the company said, an "extremely undesirable" employee who had "brought public discredit upon our employes [sic] and upon the Westinghouse Electric Corporation." If the union could reject him, Westinghouse seemed to be saying, the company might as well also. Frank Panzino was discharged on the same day for the same reason. The company noted that both men had cited the Fifth in refusing to answer questions posed by the Butler subcommittee and HUAC. Local IUE officials filed grievances on their behalf. But Carey ordered the complaints dropped, saying—according to Quinn's interpretation—that Fitzpatrick and Panzino "should tie a rope around their necks with a heavy stone and jump into a river."

For years after their discharges, Fitzpatrick, who was fifty-two when fired, and Panzino, who was thirty-nine, had trouble finding anything more than pick-up work in the Pittsburgh area. Manufacturing companies needed skilled industrial workers, but not if they were accused of being Communists. In the meantime, both men were denied unemployment compensation. In Pennsylvania, most workers laid off or fired by their employers for anything other than willful misconduct could collect jobless pay for twenty-six weeks. But the Bureau of Unemployment Compensation, caught up in McCarthyism, had stretched willful misconduct to include use of the Fifth Amendment to avoid answering questions while under investigation. In other words, the bureau had equated invoking a constitutional right with committing a crime. It took a U.S. Supreme Court decision to jolt the agency out of this position. In a 1956 ruling, the Court would condemn "the practice of imputing a sinister meaning to the exercise of a person's constitutional right under the Fifth Amendment." This decision finally worked its way into Pennsylvania law, and in 1960—six years after Fitzpatrick and Panzino were fired—a board of review granted them jobless benefits.

It was the end of the road for both men in the labor movement. It is not clear why the UE did not offer Fitzpatrick a job on the union staff. Quinn reluctantly suggested to me that his friend may have had drinking problems, and Jim Matles might have felt that Fitzpatrick forfeited a future in the UE when he defected and joined the IUE. After Fitzpatrick lost his job, his marriage ended in divorce. By 1959 he had remarried and was working in a restaurant in New York City. Eventually, Quinn said, Fitzpatrick became a furniture repairman. He and Quinn remained friends and would meet for a drink when the UE held conventions in New York. Fitzpatrick died in 1983.[18]

Panzino had an even harder time, Quinn recalled. "He had problems with his wife, and he hit the juice a little too much. But he hung on, kept his marriage intact. We were finally able to get him a job with the county, driving a refuse truck." For several years, Panzino apparently tried to overcome his reputation as an alleged Communist in hopes of being reinstated by Westinghouse. "He is said to have two daughters of about high school age who have been seriously embarrassed, and a Catholic wife, who all want him to get squared away," noted a HUAC investigator who interviewed Panzino in 1958. But Panzino never got his job back. He died in Turtle Creek in 1985 at the age of seventy-one, a broken man. His tragedy came about not because he had violated any law or engaged in any subversive act but merely because of allegations that he had belonged to the Communist Party for three years, 1943 to 1946.[19]

What happened to Whisner, the fourth UE member subpoenaed by HUAC in 1949 along with Quinn, Fitzpatrick, and Panzino, is not entirely clear. The newspapers reported Whisner's 1934 trip to Russia in some detail and then forgot about him. Quinn remembered that he remained loyal to the UE for a year or more after its defeat in the 1950 election at Westinghouse. After that, Quinn said in 2000, "Bob sort of disappeared. I saw him very little after that." In August 2000 I located Bob Whisner's son, R. C. Whisner, who was operating his own business, manufacturing hydraulic components for various products, in the Pittsburgh area. The younger Whisner believed that his father was fired around 1951, although he could not be certain of the year or the reason for dismissal. (The *UE News* contended that Whisner had been ill for some years and that Westinghouse "used his illness as a pretext to dismiss him from the job.")

The elder Whisner's problems had started, the son told me in a telephone interview, when he appeared before HUAC in 1949. His wife was working as a high school teacher, and they had four children, including R. C. Whisner, then a student at Indiana University. "His name was in the paper all the time, and it was difficult for my mother," the son said. "I graduated from college in 1951, and I was embarrassed by what was happening. I was trying to get a career going for myself, and people kept mentioning my dad's troubles. He was a fan of Stalin. It seemed when he took the Fifth, that was an admission." The elder Whisner was forced out of Westinghouse with a pension of three dollars a month. He worked for a while in a small manufacturing firm as a machine tender. Eventually he resigned for health reasons. He weighed 260 pounds and could no longer stand at a machine for eight hours. In the final years of his life, the disability prevented Whisner from doing much of anything except drive his wife to and from school. He died of a heart attack at the age of fifty-nine in January 1962.

His father's experience embittered the younger Whisner, about both his father and labor unions. "I despised the unions for what they did to my dad. He spent most all his time down in East Pittsburgh fighting for people. His whole life was the union. My mother and I almost hated him for that. But the union never fought for him. They sold my father down the river." Whisner implies that the UE was at fault, but only the IUE had standing to contest Whisner's discharge. The UE, after all, did not forget Whisner. When he died, the *UE News* ran a story extolling him as a "pioneer unionist."[20]

The purge at Westinghouse was not over yet. In late December 1954, Joe McCarthy's Senate Permanent Investigations Subcommittee issued subpoenas to six East Pittsburgh workers, ordering them to appear before the committee on January 3, 1955. Telegrams arrived at the homes of five of the workers on that very day, notifying them they had been fired even before they had testified. Although Quinn did not officially represent the workers, he knew all five and advised them when asked. Their firing, he said, "had nothing to do with what they said or did at the hearing. They were fired merely for being subpoenaed." Three people did not even show up for the hearing, let alone take the Fifth, but were fired anyway. One was Evelyn Darin, the sister of the early Local 601 leader Margaret Darin. Becoming ill a few days before the hearings began, Evelyn was committed to a hospital in Pittsburgh with severe hypertension and could not make the trip to Washington. Alfred Oyler also was unable to travel to Washington because of illness. Both were fired on the day they were to testify, as was a man named Armenio Sardoch. Sardoch's subpoena, however, ordered him to appear at 10 p.m. on January 3—an obvious mistake because the hearings started at 10 a.m. Quinn advised him to do just what the subpoena ordered. "I told him to go down there but stay away from the Senate Office Building until late at night. Armenio walked in at 10 p.m., and a guy at the desk called someone on McCarthy's staff. The guy came down, looked at the subpoena, and said, 'Oh, there's been a mistake. I'll have to call Westinghouse right away [to stop them from firing Sardoch].'" Sardoch was fired.[21]

Almost certainly the company had conspired with the McCarthy subcommittee, a judgment that is strongly supported by another incident involving Westinghouse (see chapter 15). In 1954, Sardoch, Darin, and Oyler never uttered a word to the committee but were fired anyway. Two other men, Joseph Slater and William Heiston, appeared and took the Fifth. They were fired. A sixth man confessed that he had been a Communist and retained his job.

Since Westinghouse went out of business in 1997, there was no official spokesperson with whom I could discuss the company's actions in those discharge cases. Old personnel records might have provided some answers, but it was unclear whether they had been placed in an archive or destroyed. I interviewed two retired labor-relations executives about their experiences with the UE, but both worked in low-level management jobs at the time of the discharges and were not involved in setting the policy or carrying it out. In any case, Westinghouse's precipitous firings were not unusual in that era. General Electric discharged even more employees for claiming the Fifth; according to one source, GE and Westinghouse together fired twenty workers in 1954. Westinghouse Air Brake in Wilmerding dismissed two UE members in similar circumstances. Many other corporations and government agencies, even unions, fired employees or expelled members. During the McCarthy period, from ten thousand to twelve thousand people lost their jobs for refusing to cooperate with anti-Communist investigators or because they were identified as Communists.[22]

The Quinn boys were too young to remember, but the taunting and harassing phone calls had started in 1948 when the *Pittsburgh Press* published the names of all people who signed petitions supporting Henry Wallace. It continued when Quinn appeared before HUAC in 1949, when Matt Cvetic identified him as a Communist, when he was cited for contempt of Congress, when he was found guilty, when he appeared before the Butler subcommittee, and when he was fired. Many people shoved into the spotlight during the McCarthy era received similar, often far worse, treatment from neighbors and strangers alike. Many lives were ruined through the loss of jobs, broken marriages, family divisions. The Quinns suffered less than many and handled their situation better than most. One reason was that Quinn, hardened to adversity during his early life, was prepared to accept the consequences of adopting an unwavering stand in his beliefs and associations. Irene, in turn, accepted the life that Tom created for the family through his union work. When the accusations began, she did not play the role of the passive, long-suffering wife.[23]

"She was determined to keep things under control," Chuck Quinn said. "Mother was a very strong-willed woman. I don't recall her sitting around sobbing and crying. She wasn't that kind of person. She believed in Dad and stood by him." Moreover, she was the driving force in important decisions affecting the family's welfare. "All the social developments in our family resulted pretty much from her push," Ron Quinn said. It was she who decided in 1952 that it was time to move from the busy streets and soot, dirt, and noise of East Pittsburgh.

In 1957, the family moved again at Irene's prompting, this time renting a house in Monroeville, about a mile and a half farther into the suburbs. Located near Miracle Mile, the first huge strip mall in the Pittsburgh area, the Quinns' new home had six rooms, a finished basement, and a garage. Nearly twenty years after they got married, the

Quinns finally had a house to themselves, although they rented it rather than bought it. The family still lived paycheck to paycheck. The Quinns would never own their own home until Tom and Irene, well into their seventies, bought a condominium in Florida. In the 1950s, though, their economic journey was typical of working-class families, gradually moving upward on union-driven wage increases, removing themselves from the noise and soot of the mill or factory, spreading out across suburbia in new housing developments, shopping in large markets (eventually supermarkets) instead of neighborhood groceries, driving back into town to work.

Irene's upbringing, on the surface so different from Tom's, was similar in crucial respects. Raised in a Conservative Jewish environment, she had eloped with an orphan from an Irish-Catholic background and found herself ostracized from her own family for three or four years. But she also had grown up in near poverty, in a family struggling for a better life. "The values my father was espousing struck a chord with her," Ron said. "It became very important for her to live in that world [of unions]. She gained a great sense of self and value from what he stood for and what he was accomplishing." She accepted his union friends as hers, accompanied him to union conventions, and sang the *Star-Spangled Banner* at opening ceremonies.

"She completely adopted my father's politics," Steve Quinn said, "but she added her own softening touch. She agreed with what he was doing. She would spend hours in the kitchen and sing all afternoon while cooking. Sometimes with a radio, sometimes a cappella. It was a treat to be in the same house with her. Mother went about her business as if nothing extraordinary was going on in our lives."

Although Irene believed in Tom's work, the all-consuming nature of it caused tensions between them. He was always attending meetings in the evening, often traveling on weekends, leaving home early in the morning to walk on picket lines, sometimes drinking too much. "At some point," Ron said, "she felt she was too much alone, trying to raise three children. Dad never stopped doing what he needed to do, but there was tension around him not needing to do all those things." Those tensions, however, were never severe enough to threaten the family's stability.

Tom and Irene also had differences over religion. Tom thought of himself as an atheist. Irene was not deeply religious, but she never lost her fondness for Jewish ritual. "It wasn't important to her for us to be theologically Jewish," Ron said, "but she wanted us to have the trappings of a Jewish lifestyle." Both he and Chuck recalled that Irene would take them to the synagogue in East Pittsburgh for services on Yom Kippur and Rosh Hashanah. "At some point my father said, 'I don't want the kids to do that. I don't want us to create a religion for them. That's their choice to make when they're old enough to make that decision.' Mom lost that battle and went on. When Chuck, Steve, and I grew up, we felt we didn't need religion."

When newspaper stories brought harassing calls, Irene never complained. The boys knew that their father was different, but it never occurred to them that he could be wrong. "The problem was with everybody else," Ron said. "We really felt that." Once he and Chuck were assaulted by a gang of boys on their way home from school, but that was over religion, not politics. The other boys taunted them about being Jewish. As the brothers grew up, they learned to disregard occasional hostility directed toward them. "Because Mother handled the situation so well, we never felt we had anything to be ashamed of," Steve said. Added Ron, "We didn't have a sense of having to prove something to people. I never felt I had to take a position to defend my father to anybody. I was a pretty self-assured kid. I wasn't fragile on this issue."

In 1958, Chuck began dating the woman he eventually married, Rochelle Zimmerman. Although she spent much time at the Quinns' home and came to know the entire family, Rochelle never heard either Irene or any of the sons speak of the accusations against Tom. "It was years before I even heard about that business," Rochelle said. "Irene was a very proud woman. She didn't let those problems get in her way. She carried herself as if nothing had happened."

The boys learned early in life to pay attention to what was happening around them. Tom would lead discussions around the dinner table about politics, unionism, and history. "It was like going to a seminar," Steve recalled. "Dad didn't talk about Marxism or capitalism as such. He always stressed equality and human justice. He'd tell us about the unfair things that were going on in America, that people ought not to discriminate." Tom usually led these discussions in a low-key, almost jovial spirit. But there was an exception. "If the name Father Rice came up," Steve said, "there'd be a brief silence and then Dad would fly into a rage and throw out a string of profanities. He'd curse Rice for destroying our union and destroying lives. It was really something. Normally, Dad tolerated people he didn't like. Not Father Rice." Quinn cursed a lot in those years.

"When he was an organizer," Steve recalled, "at least once a week Dad would receive a call while we were at dinner and he'd hear something he didn't like. He'd say, 'That dirty son of a bitch.' My mother would go, 'Oh, Tommy!' Then he'd go back to being the normal Tom."

"We grew up in a world of unions, and bosses weren't always the good guys that everybody thought they were," Ron said. "We had a sense of how things happened in the world because our dad knew how it really worked. But it wasn't proselytizing. There were never any 'isms.' It wasn't intellectual. It was about human decency and standards. We were living in a world where it was wrong to be a racist, wrong for people to be suffering because they didn't have resources. Early on, I learned to be for the underdog." With this upbringing, Chuck noted, it was not surprising that the three brothers took up occupations that involved serving people. Chuck and Steve became teachers and Ron became head of a county bureau that provides job training for dislocated workers, high school dropouts, welfare recipients, and other low-income people.

By 1954 the Quinn family had been tested many times and had survived intact, probably stronger than ever. But Tom's tribulations had yet to run their full course.

15

SUBPOENAED AGAIN

W HEN I came home from the army in June 1955, Harry had
moved out of the McKeesporter and was living in Pittsburgh.
My mother and her sisters were disappointed with him. What
had started as a temporary arrangement—sharing the apartment and
taking care of Grandmother Davenport, paying no rent, while he wrote
his book or got a job—had turned into a long-term residence at the family's expense. He had neither found a job nor produced a book. We
never found out what happened to the hundreds (or perhaps only
dozens) of handwritten manuscript pages he had labored over. Before
going to Washington, Uncle Harry had been industrious and hard driving, a man who never stood still. Now he was stuck in some sort of life sta-
sis at the age of only fifty-three. When Grandmother was hospitalized
with a long-term illness, he had no reason to stay in McKeesport. Neither
did I. Having paid off all its debts, my mother sold the hotel and moved
to Detroit with her second husband. My sister went with them. I returned
to school to work on a graduate degree.

The destructive force of the McCarthy era was beginning to fade in
the midfifties. Stationed in France for most of 1954, I had missed the
final, dramatic events of Joe McCarthy's career—his outrageous bullying
and slandering of witnesses during the Army-McCarthy hearings and the

vote of his Senate colleagues to censure him in December 1954. During
his four years as a Red hunter, McCarthy had not exposed a single Communist who was not already identified as one. At most, concludes a biography, he "produced evidence that the government's security procedures
were sometimes remiss." I read about these events, of course, but I was
not immersed in them as were stateside audiences of the televised hearings. I recalled that Harry had spoken derisively of McCarthy, but it did
not occur to me that my uncle's downfall was connected somehow with
the purges of the McCarthy period. I rarely thought about Harry during
the next several years. Bored with the academic ritual of graduate school,
I quit after one semester. Almost by chance I slipped into journalism,
starting as a reporter for United Press in Newark and Trenton, New Jersey. For most of the next decade, I would move from city to city, working
as a reporter, in some sense a journalistic boomer as Uncle Harry had
been an advertising boomer.[1]

Through most of the 1950s, Father Rice and Uncle Harry were
haunted by things past. Quinn, on the other hand, lived under a constant threat from that past—until May 23, 1955. On that day the U.S.
Supreme Court handed down its decision in *Quinn v. United States,* a ruling that became a bulwark in guaranteeing constitutional protections for
witnesses before investigative committees. In an opinion written by Chief
Justice Earl Warren, the court declared that Quinn had properly invoked
the Fifth Amendment's privilege against self-incrimination when he
appeared before HUAC. "The fact that a witness expresses his intention
in vague terms is immaterial so long as the claim is sufficiently definite
to apprise the committee of his intention," Warren wrote. If Quinn's
claim of protection seemed vague, the committee should have asked if
he was attempting to invoke the Fifth. Moreover, HUAC failed to confront Quinn "with a clear-cut choice between compliance and noncom-
pliance," a precondition for establishing criminal intent to violate the
law. A majority of the court voted to reverse Quinn's conviction. Julius
Emspak and a third man convicted of contempt of Congress also were
acquitted by this decision.[2]

Quinn and his family, of course, were delighted, but the ruling did
not change their lives. The one difference, a very large one indeed, was
that for the first time in nearly five years, Tom had no criminal complaint
pending against him. The Supreme Court decision had cleared him, but
it would not purge his record. There was no legitimate legal reason that

Quinn's appearance before HUAC in 1949 should keep intruding on his life. But HUAC had a way of inventing reasons to stay on the trail of favorite targets, and it was not done yet with Thomas Quinn.

In 1955, the CIO merged with the AFL, a consolidating move that would reduce organizing rivalries among CIO and AFL unions and perhaps increase the political power of organized labor. But the merger would have little success in combating structural upheavals in the economy and employers' growing use of union-avoidance strategies. Union strength had been declining under the assaults by employers and the government since the early postwar period. The CIO's purge of its left-wing unions further sapped labor's vitality. The 1955 merger would not—probably could not—prevent further decline.

The importance to Americans of labor's downward slide is a matter of dispute. Corporate interests and social conservatives, of course, applaud the decline of union power. On the other side, historian David Montgomery notes what was left behind when the United States fell into the grip of the Cold War in 1947. At its 1946 convention, the CIO called for unions to halt job discrimination and push for antilynching legislation and voting rights for black citizens. Seventeen years would pass before Congress dealt with these problems in the Civil Rights Act of 1963. In 1946, the CIO said it would fight for national health insurance, economic planning to replace a reliance on market forces, international control of nuclear power for peaceful purposes, and freedom for all peoples under colonial control. This ambitious program crumbled with the onset of the Cold War and the internal divisions it promoted in the United States. The CIO's economic proposals were questionable, but the overall social and economic guidelines clearly aimed for a more just and equal America. Yet, as Montgomery points out, "few Americans are even aware that a CIO claiming 6 million members and at the summit of its influence and self-confidence, had ever even proposed such a vision for America's future." Little of it has been realized.[3]

The AFL-CIO merger left cast-off unions like the UE even more isolated. Still urging labor unity, the Communist Party welcomed the merger and counseled the CIO's expelled unions to rejoin the mainstream. Jim Matles and other UE leaders, however, believed that formation of the AFL-CIO did not signal the birth of a new labor movement, as Ronald Schatz writes, but rather "the death of the old one." If right about this, they were "insensitive to" social and political factors that turned many

UE members against the union. The leaders still regarded the IUE as "the product of a conspiracy between corporate management, anti-Communist politicians, unprincipled unionists, and priests."[4]

As myopic as this view was, the IUE did prove to be less able a negotiator on some issues than the UE had been and still sometimes managed to be. A full-scale confrontation with Westinghouse produced a 154-day strike in 1955–1956 at all plants. The two unions coordinated bargaining to some degree, but the IUE—now the dominant union—gave way to management in its long fight to curb incentive earnings. Westinghouse won the right to replace incentive pay, for most workers in IUE-represented plants, with hourly wage rates based on measured production standards. The UE rejected that proposal in the one large plant where it still had bargaining rights, at Lester, Pennsylvania. As a result, the earnings of IUE members at East Pittsburgh would suffer in comparison with earnings at Lester. This disparity could not have mattered much to the outside world, but it demonstrated that different unions really could produce different outcomes.[5]

Through raids by other unions and mass defections, by entire districts in some cases, the UE's membership fell from 203,000 in 1953 to 58,000 in 1960. In December 1955, the U.S. attorney general filed charges before the Subversive Activities Control Board, contending that the UE was controlled by the Communist Party. If the attempt succeeded, the UE would lose all bargaining and representation rights and probably be destroyed. But the government could never make an effective case because UE officers refused to testify. If forced to testify under oath that the union was Communist dominated, a witness essentially would have to acknowledge that he or she was a member of the CPUSA—and in the process incriminate himself or herself. The government abandoned the SACB case in 1959.[6]

A separate U.S. action against Matles also ended in failure. FBI files reveal how the government attempted to suppress exculpatory evidence in this case. In 1957, a federal judge found Matles guilty of lying on his 1934 application for citizenship when he stated that he had never belonged to an organization advocating overthrow of the government. If the verdict held up on appeal, Matles would have been deported to Romania. In all likelihood, he was a CPUSA member when he applied for citizenship. But the government's case was flawed. It rested on allegations excerpted selectively from FBI reports on three informers who told investigators that they knew Matles as a Communist Party member in the early 1930s. Citing a 1956 Supreme Court decision, the judge granted a new trial on grounds that Matles had the right to review the full contents of the reports. Matles's FBI file indicates that the agency resisted furnishing the reports because they "reflect activities of Matles in opposition to instructions, plans, or programs of the Communist Party [which] would undoubtedly be helpful to the defense." If it became known that Matles "has pursued an anti-Communist course at times," the government would have a harder time proving that the UE was controlled by the CPUSA (in the SACB case). Eventually Matles's attorneys cross-examined the informers and discredited some of their testimony. The government dropped the case in 1958 because of other procedural problems. But the FBI's reasons for keeping its informers under wraps were never made public, leaving the impression that the UE always had marched wherever the Communist Party told it to march.[7]

In 1958, the FBI's New York office also conceded, in a confidential report, that it had found no evidence of Communist activity by Matles since he first signed a non-Communist affidavit in 1949 and that "he has become isolated from the Party." The party itself was disintegrating. The turning point came in 1956, the year that Soviet premier Nikita Khrushchev made startling revelations about Stalin's crimes against his own people and the year that the Soviet Union brutally crushed a rebellion in Hungary. The CPUSA, nonetheless, refused to break away from fealty to the Soviet Union, and important functionaries, including Steve Nelson, began dropping out of the party as it stumbled toward its death. In a revelatory passage in his autobiography, Nelson says that he was most angry "with myself and others who had been so blind in our adherence to Soviet policy and so mechanical in our application of Marxism." The party had been undone in large part by concerted attacks on labor's radical left wing by the government, corporations, and anti-Communist unions. Whether one regards this onslaught as fully justified or as an excessive reaction to the degree of threat involved (my view), it should be acknowledged that many, many people were harassed well beyond what the facts or the threat warranted. And the assault was not over yet.[8]

The fear of Communist subversion had waned practically everywhere in 1959, except in the pages of conservative journals and the deliberations of the Un-American Activities Committee. In March, HUAC took its road show to Pittsburgh for a three-day visitation. Pittsburgh remained as alluring for anti-Communists in the fifties as Hollywood had been in the forties. In the earlier decade, the film industry was rife with left-wing writers and directors, according to Red hunters, and now Pittsburgh's industrial plants were brimming over with radicalized workers awaiting the right moment to jam a stick in the gears of defense production. A three-member HUAC panel landed in Pittsburgh on March 10, announcing its intent to find out whether the "Communist conspiracy in the United States" had "direct or indirect control," through the UE, over manufacturing plants with defense contracts. Forty-one men and women identified as "key people" in the UE in western Pennsylvania were subpoenaed.[9]

Quinn was the first witness called on the second day. More mature and certain of himself than he had been in 1949, he challenged the subcommittee from the outset. Asked to identify himself, Quinn said he was a field organizer for the UE, "the union you just lied about one hour ago." From this point, the exchange grew sharper. The subcommittee's staff director, Richard Arens, continued the questioning.

ARENS: Now as to you, sir, you have been repeatedly identified by live
    witnesses under oath before congressional committees as a hard-
    core member of the Communist conspiracy—
QUINN: That's a lie.
ARENS: —one who is dedicated to the overthrow of the Government
    of the United States—
QUINN: That is a lie.
ARENS: —by force and violence.
QUINN: That's a lie. You still haven't answered my question why you
    called me here.

Quinn made these declarations "heatedly," according to one newspaper account. Perceiving that Quinn was going to be difficult, Arens quickly arrived at the key question: "Were you at any time a member of the Communist Party during your employment at Westinghouse?"

Before answering the question, the hearing transcript notes, Quinn "conferred with counsel." His lawyer on this occasion was Frank J. Donner, who had succeeded David Scribner as UE general counsel. Later in the hearings, Donner himself would testify under subpoena and would be labeled a Communist. Now he advised Quinn to invoke the Fifth Amendment and refuse to answer Arens's question. Quinn, however, decided to take a different approach. He explained it to me during an interview in 2000. "Our union had weathered the initial attacks that began ten years before. But other unions were still [attacking us], luring away local officers, offering them payoffs and positions. We still had the Church and Rice around, and he might stick his hand in. I was concerned that the union would be in worse shape if we all walked out of the courtroom that day saying that we were taking the Fifth Amendment. I told Donner, 'How long do we continue to go through this with these guys? Time after time they bring me in, and I plead the Fifth. What does that get us? What does that get anybody? We've got to put an end to this. We've got to challenge them.'"

Quinn turned to Arens and demanded to know the relevance of the last question. The two sparred for a minute or two. Arens then repeated the question, "Are you now or have you ever been a member of the Communist Party?" Quinn had to give an answer or face a contempt citation. In what one reporter described as a "rousing baritone," Quinn replied, "I am not now, and never was, a member of the Communist Party."

A bit later, Senator Gordon H. Scherer, a Republican committee member from Ohio, demanded that Quinn acknowledge that the CIO had expelled the UE because of Communist domination. When Quinn stated only that the UE had quit the federation, Scherer threatened to recommend that Quinn be cited for contempt of Congress. The exchange continued:

QUINN: I don't have contempt for Congress, just contempt of this
   committee. Make that clear.
SCHERER: I understand that.
QUINN: I have every respect for the institutions of our country, includ-
   ing the Congress.
SCHERER: All Communists have contempt for this committee.
QUINN: Don't call me a Communist because I told the director that is
   a lie.

He could hardly have put the challenge in more direct terms. And there was more. The panel members tried to imply that as a field organizer Quinn had open access to plants engaged in defense production, presumably to obtain secret information or commit sabotage. But they got nowhere on this issue, Quinn pointing out that he could enter a plant only at the invitation of management. Arens took over the questioning and asked whether Quinn was aware that he had been identified before a congressional committee as a Communist. But he refused to name Quinn's accuser.

QUINN: I suppose you are referring to [Matt] Cvetic or [Joseph] Mazzei or some of these guys, the guys that are described as FBI undercover men. Is that who are you talking about identifying me?
ARENS: Would you kindly answer the question?
QUINN: I am aware that people like that lied about me.
SCHERER: Did they lie when they said you were a member of the Communist Party?
QUINN: They did.[10]

Quinn's hostility enraged the subcommittee members. After he was excused, they adopted a resolution recommending that he be prosecuted for perjury. Even if there was no evidence that he lied under oath, Quinn realized that he had taken a risk in calling the committee's bluff. The government might dredge up a witness willing to give false testimony in a trial. That was a worrisome possibility, another sword hanging over his head as the contempt conviction had done before the Supreme Court cleared him. In fact, the evidence against Quinn was flimsy in the extreme and always had been. In 2001, thirty years after HUAC was dissolved, its internal records were first opened to the public at the National Archives in Washington. Among other material, I found memos written by a HUAC investigator who, in November 1958, interviewed informants in Pittsburgh as background for the 1959 hearings. "Subject [Quinn] was not interviewed on my trip to Pittsburgh, Nov. 12 to 15," one memo states. "But Derdock, Paul Clark, and Juricich all stated that he was not a CPUSA member. Juricich said Cvetic was in error in this identification." No first names were given for Derdock and Juricich, but Quinn told me that he knew of a Matthew Juricich, who worked at the Air Brake plant in Wilmerding and made no secret of his party ties. In a final memo, the investigator concludes that he "cannot make positive identification" of Quinn as a party member. During the hearings a few months later, however, the committee treated Quinn as if he were a known Communist, obviously relying on allegations by Cvetic and Mazzei.[11]

A review of Quinn's FBI file revealed why the threat to bring contempt charges against him never came to fruition. In March 1959, Richard Arens asked the FBI whether it could furnish the names of potential witnesses who might refute Quinn's denial of CPUSA membership. This led to a flurry of memos between Director J. Edgar Hoover's top aides in Washington and the FBI's Pittsburgh office. Hoover's aides criticized bureau personnel in Pittsburgh for "mishandling" two informants whose names are blacked out but who presumably are Matt Cvetic and Joseph Mazzei. Pittsburgh replied with what appears to be a rundown of dates and places provided by two informants (undoubtedly Cvetic and Mazzei) used to link Quinn with Communist activity. Much of the cited evidence is circumstantial and, in some cases, even laughable.

One informant "reported that a trolley fare increase protest meeting was held on 1/23/48 at the courthouse, Pittsburgh, Pa., and [blacked out] there were approximately 50 people present, 80% of whom belonged to the Communist Party." How one is able to count Communists in a milling crowd is not explained. Quinn, however, was present and therefore was forever after associated, in the long bureaucratic memory of the FBI, with the Communist Party. The Pittsburgh memo goes on to say that "no other reports [presumably by this informant, either Cvetic or Mazzei] could be located wherein the name Quinn was mentioned, and [another informant, presumably Cvetic or Mazzei] never identified Quinn as a Communist Party member to the Pittsburgh office."

This suggests at the very least that both Cvetic and Mazzei embellished public testimony in which they identified Quinn as a Communist. Furthermore, the Pittsburgh office mentioned other undercover informants who said that Quinn was not a Communist. In the end, Hoover's office informed HUAC that Cvetic and Mazzei "are the only 2 known potential witnesses" against Quinn. Since both men already had been discredited as witnesses, the FBI refused to recommend prosecution. HUAC did not pursue the matter further.[12]

Quinn's honesty and patriotism had been publicly impugned, but the committee never retracted its suggestion that he had committed perjury. This episode indicated, though, that by 1959 the American public perhaps had learned to be wary of the endless stream of Communist accusations. Steve Quinn, who was thirteen at the time, recalled "being afraid to go to school the next day [after Quinn testified] because people would point me out and call me a Commie. Except for one nasty kid who said something, nobody gave me a hard time." Ron Quinn was a high school senior that year. "I have a vivid memory," he said, "of a newspaper article about the hearings, in the *Sun-Telly* [*Sun-Telegraph*], I think. The headline seemed to take up half a page—'Quinn called a Commie.' I was running for president of student government, and I said to myself, 'How is this going to play out?' But nobody said anything, and I won the election. Whatever they'd heard about my dad wasn't going to change their minds about who I was."[13]

Americans perhaps were beginning to recognize guilt by association for what it was.

Some corporate executives also were rebelling against the purge mentality of the McCarthy period. In 1959, Mark Cresap, the president and chief executive officer of Westinghouse Electric, quietly reversed the company policy of cooperating with HUAC. Under Cresap's predecessor in 1954, Westinghouse had furnished the committee with names of suspected Communists and then fired workers who were subpoenaed to testify or who claimed the Fifth. Cresap refused to continue this practice when HUAC came to Pittsburgh in the spring of 1959. His actions, known only to a few corporate insiders, were never disclosed to the public. A former Westinghouse lawyer named Thomas Kerr, whom I knew through my work as a reporter in the seventies, told me about this fascinating episode in 2004. Kerr worked as a lawyer for Westinghouse from 1956 to 1964 and later taught law at Carnegie-Mellon University for forty years. He also, improbable as it may seem, headed the Pittsburgh chapter of the American Civil Liberties Union (ACLU) while serving on Westinghouse's legal staff. He later directed the Pennsylvania ACLU and was a member of the ACLU national board.

In 1959, Kerr was assigned to advise Cresap on legal matters relating to HUAC hearings that would be held in Pittsburgh. Cresap told Kerr that several Pittsburgh corporations had agreed to invite the committee to Pittsburgh with promises they would furnish the names of union leaders who might be subpoenaed to testify. The companies hoped to cast suspicion on, and then fire, the unionists. Cresap opposed the plan from the beginning. Kerr was present at a meeting in Cresap's office when a high-level personnel executive argued in favor of cooperating with HUAC. Even without proof of CPUSA membership or subversive activity, the personnel man wanted to arrange for several militant unionists at East Pittsburgh to be subpoenaed so they could be fired.

Kerr recalled that the personnel executive explained the plan in approximately these words: "'This is a good chance to get rid of these guys. When asked if they're members of the Communist Party, they can either deny the charge or plead the Fifth Amendment. Either way we've got them. If they deny it, we fire them for lying, and if they take the Fifth, we fire them for refusing to testify.'"

Cresap immediately squashed the plan and said that Westinghouse would not cooperate with the committee. The company submitted no names to HUAC. (The committee subpoenaed Tom Quinn not because Westinghouse supplied his name as a former employee but because HUAC knew him from the past.) Of Cresap's decision, Kerr said, "I thought it was a remarkably decent thing to do in view of the history of that committee and how they had blackened people's reputations." Not only was the plan unfair to the workers, Cresap did not want to set a precedent of firing people for invoking the Fifth Amendment. It would be wrong, in effect, to deny a constitutional right to all Westinghouse employees in the future, including executives.

Only a year later, in 1960, Westinghouse and several other corporations were indicted in a giant price-fixing case in the electrical industry. Cresap was one of several Westinghouse executives subpoenaed to testify in criminal proceedings. Kerr advised him that he could either testify or claim protection under the Fifth Amendment. Reflecting on his decision in the HUAC situation, Cresap said, in a bemused way, "If I took the Fifth, I wouldn't have to fire myself." In the end he was not called to testify and therefore was spared that decision. But Westinghouse and many other corporations were found guilty and assessed large fines. Although Cresap was not involved in the price fixing, Kerr said, worry over the scandal ruined his health, and he died a few years later.[14]

Quinn's defiant "That's a lie!" was the talk of political circles in Pittsburgh on the day he testified in March 1959. The *Sun-Telegraph* splashed Quinn's anger across four columns with the headline "I'm Not a Red, Quinn Roars." Uncle Harry, always attuned to current events, could not have missed the news. He may even have attended the hearing, merging inconspicuously in what was described as a standing-room-only crowd in the Federal Building. I can only guess what went through Harry's mind, but I came to know him fairly well, so my guess may be accurate. The hearing would have dredged up many memories: of his own quixotic effort to abolish HUAC ten years earlier; of the way he rejected Quinn in 1949 when, although he could not alter events, a few sympathetic words might have saved their friendship; of his buckling under to Dave Lawrence's demand that he denounce the UE. Harry may have felt a twinge of envy when he read about, or watched, Quinn demonstrate an unswerving devotion to his principles.[15]

Harry was well into his fifties now. He had never gotten, probably never applied for, a nine-to-five job. He lived alone in tiny rented rooms, I suppose, and certainly, later, in a bathhouse. My cousin Jake Osterman and my brother-in-law, Ronald McKay, both lawyers in Pittsburgh, would give him money, even old suits, when he showed up at their offices. Every now and then he approached John Connelly, whose marketing-promotions business was doing very well. "Poor Harry!" Connelly said. "He needed the money so badly. I knew it broke his heart to ask, 'Can you help me?' He was always very nice about it, not ingratiating. I'd give him a hundred dollar bill."[16]

While the Davenports may not have thought so, there was purpose in Harry's seeming indolence during the late fifties. He spent much of that time plotting and carrying out schemes to exact revenge on the man he viewed as responsible for his downfall, David Lawrence. I was not in Pittsburgh then, but this conclusion leaped out at me when I read news accounts of Harry's political activities during those years. A skilled publicist, he put his pen to work in the service of defeating Lawrence when he ran for office and embarrassing the Democratic organization he headed. If Harry had to switch to the Republican side to hurt Lawrence or his favored underlings, he did that, too, without any qualms. The *Post-Gazette*'s political writer, Pat O'Neill, wrote in one 1959 column that since Harry was turned out of Congress in 1950, he "has been outspokenly anti-Lawrence," and in another column that Harry "has served factions in the [Democratic] organization as a publicist, and has displayed a sharp and biting pen."[17]

Lawrence was serving his third term as Pittsburgh mayor in 1958 when the Democratic governor of Pennsylvania, George Leader, decided not to seek reelection. A scramble among Democrats ensued, and Lawrence agreed to seek the post. Harry wrote brochures for the man who vied with Lawrence for the Democratic gubernatorial nomination, Lieutenant Governor Roy Furman. Lawrence prevailed and took on Republican Arthur T. McGonigle, a millionaire pretzel manufacturer from Reading, in the general elections. Jumping party lines, Harry publicly announced his support for McGonigle and may have fed ideas to him behind the scenes. I see flashes of Harry's handiwork in McGonigle's reference to himself as "the man with the dough" and in his attacks on Lawrence as the "political boss" of a city that protected racketeers. McGonigle fared much better than expected against Pennsylvania's most powerful Democrat, losing to Lawrence by only seventy-six thousand votes.[18]

In 1959, Harry again took on the Democratic organization, campaigning against Lawrence's choice to succeed himself as mayor of Pittsburgh, Joseph M. Barr, long a Lawrence protégé. Working for the Republican candidate, Paul B. Reinhold, Harry invented the campaign slogan What Pittsburgh Needs is a Good Dutch Cleanser. Barr won easily, as everybody knew he would in a city with an overwhelming Democratic registration lead. But winning was not Harry's objective; he wanted to get in his licks at Lawrence and his organization. This was a bizarre thing to do in view of Harry's next move.

In the spring of 1960 he entered the Democratic primary for the congressional seat representing Allegheny County's Twenty-eighth District (the Twenty-ninth had been eliminated and pieces of it parceled out to other districts). The incumbent, Democrat William S. Moorhead, had the party's endorsement for a second term. Harry had spent the better part of two years contending with the Lawrence organization and yet somehow expected to beat the party-endorsed incumbent. Willing now to try any gambit, or deal with any devil, to get back to Washington, he set out to win the favor of Teamsters president Jimmy Hoffa. The AFL-CIO had ousted the Teamsters Union on the grounds that it was under the influence of organized crime, and the federal government was trying to indict and prosecute Hoffa for various kinds of criminal activity. Harry published a brochure, sympathizing with Hoffa and appealing for his support, in return for which Harry would vote to repeal recently enacted legislation that gave the government additional tools to go after Hoffa and his union. There was no sign that Hoffa or the Teamsters reciprocated.[19]

After his easily predictable loss to Moorhead, Harry took an enforced vacation from electoral struggles. He had emptied his pockets, temporarily at least, of political tricks and quills for his "sharp and biting pen." Ten years had passed since he committed the biggest mistakes of his life, and he still could not find a path back to political favor.

Father Rice, on the other hand, had turned away from his anti-Communist obsessions and was starting a new life.

16

MAKING AMENDS AND
MAKING FRIENDS

I N March 1959, Bishop John J. Wright of New Orleans succeeded
John Deardon as spiritual leader of the Pittsburgh Catholic diocese.
The advent of Wright's episcopacy marked the beginning of a new
public life for Charles Owen Rice, who then was serving as pastor of a
parish in Little Washington. Wright, a political liberal with a growing reputation in the Catholic hierarchy (ten years later he would be elevated to
cardinal and transferred to the Vatican), had heard of Pittsburgh's labor
priest and soon brought Rice into his inner circle. The two men thought
alike on social and religious issues, and both supported Church reforms
that grew out of the papacy of John XXIII. Rice became Wright's representative to organized labor, a personal adviser on a range of labor, civil-
rights, and political issues and a member of the diocesan Board of
Consultors. In 1960, he began appearing again in the *Pittsburgh Catholic*
as author of a weekly column that commented freely and liberally on
political topics of the day. In his early fifties, back in favor and leading a
comfortable life, Rice might have been expected to back away from the
combat and fiery pronouncements of his earlier years and, as Patrick
McGeever puts it, "pass from a 'radical' (or at least liberal) youth to a
mellow and conservative middle age." Rice, instead, went in the opposite
direction.[1]

Among other things, he reexamined his anti-Communist career. It had culminated in 1950 with the partial breakup of the UE. Perhaps the highest tribute to Rice's effectiveness as an opponent came from Jim Matles. Rice, he says in his 1974 book, *Them and Us*, "had few rivals in hostility toward the UE and few who could be said to have helped more to weaken and split the union." By the early sixties, Rice was having second thoughts about his anti-Communist days. In a 1962 column he attacked HUAC, the committee that he had conspired with in an attempt to bring down the UE national leadership. HUAC, Rice wrote, "has often used its power of subpoena to bedevil and smear non and anti-communist political opponents. Its 'findings' have been misused by others, and what good it has accomplished seems to have been done by accident."[2]

According to his own account, two events in 1965 led Rice to reevaluate his early Cold War activism. They were President Lyndon Johnson's decisions, first, to invade the Dominican Republic to quell an uprising and second, to greatly increase America's military involvement in a war between the corrupt South Vietnamese government and Communist rebels backed by North Vietnam. In both instances, Rice believed, America was acting in bad faith. In the Dominican Republic, Johnson's real goal was not to protect American lives but to keep leftist insurgents from gaining control. In Vietnam, Rice argued, America's vital interests were not at stake in the Vietnamese civil war, as the United States falsely contended.[3]

Rice's developing perceptions about the gap between American ideals and actions abroad also extended to domestic policy. He always had condemned racial segregation, whether the overt de jure form in the South or the hypocritical de facto segregation in the North. In the early sixties, Rice felt a deep affinity to the civil-rights movement as it came boiling out of the South. He saw a connection between opposition to racial equality in the union and Catholic communities, with their support for the escalating war in Vietnam. Wanting to take an active civil-rights role, he asked Bishop Wright to transfer him from his comfortable parish in Little Washington to Holy Rosary parish in the Homewood section of Pittsburgh, one of the city's largest black communities and one that was seething with discontent. Wright complied, and in January 1966, Monsignor Charles Owen Rice (he had attained the rank of domestic prelate, with the title of right reverend monsignor, in 1964) took up residence in Homewood as pastor of Holy Rosary, becoming

"Wright's ambassador to the angry, disenfranchised blacks of Pittsburgh's ghetto."[4]

Now began one of the most controversial periods in Rice's life, especially as viewed by socially conservative union members. On the national level, he took an active role in organizations such as the NAACP (National Association for the Advancement of Colored People), Catholic Interracial Council, Citizens Against Slum Housing, Student Non-Violent Coordinating Committee, and Urban League. In Homewood, he became deeply involved with two neighborhood groups formed by young black militants, Forever Action Together and United Movement for Progress. Rice helped obtain funds from the Catholic diocese and other religious groups and in some instances participated in the two groups' activities, setting up programs to deal with inner-city problems, including high unemployment, lack of job training, and poor housing. The last half-decade of the 1960s was a particularly combative time in white-black relations in Pittsburgh, and Rice popped up in the thick of all kinds of scraps and controversies. In 1969–1970 he supported Pittsburgh blacks in demanding entry to all-white building-trade unions so they could work on construction jobs. In this campaign, he took a highly visible role, participating in demonstration marches and in his columns boldly attacking unions for their racial policies. Once a friend of these unions, he became their enemy. But he said he would "shed no tears if their bungling arrogance in the race crisis leads to their destruction."[5]

"Rice used his unique vantage point to try to explain the black rage and rebellion that was engulfing America's streets to the white working-class 'ethnics' who were the backbone of the Pittsburgh Church," says Charles McCollester in *Fighter With a Heart*. But Rice did more than explain. He often sided with militant groups against city officials and establishment organizations, allying himself in particular with Bouie Haden, the head of United Movement for Progress, and later with Nate Smith of Operation Dig in contending for construction jobs. Haden aroused fear and loathing among many whites, particularly since he had a record as a petty criminal. But Rice stood by him because Haden initiated job training for unemployed blacks and helped them obtain jobs, sometimes employing intimidating tactics such as boycotts and demonstrations. Whatever they did, both Rice and Haden made news. Implicated in their activities by extension, Bishop Wright received hate mail and was even hung in effigy by angry white Catholics.[6]

The black-power self-help groups had their share of hustlers, but they also produced astonishing local leaders who took responsibility for making change occur. Pittsburgh blacks may not have won any grand victories during the confrontational years of the 1960s and 1970s. But with that brilliant flair of activism, the militants forcibly opened society's eyes to the festering sores of oppression and, to some degree, frightened white America into opening jobs and other opportunities that had long been denied. In the process, blacks and whites began to lay the foundations for the improvements in employment, housing, education, and public accommodations that were to come. Rice was by no means the only priest who played a supporting role in this movement; in Pittsburgh, the younger Father Donald McIlvane followed a more confrontational approach than Rice and often landed in jail.[7]

Rice also became deeply involved in the antiwar movement. He first attacked U.S. intervention in the Vietnam War in a prescient 1965 column and later helped organize, and participated in, many antiwar demonstrations. In April 1967, he marched with Rev. Martin Luther King and Dr. Benjamin Spock at the head of three hundred thousand demonstrators in New York in the Spring Mobilization for Peace. (It was on this march that he and Spock were positioned on either side of King to protect him from would-be assassins.) Rice later wrote that as he walked arm in arm with King, "we shared our wonder that Christian ministers in an allegedly Christian country should be expected to apologize for demanding an end to a war." In the same year, Rice was a leader of the October 21 March on the Pentagon. In *The Armies of the Night*, Norman Mailer tells of meeting Rice on the day of the march. When Mailer's friend, the poet Robert Lowell, confessed to Rice that he was a lapsed Catholic, Mailer writes, the priest gave a "thoughtful, non-approving grunt." Some Catholics criticized Rice for wearing his clerical collar while marching in demonstrations, but Rice replied that the clergy must speak up as clergy. He contended that atrocities in Hitler's Germany occurred partly because clergy and other moral leaders remained silent.[8]

These years of political activism, directed in large part against government duplicity, seemed to sharpen Rice's awareness of his own shortcomings as a political thinker in the 1940s. It was as if, in opening his window on the world, Rice allowed in a flood of light that illuminated dark corners in his own room. Starting in the mid-1960s, Rice began an intermittent reappraisal of his role in the anti-Communist battles of the

1940s and concluded that, in a sense, he had succeeded too well.

Rice's recantations began in a *Pittsburgh Catholic* column in 1966. Reporting that labor negotiations would soon begin at Westinghouse and General Electric, Rice noted that nine different unions now represented workers at the two companies, compared with only two before the CIO split in 1949 (the UE and a salaried workers' union). Rice said he had "reflected upon it [his fight against the UE] a great deal in recent years" and had concluded that, contrary to his own statements in the forties, the UE had been "doing a good job as a labor organization." The trouble was, he wrote, "certain doctrinaire Stalinists insisted on carrying party propaganda in its [the UE's] journals and equipping some staff people with the same sort of nonsense." Consequently, the UE became "a sitting duck for the hysteria" of McCarthyism that broke out during the Korean War. "Those eager and blindly obedient Stalinists made easy the wrecking of a great union," Rice wrote. At this time he still accepted the notion, already partly disproved, that some "Stalinist" UE leaders, whom he did not name, operated under party control.[9]

Rice's thinking would evolve further, but for a first shot to the rear these comments represented a remarkable change of mind. This column was published shortly before the UE opened its 1966 convention in Pittsburgh. In *Them and Us*, Matles recounts that Rice telephoned Albert Fitzgerald, the UE president, when he arrived in Pittsburgh for the meeting. "'Fitzie,' he said, 'you are surprised to hear from me. I read the news that your convention is in town and I'm calling to wish you well.' When Fitzgerald replied that the good wishes were coming twenty years too late, Monsignor Rice said 'Even twenty years is not too long for a man to change his mind.'" Fitzgerald repeated this conversation to delegates at the convention, saying that Rice regretted "all the losses" suffered by the union over that twenty-year period. "'I forgive him and I suppose you do, too,'" Fitzgerald said. Matles does not say that he forgave Rice at that time, and certainly Tom Quinn did not.[10]

In an oral history interview in 1968, Rice revealed further ambivalence about his anti-Communist campaign, disclosing for the first time that Phil Murray had put Steelworker funds into that fight. This interview was not circulated for several years, but in any case it held more interest for historians than for the general public. The same was true of Rice's next expression of regret, published in an obscure religious magazine in 1977. During the 1940s, he says, he was "more of an unblinking

American-style patriot than I should have been." In consequence, he writes, "What bothers me personally, most of all, is that, in the very bad days of the Cold War, The Day of the Toad, Scoundrel Time, I did not defend all the victims. . . . I did not defend brave people whose careers and lives were destroyed by McCarthyism because of membership, alliance or mere flirtation with Communism."[11]

When Jim Matles died in 1975, Rice praised him as "a great trade union leader, who was magnificent in adversity and always served the working man." He continued, "Intense, selfless, incorruptible, humorless [here Rice misspoke] and dedicated, he was part of a union against which there was no breath of scandal and which did its best. May he rest in peace, although I am afraid he wanted no prayers of mine." Writing about the local UE leader that he had vied with most often, Tom Fitzpatrick, Rice called him a "splendid, local grass roots leader." When Steve Nelson, the former Communist leader in Pittsburgh, died in 1993, Rice wrote sympathetically about him and his career. The two had cooperated a few years earlier in remonstrating with the Spanish government for prosecuting a group of workers merely because they had tried to hold a union meeting.[12]

Rice's most extensive mea culpa came in a 1989 article written for *Labor History*, a journal edited by and for professional historians. He describes how, as a great believer in unions, he had worried that Communists might take control of the labor movement. "Their takeover would have been a disaster because of the reaction it would provoke; but there was no chance, absolutely no chance, of that happening." In coming to this conclusion, Rice says, he was "witness to a tremendous personal change of attitude and conviction." His "regrets about the whole business," Rice adds, "cluster around my over-intensity and my unremitting enmity, almost a blood feud that went on and on until well after they [Communists] ceased to be a domestic threat along with my complete acceptance of our country's Cold War stance and rhetoric." He remained deeply critical of those Communists who insisted on secrecy and loyalty to the party. They were "dishonest" in accepting and justifying the "horrors of the Stalin era." But many Communists themselves were "wonderful, idealistic people, deceived and deceiving, crafty but noble—and eventually so often destroyed along with what they had exhausted and broken themselves to build."[13]

Taken together, these writings amount to a strange combination of remorse, regret, and extensive—though not complete—repudiation of Rice's anti-Communist activities. Mixed in with this porridge was Rice's often-expressed pride in the effectiveness with which he battled trade-union Communists and people associated with them, subversive or not. When it comes to a retrospective on history, there are few more telling critics of a movement than one of its own leaders. Rice's confessions, as he once termed them, throw into sharp relief one of the most controversial periods in modern American history. They suggest that much of the accusatory activity and the accompanying suffering should not have occurred.

A small contingent of historians have analyzed Rice's statements and tried to imagine how history would have changed if he had not employed his formidable energies against labor's left wing. But even if Rice had never said a word against union Communists, the public hysteria of the 1949–1954 period would have penetrated the CIO. Phil Murray still would have had to contend with growing rank-and-file sentiment to sever relations with organizations that appeared to support Stalinism; powerful leaders like Walter Reuther still would have demanded that the left-wing unions be purged; on the other side, the UE still would have demanded political autonomy within the federation and the right to admit Communists as members. Without Rice's interventions, it is true, even an expelled UE might have avoided being stripped of its members in East Pittsburgh and other places, and the lives of individual UE members such as Bob Whisner, Frank Panzino, and Tom Quinn might not have been disrupted. But this is conjecture: a historical image of those times without Rice is just as murky as it is with him.

As a reporter, I frequently saw and spoke with Rice in Pittsburgh during the late sixties. I first interviewed him during the election battle between two top officers of the United Steelworkers, Dave McDonald and I. W. Abel, for presidency of the union in 1965. Having just begun covering the union, I was told that Rice could supply perceptive background on the political split. Although still living in Little Washington, he readily agreed to drive to Pittsburgh and meet me for lunch, displaying one facet of his personality that did not change much over the years: he enjoyed the role of expert commentator and gave generously of his time and thoughts to reporters and historical researchers. This was true even later in life when he knew that interviewers hoped to draw out embarrassing disclosures about his anti-Communist period. Talking about the Steelworkers in 1965, however, he appeared almost indifferent to his subject. He had little good to say about either McDonald or Abel and seemed uninterested in who would win, though he gave nominal support to McDonald, the incumbent. (Demonstrating a subsequent change in his attitude about many things political, Rice thereafter would support rank-and-file rebels such as Ed Sadlowski and Ron Weisen in their battles with the Steelworkers hierarchy.)

In contrast to the slightly bored, semiretired priest speaking in disparaging terms, I saw a much different Monsignor Rice the next time I spoke with him, in 1966. By then he was deeply engaged with black people in Homewood. At the age of fifty-eight he seemed to have found a political vocation to go with the religious, and he made his enthusiasm known to the entire city. At practically every public demonstration in support of equal rights, there would be Rice, cajoling, demanding, condemning. No longer the pious priest dutifully dabbling in civic affairs, Rice now talked and acted like a fast-thinking tactical commander in a great and noble, if uncontrollable, movement. Every Sunday my wife, Joanne, and I picked up a copy of the *Pittsburgh Catholic* at Mass for the sole purpose of reading Rice's column. On the Vietnam War and civil rights, he wrote trenchantly and with passion. He was riding a wave, and although he might not have been sure where it was carrying him, he rode with great authority.

Rev. Martin Luther King was assassinated in Memphis on April 4, 1968. As in many other cities, rioting, looting, and burning broke out in Pittsburgh's black neighborhoods and lasted for four days. National Guard units and police patrolled downtown streets and broke up all gatherings of more than ten people under a state-of-emergency ordinance. King's murder and the resulting violence brought the entire movement to a dramatic decision point: would black and white America now go in opposite directions, or would they pull closer together and proceed toward an integrated society? Many whites, angry about the assassination, wanted to demonstrate in favor of the latter course. On Sunday, April 7, the police reluctantly allowed about thirty-five hundred blacks and whites to march through downtown Pittsburgh along a route lined with guardsmen and police. I put aside my reporter's notebook and marched with my wife. The next day, with the emergency decree still in force, nervous authorities refused to condone another street demonstration, this

one planned by Rice and several other ministers. The meeting was shifted indoors, and there I saw Rice, reacting with swift presence of mind,
prevent what might have been a violent incident involving hundreds of
people.

The religious leaders had called for a mass meeting with the slogan
Bury White Racism. As I walked from my office to the designated place,
I saw squads of police equipped with riot gear stationed at street corners.
National guardsmen and state troopers were patrolling in the Hill Dis-
trict and Homewood, and a large number were bivouacked at the Civic
Arena, prepared to rush to trouble spots. On downtown streets, I wrote
in my journal, "tensions showed on every face." Told that the police for-
bade an open-air assembly, the ministers convened the meeting at the
First Lutheran Church on Grant Street, about a quarter mile north of the
county courthouse.

About five hundred mostly white people eventually gathered in an
auditorium-like hall at First Lutheran. Included were a large number of
young people, presumably students eager to demonstrate their fervor.
Sitting near the front row, I noted that when Rice tried to speak about
the King assassination and its aftermath in Pittsburgh, he appeared to be
close to tears and said he was at a loss for words. A Protestant minister
named Rev. James Gardner, however, made some eloquent comments.
White people should "avoid breast-beating and self-flagellation," he said.
"It is not for us to tell the Negro how to cry." But neither his eloquence
nor Rice's tears suggested an agenda that could be followed to "bury
white racism." The demeanor of the meeting changed dramatically when
the next speaker, a militant white antipoverty leader, demanded immediate action on political reforms that would give blacks a stronger voice
in city government. Urging the audience to rise up on the instant and
march to the mayor's office, he left the stage and strode toward the rear
of the church. Other people rose and followed him. The idea of an
unruly crowd bursting into the street to form up as marchers, with
dozens of cops stationed outside on foot and horseback, struck me as
particularly foolish. Most of the other leaders seemed struck dumb, not
knowing what to do. Father Rice rushed to the podium and, speaking in
an urgent tone, pleaded with people to stay in their seats. "Do not do
this!" he said over and over. The police were tired and tensions were taut,
he said, and this was not the time or place to mount a protest march.

Many people applauded Rice, but others continued to leave their seats. A young white woman rose in the audience and challenged Rice, intimating that he was betraying African Americans for not taking to the streets. More people, mainly younger ones that I took for college students, whistled and clapped and moved toward the doorway. Rice made a final effort, walking to the edge of the stage and shouting again, "Do not do this!" He projected a tangible sense of danger, not as a hypothetical possibility, but as an inevitable outcome, a warning coming from a man who had walked many a picket line and had sized up dangerous situations. He clearly swayed a large majority of the audience. They filed peacefully out the doors onto the sidewalk. Two dozen white-helmeted cops stood at curbside. If hundreds of people had poured out of the church, shouting and shaking fists, the cops surely would have surged forward. As I walked out of the church, cops were ordering people to keep moving. The young woman who had challenged Rice in the church sat in the middle of the sidewalk, holding a White Racism sign. Three or four cops approached and ordered her to move. She refused to budge. Rice came along and urged her to walk away. "Your self-dramatization is doing no good," he told her. But she was adamant. Four cops picked her up bodily and deposited her in a paddy wagon.[14]

When I left the church area, the last stragglers were dispersing. Eventually, I later learned, seventeen students attempted a march to the City-County Building and were arrested without incident. Almost single-handedly, Rice had averted what could have been a bloody confrontation. For all his militant words and actions, he was no wild-eyed radical interested only in fomenting rebellion. I would see him in many other situations and interview him on other occasions, but his inability to speak through his tears after Rev. Martin Luther King's assassination on that day at First Lutheran, followed by his urgent plea, "Do not do this!" to people on the verge of acting rashly in the name of morality, would always stay with me as a measure of the man.

Rice's political persona seemed to undergo a transformation once every decade or so as the world changed. In the thirties and forties, his fierce embrace of unionism and fight against Communists made him a hero of working-class Catholics. In the sixties, he alienated the same group with his civil-rights and antiwar activities. In the seventies, when the issues of women's rights and the Church's positions on abortion and birth control were prominent, Rice assumed a more traditionalist posture and lost many allies he had formed in the civil-rights and antiwar struggles. He had never deviated from Church teaching, however; it was simply that the reproductive issues did not emerge as topics in political discourse until the seventies. He did not change to appeal to his earlier following, and it is doubtful that they came back to his corner.[15]

The civil-rights movement gradually waned through the 1970s, and the fierce young black militants either became community leaders or drifted off. Rice felt his usefulness in Homewood had run its course. He asked to be transferred to St. Anne's in Castle Shannon, a suburb south of Pittsburgh, to fill a vacant pastorate. Phil Murray and his family had lived in an unimposing home in Castle Shannon and belonged to St. Anne's parish. He and his wife were buried in the parish cemetery, and a bell tower erected in his honor resounded with the tolling of hours. Rice became pastor of St. Anne's in May 1976. Retiring in 1986, he stayed on at the rectory near the grave of his friend.[16]

Tom Quinn met Monsignor Rice in person once or twice when both spoke at antiwar rallies. One occasion in particular stuck in Quinn's memory. "I remember it was down in Market Square," he said. "When Rice got up to talk, he made a speech about what great friends we were." Quinn laughed at the recollection. Did Rice apologize to him for arranging the HUAC hearing in 1949? "Nah! He never did. We never talked a lot, he and I, about anything." Perhaps the complimentary words were Rice's way of apologizing.

As time passed, Quinn's anger had faded, though it never completely disappeared. As late as 2003, he still blamed Rice for "ruining a good union." Once Quinn determined that a grave wrong had been committed against anyone, he seldom forgot or forgave the offense, though he tolerated the offender. The only time he sought revenge was when Uncle Harry ran for reelection in 1950, but he viewed that as more a political than a personal matter. Quinn had a sense of right and wrong that would not bend in any wind. I saw that certitude when I first interviewed him in 1966. He was direct, forceful, and entirely lacking in equivocation. Yet he exuded pleasantness and good humor. The only mystery about Tom Quinn was how such singularity of purpose and utter friendliness could live together in one nature without coming to blows. Edwin Wintermyer, a labor mediator who later worked under Quinn, observed of him that "he never wavers, never changes, never has. Everybody knows where he's coming from. Tom is no phony."[17]

Circumstances changed significantly for Quinn and his family in the sixties. Still employed by the UE as an international representative, he was appointed business agent of Local 610 in 1962. The local represented more than five thousand workers at the Air Brake plant in Wilmerding and Union Switch and Signal in Swissvale. As business agent, Quinn served as the full-time administrative head of the local and chief negotiator in contract bargaining. He also continued to negotiate for smaller locals in western Pennsylvania. The UE had surmounted most of its Cold War difficulties and was successfully organizing new members. From a low of 90,000 members in the midfifties, the UE grew to about 165,000 in 1966. The IUE was still much larger, but dissatisfaction over Jim Carey's leadership had resulted in a disgraceful episode of attempted vote stealing. In a 1964 mail-ballot election of officers, Carey's vote counters announced that Carey had won. The opposition, led by presidential candidate Paul Jennings and including local leaders such as John Vento of East Pittsburgh, charged vote fraud and sought judicial intervention. Eventually, the U.S. Labor Department recounted impounded ballots and declared Jennings the victor. He took over the union, and Carey retired in 1965.[18]

As the Quinns' sons grew to manhood and spent more time away from home, Irene needed something to occupy her time. "The empty-nest syndrome," Chuck Quinn said. "Her whole life was built around taking care of her boys, and she didn't have anything to do when we moved out." Tom, still traveling frequently on union business, could not fill the empty hours. The mother who had always seemed so secure and serene was vulnerable to loneliness. She took a job in a nearby shopping center and eventually became a jewelry sales clerk. When Tom saw that Irene enjoyed working outside the home, he talked to a friend in county government, who found an office job for her. She later switched to a clerical position at the State Department of Revenue office in Pittsburgh. The jobs gave Irene a sense of accomplishment and extra income to buy clothing and decorative objects for the house.

Irene and Tom always had urged, even demanded, that their sons get a college education, although Tom's UE salary precluded setting up a college fund. The boys, nonetheless, used a combination of income from part-time jobs and scholarships to earn an impressive array of college degrees. Chuck, the oldest, graduated from the University of Pittsburgh, obtained a doctorate in history at Carnegie-Mellon University, and became a teacher. He and his wife, Rochelle, brought up four children. Ron received a bachelor's in music at Duquesne University and a master's in performance at Yale University. An illness prevented him from becoming a professional bassoonist, but he performs regularly with semi-professional orchestras and a woodwind quintet in the Pittsburgh area. Steve Quinn graduated from the University of Pittsburgh, earned a master's in political science at the University of Wisconsin, and also became a teacher. He married in 1972 and has one daughter.[19]

The family had made it through the long, dark tunnel of 1950s Red baiting with only a few bad memories. Quinn guessed that he was still under FBI surveillance, and his FBI file indicates that a pro forma monitoring continued until 1970. But he no longer felt that some government agency or congressional committee hovered in the vicinity, prepared to pounce. In his union work, he gradually evolved from a fierce young warrior to a leader with broader community interests. One immediate concern was the deteriorating situation of workers and communities in the Turtle Creek and Monongahela valleys. Manufacturing employment had declined, and many mill and factory towns were losing jobs, population, tax revenues, and whatever allure they once had for new businesses. Some of the towns were trying with little success to cope with massive problems, including smoke, dirt, polluted skies and waterways, obsolete plants and equipment, old housing, rundown business districts, and inadequate highways in and out of the valleys. In 1963, Westinghouse Air Brake threatened to move out of Wilmerding unless improvements were made.[20]

Although constantly at odds with WABCO over wages, benefits, and working conditions in the plant, Quinn sided with the company on the need to act. He helped form the Wilmerding Community Improvement Advisory Committee, made up of representatives from corporations, private businesses, labor, government agencies, schools, and the legal and medical professions. It obtained county and federal help to demolish and reconstruct portions of the community and to build a highway system linking towns in the Turtle Creek Valley and facilitating truck traffic to and from the plants. The committee also initiated social-service programs and oversaw construction of new housing and recreation sites. "We transformed an old mill town into a rehabilitated, newer-concept mill-town community," said Henry Slaczka, who served as committee chairman for fifteen years. "Local 610 was a key player," Slaczka said, "and Tom was always available if I needed any assistance." This group was still functioning in 2004. Wilmerding fared much better than the larger mill towns along the Monongahela. "I'm proud of what happened in Wilmerding," Quinn said. "We had a strong committee, which didn't allow the politicians to take over and hand out contracts to their friends, as happened in some of the steel towns."[21]

Quinn also threw himself into politics. After the Progressive Party disbanded he had switched to the Democratic Party and gradually expanded his and the UE's influence in local and state contests. He eventually would become a member of the Democratic State Committee. Meanwhile, working as a party organizer and perennially involved in election contests, he formed friendships on all sides, from left to right. His Republican friends included Elsie Hillman, head of the Allegheny County Republican Committee and for many years a Republican national committeewoman from Pennsylvania, and Dick Thornburgh, the U.S. attorney in Pittsburgh, who would go on to serve two terms as governor of Pennsylvania and as U.S. attorney general under Presidents Ronald Reagan and George H. W. Bush. Quinn even supported Thornburgh in his failing bid for a congressional seat in 1966.[22]

In 1971, Quinn was impressed by a young Republican named H. John Heinz III, thirty-three, grandson of the founder of H. J. Heinz and Company. He was seeking a seat in the House of Representatives from a district that encompassed North Side Pittsburgh and communities along the Allegheny River. At Quinn's urging, the UE endorsed Heinz, largely because of his stands on labor, trade, and benefits for the elderly and because he ran a smart, well-financed campaign. In a strange twist of history, his opponent was John Connelly, Uncle Harry's former congressional aide. By this time, Connelly's marketing-promotion business was flourishing, and he had plenty of money too. Quinn respected Connelly and his liberal credentials but thought that Heinz was more likely to win and stay in Congress a long time.

"The papers called it the Battle of the Millionaires," Connelly told me. "I had assets of maybe 5 million dollars. John had hundreds of millions." He laughed. Harry offered to help Connelly. Appearing at meetings with the candidate, Harry "told people what a good assistant I'd been, and I would be a credit in Congress." But the Heinz name and fortune gave the Republican an overwhelming advantage. He won handily, and Connelly never again ran for elective office. Heinz later shifted to the U.S. Senate. He died in a plane crash on April 4, 1991.[23]

My cousin Jake Osterman, who worked in many Republican campaigns in the sixties, met Quinn often and got along well with him. "Tom Quinn was on the left, yes," Jake said, "but he was an intelligent leftist. He could see the other side and work with the other side as long as they were reasonable and decent." [24]

On one issue, however, Quinn would not compromise. He had opposed the Vietnam War from its earliest days, objecting to U.S. involvement as a political and humanitarian mistake of tragic proportions. Speaking at rallies, meetings, and seminars, he urged workers and unions to organize in protest against the war. His outspoken antiwar stand drew unexpected criticism from some Local 610 UE members. At about the same time, an even more important conflict with Jim Matles forced Quinn to reassess his position in the UE. Eventually he would leave the union that he had served for more than thirty years.

17

DECLINE AND ASCENT

SHORTLY after returning to the Pittsburgh area in December 1964 following a ten-year absence, I began asking in the Davenport family about Uncle Harry's whereabouts. My mother wondered why I wanted to see him. She had detected in me signs of a do-gooder looking for causes to fight for and unfortunates to lift out of poverty and misery. I had done none of that, but Mother always thought she knew me better than I knew myself. As for Harry, she had lost all hope that he would rejuvenate himself, get a regular job, and live a "normal" life. "Don't think you're going to save him," Mother warned.

Save is not a word I would have used, but I did have vague thoughts of reconnecting him with the family, as well as learning something about my eccentric uncle. It was not that the family had neglected Harry. My sister and her husband, Ronald McKay, had helped him in various ways, as had Mother and her sisters, before I moved back to town. But Harry seemed to take from other people and never give anything of himself in return. I thought a show of concern by another member of the younger generation might reel him back in. Inclined to romantic notions about people at odds with society, I may have overdramatized his situation. Nonetheless, that is what I was thinking when I called the bathhouse where Harry was living. We arranged to meet for a drink one evening after work.

I recognized him through the front window of the saloon on Forbes Avenue. He was standing at the bar, restlessly swiveling left and right to survey the nearly empty taproom, prepared to acknowledge admiring glances that might be coming his way. I knew that personality tic.[1]

His arc of search, swinging toward the door just as I entered, stopped abruptly. Harry had found his audience. He took my outstretched hand, his lips curling in the same droll grin I had seen so often in the past. "You're not as tall as your father was," he said.

"No," I replied, instantly recalling how he had sent me off to the army in 1953, "but I'm as nice a guy as he was." I ordered beers for both of us.

We had met at my sister's home the previous year when I briefly visited Pittsburgh. But there we had been among a lot of people. This was an intimate tête-à-tête between an uncle and nephew who had swum laps together at the McKeesport YMCA. After a few polite inquiries about his general well-being, I stopped posing questions. I felt it would be cruel to ask what he was doing these days because I sensed that he was not doing much of anything except reading, walking around, and dabbling in politics. Taking over the conversation by default, Harry asked about my current reading. When I mentioned a couple of novels, he told me I ought to read more history and political theory. We needed intellectuals to replace the ideological poseurs and military brassheads who had led us into a dead end of eternal world conflict. I responded with a hearty "Uh-huh!"

I had feared that Harry might be destitute. But, like the Harry of old, he wore a suit and tie, of respectable age. A neatly folded overcoat lay on the stool beside him. Aside from sagging cheek flesh, his outward shape had not changed much. But by the end of our conversation, I saw that the man inside had somehow shriveled without reducing his bulk. There was no talk of writing a book or running for office, or seeking revenge on anyone. All ambition to do good, or ill, had died out. Harry had become a professional former congressman.

I invited Harry to dinner the following weekend to see Joanne and our children. As we stood outside the saloon, pulling up our coat collars and preparing to set off in different directions, Harry averted his head and muttered, in a voice so low I had to strain to make it out, "D'ya have a few extra bucks?" I gave my uncle a ten-dollar bill.

We met every month or two when I was not traveling. We would generally have a few drinks at one or more saloons of his choosing in downtown Pittsburgh. Although he knew I would pay, Harry always led me to an ordinary beer joint—of which he had an extraordinary collection stored in his memory—rather than an expensive habitat of martini drinkers. On each occasion, as we parted, I would slip him a five or ten, depending on how much cash I had left for the bus home and a bus back to work in the morning. We usually talked about current events, guided by Harry's recent reading. I remember a conversation about labor unions. I had mentioned something about Walter Reuther, I believe. Harry waved dismissively. "Reuther's like all the others. All union leaders have sold out, lost their way. Whatever happened to the shorter work week and the guaranteed annual wage?" Recalling those labor slogans from a far-off time, he shook his head. "Unions meant something in those days. Today it's all business unionism. Take the money and run. There's no backbone in the labor movement any more."

And so the conversation went . . . and so conversations with Harry usually went: all abstractions and politics. He had left behind sensuality, family intimacy, friendship, and religion and lived in an intellectualized world of politics and political history. If there was love in his world, it remained in the attic, crammed into a steamer trunk with a rusted lock. He had no curiosity about his sisters and their husbands and children. After he met Joanne, whom he took a liking to, and our children, he occasionally would ask about them. Now and then I managed to drag out of him reminiscences about family history. His father, he said, laughing, was a "hard man," but Harry abruptly moved to another subject. The conversation would never linger in the past but always return to current events. The more that American involvement in Vietnam escalated, the louder Harry demanded Lyndon Johnson's impeachment—and the more I glanced apprehensively at our bar companions. He praised the Berkeley free-speech movement and the SDS (Students for a Democratic Society), and he talked a lot about how Americans, especially liberals, had been co-opted by our materialistic culture.

On Thanksgiving or Christmas I would drive into Pittsburgh and pick up Harry at the Arena Baths on Forbes Avenue, where he lived, and bring him to our home in the suburbs for dinner and a stay overnight. He fascinated our boys with tricks and funny stories. My older son, Peter, remembered those visits. "He was the kind of guy who pulls quarters out of kids' ears," Peter said. "He always wore a suit and was sort of impressive. I liked him. But in the morning, I'd go into the living room and see this old man sleeping on the couch. It was scary."

On Thanksgiving in 1965, both Mother and Harry came for dinner, as well as Lynn and Ron McKay. We had a wonderful time listening to sister and brother trading stories about growing up on Jenny Lind Street in McKeesport. Mother remembered their father dominating the dinner table, demanding rigid behavior. Harry, she said, would bend over to pick up a spoon or fork that had conveniently fallen and, coming back up, would make a funny face as their father carved a roast beef or leg of lamb. Mother and her sisters could not help but giggle, and their father would make the girls sit at the table after dessert. Harry would get several whacks on the backside. That Thanksgiving evening, listening to their stories, was as enjoyable as any I had spent in Harry's presence, and I felt good about bringing him and Mother together. As usual, though, he drank too much. He fell silent for a while, then erupted with sarcastic remarks. My mother turned away in disgust.

Harry told me that he now and then earned money by writing publicity material and "selling stuff." As an ad man he was in part a con man and could sell anything to anybody, as Joanne and I found out. He came to dinner one evening with brochures advertising the Great Books of the Western World series, a fifty-five-volume set edited by University of Chicago professors and published by the Encyclopedia Britannica. My salary in those days only barely kept us ahead of ordinary bills, and we politely resisted Harry's spiel for a week or two before giving in and buying the set on an installment plan. I do not know how much commission he received, but I imagine it paid for room, meals, and booze for a couple of weeks. At about the same time, I discovered that although Harry had turned sixty-five, he had not applied for Social Security. I was astounded. Harry had registered for Social Security in 1938 and as a congressman had voted to increase benefits paid to the elderly. Nonetheless, he seemed to feel there was something ignoble about collecting benefits. I pointed out that it was not the same as receiving welfare. Yes, of course he knew that, he grumbled, but he just did not want to apply. I pressed more. Finally he said, "I don't want to answer a lot of questions from a lot of bureaucrats. And I don't want to talk any more about it."

Some months later Harry ran out of money, fell behind in his room rent at the Arena Baths, and sought legal advice from Ron McKay. He reluctantly agreed to apply for Social Security but worried that the bath-house management might confiscate the monthly check when it arrived in the mail. Ron set up a plan under which the government mailed the benefit check, amounting to about $150, to Ron's office. After Harry endorsed the check, Ron would deposit it in a trustee account at a bank. When Harry needed money, he would stop at the office, pick up a check written against the trustee account, and cash it for rent and other expenses. Ron's system protected Harry from the bathhouse manage-ment—and from himself.

The Arena Baths served Harry's purposes in a number of ways. A bathhouse dormitory was a relatively cheap place to sleep; the steam room catered to Harry's fetish, as John Connelly described it, for clean-liness; and the Arena was located near downtown Pittsburgh. The reality of the place was not as bad as I had imagined it. Harry took me there a couple of times, and I especially recall the first visit. After we undressed and wrapped our midsections in towels, Harry took me into the sauna, where we climbed to the top level of tiered wooden benches on which lounged two elderly men desultorily swatting themselves with oak-leaf shoots. As we sat there sweating, Harry began a learned discussion of a contemporary sociopolitical work, C. Wright Mills's *The Power Elite*, as I recall, which he urged me to read. From the sauna, I followed him into the steam room and after a few minutes, groping around in clouds of steam, we escaped through another door to take a dip in a small pool. Then back into the steam room for a while, followed by immersion in cold showers.

After we dressed, Harry asked if I wanted to see where he slept. "Sure," I said, though I was by no means sure. We went upstairs to a sec-ond-floor dormitory consisting of a couple of rows of single beds. This was a segregated bathhouse, Harry told me with a laugh. Homosexuals slept, or whatever, in tiny private rooms on the third floor.

"And this is my bedroom," he said with mock pride, pointing to a bed with a rumpled brown blanket. Books were piled on the floor under the bed. There were more books in a nearby locker where he kept a few clothes. He never bought books, rather stealing them from libraries because he detested having to go through the checkout routine. He had perfected a means of secreting books on his person when taking them from the library—and bringing them back, as he always did.

I stood staring at my sixty-six-year-old uncle's bed, a six-by-three-foot slice of personal space in a room of snoring, farting, coughing men. It was like any number of army barracks I had lived in, though most of my barracks mates and I knew we were not stuck for the rest of our lives in those quarters.

Harry saw me hesitate. "Sometimes it gets a little . . . stuffy in here," he said with a laugh. "But usually it's okay."

I urged him to get reacquainted with the family, to call his sisters now and then and see how they were doing. He talked occasionally with Sister Catherine but never to my mother or Aunt Annamae (Kate had died in 1965). Everyone in the family had given him various kinds of help over the years, but he showed little interest in them.

Once, though, Harry made an effort to be nice. He told me he had received a check for work as a political consultant and wanted to invite the entire family to dinner at a "wonderful" Chinese restaurant. Would I spread the word? In due course, the arrangements were made, and about ten family members (without children), met Harry at a restaurant in Pittsburgh's "Chinatown," the full extent of which included three or four buildings on Second and Third Avenues. Harry acted as host. He kissed all the women, told funny stories, ordered a second round of cocktails. He offered a toast to "my loving sisters and their wonderful families." It was, indeed, a good meal. At the height of the merriment, as we sipped after-dinner drinks, Harry disappeared. I assumed he had gone to the men's room. But our host never returned. We guests had to split the check.

The tragic and spectacular events of 1968—the assassinations of Robert Kennedy and Rev. Martin Luther King, police beating of protesters in the streets of Chicago during the Democratic National Convention, Johnson's decision not to run for a second term, and Richard Nixon's election as president—rang a fire bell for Harry. Early in the year, when Eugene J. McCarthy, the moody, quirky Democrat from Minnesota, suddenly spurted to the top of a list of candidates for the Democratic presidential nomination, Harry joined McCarthy's campaign. He and McCarthy had become friends when both served as freshmen representatives in 1949–1950, Harry told me excitedly. He signed on as publicity chairman of the Citizens for McCarthy campaign in Pittsburgh, hoping that the future President McCarthy would not only end the war in Vietnam but also, perhaps, take his old congressional friend back to Washington. In 2003, I talked with Daniel Berger, who had served as chairman of Citizens for McCarthy in Pittsburgh. He recalled that Harry produced leaflets, posters, and a throwaway newspaper touting McCarthy's qualifications and appeared at a rally with him in Pittsburgh.[2]

I saw Harry in action one day about a month before the Democratic convention in 1968 and recorded the following scene and conversations in my journal. The Steelworkers union frequently held conferences and meetings at the Penn-Sheraton Hotel, known today as the Omni William Penn. The hotel was a frequent stopping place for Harry on his daily strolls in the courthouse area. I would occasionally see him in the lobby sitting room, a large rectangular area with forty or fifty chairs of all descriptions arranged around the perimeter. With its ornate decor, the room appeared to have been imported from the Gilded Era. Yet it served well enough as a place of respite for anybody who wandered in. Harry would sit there reading or scrawling notes, frequently gazing around to see who was passing through. One day in early July, when hundreds of union officials from locals around the country were attending a national bargaining conference at the hotel, I sauntered into the sitting room at noontime to catch union people on their way to lunch. Uncle Harry caught me first. Carrying a bulging briefcase, he wore a Citizens for McCarthy button on his coat lapel. The committee, he said, was wooing union members and blacks, two groups of Americans who seemed resistant to McCarthy's appeal, and he wanted me to introduce him to some of the union officials.

Dozens of local presidents were streaming toward the door, on their way to restaurants in the area. I introduced Harry to a large, florid-faced man from a Steelworkers local in Gary, Indiana. I shall call him Charlie. "Hi ya, Charlie," Harry said, pumping his hand. "I'm working for the man I think will be the next president of the United States. Who are you supporting?" No subterfuge there. Avoiding a direct answer, Charlie said he had not made up his mind but he could tell us about the situation in Gary. His voice rising with indignation, Charlie declared that Richard Hatcher, the first black mayor of Gary, was discriminating against white people. Most of the white steelworkers he knew, Charlie said, intended to vote for George Wallace, the segregationist Alabama governor who was running on a third-party ticket.

"Oh, no!" Harry said. "You have got to stop that movement. Don't you know Wallace is antilabor and a racist?"

I thought, "Uh-oh." Charlie was the wrong man to engage on this issue. Only a few days before I had heard him refer to blacks as "jungle bunnies" and "niggers."

Charlie did not appreciate being lectured to. "Look," he said, moving closer to Harry, "you asked my opinion and I gave it to you. You come out to Gary, you'll see. The streets are so unsafe, our members are afraid to go to union meetings at night." He listed a few more items in his litany of anti-Hatcher feelings, talking over Harry's attempts to praise McCarthy.

Harry stood his ground and shook his head as Charlie raved on. By this time several other men had gathered around, attracted by Charlie's gravelly voice. One was Bernard Novak, president of the U.S. Steel Irvin Works local in West Mifflin. I nudged Bernie forward and introduced him to Harry, noting that Bernie was running for the state legislature as a Democrat. Harry immediately dismissed Charlie as a no-sale and focused on Bernie, jabbing a finger for emphasis as he ticked off points in McCarthy's prolabor program. He opened his briefcase and pulled out layouts he had prepared for McCarthy leaflets, talking all the while. "We can assure your election if you work for McCarthy," Harry told Novak. "I can put 250 kids on a house-to-house campaign, for free." Harry drew a pen from an inside pocket. "Let's set up a meeting to work out the details."

Bernie begged off, saying he had to take care of union business. "I'll see you later," he said, flashing a politician's smile.

Dan Hannan, president of the Steelworkers local at the Clairton Works of U.S. Steel, was standing on the edge of the group. I gave a come-on wave. Hannan was a quiet, thoughtful man for whom I had deep respect. He had to fight both the company and his own international union to win relief for Clairton coke-oven workers, mostly black men, who were exposed to excessive, cancer-producing smoke. Dan took a step or two toward us. But when he saw Harry's McCarthy badge, he stopped and blurted out, "I'm not gonna talk to any McCarthy man, not when McCarthy's against the war!" He walked off angrily.

Others in the group surrounding Harry, as if echoing Dan's and Charlie's views, also drifted away. Harry and I walked back through the lobby toward Grant Street, I musing to myself that working-class politics were not as simple as they might have been in the thirties. "It looks like you'll have trouble bringing out a labor vote for McCarthy," I said, putting it mildly.

My uncle shrugged. "Unions aren't imparting the right values. These days it's all about money. Cash register unionism. To hell with brother-hood and social progress."

Harry already sensed that the McCarthy campaign was fading, and with it his own hopes for a political rebirth. (In August, delegates at the Democratic National Convention in Chicago would vote overwhelming-ly to nominate Vice President Hubert Humphrey for president.) On a deeper level, Harry's outburst expressed disillusionment with a cause in which he had placed soaring hopes more than thirty years before—the industrial union movement as embodied in the CIO. In the early, explo-sive years of growth, it seemed to have the potential for remaking a soci-ety dominated by corporate interests and indifferent to racism and the welfare of people at the bottom. By the fifties, CIO unions had boosted elite groups of industrial workers several rungs up the economic ladder. But in the sixties, the nation's first real progress toward racial equality stripped away illusions of brotherhood in what was left of the labor movement, revealing a deep strain of bigotry among white blue-collar union members. Most unions and their members also had drifted into unquestioning support for the Vietnam War. All great social and politi-cal movements eventually take erratic turns to left or right, invariably disappointing many original followers. Harry was left stranded on an idealistic atoll with many other disillusioned believers, including the two men whose words and actions had led to his downfall, Father Rice and Tom Quinn.

The Vietnam War had lasted nearly ten years by the early 1970s and still America had not extricated itself. During all that time Quinn had continued his public condemnation of the war. He was acting on his own convictions, but the UE could hardly complain about his public appearances because the international union had adopted a resolution against the war in the midsixties. Individual members, of course, were not bound by this resolution, and many strongly supported the war. A group of prowar activists in Local 610 complained about Quinn identi-fying himself as business agent of the local when he spoke publicly. "Some stewards in the local said they didn't want to be associated with someone who opposed the war," Quinn said. "My answer was, I wasn't say-ing anything that is not the policy of the UE. But the local officers prevailed on national officers, including [Jim] Matles, to order me to stop identifying myself with Local 610. That didn't sit well with me."

Quinn had another problem in the UE. His experience and loyalty amply qualified him for a higher elected post, even in the top-level tier of officers. But the path upward was blocked. In most unions, the politically ambitious move up one step at a time. The next step for Quinn would be getting elected as president of UE District 6 and a member of the union's executive board. But this would have meant running against a good friend, the incumbent Daniel Marguerite. There might have been other routes to the top in the UE, but Quinn received no encouragement from the one man whose support was essential, Matles.

"When that didn't happen," Ron Quinn said, "Dad decided to go in another direction. There was a disappointment, a reaction, and a new plan." He decided to leave the UE if he could find another job, no easy matter for a fifty-seven-year-old man with a radical past. At the suggestion of a friend, he took and passed a state civil service test for a position as labor mediator with the Pennsylvania Bureau of Mediation. "Once he did that," Ron added, "he shifted gears and became very enthusiastic about being a mediator." In 1974, Quinn applied for a job in the bureau's Pittsburgh office.[3]

By chance Quinn's timing could not have been more propitious. The state mediation bureau was not recognized as a first-rate service when compared with the Federal Mediation and Conciliation Service. If major corporations and their unions needed help in avoiding a strike, they normally requested the assistance of federal mediators. State mediators generally entered bargaining situations at smaller employers in the private sector. This was about to change, however. In 1974, the very year that Quinn applied for a job, a new state law became effective, greatly increasing the mediation bureau's scope of responsibility. Public Employee Act 195 extended collective bargaining rights to many thousands of public employees in schools and government units and directed the bureau to help employers and unions reach peaceful settlements. The new law portended significant, potentially disruptive changes in relations between teachers and school boards in more than five hundred school districts throughout Pennsylvania. Teachers' unions existed at most schools, but in the past they had had only a consultative role in determining wages and working conditions. Now they would negotiate the terms of employment, with a right to strike after a required bargaining period elapsed and if mediation proved unsuccessful. Most local union leaders had little experience in bargaining, and school administrators, who had even less, objected to the very idea of negotiating with teachers.

Although aware of the new law, Quinn still was surprised when the bureau's regional director in Pittsburgh, James Rush, offered him a job. "We were really swamped," Rush told me. "The teachers were ready to go. They wanted to negotiate, and if we weren't there they would go on strike." A former industrial-relations executive with U.S. Steel, Rush had spent much of his career dealing with unions before turning to mediation in 1960. More than ten years had passed since the last vestiges of McCarthyism faded away, and Rush dismissed the old Communist allegations against Quinn. The only relevant part of Quinn's long association with the left-wing UE, Rush thought, was his extensive bargaining experience. Negotiating labor contracts had little to do with political ideology. American workers wanted contracts that were strong on wages, benefits, and job security and short on ideology, and they would quickly unelect a leader who injected political issues into bargaining at the expense of bread-and-butter concerns.

As a successful negotiator for more than twenty years, Quinn also possessed one skill essential to a mediator: the ability to apply objective analysis to bargaining situations. A union bargainer could not afford to mislead himself or his members about an employer's financial condition or to lead a strike in which the members lost more than they gained. A union leader had to be objective enough to recognize a realistic management offer and forceful enough to convince his constituents to accept it. One could not learn this in school; it came only through experience, and Rush was impressed by Quinn's record in the UE.

Peaceful bargaining was the primary goal of labor mediation, and Quinn was well suited to the task. Ever since he and his family had scraped through the four-month strike at Westinghouse in 1946, he had focused his efforts as a UE negotiator on settling disputes without a work stoppage. Quinn succeeded not by bending to the will of the employer, but by deciding—sometimes in a process akin to divination—how to draw from the employer his best possible offer and then persuading the members that the time had come to say yes.

Ron Quinn remembered hearing his father talk often about negotiating contracts. "For Dad, it wasn't about rabble-rousing and striking. You only went on strike when you couldn't get it to work any other way."

Quinn settled into his new job with ease. He worked initially with a mediator named Hyman Richman, who had joined the mediation service after an administrative career with the federal government. "Tom was a trainee under me, but he had such a better background than I did," Richman said in a 2000 interview. Management negotiators soon learned that Quinn prodded both sides equally to reach a peaceful settlement. As Richman put it, "when Tom walked in the door, he was the only truly objective person in the room." He would analyze a company's or school board's financial situation the way he had done as a UE negotiator to suggest solutions to bargaining impasses. He knew almost by instinct when a union leader was reluctant to reach an agreement on reasonable terms because of internal union politics. Jim Rush told this story: "We had a meeting with school teachers in Pittsburgh or Harrisburg, and Tom was in the meeting. The teachers started complaining, blaming their difficulties on mediation. Tom gave them a pretty strong talking to. 'I've been where you are, I know you have to get the people wound up for a strike. It's your fault not mediation's that you don't have a contract. You're not getting the job done.' He knew very well what an organizer goes through." In this case, the lecture worked. The union made an agreement. "Union guys might have mumbled to themselves, 'This isn't the old Tom.' But they were wrong," Richman said. "Tom has never sold out."

The old allegations against Quinn caused surprisingly little difficulty. Rush recalled only one occasion in which a management representative objected to mediation by a man once accused of being a Communist. "It didn't mean anything to me," Rush said, "but a guy like that could make mediation unpleasant and Tom had a right to know about it. When I told him, he said, 'To hell with him' and asked to be reassigned."[4]

In the first years of school bargaining, many strikes occurred because of inexperience on both sides of the bargaining table. Quinn and his colleagues often had to instruct the negotiators on how to get past the demand, counterdemand stage to find common ground for agreement. One interesting complication occurred where school boards, reflecting the character of their urban populations, were made up in part by blue-collar workers from the steel, electrical, and other unionized industries. Although they had walked picket lines to enforce their own unions' demands, many of these board members opposed teachers having the right to strike. In their view there was a fundamental difference between striking to win a greater share of a company's profits and striking for wages that came out of taxpayer revenues. They could not see teaching as remotely comparable to industrial labor. Quinn remembered mediating in many such situations. "I think my background helped me understand the politics of the situation and gave me credibility with those board members and even with those who weren't workers."

Over the next several years, Quinn mediated hundreds of labor-management disputes and earned recognition as a top-ranked mediator. He enjoyed this work, and in 1980, when the director of the mediation bureau resigned, Quinn let it be known that he would like to be considered as a replacement. An outside observer might have rated Quinn's chances as low. Several other mediators had longer tenure with the bureau. More important, as a well-known Democratic Party activist and former labor leader with a radical past, Quinn did not seem a likely candidate for a high-level position in a Republican administration. In Pennsylvania at that time, appointment to cabinet and subcabinet posts and even third-level bureau directorships depended almost as much on party registration as on qualifications for the job. Quinn, however, had made many friends over the years among Republicans and had shown his willingness to work in bipartisan fashion.

Fortunately, the cabinet officer who oversaw the mediation bureau, Charles Lieberth, secretary of labor and industry, valued skill and ability above party registration and had a reputation for independent action. He recommended Quinn for the job to Dick Thornburgh, then serving his first term as Pennsylvania governor. Thornburgh regarded himself as a moderate Republican. He had publicly criticized his party for ceding control to its radical right during Barry Goldwater's presidential bid in 1964. Thornburgh also had served on the executive board of the American Civil Liberties Union chapter in Pittsburgh and first met Quinn at ACLU meetings. In the spring of 1980, Thornburgh appointed Quinn as acting director. He became director in September.[5]

There may have been "some raised eyebrows" when the appointment was announced, Quinn acknowledged, but nothing approaching an outcry. (In Quinn's archived papers, I found a letter from a western Pennsylvania resident to his state assemblyman, decrying the elevation of a "Communist" to the office of head mediator. As far as I could determine, the letter went unanswered.) Quinn and Irene moved to Harrisburg and rented an apartment close to the state offices. Quinn persuaded the State Department of Revenue to give Irene a job in Harrisburg similar to the one she had in Pittsburgh. With her earnings added to Quinn's salary, which started at $29,200, "their situation improved materially," Chuck Quinn said. "They developed a very comfortable lifestyle, and Mother started getting fur coats and jewelry. It came late in life for her."[6]

Quinn managed a staff of twenty-four mediators working throughout Pennsylvania. He occasionally acted as mediator in large, statewide labor disputes, such as negotiations between the state and unions representing many thousands of workers employed by government agencies. But his time was consumed mainly with administrative duties, handling payroll and staff issues, dealing with legislators and other agencies, monitoring the work of mediators around the state, and seeking out new mediators. "Tom attracted excellent people, and the quality of our mediators was higher than those in the Federal Mediation Service by the time I retired," Hy Richman said.[7]

Among other new people, Quinn hired the first woman mediator ever employed by the Pennsylvania Bureau of Mediation. She was Jill Leeds Rivera, a former union staff member who worked nearly eleven years as a mediator for the state of Minnesota before deciding, for personal reasons, to live in Pennsylvania. While attending the annual conference of the Association of Labor Relations Agencies in 1987, she heard Quinn speak. "He had an aura of goodness and integrity that was just screaming at me," Rivera remembered in 2003. "He reminded me of people I had known in the early sixties in the labor movement. I met him and said, 'I want to work for you.'" She moved to Philadelphia, went through the application process, and was hired in 1988. "In those days," Rivera said, "most of the men did not want women doing what they did because it would ruin the whole image of mediators if a woman could do it." She had some trouble with her fellow mediators. But Quinn always gave her strong support, and the hostility vanished after a while. Rivera was still working as a state mediator in 2003.[8]

The hiring of Ed Wintermyer could have generated a different kind of controversy. Wintermyer was one of more than eleven thousand members of the Professional Air Traffic Controllers Organization who went on strike in 1981 despite a law banning strikes by federal employees. President Ronald Reagan fired the entire group and barred their return to government jobs. For six years, Wintermyer could not find a permanent job and felt, though he could not prove, that he had been blacklisted. Finally he applied to the mediation bureau and was hired by

Quinn in 1987. Quinn's own experience with Communist allegations, Wintermyer felt, enabled him to dismiss the controllers controversy as an employment consideration. By 2004, Wintermyer was heading the Pittsburgh region of the mediation bureau. "This guy," Wintermyer said, referring to Quinn, "was the most highly regarded individual that ever held that position [bureau director]. He was the driving force behind making the bureau what it is today."[9]

In the last decade of his career, Quinn began receiving notice both for his mediation work and for the unusual arc of his life. Newspapers no longer referred to him suggestively as the Communist-tainted Tommy Quinn but as Thomas Quinn, the labor peacemaker, who had become, as one reporter wrote, with more than a little exaggeration, "more of a silver-haired ex-seminarian than a Goliath for rough and tumble bargaining brawls." He and his family devoted time and money to preserving the historical record of Quinn's colorful past. In 1987, for example, Quinn's sons raised nearly six thousand dollars from Tom's friends and associates to establish the Thomas J. Quinn Labor Archives Fund for the purpose of maintaining the large UE Archives at the University of Pittsburgh's Archives Service Center in Pittsburgh. By then not many people remembered the factional battles of the forties during which workers informed on fellow workers.[10]

Ten years earlier, however, when Quinn and the labor historian David Montgomery, a former UE member himself, helped set up the UE Archives, many people retained powerful memories of that period. As Montgomery remembered, in about 1975 or 1976, he and Quinn, appearing on a local television program, described the grim atmosphere in East Pittsburgh during the time of fear and allegations, charge and countercharge, between the opposing union factions. The discussion brought out what Quinn always had suspected, that the public testimony of a few dozen informers and anti-Communists in the late forties and early fifties represented only the tip of an iceberg: many more workers told tales on one another in private interviews with investigators. At the end of the broadcast, "the station's switchboard lit up like a Christmas tree with people wanting to tell what they recalled," Montgomery said. "Often it was people who had turned in or done in fellow union members who stood by the UE and quite literally wanted to make amends. In fact one such person saw me on the street a few days later and stopped his car to offer a confession. On the other hand, those who had been on the Left and were targets of the attack tended to remain very quiet, in fear of reviving the bad old days."[11]

In August 1991, after eleven years as mediation bureau director, Quinn retired at the age of seventy-four. Irene already had retired from her job in Harrisburg, and the couple decided the time had come to live at a slower pace. There was a flurry of parties for the Quinns, culminating in a tribute dinner attended by fifty to sixty people at the William Penn Hotel in November 1991. Guests included officials of the Commonwealth of Pennsylvania and the mediation bureau, lawyers who represented both management and labor, old union associates, and friends and relatives.[12]

They had come a long way, the Jewish girl who wanted to sing and take care of her family and the Irish Catholic orphan who evolved from Depression-era industrial worker to union steward on the radical left to UE representative publicly tainted as an accused Communist to well-regarded labor leader who made friends on all sides to director of a statewide agency charged with finding peaceful solutions to labor-management disputes. He and Irene had persisted and made a remarkable life out of adversity.

Chuck Quinn recalled a vow his father made in the fifties, when he was particularly angered by a new round of Red baiting or unfounded accusations. "I'll outlive all those bastards," Quinn declared, referring to the informers, congressional inquisitors, and union and management enemies who were making the Quinns' life difficult. He meant more than merely living longer than his adversaries, though he did that. The more important thing was that he had survived everything they had thrown at him and not only barely survived but achieved distinction in a public-service career, remained close to his family, and—with Irene—raised three accomplished sons.[13]

By 2000, many of the organizations that Quinn had contended with no longer existed. The House Un-American Activities Committee was dissolved in 1969, exactly twenty years after Harry Davenport proposed its abolition. The IUE in 2000 merged with, and became a division of, the Communications Workers of America. Because of shifts in technology and consumer products, the transfer of manufacturing to overseas plants, and company opposition to union organizing in the United States, the IUE had shrunk from 279,000 members in 1979 to about 115,000. At the same time, the UE remained proudly on its own, still unaffiliated with the AFL-CIO, though also much smaller in size, claiming a membership of about 30,000.[14]

Westinghouse Electric succumbed to a series of disastrous management decisions in 1997. For a brief time in the 1950s, Westinghouse had acted unfairly against a small group of employees engaged in political dissent. Few organizations of any kind, including unions, came out of that period with an unsullied record on civil-liberties issues. It was an ugly interval for all Americans. In the long run, however, Westinghouse Electric's contributions to the national welfare and economy overshadowed those repressive acts. For more than a century, the company provided decent jobs for thousands upon thousands of people and ranked among the most technologically innovative companies in the world. As for labor relations, both Westinghouse and its unions sometimes bent the truth or unfairly exploited a temporary advantage or made out-of-line demands or took unnecessarily harsh actions. Having known people on both sides of the divide, I believe—as relative as it may seem—that the company and union negotiators represented the interests of their constituents with equal honesty and integrity.[15]

Quinn also outlasted most of his friends in the UE and most of the people who, secretly or in public session, had accused him of being a Communist subversive. Father Rice was still alive but retired. Quinn had no idea what had become of Harry Davenport, the man he once regarded as a friend and who might have become an excellent congressman. For a while Harry's name occasionally appeared in the newspapers, but by the seventies he had dropped out of sight. One day, out of the past, there came a message from Harry, relayed to Quinn by a distant relative of Irene's who operated a store in the town of Millvale. It was vague and a bit mysterious and seemed to invite Quinn to reopen a part of his life that he considered closed. He never responded and forgot about the incident until many years further on, when he and I exchanged information about the final episode in my uncle's life.

18

MILLVALE REVISITED

FTER Tom retired in 1991, he and Irene continued to live in
Harrisburg but spent six months of each year in Pompano Beach,
Florida, where they rented a friend's apartment. Eventually, Tom
tired of this "snowbird" life. In 1996, on their annual trip to Florida, he
surprised Irene by taking her to a condominium complex. He led her to
the fifth floor, opened the door to a handsomely furnished apartment,
and said, "This is ours." He had purchased the condominium with a one-
hundred-thousand-dollar cash payment.

"It was an amazing change," Ron Quinn said. "They had been penurious for so many years when Dad was with the UE. Now he could buy a
condominium outright." In his final years with the mediation bureau,
Quinn had collected partial Social Security benefits while earning a full-
time salary, and he had invested the savings. He retired with a pension
and full medical benefits for himself and Irene provided by the Commonwealth of Pennsylvania. During those penurious years with the UE,
Tom Quinn, the labor organizer with a leftist ideology, had learned some
of the ways of capitalists, namely, that they conserved their wealth in
secure investments but did not hesitate to spend a lot of money to purchase things of value. In selecting a well-maintained condominium complex out of the many available in Pompano Beach, Quinn told Ron, "I

looked at the place where I thought people had the most money, and I decided to go there because I knew they would make sure their investments were being take care of."

Their apartment contained a large master bedroom, a combined living and dining room, a studio with a fold-out sofa bed, a kitchen, a bathroom with walk-in closets, and a screened balcony overlooking a golf course. The complex also had two outdoor pools. Tom swam often, played golf almost every day, and served on the condominium board. The Quinns occasionally traveled back to Pittsburgh, and their sons and grandchildren visited them frequently in Florida. These were years of contentment. "That life," Steve Quinn said, "was my father's dream. I don't think Mother was ever quite as happy there. She took joy in the beautiful apartment with all its amenities, but she longed to be with her family." Tom was solicitous of her needs and handled most of the household chores—as he had for many years—except cooking. "I think Dad conceded that she was worn out," Steve added.[1]

The good years were followed, as is inevitably the case, by illness, grief, and death. In 1999 Irene was diagnosed with ovarian cancer. Tom gave up golf and his other activities and took care of her himself, rarely leaving the apartment. Eventually the stress proved too much, and he became depressed. Chuck, Ron, and Steve Quinn saw what was happening and brought their parents back to Pittsburgh, where Irene was treated for cancer in a nursing home. Tom suffered a nervous breakdown. He recovered, but she died in October 2000.

Unknowing, I inserted myself into Tom's life in April 2000 as Irene lay terminally ill. We met for the first time in more than a dozen years at Ron Quinn's home in Forest Hills. I was still trying to determine whether the relationship between Tom Quinn and Harry Davenport contained enough historical interest or drama to justify further research. Quinn's memory of events and people from the long ago seemed not to have suffered from his bout of depression. He surprised me, first, by remembering that one of Harry's sisters was a nun named Sister Catherine. About a third of the way through a tape-recorded conversation during dinner, he startled me for the second time. As I talked about my initial efforts to fill out the details of Harry's life, Tom suddenly interjected, "There's one thing. Why did he spend so much time in Millvale? Was there somebody there?"

After a confused pause, I asked Quinn how he happened to associate Harry with Millvale. He had not seen or talked with Harry in fifty years. I had only just confirmed, through the receipt of a death certificate, that Harry had died in that town, and I had yet to make inquiries there. Quinn replied that a man named Sid Garfinkel, the husband of one of Irene's cousins, had owned a grocery store in Millvale and once told Quinn that a man named Harry Davenport had asked him to relay a message to Quinn. It was a brief, somewhat vague message, but in those few sentences I heard the nub of a story that I very much wanted to write. If I could verify the circumstances of Garfinkel's message, what he said would round out my story and provide a final revelation about a severed friendship.

And so my search for Uncle Harry began. My next stop would be Millvale, the little town on the north bank of the Allegheny River where Harry had spent his last days.

Harry's death in December 1977 received little notice aside from short obituaries in the Pittsburgh and McKeesport papers. The family did what it could to honor his memory. Mother and Aunt Annamae had not seen him in several years. They and Sister Catherine decided to have Harry's body sent to a funeral home in White Oak, where Mother and Annamae lived. I was working in New York then and did not travel back to Pennsylvania for the funeral. Perhaps two dozen people, including relatives, showed up for the viewing. My sister's two sons, Tim and Pat McKay, served as altar boys at the funeral Mass. We nephews and nieces split the cost of the funeral that was not covered by Harry's Social Security death benefit.

That would have been the end of Harry's story if Tom Quinn had not excited my interest with his tale of a broken friendship. Curious, I went to Millvale in June 2000 and talked to people at Ulrich's Hotel, where Harry died. Located at the corner of Howard Street and North Avenue near the center of town, it was a plain, three-story building, unadorned except for whitewashed brick on the ground floor and a Stroh's Beer sign glowing in the barroom window. Inside was a long bar and a dining room with a half-dozen tables. Many hotel residents drifted from their rooms down to the dining room for breakfast, then sat at the bar, drinking coffee or nursing a beer, watching television. Millvale was not brimming with activities for senior citizens.

Teresa Ulrich, the daughter-in-law of one of the original owners of Ulrich's Hotel, worked there as a cook and waitress in the 1970s. She recalled that Harry ate breakfast and lunch in the dining room. "He usually sat alone," she said. "He always wore a suit and tie and was reading a book. He made you feel as if he was lonesome. He was an educated man, and most of the people in the barroom were common laborers. They were nice people, but Harry didn't sit at the bar and chat with them." Harry paid his hotel bill on time. His few friends included a retired Millvale policeman and a man who had an administrative job in the county sheriff's department in Pittsburgh. It was the latter man, a Millvale resident, who first brought Harry to Ulrich's in late 1975 or 1976, according to John Ulrich, a former owner of the hotel. This solved the minor mystery of how Harry came to be in Millvale.[2]

When my family and I left Pittsburgh in April 1975, Harry was still living at the Arena Baths. Turning seventy-three in August of that year, he was getting rather old to live comfortably in a bathhouse dormitory, lacking privacy and exposed to the random behavior of a migrant clientele. A fire that swept through the Arena in 1975 or 1976 also probably helped convince Harry that he should move. My guess is that the man who worked in the sheriff's office (several people gave me his name) and Harry were friends, possibly drinking pals, who met frequently at restaurants or bars in Pittsburgh's courthouse area. When Harry spoke of needing a new place to live, his friend introduced him to Ulrich's in Millvale. The hotel had only thirteen guest rooms, all securely placed on upper floors with access only through a locked steel door at ground level. The hotel offered safety and a minimum amount of privacy and, in a sense, catered to the needs of elderly and disabled men. That much settled, Harry only had to pass the time in a town which may have come close to meeting the definition of a place where time stood still.

Like many old towns in the Pittsburgh region, Millvale has a more interesting past than present. It is located where Girty's Run, named for an early white settler, flows into the Allegheny River opposite Pittsburgh. The Girtys and a few other frontier families lived along the creek for several decades in the late 1700s, frequently under attack by Indians. In the nineteenth century, small industrial enterprises, commercial establishments, and homes sprang up on the river front. An iron-rolling mill, for which Millvale was probably named, began operations in the 1860s and went out of business in 1888.[3]

Millvale entered a postindustrial phase decades before the term itself came into use, though it apparently never had been intensely industrial. The town had nothing to export except its unemployed young people. Former factory towns are too often described in disparaging terms, as if they were industrial Sodoms and Gomorrahs whose inhabitants got what was coming to them through moral laxity. Industry left Millvale for economic reasons, and the town shriveled into a small, unpretentious living place for people who worked elsewhere or had retired. I spent most of a day there in 2000, asking questions, walking the streets, and getting historical information from clerks in the borough office, and everybody was pleasant and helpful.

Although there was not much for Harry to do and see in Millvale, the famous murals of St. Nicholas Croatian Church offered one outstanding attraction. Located several blocks from Ulrich's, St. Nicholas was built in 1900 to serve Croatian immigrants who had come to Pittsburgh to work in the steel mills. Following a fire that gutted St. Nicholas, a Croatian artist, Maxo Vanka, was commissioned in 1937 to paint the inside of a new church built on the site. A pacifist who had seen the harsh treatment of peasants in his homeland, Vanka covered the walls and ceiling with twenty-two stunning murals depicting religious, antifacist, and antiwar scenes. Vanka's subjects are rural Croatian peasants, industrial workers and working-class families in America, women lamenting over a dead coal miner and a soldier's coffin, a crucified Jesus whose side has been split by the bayonet of a twentieth-century soldier, and a capitalist reading a stock report while being served dinner by a black servant. Harry, who never became the hero of the oppressed that he longed to be, would have felt at home amongst Vanka's angry images.[4]

Harry undoubtedly passed much of the time reading whatever he could lay his hands on. Bill Sitzman, Harry's next-door neighbor at Ulrich's and the man who saw him lying dead in his room in 1977, told me that he often saw Harry reading a book as he strolled through town. His walking trips would have been limited by topography. He might walk a few blocks west on Howard Street until the grade became too steep. Walking eastward, he would have found his way blocked by the Route 28 expressway running along the river's edge. He might go two blocks south on North Avenue before it dead-ended in a wooded hill. He could have walked miles in the opposite direction on North, which eventually left Millvale behind and continued up the valley, but there was nothing to see except houses and occasional retail stores. The streets, however, were clean and quiet; traffic noises were so faint as to be unnoticeable. On my visit, I had the romantic notion that Millvale was a place utterly beyond worldly ambitions, devoid of the political and legal hustlers that Harry had brushed shoulders with every day in Pittsburgh. The silence would have nourished his introspectiveness, his secretiveness—and his memories.

Room 6, Harry's room, was on the south side of Ulrich's, and his window gave him a view of a steeply pitched hill topped by Holy Spirit Roman Catholic Church, a large, yellow-brick edifice with castlelike twin towers. Sitting next to it were parish administrative offices, the rectory, and an elementary school. On Sunday mornings, Harry could have watched worshipers climbing the broad, steep steps to the church's oaken front doors. The scene might have reminded him of St. Peter's in McKeesport, where he served as an altar boy and attended school before being tossed out. St. Peter's also had broad oaken doors that banged and rattled if you pulled or pushed too hard upon entering or leaving, causing everybody to turn around and nuns to emblazon in memory the faces of young boys who arrived late for Mass and who, the next day in the parish school, would be ordered to stand in a corner. Back in those days, Harry would have had a panoramic view of downtown McKeesport as he looked south from the Davenports' backyard on Jenny Lind Street. He would have seen the spires, steeples, and onion-bulb cupolas of many churches, including St. Peter's, in the town below, along with mill stacks, a bridge going across the Youghiogheny River, and a sliver of the Monongahela where it wound to the southeast, disappearing between wooded bluffs. He had dreamed of getting out of McKeesport and seeing the world on the other side of those bluffs. At the end of his life, he had come to rest in another old mill town, this one hemmed in by a river and its bluffs. When he gazed out the window of his final home in Ulrich's Hotel, Harry could see little more than a few houses and a steep hill crowned by a church.

I believe that when Harry moved to Millvale, he guessed that his time was almost up. Since he died of a gastrointestinal hemorrhage, he must have had an active ulcer for some time, as well as other ailments that accompany aging. But Harry never complained about his health or asked the family's help in paying medical bills. He simply avoided doctors and lived with his pain and discomfort. For all his mistakes—and he made many in his personal and political life—I give Harry one thing. He did not cry out for help and throw himself on the mercy of his sisters, nephews, and nieces. He may simply not have cared, either about them or himself. But I think he retreated from family and old friends because he felt he had not earned, or had lost, their respect. In life Harry never achieved the celebrity and honor that he craved. I believe he did achieve, before death, the dignity of accepting his failures and, in his own way, asking forgiveness.

This is where Sid Garfinkel enters the story. When Harry lived in Millvale, Garfinkel's grocery store stood on Howard Street across from Ulrich's Hotel. By 2000, when I visited the town, Garfinkel's no longer existed, having been torn down many years before. The site was occupied by a tiny, fenced-in park with a spiral sliding board and a small jungle climb for young children. But I talked to several people who remembered Garfinkel's as a rundown little place with one unusual feature. Garfinkel had a beer license and ran a tiny barroom in the rear of the store. Known as the Blue Room because it was lit by an overhead blue bulb, the place was little more than "a sitting room with beer," as John Ulrich scornfully described it. Old Millvale cronies would hang out there, gossiping and chatting about local and national news. Harry spent much time in the Blue Room, more at home among its habitués than with the clientele of the hotel bar. It may have reminded him of speakeasies he had known in the twenties.

One day, when the Blue Room group was reminiscing about old times, it somehow emerged that Harry and Sid both knew (in Harry's case once knew) Tom Quinn. What happened next was related to me by Quinn during the dinner at his son's home in 2000. "Sid got hold of me one day many years ago," Quinn said. "He asked me, 'Do you remember Harry Davenport?' I said yeah. He said, 'Harry hangs out in the store a lot and he'd like to talk to you.' I asked what about. 'Well,' he says, 'Harry said you didn't understand what his problems were, the pressures he was under, and he wants to talk to you.' It seems that Harry confided in Sid. I said I'd try to do that sometime."

Garfinkel's message may have seemed vague, but I had been thinking about the relationship between Harry and Tom for some time, and I believed I knew what it meant. "Maybe Harry wanted to apologize," I said.

Quinn shrugged.

"Did you ever see or talk to him after that?"

Quinn shook his head. "It was sort of late for that."

I had found the end of my story before I knew the middle of it. Two years later, in one of my many phone conversations with Quinn, I was describing Harry's long slide downhill. I had not expected Quinn to comment, but suddenly he interjected, "I'm sorry about what happened to your uncle." I thanked him for the sentiment and went on to say that I had not begun my search with the idea of eliciting sorrow or guilt on anybody's part.

One final irony about Harry is that he had spent much of his life studying history (even if he did not always learn from it), only to be randomly dropped from most accounts of the history of his time. It might be said that Quinn and many others made it possible to reinsert Harry's cautionary tale into that history, making neither more of it than it amounted to, nor less.

NOTES

Acronyms are used for newspapers referred to frequently: *NYT, New York Times; PC, Pittsburgh Catholic; PP, Pittsburgh Press; PPG, Pittsburgh Post-Gazette; PST, Pittsburgh Sun-Telegraph; WG, Wilkinsburg Gazette.*

PROLOGUE: A DEATH IN MILLVALE

1. Harry's death: Commonwealth of Pennsylvania, Department of Health, Coroner's Certificate of Death No. 108695, Millvale, PA, December 19, 1977. Harry's election: "McDowell Loses Seat," *NYT*, Nov. 3, 1948.

CHAPTER 1: A TALE OF TWO HARRYS

1. Westinghouse's 1887 purchase: *History of Forest Hills*, booklet published by Borough of Forest Hills, PA. Also see exhibits and accounts of George Westinghouse's life at the George Westinghouse Museum, Wilmerding, PA.

2. *WABCO News*, December 28, 1926; Katherine Dawson testimony: *Pittsburgh Gazette*, December 13, 1926; see also *Daily News* (McKeesport), January 14, 1927. Death of Harry F. Davenport: County of Allegheny, *Coroner's Jury Verdict*, January 14, 1927.

3. UE membership in late 1940s: Bert Cochran, *Labor and Communism: The Conflict that Shaped American Unions* (Princeton, NJ: Princeton University Press, 1977), 283 (citing figures calculated by Leo Troy).

4. Quinn and cousin Charles: Quinn oral history, Western Pennsylvania Electrical Workers Oral History Interviews, conducted by Ronald Schatz, April 14, 1977, UE Archives and Labor Collections, Archives Service Center, University of Pittsburgh (hereafter UE/Lab), 91:15.

5. Description of Hill District: *Wylie Avenue Days*, video produced by QED Communications, 1991.

CHAPTER 2: LABOR TURMOIL, 1937

1. Founding of the CIO and John L. Lewis: I drew from many books and articles, especially Robert H. Zieger, *The CIO: 1935-1955* (Chapel Hill: University of North Carolina Press, 1995) and Melvyn Dubofsky and Warren Van Tine, *John L. Lewis, A Biography* (New York: Quadrangle, 1977), as well as from personal memo-

ries of the CIO in McKeesport. Thanks to Russell Gibbons and Tony Slomkoski for calling my attention to the CIO Pilsener label.

2. CIO history: Zieger, *CIO*; Dubofsky and Van Tine, *John L. Lewis*. Number of jobless in 1933: David M. Kennedy, *Freedom from Fear: The American People in Depression and War, 1929–45* (New York: Oxford University Press, 1999), 163.

3. Legal challenge to the Wagner Act: Harry A. Millis and Emily Clark Brown, *From the Wagner Act to Taft-Hartley: A Study of National Labor Policy and Labor Relations* (University of Chicago Press, 1950), 96–98.

4. Supreme Court decision, strike, NLRB vote: Millis and Brown, *Wagner Act*, 97. Strike details: Steve Kocherzat and Charles McCollester, "Aliquippa's Struggle and Labor Law Reform," historical marker dedication, Aliquippa, April 8, 2000. Strike settlement: Zieger, *CIO*, 59–61.

5. Popular Front discussion: Fraser M. Ottanelli, *The Communist Party of the United States: From the Depression to World War II* (New Brunswick, NJ: Rutgers University Press, 1991), 107–36. Mao Zedong apparently made an effort to quell prostitution at various times during his career. When he led a rural guerilla government called the Jiangxi Soviet on the Jiangxi-Fujian border from 1929 to 1934, "prostitutes were freed from their demeaning contracts." Jonathan Spence and Annping Chin, *The Chinese Century* (London: HarperCollins, 1996), 113–14.

6. Internal Revenue Service, U.S. Social Security Act, Application for Account Number, Harry J. Davenport, Detroit, December 13, 1938.

7. John's death: Pittsburgh *Gazette*, March 23, 1925.

8. Skating championships: *Daily News*, April 9, 1920. William's death: ibid., September 30, 1885. Spurning a final drink: ibid., March 23, 1925.

9. Utica store: *Daily News*, June 30, 1927; Ed Davenport's career: *The National Cyclopaedia of American Biography* (New York: James T. White, 1954), 29:615.

10. Charles Owen Rice interview, June 8, 2000.

11. Rice oral history, interviews recorded by Ronald Filippelli, October 17, 1967, and April 5, 1968, Historical Collections and Labor Archives, Pennsylvania State University Library; Charles Owen Rice Papers, Archives of an Industrial Society (hereafter AIS), Archives Service Center, University of Pittsburgh, 76:11; Charles McCollester, ed., *Fighter with a Heart: Writings of Charles Owen Rice* (University of Pittsburgh Press, 1996); Patrick J. McGeever, *Rev. Charles Owen Rice: Apostle of Contradiction* (Pittsburgh: Duquesne University Press, 1989).

12. Heinz picketing: *Time*, June 28, 1937, 62–63; McGeever, *Apostle of Contradiction*, 46–47; *Pittsburgh & Western Pennsylvania Labor Legacy*, "Canning and Pickle Workers Union," http://www.library.pitt.edu/labor_legacy/heinz.html.

13. Father Cox: McGeever, *Apostle of Contradiction*, 41. CRA: ibid., 37–40.

14. Rice and Dorothy Day: McGeever, *Apostle of Contradiction*, 42–45, 54. Church's sanction: McCollester, *Fighter*, xiv.

15. Rice's early life: McGeever, *Apostle of Contradiction*, 1–3. Catholic labor doctrine: ibid., 24–27.

16. Communists, unions, and Lewis: ibid., 97–98; Dubofsky and Van Tine, *John L. Lewis*, 288–89, 309; Charles Owen Rice, "Confessions of an Anti-Communist," *Labor History* 30 (Summer 1989): 461–62. Relations with Murray: Rice interview, June 8, 2000.

CHAPTER 3: WORKING-CLASS POLITICS IN ELECTRIC VALLEY

1. Ronald Quinn interview, January 8, 2001.

2. Quinn sons: Interviews with Ron Quinn (January 8, 2001), Chuck Quinn (August 12, 2000), and Steve Quinn (November 29, 2000).

3. Bridge dimensions: *The Bridges of Pittsburgh and Allegheny County*, published by Allegheny County, PA, Carnegie Library of Pittsburgh. Twenty-two thousand employees: Ronald W. Schatz, *The Electrical Workers: A History of Labor at General Electric and Westinghouse, 1923–1960* (Urbana: University of Illinois Press, 1983), 199.

4. Area and population of three towns: Schatz, ibid., 189. Election statistics: *Smull's Legislative Handbook and Manual of the State of Pennsylvania* (Harrisburg: State of Pennsylvania, 1913), 581–602. George Westinghouse and Westinghouse Electric: Henry G. Prout, *A Life of George Westinghouse* (Arno Press, 1921), 278–81. Strikes in 1914 and 1916: Charles J. McCollester, "Turtle Creek Fights Taylorism: The Westinghouse Strike of 1914," *Labor's Heritage* (Summer 1992): 4–27; Carl I. Meyerhuber Jr., *Less Than Forever: The Rise and Decline of Union Solidarity in Western Pennsylvania, 1914–1948* (London: Associated University Presses, 1987), 17–41; David Montgomery, *The Fall of the House of Labor: The Workplace, the State, and American Labor Activism, 1865–1925* (Cambridge: Cambridge University Press, 1987), 317–27.

5. Radicals, Burkhart: Schatz, *Electrical Workers*, 190. Alex Staber interview, May 15, 2002. Independent union and Local 601 political groupings: Schatz, *Electrical Workers*, 190, 196.

CHAPTER 4: BUDDING POLITICIAN AND LABOR PRIEST

1. East Liberty history: John F. Collins Jr., *Stringtown on the Pike* (East Liberty Chamber of Commerce); "The Land That Retail Forgot," *PPG*, May 24, 2000.

2. Sister Catherine's return: *PPG*, December 6, 1941. East Liberty speech: "China Thrives on War, Missionary Tells Group," *PST*, February 5, 1942.

3. Harry J. Davenport FBI file, 100-HQ-185330.

4. John Connelly interview, April 13, 2000 (all Connelly comments in this chapter).

5. Rice photographs: McCollester, *Fighter*, various pages. CPUSA membership: Harvey Klehr and John Earl Haynes, *The American Communist Movement: Storming Heaven Itself* (New York: Twayne, 1992), 85–86. Same instincts: Steve Rosswurm, "The Catholic Church and the Left-Led Unions: Labor Priests, Labor Schools, and the ACTU," in Steve Rosswurm, ed., *The CIO's Left-Led Unions* (New Brunswick, NJ: Rutgers University Press, 1992), 120.

6. Rice as anti-Communist: http:www.library.pitt.edu/labor_legacy/heinz.html; as anti-fascist: McCollester, *Fighter*, xv; Rice, "New Communist Line," *PC*, June 26, 1941, quoted in McCollester, *Fighter*, 64. ACTU: McGeever, *Apostle of Contradiction*, 45, 61. Rice and Local 601, ambulance dispute: Schatz, *Electrical Workers*, 191–93; Ronald L. Filippelli and Mark D. McColloch, *Cold War in the Working Class: The Rise and Decline of the United Electrical Workers* (Albany: State University of New York Press, 1995), 57. Labor school: McCollester, *Fighter*, xv.

7. UE's Catholic members: Schatz, *Electrical Workers*, 29–30. Charles Newell to Bishop Boyle, August 13, 1941, Charles Newell Papers, UE/Lab, National Office Records, folder 30. Number of UE members: Quinn to author, December 1999 (in 1948, Locals 601 and 610 had a total of twenty thousand members, and the UE represented more than five thousand workers at other shops in the region).

8. UE history: Filippelli and McColloch, *Cold War*, 13–32. CPUSA membership of Matles and Emspak: ibid., 21–22, 44 (Matles), 30 (Emspak); Schatz, *Electrical Workers*, 64 (Matles), 92–95 (Emspak), 176–77 (both). See chapter 7 in this book for evidence of Matles's CPUSA membership.

9. Communist ban, Carey defeat: Filippelli and McColloch, *Cold War*, 51, 58–64. UE staff: Filippelli and McColloch, *Cold War*, 44 (the source was a story in the May 22, 1950, issue of the *IUE News*, official newspaper of the union that displaced the UE in many plants). Largest Communist-led institution: Schatz, *Electrical Workers*, xiii. Steve Rosswurm calculates that less than 1 percent of the members of all CIO unions were Communist Party members in 1948: "Introduction," in Rosswurm, *CIO's Left-Led Unions*, 6.

10. Rice oral history, April 5, 1968.

11. OPA czar: McGeever, *Charles Owen Rice*, 74–82.

CHAPTER 5: THE MAKING OF A UNION RADICAL

1. Steve Quinn interview, May 28, 2003.

2. Union membership in manufacturing, 1947: Leo Troy and Neil Sheflin, *Union Sourcebook* (West Orange, NJ: Industrial Relations Data and Information Services, 1985), 3–15.

3. Quinn's problem: Quinn oral history, 12–13.

4. Samuel O. Lemon Jr. to author, August 17, 2002.

5. The UE's incentive policies: Schatz, *Electrical Workers*, 137–50; Mark McColloch, "The Shop-Floor Dimension of Union Rivalry: The Case of Westinghouse in the 1950s," in Rosswurm, *CIO's Left-Led Unions*, 183–99. After replacing the UE at East Pittsburgh, the IUE conducted a long strike in 1955–1956 and as part of the settlement agreed to gradually eliminate the Standard Time Incentive Plan and replace it with a system that produced more moderate gains for workers (see chapter 15).

6. Fitzpatrick background: Schatz, *Electrical Workers*, 188–200.

7. Progressives' association with CPUSA: ibid., 196. Core Progressive group: ibid., 219. Quinn quotes: Interviews with author and Quinn oral history.

8. CPUSA and Local 601: Testimony of Francis Nestler, *Subversive Influence in the*

United Electrical, Radio, and Machine Workers of America, Senate Internal Security Sub-committee, Pittsburgh, November 9, 1953, 43–45.

9. Union membership as a percentage of nonfarm employment peaked at 32.5 percent in 1953: Troy and Sheflin, *Union Sourcebook,* 3–10.

10. The 1946 strikes: Zieger, *CIO,* 217–27; James J. Matles and James Higgins, *Them and Us: Struggles of a Rank-and-File Union* (Englewood Cliffs, NJ: Prentice-Hall, 1974), 139–47.

CHAPTER 6: A PROMISING BID FOR CONGRESS

1. Formation of Twenty-ninth District, 1944 presidential vote: "Congressional Drive in 29th District Takes on Angry and Confused Aspect," *PPG,* October 28, 1946.

2. Lawrence's political power: Michael P. Weber, *Don't Call Me Boss: David L. Lawrence* (University of Pittsburgh Press, 1988), chap. 2–11; Thomas J. Donaghy, *Keystone Democrat: David Lawrence Remembered* (New York: Vantage, 1986). Davenport's committee: *PPG,* October 28, 1946. LaGuardia meeting: "If He Were Elected Mayor . . ." *PP,* August 25, 1945; see also an anecdote about this trip in Weber, *David L. Lawrence,* 173.

3. John Connelly interview, April 13, 2000.

4. UE members in Twenty-ninth District: Tom Quinn to author, December 1999.

5. John McDowell, "The Country Editor," *Wilkinsburg Gazette* (columns referred to hereafter as McDowell, *WG*), May 24, 1946.

6. Milton K. Susman, *Jewish Criterion* (articles referred to hereafter as Susman, *Criterion*), August 16, 1946.

7. Harry's New Deal allegiance: *Post-Gazette,* October 28, 1946. McDowell's complaint: McDowell, *WG,* November 11, 1946.

8. Jewish population of Pittsburgh: Jacob Rader Marcus, *To Count a People: American Jewish Population Data, 1584–1984* (Lanham, MD: University Press of America, 1990), 195.

9. "Climbing like flies": Susman, *Criterion,* August 16, 1946. Jewish writers: ibid., September 13, 1946. Endorsement of Davenport: ibid., November 1, 1946. McDowell's reply and Klan comment: *WG,* November 1, 1946; political ad, ibid.

10. Davenport endorsement: *Pittsburgh Courier,* October 19, 1946. *Courier* advertisement, ibid., November 2, 1946. Critique of McDowell, ibid., October 19, 1946.

11. UE endorsement: *District 6 Progress,* October 30, 1946, UE/Lab.

12. Election results: Commonwealth of Pennsylvania, *The Pennsylvania Manual,* vol. 88, 1947–1948. Fourteenth Ward vote: *PST,* November 10, 1946. Election post-mortem: "UE Helps Pile Up Votes for Davenport," *District 6 Progress,* November 21, 1946, UE/Lab.

CHAPTER 7: TAKING ON THE UE

1. Rice at Duquesne: McGeever, *Charles Owen Rice,* 105.

2. *Sunday Visitor:* Rice oral history, April 5, 1968. *Visitor* articles, pamphlet: ibid.,

102–3. "How to Decontrol Your Union of Communists," excerpts reprinted in McCollester, *Fighter*, 77.

3. ACTU: McGeever, *Charles Owen Rice*, 106. Michael Harrington, "Catholics in the Labor Movement: A Case History," *Labor History* 1, no. 3 (Fall 1960): 231–63. Duffy: McGeever, *Charles Owen Rice*, 114. Dossier: ibid., 103–4; Rice comment: Rice oral history, April 5, 1968.

4. Rice interview, June 8, 2000.

5. Rice-Murray: McGeever, *Charles Owen Rice*, 98–99. CIO membership loss: Zieger, *CIO*, 277. Murray's reluctance: Rice oral history, October 17, 1967. Murray's funding: Rice oral history, April 5, 1968.

6. Murray's shift: Filippelli and McColloch, *Cold War*, 92–96.

7. Atomic Energy Commission: David Caute, *The Great Fear: The Anti-Communist Purge under Truman and Eisenhower* (New York: Simon & Schuster, 1978), 377. Government attacks: Schatz, *Electrical Workers*, 175–78; Filippelli and McColloch, *Cold War*, 103.

8. Taft-Hartley Act: Zieger, *CIO*, 246–48. Corpse quote: Rice oral history, April 5, 1968. Raids: Schatz, *Electrical Workers*, 180.

9. UE conventions, 1946–1949: Filippelli and McColloch, *Cold War*, 117–34.

10. Informant accusation: McGeever, *Charles Owen Rice*, 106–7; Rice's rebuttal: Letter to editor, *PPG*, November 1989. Grave error quote: Sigmund Diamond, "Labor History vs. Labor Historiography: The FBI, James B. Carey, and the Association of Catholic Trade Unionists," essay included in a festschrift honoring Professor Yehoshua Arieli of Hebrew University, *Religion, Ideology and Nationalism in Europe and America* (Jerusalem: 1986), 325–26, copy in Rice Papers, AIS 76:11, "Rice Recollections/Carey FBI."

11. Matles background: Filippelli, and McColloch, *Cold War*, 20–41; Matles and Higgins, *Them and Us*, 21–22.

12. Convention speech: *UE 38th Convention Proceedings*, Pittsburgh, 1973, 295–96.

13. Former Vanderbilt townhouse: Matles and Higgins, *Them and Us*, 269.

14. Audiotape of August 1975 interview in author's possession.

15. Sam Lemon to author, August 17, 2002.

16. Company couch: Robert McCoy interview, October 18, 2002.

17. "James J. Matles, a Top Official of Electrical Workers, 66, Dies," *NYT*, September 17, 1975.

18. Matles and CPUSA membership: Filippelli and McColloch, *Cold War*, 44.

19. "Records of the Communist Party USA Opened," *Library of Congress Information Bulletin*, February 2001, http://www.loc.gov/loc/lcib/0102/index.html. Internal Records of Communist Party, USA, 1919–1937, original collection (Fond 515) archived at Russian Center for the Preservation and Study of Documents of Recent History, Moscow, available on microfilm at National Archives, Washington, DC, and Tamiment Library, New York University (hereafter CPUSA Records).

20. Matles in TUUL, IAM, and UE: Matles and Higgins, *Them and Us*, 43–49; Schatz, *Electrical Workers*, 231; Matles oral history interviews by Ronald Filippelli, May 6, 1968, Historical Collections and Labor Archives, Pennsylvania State University. Few TUUL members in CPUSA: Cochran, *Labor and Communism*, 357, note 2. Matles at 1934 TUUL meetings: CPUSA Records, file 3657; at 1935 TUC meetings and report on IAM negotiations: file 3770; Matles letter: file 3774; other Matles appearances at TUC meetings: files 3910, 3911 (1935) and 3985 (1936).

21. File of James J. Matles, 122-186, included in copies of FBI files on the UE, UE/Lab, 98:46, obtained through a Freedom of Information Act request submitted by the Samuel Gruber Education Fund on behalf of the UE (hereafter Matles FBI file). Search for job-related actions: Ellen Schrecker, *Many Are the Crimes: McCarthyism in America*, paperback ed. (Princeton, NJ: Princeton University Press, 1999), 31. North American Aviation and other strikes: ibid., 99–101; Zieger, *CIO*, 127–30.

22. UE convictions: Filippelli and McColloch, *Cold War*, 157.

23. Criticism of U.S. foreign policy before 1949: Filippelli and McColloch, *Cold War*, 59–62, 83–84, 94–95, 108–9. After 1949: I scanned scores of issues of the *UE News* published in the 1950s, 1960s, and 1970s on microfilm at the University of Pittsburgh's Archives Service Center in June 2004. Starting the Cold War: "McCarthyism Is Hitlerism," *UE News*, November 16, 1953 (". . . Cold War first launched by the Truman administration").

24. Mindszenty affair: *PP*, Feb. 14, 1949, UE/Lab, 67.2, box 3, folder X. Darin on Mindszenty: Margaret Darin Stasik oral history interview conducted by Ronald Schatz, January 7, 1977, UE/Lab, 91:15.

25. Ellen Schrecker, "McCarthyism and the Labor Movement," in Rosswurm, *CIO's Left-Led Unions*, 141.

CHAPTER 8: THE HARRY-TOM CONNECTION

1. Connelly profile: "Master Salesman Puts a New Spin on River Business," *PPG*, May 28, 1990. Connelly interview, April 13, 2000 (all comments by Connelly in this chapter are from this interview).

2. Democratic support: "UE Support Prompts Running of Davenport Against House Prober," *PPG*, October 14, 1948.

3. Consumer price statistics, 1946–1947: Bureau of Labor Statistics.

4. Radio talk: "Palestine Betrayed," broadcast April 2, 1948, radio station WCAE, UE/Lab, National Office Records, Washington Office, box B, folder "Wallace Material—Dist. 6 1948."

5. Wallace's presidential quest: John C. Culver and John Hyde, *American Dreamer: The Life and Times of Henry A. Wallace* (New York: Norton, 2000), 452–57. Communist dupe: ibid., 464–67. Hatred and hysteria: ibid., 443. Gifted: McDowell, *WG*, October 15, 1948. Communists and dupes: ibid, October 22, 1948.

6. Publication of Wallace list: Culver and Hyde, *American Dreamer*, 469; *PP*, April 11–30, 1948.

7. Quinn's 1948 vote total: Quinn FBI file, 100-362-956, Thomas J. Quinn Papers, UE/Lab, 73:9, obtained by Thomas Quinn through a Freedom of Information Act request and cited with his permission (hereafter Quinn FBI file). Truman and Taft-Hartley: Zieger also notes that Truman abandoned the fight against Taft-Hartley, *CIO*, 275.

8. Loyalty Review Boards: William Manchester, *The Glory and the Dream: A Narrative History of America, 1932–1972* (New York: Bantam, 1975), 494–98.

9. HUAC history: Caute, *Great Fear*, 88–97. Hollywood Ten: ibid., 490–95.

10. McDowell on Marx: Caute, *Great Fear*, 91. Condon affair: ibid., 470–71. HUAC attacks Nelson: Steve Nelson, James R. Barratt, and Rob Ruck, *Steve Nelson, American Radical* (Pittsburgh: University of Pittsburgh Press), 293–95. News stories on Nelson episode: "Indictment of Five Is Urged in Report on Atomic Spying," *NYT*, September 28, 1948; "Clark Agency Hits Spy Investigations, Bars Trials Now," *NYT*, September 30, 1948; "Impeaching Clark Urged If He Fails to Prosecute Spies," *NYT*, October 1, 1948; "M'Dowell Denies Slur on M'Gohey," *NYT*, October 9, 1948.

11. *Post-Gazette* editorials: "Turn McDowell Out," October 22, 1948; "McDowell's Major Offense," November 2, 1948.

12. CPUSA's anti-McDowell campaign: "McDowell, An Un-American, in Fight for Re-election," *The Worker*, October 10, 1948, Sunday edition; also see ibid., October 10 and 31, 1948, and "Frankly Speaking, John McDowell and Carey's IUE," April 23, 1950.

13. Gallup poll: Manchester, *Glory*, 466.

14. *Post-Gazette* election stories on November 3, 1948: "Truman leading; Democrats Take House and Senate," "McDowell Is Defeated in Race for Re-election." Vote totals for Twenty-ninth District: "Official Tabulation of Votes Cast, November 2, 1948," Allegheny County Bureau of Elections. Harry's victory: "McDowell Loses Seat," *NYT*, November 3, 1948.

15. National results: Manchester, *Glory*, 458, 470–71; *Congressional Quarterly's Guide to U.S. Elections*, 4th ed. (Washington, DC: CQ Press, 2001).

CHAPTER 9: BLONDE SPY QUEEN TELLS ALL

1. Bentley's background: Kathryn S. Olmsted, *Red Spy Queen: A Biography of Elizabeth Bentley* (Chapel Hill: University of North Carolina Press, 2002), chap. 1–6; Lauren Kessler, *Clever Girl: Elizabeth Bentley, the Spy Who Ushered in the McCarthy Era* (New York: Harper Collins, 2003), chap. 1–12. Aftermath of Bentley's confessions: Harvey Klehr, John Earl Haynes, and Fridrikh Igorevich Firsov, *The Secret World of American Communism* (New Haven, CT: Yale University Press, 1995), 309–13. Spies identified: Kessler, *Clever Girl*, 132. Bentley's appearance: Olmstead, *Red Spy Queen*, 125. HUAC, *Hearings Regarding Communist Espionage in the United States Government*, 80th Cong., 2nd sess., July 31, 1948.

2. "Red Spy Spent Early Years of Her Life in McKeesport," *PP*, August 3, 1948.

3. Bentley in McKeesport: Elizabeth Bentley, *Out of Bondage: The Story of Elizabeth Bentley* (New York: Devin-Adair, 1951), 12; Kessler, *Clever Girl*, 15–16; *PP*, August 3,

1948; "'Spy Queen Lived in City,'" *Daily News* (McKeesport), August 3, 1948; the two stories contain essentially the same facts, indicating that the *Daily News* reporter probably acted as a stringer for the *Press.*

4. Quote from "Spy Queen Lived in City," *Daily News.*

5. Bentley's embellishments: Olmsted, *Red Spy Queen*, 133. Obituary: "Elizabeth Bentley Is Dead at 55; Soviet Spy Later Aided U.S.," *NYT*, December 4, 1963.

6. Gouzenko: Klehr, Haynes, and Firsov, *Secret World*, 168. Bentley's testimony confirmed: ibid., 311. End of spying: Allen Weinstein and Alexander Vassiliev, *The Haunted Wood: Soviet Espionage in America—the Stalin Era* (New York: Random House, 1999), 340.

7. Foundation of Red Scare: Olmsted, *Red Spy Queen*, 117.

8. Charles Owen Rice to Rev. Benjamin L. Masse, October 30, 1946, reprinted in McCollester, *Fighter*, 68.

9. Ron Quinn interview, January 8, 2001.

10. John Vento interviews, April 29, 2002, and February 10, 2004.

11. CRC background: Caute, *Great Fear*, 178–79. Aid for twelve top CPUSA members: ibid., note 3, 583.

12. Rally fracas: McGeever, *Charles Owen Rice*, 121–22; "Pickets Push Reds as Rally Breaks Up In Wild Riot," *PG*, April 3, 1949.

13. Fitzpatrick brothers: *PP*, January 13, 1949 (headline missing).

14. Undercurrent in American life: James T. Patterson, *Grand Expectations: The United States, 1945–1974* (New York: Oxford University Press, 1996), 169. The term Red Scare originally referred to an episode of severe repression of left-wing radicals in 1919. However, many historians, such as Patterson and David Caute, have applied the term to the post–World War II period. CPUSA members in Pittsburgh: Nelson, Barrett, and Ruck, *American Radical*, 299.

15. Homegrown radicals: Schatz, *Electrical Workers*, 190–96.

16. Violent epicenter: Caute, *Great Fear*, 216.

17. Cvetic's emergence and resultant ostracism of accused: Caute, *Great Fear*, 217. Lost jobs: Frank J. Donner, *The Un-Americans* (New York: Ballantine Books, 1961), 143. Teachers fired: ibid., 144. Musician fired: Caute, *Great Fear*, 143. *PP* quoted in Donner, *Un-Americans*, 143.

18. Musmanno's background and dismissal of juror: Donner, *Un-Americans*, 145–46.

19. Musmanno's raid: Caute, *Great Fear*, 218.

20. Nelson trial: ibid., 219–21. Convictions thrown out: Nelson, Barrett, and Ruck, *American Radical*, 378.

21. Survey: Schrecker, *McCarthyism in America*, 142.

22. Pechan Law: Philip Jenkins, *Cold War at Home: The Red Scare in Pennsylvania, 1945–1960* (University of North Carolina Press, 1999), 137–38.

CHAPTER 10: HARRY'S BID FOR GLORY

1. Opening day 1949: "Flood of 600 Bills Inundates House," *NYT*, January 4, 1949; "Action Delayed for Davenport," *PPG*, January 4, 1949. Connelly interview,

April 13, 2000. Rules Committee: "Truman Forces Win Test, *NYT*, January 4, 1949. Resolution 36: *Congressional Record 1949* (hereafter *CR1949*), 288. "Congress Clears the Decks," *New Republic*, January 17, 1949. HUAC expenses: *CR1949*, 1044–45.

2. Clipping of photograph of Harry and Peggy Ann in author's possession, unknown newspaper, February 24, 1949.

3. Davenport on steel pricing: *CR1949*, 8799–800.

4. Poll tax debate: *CR1949*, 10221–24; "Anti-Poll Tax Bill Is Passed by House by Vote of 273-116," *NYT*, July 27, 1949. Poll tax committee: *CR1949*, 13575. Elimination of poll tax: *Harper v. Virginia Bd. of Elections*, 383 U.S. 663 (1966), which also cites Twenty-fourth Amendment to the U.S. Constitution for banning poll tax in federal elections.

5. CPUSA backs third party: Klehr and Haynes, *American Communist Movement*, 114. CIO and CPUSA political goals: ibid., 117. CIO board decision: Klehr and Haynes, *American Communist Movement*, 116–17; Zieger, *CIO*, 269–75. Underlying irony: Schatz, *Electrical Workers*, 184. UE and Wallace: Filippelli and McColloch, *Cold War*, 125. The Wallace vote and aftermath: Klehr and Haynes, *American Communist Movement*, 122–23.

6. Raids on UE: Filippelli and McColloch, *Cold War*, 133.

7. Harry's anti-Communist speech: *CR1949*, 8799–800. Liberals shift positions: Schrecker, *McCarthyism in America*, 81–85; 249.

8. HUAC hearings revealed: Ingrid Jewell, "Reds Bore in U.E. at Westinghouse," *PPG*, July 31, 1949.

9. Local 601 had 152 votes: *UE 14th Convention Proceedings*, Cleveland, September 19–23, 1949, 142.

10. Rice's publicity campaign: McGeever, *Charles Owen Rice*, 124–25. Jewell's second story: "Probe Tied to UE Election," *PPG*, August 7, 1949. Rice later claimed that Walter had promised not to reveal his identity. See McGeever, *Charles Owen Rice*, 125; also in author's interview with Rice, June 8, 2000.

11. Hollywood Ten: Schrecker, *McCarthyism in America*, 316–29.

CHAPTER 11: HUAC HEARINGS

1. All comments at the hearings are drawn from House Un-American Activities Committee, *Hearings Regarding Communist Infiltration of Labor Unions—Part 1 (Local 601, United Electrical, Radio, and Machine Workers of America, CIO, Pittsburgh, Pa.)*, August 9–11, 1949 (hereafter *HUAC 1949*). Crowded hearing room: "Fitzpatrick Silent on Reds in UE," *PP*, August 11, 1949.

2. No current defense projects: *HUAC 1949*, 544. Copeland testimony: HUAC 1949, 583–87. Peeler testimony: HUAC 1949, 587–91. (Although Quinn couldn't recall in 2003 why Peeler testified that he [Quinn] had helped get "Negro girls into the plant," historian David Montgomery provided the answer after reading the manuscript of this book. In an interview in the 1970s, Peeler told Montgomery that Quinn had helped persuade Westinghouse to hire the first black women it had ever employed. Montgomery to author, July 2, 2004.) Testimony by right-wing witnesses Blair Seese and Stanley Glass: *HUAC 1949*, 591–97.

3. Statement of William H. Peeler Sr., August 28, 1952, UE/Lab, National Office Records, District/Local Group, Local 601, folder 308. Peeler's statement is self-serving in some respects and contains errors of fact. Thus he says that in the election for convention delegate, "the Right-Wing Rank and File took all the offices in the election and the UE men were branded for good." Only the latter part of this statement is true. Generally, though, the statement is credible.

4. Fitzpatrick testimony: *HUAC 1949*, 599–607.

5. Panzino testimony: *HUAC 1949*, 607–10.

6. Whisner testimony: *HUAC 1949*, 611–31.

7. Buchanan: 1948 victory reported in "McDowell Is Defeated in Race for Reelection," *PPG*, November 3, 1948. Vote against HUAC funding: *CR 1949*, 1044–45.

8. The meeting: Thomas Quinn to author, December 1999, and subsequent interviews.

9. Anger toward Davenport: Thomas Quinn to author, December 1999. Scribner absent: *Quinn v. U.S.*, 349 U.S. 155 (1955).

10. Quinn testimony: *HUAC 1949*, 633–36.

11. Quinn's punch: Rice, *PC*, August 18, 1949. (Tommy Sullivan later served as a borough councilman in East Pittsburgh: Charles McCollester to author, June 2, 2004.)

12. Clerical pronouncement: Sunday bulletin, Saint Regis Church, Trafford, August 14, 1949, UE/Lab, Local 601 Records, box 7, folder 1. Election day: "3,000 Vote In Election at UE-601," *PPG*, August 15, 1949; "How to Beat the Communists," *Life*, August 29, 1949. The vault: "UE Counts Record Vote Here," *PST*, August 15, 1949.

13. Number of Local 601 votes at convention: *UE 14th Convention Proceedings*, Cleveland, September 19–23, 1949, 142.

14. Davenport, Lawrence, Leonard: John Connelly interview, April 13, 2000. Leonard primary challenge: Weber, *David L. Lawrence*, 247–52; Thomas J. Donaghy, *Keystone Democrat: David Lawrence Remembered* (New York: Vantage, 1986), 32–35.

15. Rice's remorse: McGeever, *Charles Owen Rice*, 125; "The Un-Americans," BBC documentary, ca. 1990; Rice interview, June 8, 2000.

16. UE election results: *UE 14th Convention Proceedings*, 142. Carey forces stronger: "UE Session Ends, Charges Treason," *NYT*, September 17, 1949. HUAC goal of exposure: Donner, *Un-Americans*, chap. 4.

17. Directing from the gallery: Charles Owen Rice, *PC*, October 13, 1949. Vicious reactionaries: Charles Owen Rice, *PC*, October 20, 1949.

18. Convention actions: Filippelli and McColloch, *Cold War*, 134–38. UE ultimatum: UE officers to Philip Murray, October 7, 1949, UE/Lab, Local 601 Records, box 1, folder 5 (Correspondence-ACTU).

19. Oath signing: "UE Chiefs Sign non-Communist Affidavits," *NYT*, October 22, 1949. Imprisonment predicted: Charles Owen Rice, *PC*, October 27, 1949. Expulsion: "UE Session Ends, Charges 'Treason,'" *NYT*, September 24, 1949.

CHAPTER 12: CIO SPLIT

1. All references to 1949 steel negotiations, strike, and settlement terms, throughout: *Collective Bargaining in the Basic Steel Industry* (Washington: U.S. Department of Labor, 1961), 261–69. Estimate of sixty thousand steel strikers in the Monongahela Valley comes from my calculation of Steelworkers members based on a local union survey: John Hoerr, *And the Wolf Finally Came: The Decline of the American Steel Industry* (Pittsburgh: University of Pittsburgh Press, 1988), 633, note 10.

2. Coal negotiations and strike: Dubofsky and Van Tine, *John L. Lewis*, 486–89.

3: UE attack on Murray: UE leaflet, "What's Behind the CIO Split?" UE/Lab, Local 601 Records, box 7, folder F-D. Attacks anger Murray: Harvey A. Levenstein, *Communism, Anticommunism, and the CIO* (New York: Greenwood, 1981), 298.

4. Coverage of CIO convention and union expulsions: Filippelli and McCulloch, *Cold War*, 113–40; Zieger, *CIO*, 253–93; Levenstein, *Communism*, 298–301; Matles oral history, 77–80. One million purged: Zieger, *CIO*, 277, 339 (he points out that the CIO's membership figures were inflated to an unknown degree). David J. McDonald, Steelworkers secretary-treasurer under Murray, who served on panels that tried the Communist union leaders, referred to them as kangaroo courts in his autobiography: David J. McDonald, *Union Man: The Life of a Labor Statesman* (New York: E. P. Dutton, 1969), 211.

5. Indictment against the UE: Filippelli and McCulloch, *Cold War*, 139; Levenstein, *Communism*, 301. "Masquerading": ibid., 300. CPUSA against split: Schatz, *Electrical Workers*, 185; Editorial, "The Peril Facing CIO," *The Worker*, October 2, 1949, Sunday edition.

6. Rice on IUE: Charles Owen Rice, *PC*, November 11, 1949. Charles McCollester interview, June 1, 2004. Rice, however, occasionally claimed that he pushed Murray to create the IUE (see chapter 7). Rice as outside observer: Charles Owen Rice, *PC*, September 29 and October 27, 1949; McGeever, *Charles Owen Rice*, 126. Lavish praise: Charles Owen Rice, *PC*, November 11, 1949, and February 16, 1950.

7. CIO ban on Communists: Levenstein, *Communism*, 299.

8. U.S. Steel settlement: *Collective Bargaining in the Basic Steel Industry*, 268–69. Steelworker pensions: Interview with Thomas Duzak, executive director, Steelworkers Health and Welfare Fund, July 14, 2004. Duzak obtained the estimate of three hundred thousand workers who have retired on a pension at U.S. Steel from a company pension executive. Since U.S. Steel represented about a third of the steel industry from the 1940s to the 1990s, a total of roughly nine hundred thousand workers probably retired from all companies during that time.

9. Growth of defined-benefit plans: David Rajnes, "An Evolving Pension System: Trends in Defined Benefit and Defined Contribution Plans," *EBRI Issue Brief Number 249*, Employee Benefit Research Institute, September 2002. Coverage estimate: "The Benefits Trap," *Business Week*, July 19, 2004, 64–72. Another level of complexity is added to the pension story by Seth Wigderson in "How the CIO Saved Social Security," *Labor History* 44, no. 4 (2003): 483–507. Wigderson demonstrates that the union demands for pensions in 1949–1950 were linked with an eventually

successful CIO effort to improve Social Security benefits and prevent business interests from gutting the Social Security system.

10. Eddie Davenport's council career: "Councilman Ed Davenport Dies in Sleep," *Los Angeles Times*, June 25, 1953.

11. Harry's behavior: John Connelly interview, April 13, 2000.

12. Westinghouse petition and NLRB decision: W. O. Lippman, vice president, to Westinghouse employees, January 27, 1950, IUE Archives, box 53, folder 14. Easing the way for IUE: Matles and Higgins, *Them and Us*, 198; Filippelli and McColloch, *Cold War*, 142–43; "'We Took Carey off the Hook'—GE," *UE News*, July 21, 1952.

13. Background on Hiss, Fuchs, McCarthy, and McCarthyism: Patterson, *Grand Expectations*, 178–205; Manchester, *Glory*, 511–30; David M. Oshinsky, *A Conspiracy So Immense: The World of Joe McCarthy* (New York: Free Press, 1983), 173–507; Klehr, Haynes, and Firsov, *Secret World*, 15–16.

14. NLRB elections: Filippelli and McColloch, *Cold War*, 148.

15. CIO ad campaign: ibid., 143. Campaign incidents and false Truman report: Schatz, *Electrical Workers*, 202; UE, "Memo To Defend the UE Committee," April 25, 1950, UE/Lab, Local 601 Records, box 1, folder L(2).

16. Cvetic surfaces: "'Commie' Leader Here Unmasks Self as FBI Agent for Nine Years," *PP*, February 19, 1950. Cvetic background: Daniel J. Leab, *I Was a Communist for the FBI: The Unhappy Life and Times of Matt Cvetic* (University Park: Pennsylvania State University Press, 2000), 6–17. Fired by FBI: ibid., 25–26. After Cvetic began testifying, it was disclosed that his former wife had filed suit against him for nonsupport and charged him with assaulting another woman. It was more than twenty years before biographer Daniel Leab found that the FBI actually fired Cvetic in January 1950. After Cvetic had testified on numerous occasions, a federal appeals court in 1955 declared that his testimony in a deportation case was of "no more value than the tattlings from a town meeting." Cast aside by investigative agencies, Cvetic drank excessively and died of a heart attack in 1962; ibid., 25–26, 101, 122–23. Cvetic's testimony: HUAC, *Expose of the Communist Party of Western Pennsylvania, Based Upon Testimony of Matthew Cvetic*, Washington, DC, February 21, 1950, 1246.

17. Analysis of Cvetic's testimony about Quinn: Quinn FBI file.

18. Cvetic at East Pittsburgh: "City Called 'No. 1 Target' of Communists," *PP*, March 20, 1950; audio tape recorded by Hymen Schlessinger, March 19, 1950, Hymen Schlessinger Papers, UE/Lab, 77:33.

19. Attack on the UE: Charles Owen Rice, *PC*, April 6, 1950. McDonald's role: McDonald, *Union Man*, 212; Matles oral history, 83.

20. Church activities: UE leaflet, "Facts on Church Interference," April 27, 1950, Charles Newell Papers, UE/Lab. Mimeographed statement distributed at St. William's Church, East Liberty, April 23, 1950, UE/Lab, Local 601 Records, box 7, folder F(2).

21. Endorsements: "Your Government Speaks Out for IUE," reprints of state-

ments by Truman, Tobin, and Symington, UE/Lab, Local 601 Records, box 5. Politicians' neutrality: UE, "Memo to Defend," April 14, 1950.

22. Communist involvement in Twenty-ninth District race: "'Commie' Leader Here Unmasks Self . . . ," *PP*, February 19, 1950; "Frankly Speaking," *The Worker*, April 23, 1950, Sunday edition.

23. Bawling out Peeler: UE, "Memo to Defend," April 14, 1950.

24. Lawrence and Matson: Weber, *David L. Lawrence*, 284–86.

25. Connelly's story: Interviews, May 8, 2000, and January 19, 2004.

26. Harry's story: author's journal, June 29, 1967. IUE rally: "IUE E. Pgh. Rally Turns Out a Dud," *The Worker*, April 23, 1950, Sunday edition.

27. Peeler oral history, April 20, 1977, conducted by Ronald Schatz, UE/Lab, 91:15 (original tapes in MS Group 4009, Pennsylvania Oral History Collections, Pennsylvania State Archives, Harrisburg).

28. Left-wing faker: UE, "Memo to Defend," April 18, 1950.

29. Vote results: "Westinghouse Vote gives Edge to CIO," *PP*, April 28, 1950. Runoff results and voting analysis: Schatz, *Electrical Workers*, 203.

30. Company-wide election results: Filippelli and McColloch, *Cold War*, 144; McColloch, "Shop-Floor Dimension," 184. UE's membership losses: Filippelli and McColloch, *Cold War*, 148. Local 610: ibid., 148.

CHAPTER 13: *DEATH OF A CONGRESSMAN*

1. Turnabout on HUAC: *Congressional Record 1950* (hereafter *CR1950*), March 23, 1950, 3941–44.

2. Contempt citations: ibid., August 10–11, 12283–384; Walter Goodman, *The Committee: The Extraordinary Career of the House Committee on Un-American Activities* (New York: Farrar, Straus and Giroux, 1968), 283–86; "House Cites 2 of 58 in Contempt Cases," *NYT*, August 11, 1950 (final number of citations was 56, not 58); "Contempt Citation Voted for 54 More," *NYT*, August 12, 1950.

3. McCarran Act: *CR1950*, August 29, 13721–39, September 22, 15629–32; "Conferees Delay Red Curb Decision," *NYT*, September 15, 1950. Courageous congressmen: Caute, *Great Fear*, 39. Legitimacy for McCarthy: Schrecker, *McCarthyism in America*, 249. Legal flaws: Caute, *Great Fear*, 38–39; Klehr and Haynes, *American Communist Movement*, 135–36. SACB abolished: Nelson, Barrett, and Ruck, *American Radical*, note 4, 442. Equating dissent with treason: Oshinsky, *Conspiracy*, 173.

4. Newspaper strike: "P-G Is First Paper Out In 47 Days," *PPG*, November 18, 1950.

5. All election results in this section: Allegheny County, "Official Tabulation of Votes Cast," November 2, 1948, and November 7, 1950.

6. Harry and Lawrence: John Connelly interview, April 13, 2000. Lawrence and drinking: Weber, *David L. Lawrence*, 161–62, 178; James Knox interview, June 23, 2000.

7. African American support: "Davenport Plans Naming Local Boy To Naval School," *Pittsburgh Courier*, November 4, 1950.

8. Election impact on Congress: Goodman, *Committee*, 296. Republican analysis: Republican national chairman Leonard Hall, ibid., 296.

9. Events in Rice's life, 1950–1954: McGeever, *Charles Owen Rice*, 136–41.

10. Divorce: *Mary Davenport vs. Harry J. Davenport*, Court of Common Pleas of Allegheny County, Docket No. 1238, July term, August 23, 1951.

11. Harry's state of mind: Connelly interview, April 13, 2000.

12. Ben Bast, Harry's writing: Mary Kate (Bast) Gillespie interview, May 21, 2003.

13. Ruth Ann (Baird) Molloy interview, June 6, 2004.

14. Lynn (Hoerr) McKay interview, June 15, 2004.

CHAPTER 14: FREE SPEECH AND FAMILY SOLIDARITY

1. Korean War and McCarthy's popularity: Manchester, *Glory*, 556–58.

2. Quinn trial: *U.S. v. Quinn*, U.S. District Court, Washington, DC, Criminal Case No. 1744-50; "UE Leader Quinn Guilty of Contempt," *PP*, February 27, 195.

3. Interviews with Chuck Quinn, February 20, 2004, and Ron Quinn, February 21, 2004.

4. Appeals: "UE Leader's Conviction Overruled," *PP*, December 12, 1952; "UE Official's Appeal to Be Heard in Fall," *PPG*, June 8, 1954. Three convictions: Goodman, *Committee*, 285.

5. First car: Steve Quinn interview, July 8, 2004.

6. IUE compromises: McColloch, "Shop-Floor Dimension," 183–99. 1952 election: Filippelli and McColloch, *Cold War*, 151. Wages falling behind: ibid., 159–65.

7. Murray's death and eulogy: "In Memoriam: Phil Murray," radio address excerpted in *PC*, November 13, 1952, reprinted in McCollester, *Fighter*, 115–17.

8. UE rejects CPUSA order: Cochran, *Labor and Communism*, 294. UE defections: Filippelli and McColloch, *Cold War*, 157–59. United front plan: John Vento interview, April 29, 2002.

9. Quinn's memo: Quinn to Matles, March 16, 1953, UE/Lab, District 6 Records, box 1331, folder 275.

10. Proliferation of committees: Caute, *Great Fear*, 222. Butler and Tydings: ibid., 222.

11. Hearings: SISS, *Subversive Influence in the United Electrical, Radio, and Machine Workers of America, Pittsburgh and Erie, Pa.*, 83rd Cong., 1st sess., November 9–12, 1953 (hereafter SISS transcript). Hundred meetings: ibid., 154.

12. Sherman testimony: Caute, *Great Fear*, 222; SISS transcript, 32. Mazzei testimony: ibid., 32. Quinn testimony, ibid., 92–97. Nestler: ibid., 43–45.

13. Mazzei had testified against and helped convict five Communist leaders, including Steve Nelson, when they were tried on charges of advocating overthrow

of the government. In October 1956, the U.S. Supreme Court reversed the convictions and ordered a new trial because of Mazzei's lies. "Mazzei, by his testimony," said Chief Justice Earl Warren, "has poisoned the water in this reservation and the reservoir cannot be cleansed without draining it of all impurity." In October 1956, the Court ordered that five Communists convicted in the Nelson case (*Mesarosh v. United States*, 352 U.S. 1) must be tried afresh. Eleven months later the government the dropped case for good following the recantation of another witness: Caute, *Great Fear*, 222.

14. Discussion of First Amendment trends is based on Geoffrey R. Stone, *Perilous Times: Free Speech in Wartime* (New York: Norton, 2004), 396–419. Conspiracy to advocate: ibid., 408. Douglas quote is from his dissent in *Dennis v. United States*, 341 US 494 (1951). Full weight of authority: Stone, *Perilous Times*, 413. Arrest of 145 members: ibid., 411. Yates ruling: ibid., 414; *Yates v. United States*, 354 US 298 (1957).

15. Communist Control Act: Caute, *Great Fear*, 50; Schrecker, *McCarthyism in America*, 357.

16. Quinn fired: John Vento interview, April 29, 2002; "Electric Firm Fires Leftist Union Leader," *PPG*, January 2, 1954.

17. Cordiner Policy: Matles and Higgins, *Them and Us*, 217–18.

18. Westinghouse policy and firings: Filippelli and McColloch, *Cold War*, 155. Carey halts grievances: Quinn to David Scribner, September 29, 1954, UE/Lab, District 6 Records, DD6-D47. Jobless benefits: Commonwealth of Pennsylvania, Unemployment Compensation Board of Review, re claim of Thomas J. Fitzpatrick, Appeal No. B-4-B-504, and Frank W. Panzino Jr., Appeal No. B-4-B-505, May 10, 1960. This decision cited the 1956 Supreme Court case, *Slochower v. Board of Education*, 350 U.S. 657 (1956). Fitzpatrick in New York: HUAC memo, March 4, 1959, Records of House Un-American Activities Committee, 1945–1969, record group 233, National Archives, Washington, DC (hereafter HUAC Records).

19. Embarrassed daughters: HUAC memo, Paul C. Gerhart to File, HUAC Records, November 18, 1958. Allegations of party membership: ibid., December 16, 1958. Deaths of Fitzpatrick and Panzino: Social Security Death Index.

20. Whisner's life after 1949: R. C. Whisner interview, August 23, 2000. Obituary: "Robert Whisner, Pioneer Unionist in E. Pittsburgh," *UE News*, January 15, 1962.

21. Fired for being subpoenaed: Evelyn O. Darin Papers, UE/Lab, 88:19; "Report on Discharge of East Pittsburgh Workers Subpoenaed by McCarthy Committee," undated, apparently written by Quinn, UE/Lab, UE District Reports, DD6-L18.

22. Twenty fired: Filippelli and McColloch, *Cold War*, 155. Nationwide number of firings: Schrecker, *McCarthyism in America*, 363.

23. Information about the Quinn family in this section is drawn from interviews with Chuck Quinn (February 20, 2004), Ron Quinn (January 8 and February 21, 2004), and Steve Quinn (November 28, 2000, and May 7, 2004).

CHAPTER 15: SUBPOENAED AGAIN

1. McCarthy's performance: Oshinsky, *Conspiracy*, 507. McCarthy "never identified a single subversive," says James Patterson in *Grand Expectations*, 199.

2. Quinn cleared: *Quinn v. United States*, 349 U.S. 155 (1955); "High Court Clears Three of Red Inquiry Contempt," *NYT*, May 24, 1955; "High Court Clears Quinn and Emspak," *PPG*, May 24, 1955.

3. David Montgomery, "Causes and Consequences of the CIO's Purge" (paper, presented at a conference in Turtle Creek, PA, September 18, 1998).

4. Attitude of UE leaders: Schatz, *Electrical Workers*, 231.

5. Westinghouse strike, weakened unions: Filippelli and McColloch, *Cold War*, 162–66; Schatz, *Electrical Workers*, 232–40.

6. Membership loss: ibid., 232. SACB case: Filippelli and McColloch, *Cold War*, 156.

7. Material helpful to defense: Matles FBI file, SAC New York to Director, August 2, 1957; SAC New York to Director, October 3, 1957. The 1956 Supreme Case referred to is *Jencks v. U.S.*, 353 U.S. 657 (1957). The Matles deportation case and several others were dropped in 1958 when the Supreme Court found that the government had failed to file on-time affidavits showing the basis for a denaturalization suit: "Costello Upheld in Citizen Status," *NYT*, April 8, 1958; "Matles Case Thrown out by U.S. Supreme Court," *UE News*, April 14, 1958.

8. Matles isolated: Matles FBI file, SAC NY to Director, March 12, 1958. Nelson's lament: Nelson, Barrett, and Ruck, *American Radical*, 397.

9. HUAC, *Problems of Security in Industrial Establishments Holding Defense Contracts, Greater Pittsburgh Area—Part 2*, Pittsburgh, March 10, 11, 12, 1959 (hereafter HUAC59 transcript), 396.

10. Quinn testimony: ibid., 410–23. Atmosphere at hearings: "Reds Control UE Here, Probe Told, *PP*, March 11, 1959; "I'm Not a Red, Quinn Roars As He Defies House Probers," *PST*, March 11, 1959; "Sparks Fly as Quinn Steals Probe Show," *PST*, March 12, 1959. Quinn's baritone: ibid., March 12, 1959.

11. Investigative reports on Quinn: Gerhart to File, November 19, 1958, HUAC Records; Gerhart to Arens, March 6, 1959, ibid. The same staff member tried but failed to entice Frank Panzino into testifying at the March hearings as a friendly witness—in other words, to testify against Quinn and others. Gerhart to File, February 6, 1959, ibid.

12. HUAC request and FBI internal memos: Quinn FBI file, De Loach to Tolson, March 25, 1959, Director to SAC Pittsburgh, March 26, 1959; SAC Pittsburgh to Director, April 2, 1959. No prosecution: J. F. Bland to A. H. Belmont, August 13, 1959, ibid.

13. Interviews with Steve Quinn (May 24, 2004) and Ron Quinn (February 21, 2004).

14. Thomas Kerr interview, July 19, 2004.

15. Crowded hearing: "Sparks Fly," *PST*.

16. John Connelly interview, April 13, 2000.

17. Harry against Lawrence: Pat O'Neill, "Davenport Will Oppose Moorhead," *PPG*, November 23, 1959; Harry's sharp pen: O'Neill, "Davenport Eyes Help from Hoffa," *PPG*, March 6, 1960.

18. McGonigle challenge: Weber, *David L. Lawrence*, 341–45 (Weber does not mention Davenport but provides good detail on McGonigle's campaign). Harry supports McGonigle: "Democrats for M'Gonigle," *PPG*, October 1, 1958.

19. Hoffa brochure: O'Neill, "Davenport Eyes Help."

CHAPTER 16: MAKING AMENDS AND MAKING FRIENDS

1. Wright and Rice: McGeever, *Charles Owen Rice*, 148; McCollester, *Fighter*, xviii; Kenneth J. Heineman, "Reformation: Monsignor Charles Owen Rice and the Fragmentation of the New Deal Electoral Coalition in Pittsburgh, 1960-1972," *Pennsylvania History* 71, no. 1 (Winter 2004): 58. Youth to middle age: McGeever, *Charles Owen Rice*, 152.

2. Rice as opponent: Matles and Higgins, *Them and Us*, 258. Attack on HUAC: McGeever, *Charles Owen Rice*, 153.

3. Reevaluation: Rice, "Confessions," 454.

4. Anti-civil-rights and prowar attitudes: Heineman, "Reformation," 57. Wright's ambassador: McGeever, *Charles Owen Rice*, 168.

5. Rice in Homewood: McGeever, *Charles Owen Rice*, 150, 172, 174–76. Building trades: ibid., 192.

6. Vantage point: McCollester, *Fighter*, xviii. Haden, Wright: McGeever, *Charles Owen Rice*, 177–79.

7. McIlvane: McGeever, *Charles Owen Rice*, 183–84.

8. New York march: ibid., 182. With King: Charles Owen Rice, "A Good Man," *PC*, April 12, 1968, reprinted in McCollester, *Fighter*, 137–39. Lowell: Norman Mailer, *The Armies of the Night* (New York: New American Library, 1968), 106. Clerical garb: McGeever, *Charles Owen Rice*, 206.

9. Charles Owen Rice, "'Ecumenism' in Labor," *PC*, June 9, 1966.

10. Good wishes to UE: Matles and Higgins, *Them and Us*, 259.

11. Steelworkers funds: Rice oral history, April 5, 1968. Patriot: Charles Owen Rice, "The Tragic Purge of 1948," *Blueprint for the Christian Reshaping of Society* 29, no. 6 (February 1977), reprinted in McCollester, *Fighter*, 97–98.

12. Matles death: Charles Owen Rice, "Red Gains in Italy a Paradox," *PC*, September 26, 1975. Fitzpatrick: Rice, "Confessions," 457. Nelson: Charles Owen Rice, "Steve Nelson: An Honorable Antagonist," *PC*, December 24, 1993, reprinted in McCollester, *Fighter*, 228–30. Rice-Nelson cooperation: McGeever, *Charles Owen Rice*, 228.

13. Rice, "Confessions," 449–62.

14. Rice's plea: Author's journal, April 16, 1968; "Ministers Call for Negro Aid," *PPG*, April 9, 1968.

15. Rice's changing persona: Suggested in Heineman, "Reformation," and sections of McCollester, *Fighter*.

16. Retirement: Rice interview, April 13, 2000.

17. Edwin Wintermyer interview, August 12, 2000.

18. UE membership: Matles and Higgins, *Them and Us,* 259. Contested ballots: John Vento interview, April 29, 2002; Filippelli and McColloch, *Cold War,* 169.

19. Irene's activities, sons' education: Interviews with Chuck Quinn (February 20, 2004), Ron Quinn (August 12, 2000 and May 31, 2004), and Steve Quinn (May 28, 2004).

20. Surveillance: Quinn FBI file.

21. Transforming Wilmerding: Henry Slaczka interview, December 20, 2000.

22. Bid for Congress: Dick Thornburgh, *Where the Evidence Leads: An Autobiography* (Pittsburgh: University of Pittsburgh Press, 2003), 25–30.

23. Heinz election: Connelly interview, April 13, 2000; "Heinz Stops Connelly Cold by 2-1 Margin," *PPG,* November 3, 1971. Heinz death: "John Heinz, 52, Heir to a Fortune and Senator from Pennsylvania," *NYT,* April 5, 1991.

24. Jake Osterman interview, May 19, 2000.

CHAPTER 17: DECLINE AND ASCENT

1. Anecdotes in this chapter about Harry Davenport are taken from the author's journal and conversations with relatives. The dialogue between Harry and local union officers on presidential politics in 1968 is recorded in author's journal, July 9, 1968.

2. Harry as publicist for McCarthy: Interview with Daniel Berger, August 26, 2003. Eugene McCarthy: Maurice Isserman and Michael Kazin, *America Divided: The Civil War of the 1960s* (New York: Oxford University Press, 2000), 224.

3. Quinn's problems in the UE: Ron Quinn interview, June 6, 2004.

4. Public employee bargaining law, Quinn's hiring and his experiences as mediator: Author's personal knowledge; interviews with James Rush (August 22, 2000), Ron Quinn (June 6, 2004), and Hymen Richman (May 5, 2000, and June 1, 2004).

5. Appointment as bureau director: Interview with Tom Foley, former labor and industry secretary (1991–1994) and deputy secretary (1987–1990), June 7, 2004; Hymen Richman interviews. Thornburgh-ACLU: Thornburgh, *Autobiography,* 33. "Negotiator Here Is Named Mediation Chief," *PPG,* September 17, 1980.

6. Complaint about Quinn: Charles A. Provan, MD, to Rep. David W. Sweet, January 11, 1983, Thomas J. Quinn Papers, UE/Lab, 73:9, box 11. Improved situation: Chuck Quinn interview, February 20, 2004.

7. Hymen Richman interviews.

8. Interview with Jill Leeds Rivera, May 19, 2003.

9. Interview with Edwin Wintermyer, August 12, 2000.

10. Last decade: "Once Union Radical, GOP Appointee Has Mellowed," *PP,* date missing, 1981. Archives fund: Press release, University of Pittsburgh, "Labor Archives Fund Established at Pitt," November 19, 1987.

11. TV appearance: David Montgomery to author, April 16, 2004.

12. Retirement: "A Tribute to Tom Quinn," program brochure, Westin William Penn Hotel, November 22, 1991.

13. Quinn's vow: Chuck Quinn interview, August 12, 2000.

14. IUE merger and UE status: Jim McKay, "IUE Members Back CWA Union," *PPG*, September 22, 2000; interviews with Candace Johnson, CWA (July 25, 2000), Peter Gilmore, UE (July 27, 2000).

15. Westinghouse demise: "Who Killed Westinghouse?" *PPG*, March 1, 3–7, 1998.

CHAPTER 18: MILLVALE REVISITED

1. Interviews with Ron Quinn (June 6, 2004) and Steve Quinn (June 3, 2004).

2. Interviews with John Ulrich (April 28, 2000) and Teresa Ulrich (June 12, 2000).

3. Town history: "The Gateway to the North, Millvale PA," a brief history produced for the town's centennial celebration, 1868–1968, Millvale Borough offices.

4. "Maxo Vanka's Millvale Murals," brochure distributed by St. Nicholas Croatian Church.

INDEX